A HISTORY OF

UYGHUR BUDDHISM

A HISTORY OF
UYGHUR BUDDHISM

JOHAN ELVERSKOG

Columbia University Press
New York

Columbia University Press
Publishers Since 1893
New York   Chichester, West Sussex
cup.columbia.edu
Copyright © 2024 Columbia University Press
All rights reserved

Library of Congress Cataloging-in-Publication Data
Names: Elverskog, Johan, author.
Title: A history of Uyghur Buddhism / Johan Elverskog.
Description: New York : Columbia University Press, 2024. | Includes bibliographical references and index.
Identifiers: LCCN 2023053542 (print) | LCCN 2023053543 (ebook) | ISBN 9780231215244 (hardback) | ISBN 9780231215251 (trade paperback) | ISBN 9780231560696 (ebook)
Subjects: LCSH: Buddhism—China—Xinjiang Uygur Zizhiqu—History. | Uighur (Turkic people)—Religion. | Xinjiang Uygur Zizhiqu (China)—Religion.
Classification: LCC BQ649.X56 E45 2024 (print) | LCC BQ649.X56 (ebook) | DDC 294.30951/6—dc23/eng/20231201
LC record available at https://lccn.loc.gov/2023053542
LC ebook record available at https://lccn.loc.gov/2023053543

Cover design: Elliott S. Cairns
Cover image: The *praṇidhi* scene No. 14 in Cave 20, Bezeklik, Xinjiang, China. After Le Coq, *Chotscho* (photo by author).

I had also exchanged the Chinese word "idea" or *si* (思) with another *si* word whose meaning was "death" (死). When he showed me this mistake, I laughed without thinking, because I liked these kinds of mistakes.... I picked up the Letter of Guarantee and looked through it. He still hadn't noticed that I had mistakenly written the date for one hundred years prior. Who knows, perhaps a hundred years ago his grandfather had forced my grandfather to write the same kind of letter.... That's right, the greatest thing in the world is living. There is nothing greater than living! What outraged him the most was that I was alive. It follows, then, that my ability to live must be of great value. My very existence was his greatest source of frustration.

—Perhat Tursun, *The Backstreets: A Novel from Xinjiang*

Contents

List of Illustrations ix

Acknowledgments xiii

Introduction 1
1. Becoming Buddhist 5
2. Buddhist Politics 40
3. Buddhist Economics 66
4. Uyghur Buddhisms 92
5. Becoming Muslim 135

Conclusion 170

Notes 175

Bibliography 229

Index 267

List of Illustrations

0.1. The West Uyghur Kingdom with its summer capital at Beshbaliq (Beiting) and winter capital at Qocho (Xizhou/Gaochang) 3
1.1. The First Turk Empire (552–612 CE) 6
1.2. The Uyghur Empire (744–840) 8
1.3. Uyghur migration in the mid-ninth century 10
1.4. Mural commemorating Zhang Yichao's victory over the Tibetans, Mogao Cave 156, Late Tang (875–907) 11
1.5. Cao Yijin's Ganzhou Uyghur wife (on the right), Mogao Cave 98 (c. 923–925) 13
1.6. Stake inscription for a Buddhist monastery built in 1008 16
1.7. Bema Scene, full-page book painting shown from picture-viewing direction 16
1.8. Early trilingual Sanskrit, Tokharian, and Uyghur text in Brahmi script 18
1.9. A Uyghur "Buddhist Catechism" containing questions and answers about the Dharma in Tibetan script 19
1.10. Post-Abbasid Central Asia 21
1.11. The Qara Khitai's Western Liao 24
1.12. Buddhist Asia 28
1.13. The Phoenix Temple in Kyoto, Japan 30
1.14. Page of the Khitan canon with a Uyghur inscription 31
1.15. Khitan big-script manuscript with Uyghur interlinear glosses 31
1.16. The *praṇidhi* scene No. 1 in Cave 20, Bezeklik, Xinjiang, China 32
1.17. The *praṇidhi* scene No. 14 in Cave 20, Bezeklik, Xinjiang, China 33

x   Illustrations

1.18. Bezeklik murals in Berlin's Museum für Völkerkunde before the building was bombed during World War II   34
1.19. State Hermitage *praṇidhi* scene from the Bezeklik caves, Xinjiang, China   35
1.20. Bezeklik Cave Temple Restoration Project, Ryukoku Museum   36
1.21. Tokharian monks in Cave 20, Bezeklik, Xinjiang, China   37
1.22. Chinese monks in Cave 20, Bezeklik, Xinjiang, China   38
2.1. Mural with Vaiśravaṇa from the Bezeklik Caves, Xinjiang, China   44
2.2. Avalokiteśvara with a thousand hands and a thousand eyes from Dunhuang   46
2.3. Buddha Tejaprabha's Paradise, Bezeklik, Xinjiang, China   47
2.4. Portrait of Uyghur donor Kara Totok represented as the main figure in a temple banner   49
2.5. Fifth-century Tokharian mural of king presenting an umbrella to the Buddha, Kizil Cave 38   53
2.6. Fifth-century Tokharian mural of merchant presenting treasures to the Buddha, Kizil Cave 38   54
2.7. Portrait of male Uyghur donor from Bezeklik Caves, Xinjiang, China   56
2.8. Portrait of a female Uyghur donor from Bezeklik Caves, Xinjiang, China   57
2.9. Uyghur transcription of a Chinese sutra, U5335, p. 24   63
2.10. Uyghur text with Chinese characters   63
3.1. Republics of early India   68
3.2. The Mauryan Empire   69
3.3. Cloth of gold with winged lions and griffins (ca. 1225-1275)   77
3.4. Prostitution contract   80
3.5. Horse markets in the Northern Song   81
3.6. Male donor portraits from the Bezeklik caves, Xinjiang, China   86
3.7. Female donor portraits from the Bezeklik caves, Xinjiang, China   87
4.1. Illustrated *Daśakarmapathāvadānamālā*   96
4.2. Illustrated *Viśvantara Jātaka*   103
4.3. Twelfth-century Tangut blockprint   104
4.4. Uyghur wall painting with hell realms and dais   105
4.5. Uyghur pothi manuscript   108
4.6. Illustrated *Säkiz Yükmäk Yaruk Sutra*   108

4.7. Uyghur scroll manuscript   109
4.8. Uyghur concertina manuscript   109
4.9. Uyghur codex manuscript   110
4.10. Uyghur text with Chinese amulets   111
4.11. Chinese version of *Guanyin Sutra*   111
4.12. Uyghur translation of *Guanyin Sutra*   112
4.13. Fragment of the *Scripture on the Ten Kings*: the court of one of the Ten Kings   113
4.14. Kṣitigarbha and the Ten Kings, tenth to eleventh century, Qocho   114
4.15. Veneration of Guanyin. First half of the tenth century. Central Asia, Dunhuang, Mogao Caves   115
4.16. Buddhist cave temple complex at Beshbaliq   116
4.17. Bezeklik Caves outside Qocho (Gaochang)   116
4.18. Uyghur donor of cave temple in the underground south entry to the cave temple complex at Beshbaliq   118
4.19. Mounted figures attacking a city with donors below. West wall of south chamber 105, Beshbaliq   118
4.20. The early Uyghur-based Mongol script as used on Guyuk Khan's imperial seal (r. 1246–1248)   121
4.21. Uyghur in Pakpa script   124
4.22. Ḍākinī from Bezeklik caves   126
4.23. Uyghur text with embedded Brahmi script. Mainz 713   128
4.24. A printed fragment of the *Grahamātṛkādhāraṇī* with glosses in Brahmi Script. U 4123   129
4.25. Uyghur translation of the *Madhyamāgama* (*Zhong ahanjing* 中阿含經 T. 26) with quoted Chinese passages marked with characters and circles   129
4.26. Uyghur monks wearing Tokharian style robes, from a mural at Beshbaliq   131
4.27. Temple banner dedicated to Vairocana Buddha   133
4.28. Uyghur blockprint of *The Big Dipper Sutra*   134
5.1. Buddhist sites in the Il-khanid realm   140
5.2. Body meridians in Rashid al-Din's *Tansuq Name*   142
5.3. Zhou Dunyi's 周敦頤 "Diagram of the Supreme Polarity" (*Taijitu* 太極圖) in Rashid al-Din's *Tansuq Name*   142
5.4. Chinggis Khan's conquests at the time of his death   144
5.5. The Four Ulus of the Mongol Empire   145

5.6 and 5.7. 1331 Yuan dynasty map of Central Asia (*Yuan Jingshidadian Xibeibidili Tu* 元經世大典西北嵒地里圖)   151

5.8. Fifteenth-Century Eurasia   166

Con.1. Tao Zongyi's 陶宗儀 Shushi Huiyao 書史會要 vol. 8, folio 7a–8a   171

Con.2. Chinese-Uyghur dictionary   171

Con.3. Muhammad and the angel with seventy heads, from the *Miraj Name*, Herat, Afghanistan, 1436 CE (Manuscrit Supplément Turc 190, f. 19v)   172

Con.4. Pilgrims praying at the Imam Asim *mazar*   173

Acknowledgments

If one were to read all the introductory textbooks and general surveys of Buddhism, it would be rare to come upon any mention of the Uyghurs. I therefore thank my teachers at Indiana University—Larry V. Clark, György Kara, and Jan Nattier—for introducing me to this field of study. Indeed, it was on account of their inspiration and guidance that not only enabled me to publish my first book on Uyghur Buddhism but also made it possible for me to return to the topic a quarter of a century later.

Of course, being trained and inspired to tackle a particular topic is one thing; finding the time and wherewithal to bring it to fruition is quite another. I therefore sincerely thank all those who supported this project: the American Academy in Berlin, the American Council of Learned Societies, the James P. Geiss and Margaret Y. Hsu Foundation, the Robert H.N. Ho Family Foundation, and the National Humanities Center.

Being afforded the time and solitude to write a book is a remarkable thing; however, scholarship invariably does not develop in a vacuum. I therefore thank Iselin Frydenlund, Carmen Meinert, and Diego Loukota for inviting me to talk about this project in its early stages, as well as those who provided insightful feedback during these presentations, including Amund Bjorsnes, Jens Braarvig, Volkhard Krech, Oktor Skjaervø, and Henrik H. Sørensen. I also want to especially thank my colleagues who read earlier drafts of this manuscript: Zsuzsanna Gulásci, Yukiyo Kasai, Lilla Russell-Smith, Abdrishid Yakup, and Peter Zieme. Their incisive and invaluable comments made this a much better work. All remaining mistakes and dubious interpretations are, of course, mine alone.

For believing in this manuscript before it was even written—and for contacting me about publishing it—I wish to thank Wendy Lochner. She and Lowell

Frye and many others at Columbia University Press made the final stretches of this endeavor a quick and joyful jaunt.

In the same vein, I also want to thank everyone who helped me with the images: Céline Boudias, Nadège Danet, Joyce Faust, James Kohler, Christophe Mauberret, Kristina Münchow, Roxann Prazniak, Kira Samosyuk, Neil Schmidt, Lilla Russell-Smith, Paul Jakov Smith, Rian Thum, and Susan Whitfield. And I especially want to thank Ben Pease, who with skill and wit made the maps in record time.

Finally, I wish to thank all of my family and friends for making it all worthwhile.

A HISTORY OF UYGHUR BUDDHISM

Introduction

> *The Turks and the Mongols are not a religious people. The religious imagination, zeal and abundant inquiry that was so strong among the Arabs, Iranians and Slavs was unable to have an important influence on the thoughts of the Turks, Mongols or Manchus. The religion that was most appropriate to the nature of the Turks was the faith of the Buddha. In nature, thought and temperament, the Turks were Buddhist. The one encompassing [space] that would have kept the Turks living in complete comfort would have been the faith of the Buddha.*
>
> —Ahmet Refik, *Büyük Tarih-i Umumi* (1912)[1]

Today most Uyghurs are Muslims. Yet this was not always so. For centuries they were Buddhists. In their homeland along the Silk Road in what is now northwestern China, the Uyghurs stood at the center of Buddhist Eurasia and thus drew upon all the surrounding cultures to forge their own distinctive form of the Dharma. In doing so they used their wealth and power to produce stunning Buddhist monuments not only in their own kingdom but also across Asia, from Beijing to Baghdad. In fact, the glories of Uyghur Buddhism were so renowned in the thirteenth and fourteenth centuries that the Tibetans even came to postulate that their kingdom was the mythical land of Shambhala.[2]

Yet, contrary to the myth of Shambhala—which claims that a Buddhist savior will ride forth from that hidden kingdom, annihilate the Muslims, and thereby usher in a Buddhist golden age—the opposite happened.[3] In the face of expanding Muslim power the Uyghur Buddhists converted to Islam. And as part and parcel of this conversion they rewrote their past, erasing their entire Buddhist history. In fact, because there was such a powerful historical connection between the Uyghurs and their Buddhist culture, this religious rewriting even caused their historical ethnonym to fade.[4] Instead, these new Muslims eventually came to call themselves Musulman (Muslims), Altishahris (citizens of the "Six Cities" of the Tarim Basin), or simply Kashgaris and Turfanis.[5] The time of the Uyghurs and their Buddhism was thereby forgotten.

In the beginning of the nineteenth century, however, this history was rediscovered by European orientalists. They were the first to recognize that the Turkic speakers of northwest China had their roots on the Mongolian plateau. In particular, the German philologist Julius Klaproth made clear that the Uyghurs of the Turfan Basin—who were famous as the "steppe intelligentsia" of the Mongol empire—had migrated into this area when their steppe empire collapsed in the mid-ninth century. Then, in 1849, the French scholar Stanislas Julien made it known that Buddhist texts had been translated into the Uyghur language based on his study of a catalogue of the Chinese Buddhist canon prepared under the auspices of Khubilai Khan.[6] Yet this scholarly breakthrough was to remain hypothetical until the height of the Great Game in the late nineteenth century, when European imperial powers sent out a host of expeditions to better understand the terra incognita of northwest China.[7] The Manchu Qing dynasty (1644–1912) had only conquered the area in 1757 and named it Xinjiang ("New Frontier"), but their hold on this borderland territory was already teetering in the nineteenth century. Explorers from Britain, Finland, France, Germany, Japan, Sweden, and Russia poured into Xinjiang and discovered the treasures of what we now know as the long-lost civilizations of the Silk Road.[8] Among these discoveries was a treasure trove of Uyghur Buddhist manuscripts and artwork found at sites across their ancient kingdom (see fig. 0.1).

As all of this material made its way back to Europe, scholars set about the arduous task of making sense of it. This included the Turkologists Wilhelm Radloff and S. E. Malov working on the Uyghur material brought back to Russia, as well as F. W. K. Müller working on the material brought back to Berlin by four German expeditions to Xinjiang between 1902 and 1914. Their groundbreaking work showed that the Uyghurs had—before their conversion to Islam—been not only Buddhist but also Christian and Manichaean. This led scholars to explore a range of questions: how their kingdom functioned; why they gave up their Manichaean faith for Buddhism; where the Christian Church of the East fit into all of this; and finally, why they eventually became Muslim.[9]

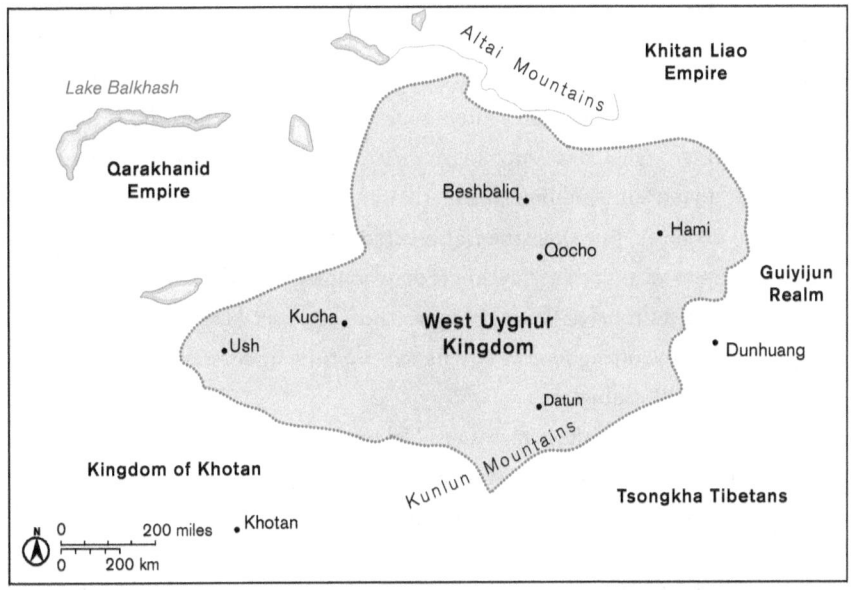

0.1 The West Uyghur Kingdom with its Summer Capital at Beshbaliq (Beiting) and Winter Capital at Qocho (Xizhou/Gaochang)

These same questions animate this book. However, this work is also shaped by three other questions or historiographical concerns. The first is how the religious history of the Uyghurs problematizes the common perceptions about the meeting of Buddhism and Islam.[10] In exploring this dynamic I draw inspiration from historian Peter Brown's exploration of conversion narratives during the Christianization of the Roman Empire: "I have long suspected that accounts of Christianization . . . are at their most misleading where they speak of the process as if it were a single block, capable of a single comprehensive description that, in turn, implies the possibility of a single, all-embracing explanation."[11] Indeed, as this book will show, neither Uyghur conversion to Buddhism nor the later conversion to Islam occurred in one fell swoop. In both cases a host of factors ranging from geopolitics to climate change and global economic shifts to technological innovation drove the adoption of a new religion. Becoming Buddhist or Muslim did not happen in a vacuum.

This observation also informs the second thematic concern, which is to better understand what it means to be Buddhist. Over the last twenty years postcolonial scholarship has amply documented how the modern and popular understanding of Buddhism came about, and in so doing has challenged many of the popular preconceptions about Buddhism.[12] Thus, contrary to the conventional view that Buddhist practice centers on meditation, scholars have shown that it has centered instead on rituals such as relic veneration, the transfer of merit, mortuary rights, and pilgrimage.[13] And it is precisely such practices—as well as the materiality of Buddhism—that inform this study of the Dharma among the Uyghurs. But this study also explores Buddhism in relation to politics, the economy, and everyday life. For example, what legal system did the Uyghur Buddhists follow? What calendar did they use? How did they make a living? Only by including such concerns will we fully understand what it meant and means to be Buddhist.

Through uncovering these facets of Uyghur Buddhism, the third aim of this project is to highlight the importance of both the Uyghurs and Buddhism in shaping the sweep of Asian history, because all too often Buddhism is imagined as being outside of history. Yet ignoring its role in Asia is the equivalent of a historian of the Mediterranean ignoring Christianity or Islam. It simply does not make sense, but sadly, it happens all the time. As Donald Lopez pointed out long ago, historians of Asia see Buddhism as "an esoteric domain entered only by the initiate, and Buddhologists are . . . often woefully ignorant of Asian history."[14] But Buddhism is the only religious system that spread over all of Asia in the premodern period, from Sri Lanka to Siberia and from Iran to Japan. As the first "pan-Asian faith," Buddhism dominated Asia's religious, sociocultural, economic, and political discourses for almost two thousand years.[15] And yet the problem remains: historians of Asia know little about Buddhism, and scholars of Buddhism care little about history.[16] The Uyghurs, however, provide an especially good opportunity to connect Buddhism to Asian history because they resided at the center of Eurasia and linked multiple worlds: China and the West, the steppe and the sown, China and Tibet, as well as the Buddhist and Muslim worlds. By explicating the history of Uyghur Buddhism and its place in Asian history, we will understand both better.

CHAPTER 1

Becoming Buddhist

The area has no rain or snow and is extremely hot . . . Their houses are white-washed, and water from the Jinling [Golden Mountain] flows between them and is circulated through the capital city to water the gardens and to turn the mills. The area produces the five cereal grains, but it lacks buckwheat. The nobles eat horse meat and the common people eat goat or fowl. In music they make much use of the pipa *[a kind of four-stringed lute] and the* konghou *[an ancient plucked instrument with seven strings like the harp]. They produce sable, cotton and brocade cotton. They are fond of archery and riding. . . . They are fond of excursions and always take along musical instruments. There are more than 50 Buddhist temples with inscribed tablets given by the Tang imperial court. In the temples the* Buddhist Tripitika, *the* Rhyming Book of the Tang, *the* Dictionary of Chinese Characters, *the* Chinese Buddhist Dictionary . . . *and other works are kept.*
—Wang Yande 王延德, *Records of an Embassy to Qocho* 使高昌記 (ca. 982 CE)[1]

Why does someone become Buddhist? Indeed, why does anyone—much less an entire civilization—adopt a new religion? The reasons for conversion are many, from the political and economic to the personal and psychological, with cultural, social, and technological influences as well. It is not a simple or singular event but a process.

No Uyghur ruler—such as Aśoka in India or Songtsen Gampo in Tibet—ushered his people into the faith. Rather, it was the Uyghur elite—the nobility and wealthy merchant class—who adopted Buddhism,[2] and they did so over centuries.[3] Two common scholarly explanations for their conversion point to the

6 *Becoming Buddhist*

threat posed by the expansionist Muslim Qarakhanids and the intellectual and social failure of their own Manichean tradition.[4] I find both unsatisfactory, as set out below. To consider these modern scholarly arguments, we need first to look back at the fortunes of the Uyghurs and their various religious entanglements, which resulted in the Uyghur migration to what is now Xinjiang province in northwest China and their subsequent adoption of Buddhism.

THE CONSOLIDATION OF A BUDDHIST UYGHUR KINGDOM

Much of the early history of Buddhism among the Uyghurs—and of the Turks more broadly—remains unclear. Nevertheless, Chinese sources provide evidence that Buddhist missionaries were active among the Turks already in the sixth century, during the First Turk Empire (552–612 CE) (see fig. 1.1).

In particular, the sources record that Xiao Min Di, the founder of the Northern Zhou dynasty (r. 556–581), had a Buddhist temple built in the capital of Chang'an (today's Xi'an) for the thousands of Turks living there. Later, his successor Ming Di added an inscription to this temple that proclaimed the Turk

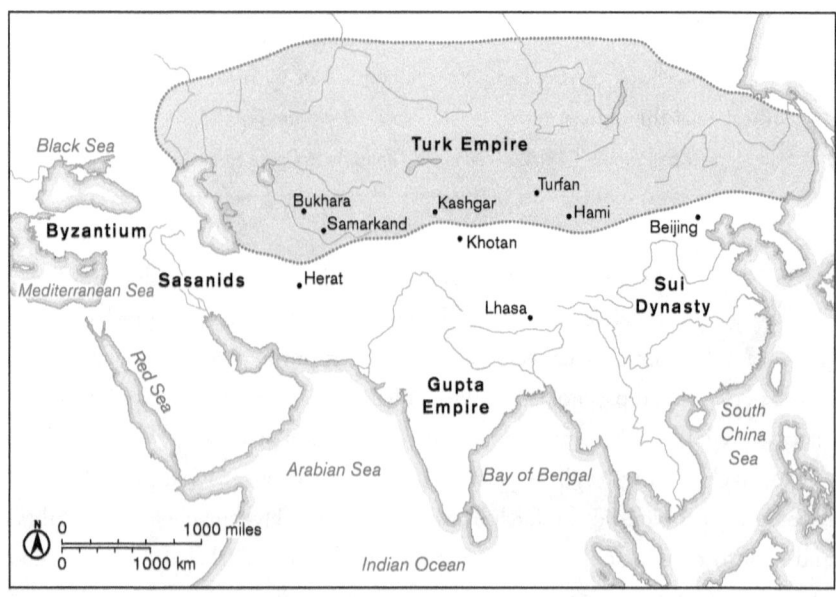

1.1 The First Turk Empire (552–612 CE)

ruler Muhan Khan (r. 553-572) had adopted Buddhism. Another Chinese source indicates that a Chinese monk named Huilin, a member of an embassy sent to the Turks' court by the emperor of the Northern Qi dynasty, converted Muhan Khan's brother and successor, Tatpar Khan (r. 572-581), to Buddhism. After his conversion the khan not only invited the Gandharan monk Jinagupta (528-605?) from Chang'an in 574 but also built a monastery and requested Buddhist texts from the Chinese court. In reply, the emperor of the Northern Qi had a copy of the *Mahāparinirvāṇa Sūtra* translated into the "language of the Turks."[5] And a few decades later, in 626, the then ruling khan welcomed the Buddhist pilgrim Prabhakhamitra to his court.[6]

These early connections between the Turks and the Dharma, however, do not seem to have taken root.[7] Sources do not mention any Buddhism among the Turks during the Second Empire (692-742).[8] In fact, the Chinese traveler Hui Chao claimed, based on his travels in Inner Asia in the 720s, that the Turks did not have the Buddha's teaching, or monasteries and monks.[9] If that was indeed the case, the Uyghurs, one of the "Nine Tribes" (Toquz Oguz) of the Second Turk Empire, were not Buddhist either.

Despite their membership in the Turk Empire, the Uyghurs forged a rebel alliance with two of the other tribes—the Basmil and Karluk—with the aim of putting the Basmil leader on the throne. They succeeded in doing so in 742, but two years later the Karluk and Uyghur turned on their erstwhile ally and deposed him. Then the Uyghur ruler Köl Bilgä Khan (Ch. Huairen, r. 744-747) took over the Orkhon Valley in what is now Mongolia and established the Uyghur empire (744-840) (see fig. 1.2).[10]

Although the rise of the Uyghurs was in many ways a local affair, it was also part of a much broader mid-eighth century reordering of political alignments in eastern Eurasia. The Abbasids overthrew the Umayyads from their base in Central Asia and forged "a Perso-Arab partnership in power."[11] In 751 they defeated a large Tang dynasty expeditionary force at the Battle of Talas in what is now Uzbekistan. Similarly, the Tang dynasty's attempt to expand its power to the south by attacking the Nanzhao Kingdom had failed. Their attempts to control the expanding power of the Tibetan empire also failed. Yet none of these setbacks to the Tang's expansionist policies compared to the devastation unleashed by the rebellion of 755-763, led by revered military commander An Lushan, which nearly brought down the dynasty. Importantly, the Tang were able to put the uprising down only with the Uyghurs' military intervention on their behalf.

8 Becoming Buddhist

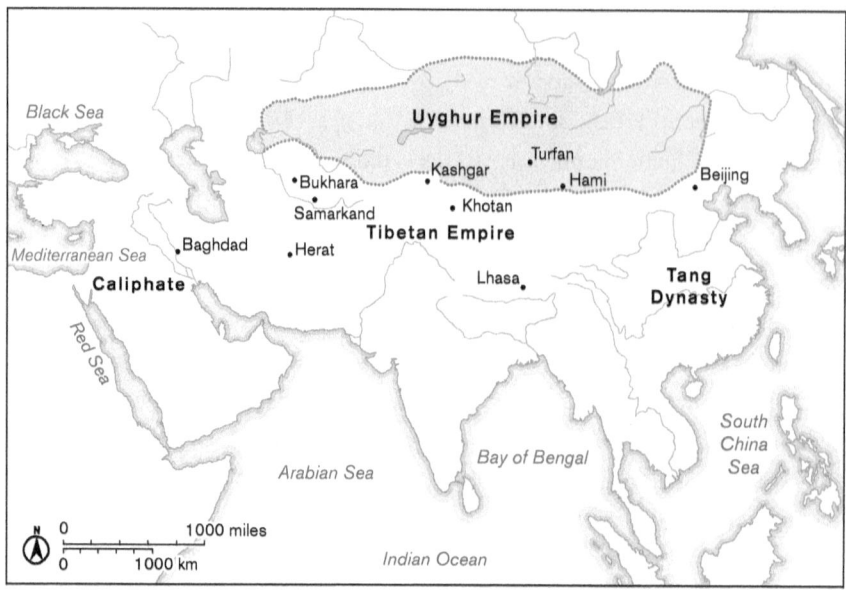

1.2 The Uyghur Empire (744–840)

The Uyghur decision to support the Tang at this critical moment secured the military and economic fortunes of their newly formed state. The weakened Tang granted the Uyghurs important trade monopolies, creating what one scholar has called a "military-commercial complex."[12] This "complex" was further enhanced when the Tibetans took advantage of the Tang's turmoil and conquered the Gansu corridor, after which the Silk Road trade moved north into Uyghur territory.[13] As a result, by the reign of Külüg Bilgä Khan (Ch. Mouyu, r. 759–779), the Uyghur realm was secure both militarily and financially. In 760 he adopted Manichaeism and promoted it as the state religion.[14]

It is unknown why Külüg Bilgä Khan took this step. It is possible that the chaos of the Tang dynasty, as well as the recent assassination of the Tibetan emperor and the Tibetan court's anti-Buddhist turn, swayed his decision.[15] He likely knew that the Tang emperor Xuanzong (r. 713–756) had recently tried to solve the problems of the state by stripping Buddhist monasteries of their assets and forcing monks to become soldiers. But perhaps what ultimately convinced him was the Manichaean tradition's strong affinities to the world of commerce.[16] The Sogdians, who had controlled the lucrative East-West trade of the Silk Road for centuries from their homeland in Central Asia, were Manichean.[17] Adopting Manichaeism brought the favor of the Sogdians as well as their unrivaled economic prowess and technology to the Uyghurs. Külüg Bilgä Khan, of course, may also have believed in the teachings of Mani.[18]

Regardless, the adoption of Manichaeism as the state religion brought the Sogdians firmly into the inner circle of Uyghur power, and on account of the Sogdians' continent-wide commercial network, the relationship served both well. Because of the troubles facing both the Tang and the Tibetans, the Uyghur empire was probably then the most powerful state in Inner Asia. But this lured them into a false sense of superiority, with catastrophic consequences. After the death of the Tang emperor Daizong in 779, the Sogdians advised Külüg Bilgä Khan to invade China at this moment of weakness. Other leading Uyghurs at the court were wary of the power that the Manichaeans held over the Uyghur ruler and disapproved of this strategy. As a result, there was a "palace revolution" that brought to power Alp Qutluq Bilgä Khan (Ch. Dunmohe Dagan, r. 779-789). Qutluq Bilgä Khan not only executed Külüg Bilgä Khan and two thousand of his close attendants but also violently suppressed the Manichaean community. This Turkic ethno-religious ideology—anti-Sogdian and anti-Manichaean—characterized the next three Uyghur rulers.[19]

While this strategy rallied the support of the Uyghur elite, it also had negative economic consequences because it fractured relations with the lucrative East-West trade. When Qutluq Bilgä Khan died young in 795, Huaixin, the grand minister of both the deceased ruler and his father, took the throne. This development had two major ramifications. First, although the Uyghurs were divided into ten clans (On Uygur), earlier Uyghur rulers had all been of the Yaglakar clan. The grand minister, however, was of the Ädiz clan, and with his ascension the ruling lineage changed and remained so until the end of the empire. Second, the grand minister, who took the lengthy title Tängridä Ülüg Bolmïš Alp Qutlug Ulug Bilgä Khan (Ch. Huaixin, r. 795-808), not only revived the Manichaean tradition but also favored the Sogdians.[20]

The reason for this return to Manichaeism and the Sogdians is not known, but it is clear that for the first few decades of the ninth century the Uyghur realm prospered, so much so that Uyghurs moved into China and became major players in the economy through trade in horses and moneylending. Moreover, the Uyghurs' insatiable demand for silk—which was used as both currency and commodity on the Silk Road—drove the Chinese economy and "influence[d] the

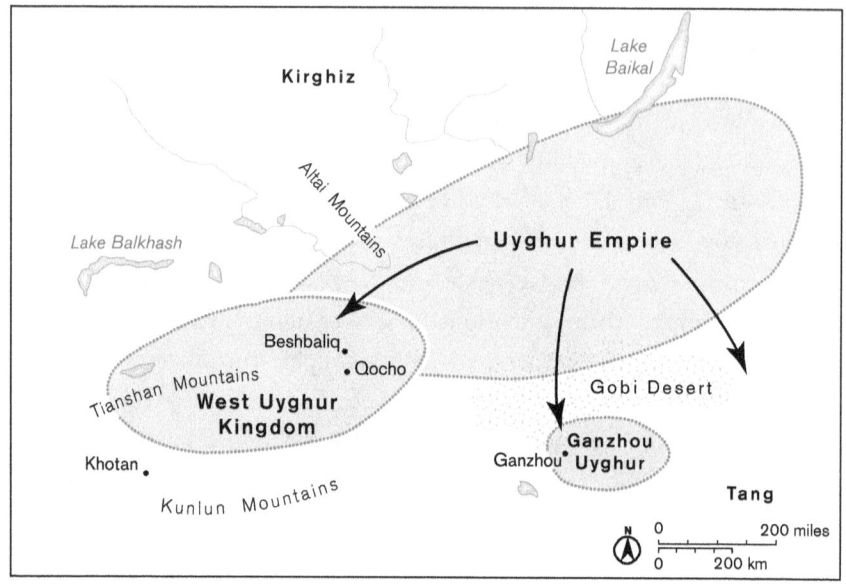

1.3 Uyghur Migration in the Mid-Ninth Century

development of silk production and commerce in Central Asia and in China from the mid-eighth to the fifteenth century."[21] Peace treaties signed among the Tang, the Tibetans, and the Uyghurs in the early 820s likely spurred this economic revival.[22] But the good times quickly came to end when in 829 the Chinese stopped trading with the Uyghurs and major environmental upheavals such as desertification and colder temperatures, as well as epidemics, took their toll throughout the 830s.[23] By the end of the decade the Uyghur state was depleted and no match for the Kirghiz who attacked from the north and defeated them.

After this invasion the Uyghur elite fled the Mongolian plateau in three distinct groups. One group went south and tried to settle in Tang territory. These Uyghurs eventually melded into the Sino-Turkic world of ninth-century north China.[24] A second group, led by a ruler of the Yaglakar clan (the original ruling lineage), moved southeast into the area of Ganzhou in the Gansu corridor and came to establish the Ganzhou Uyghur Kingdom.[25] The third group, led by Mäng Tekin of the Ädiz clan, first took over Beshbaliq on the northern slopes of the Tianshan mountains and set about establishing the West Uyghur Kingdom (see fig. 1.3).

Of course, the establishment of the Ganzhou Uyghur and the West Uyghur Kingdoms did not happen overnight. Both areas had recently been under the control of the Tibetan empire. The Uyghurs, however, had pushed the Tibetans out of Beshbaliq in 792, and in the wake of the Tibetan emperor Langdarma's death in 841 the empire had started to fall apart.[26] In 848 the local Chinese warlord Zhang Yichao (798-872) pushed the Tibetans out of Dunhuang, the pivotal Silk Road city that linked China with the West (see fig. 1.4).

To solidify his control over Dunhuang and the surrounding area Zhang sent an embassy to the Tang court, which appointed him military commissioner of the Guiyijun ("Return to Righteousness Army"). And with this imperial recognition Zhang began projecting the power of the nascent Guiyijun state beyond Dunhuang.

Yet as Tibetan power retreated in the Ganzhou area, the local inhabitants, known as the Dum—or, in Chinese, as the Longjia, "dragon families"—also reasserted their authority. The expanding Guiyijun thwarted their attempt at independence until the Uyghurs moved into the neighboring territory with their nomadic horse power. In 884 the Dum entered a treaty with the Ganzhou Uyghurs to become "one family" in order to reclaim their sovereignty from the

1.4 Mural commemorating Zhang Yichao's victory over the Tibetans, Mogao Cave 156, Late Tang (875-907)
Wikimedia Commons

Guiyijun.[27] Ultimately this was a fool's bargain because the more powerful Uyghurs soon took over and established their own state.

As all of this was unfolding in the Gansu corridor, the Uyghurs of the Western Kingdom were similarly trying to establish their rule. To this end they sent an envoy to the Tang court in 856 requesting imperial recognition, who died en route. And as tensions among all of these groups were rising, the Ganzhou Uyghurs tried to assert their power by attacking Dunhuang in 870, but Guiyijun forces repelled them. But in the 890s the Guiyijun leader Zhang Huaishen and his family were killed, as was his successor, whereupon the underage Zhang Chengfeng (894-910) was put on the throne. This unstable situation among the Guiyijun enabled the Ganzhou Uyghurs to consolidate their power. They attacked Dunhuang and in 901 burned the large pavilion at the Cave of a Thousand Buddhas. By 907 the troubled Zhang Changfeng declared the founding of a new dynasty, the Kingdom of the Golden Mountain of the Western Han, and proclaimed himself Emperor White Robe. In this new guise he rejected the pleas of his subjects and set about attacking the more powerful Ganzhou Uyghurs, which resulted in protracted warfare.

In 914 Cao Yijin (d. 935) ultimately repelled the Ganzhou Uyghurs and reestablished the Guiyijun. He also made peace with the Ganzhou Uyghurs by marrying the daughter of their khan. During the Five Dynasties period (907-960), Cao Yijin was able to secure his realm by taking control of the Gansu corridor trade. As relations between Guiyijun and the two Uyghur kingdoms became peaceful and stabilized, the economy blossomed and glorious Buddhist artwork was produced in Dunhuang.

Cao Yijin, for example, had one of the largest cave temples built at the Mogao caves in the years 923-925, which even includes a portrait of his Ganzhou Uyghur wife, Lady Li (see fig. 1.5).

This initial Uyghur involvement with Buddhism via the Cao family was probably not the first, and it was certainly not the last. In 925, the very year Cave 98 was completed, a delegation of Ganzhou Uyghurs came to Dunhuang to worship at the Mogao caves. Throughout the Cao family's rule there were numerous such envoy exchanges between the Ganzhou Uyghurs and the West Uyghur Kingdom.

These sociopolitical exchanges typically involved the gifting of Buddhist texts and relics. In 956, for example, the monk Fabao of Sanjie monastery in Dunhuang sent Buddhist texts to the West Uyghur Kingdom, including copies

1.5 Cao Yijin's Ganzhou Uyghur wife (on the right), Mogao Cave 98 (c. 923-925)

After Dunhuang Wenwu Yanjiusuo 敦煌文物研究所, ed., *Zhongguo shiku.5. Dunhuang Mogaoku* 中國石窟. 敦煌莫高窟 5 (Beijing: Wenwu Chubanshe, 1987), pl. 12

of the "transformation texts" (*bianwen*) that were then popular. Similarly, in 966 the then ruler Cao Yuanzhang and his wife visited the Mogao caves and ordered monks to make seventeen copies of *The Names of the Buddha Sutra* (*Foming Jing* 佛名經), which were to be distributed to the sixteen great temples in Dunhuang and one gifted to the West Uyghur Kingdom.[28] Of course, not all exchanges entailed such grand gestures. Based on extant Chinese loan contracts, most involved more quotidian matters, such as a Dunhuang envoy borrowing silk with interest while visiting the Ganzhou Uyghurs in 923 or another envoy from Dunhuang renting a camel to travel to the West Uyghur Kingdom.[29]

Although such political and economic exchanges—often greased with Buddhist ritual exchanges—enabled the three dynasties of Guiyijun, the Ganzhou Uyghurs, and the West Uyghur Kingdom to flourish during the early tenth century, they were not the only reasons for this cultural florescence. That depended on the relations that all three maintained with the ruling dynasties in China, especially the Song in the south and the Khitan Liao in the north. The Guiyijun, for example, sent tribute missions to both the Song and Liao every two or three years until their demise in 1024.[30] The Ganzhou Uyghurs favored the Liao and therefore sent numerous missions to the Khitan court. In 976 the Ganzhou Uyghur Khan began sending envoys to the Song, and these missions occurred uninterrupted between 984 and 996. The trade missions most likely financed the cultural flowering so evident in the Buddhist monuments of tenth-century Dunhuang.

Yet, as hinted at above by the Cao family's demise in 1024, the situation at the turn of the millennium was changing dramatically. There arose at this time two powerful and expansionist Buddhist states: the Tangut's Xixia dynasty and the Hexi Tibetan's Tsongkha kingdom. The Tsongkha Tibetans were based at Xiliangfu (today's Liangzhou) and had strong connections with the Song court, on whose behalf they fought against the Tanguts. Since the Tanguts were also threatening the Ganzhou Uyghurs, their ruler asked to form a marriage alliance with the Tsongkha Tibetans in 1012. The Tsongkha ruler, however, not only refused but also banned Uyghur traders from passing through his territory. This policy was damaging to the Ganzhou Uyghurs since their trade routes to China were otherwise blocked by the Tanguts. Nevertheless, several years later, in 1018, the Tsongkha ruler acquiesced and Uyghur trade with the Song resumed. Trade continued until 1028 when the Ganzhou Uyghurs suffered a devastating attack by the Tanguts from which they never recovered. Although they held out for another seven years, the Ganzhou Uyghurs eventually fled their kingdom and resettled in Tsongkha territory,[31] where they survived and are now a recognized minority in the People's Republic of China: the Yellow Uyghurs.[32] The Ganzhou Uyghur realm, however, was no more. The Tanguts conquered Dunhuang and put an end to the Cao family's Guiyijun regime as well.

During these tumultuous upheavals the West Uyghur Kingdom not only survived but thrived, and they began to convert to Buddhism in earnest. One reason they were able to resist the Tanguts—as well as maintain their independence for centuries thereafter—is that they never abandoned their nomadic heritage. Maintaining their summer capital at Beshbaliq on the steppe north of the Tianshan mountains, they continued their horse-riding military culture and thus were readily able to fend off the Tanguts. But perhaps even more important was their decision to become vassals of the powerful Khitan Liao dynasty around 925.[33] This relationship gave them military protection and enabled them to trade with the Liao, then the major driver of both Asia's economy and its Buddhist culture.

Still, both the ruler and the nobility of the West Uyghur Kingdom continued to profess their Manichaean faith for more than a century after they moved into their new homeland in the 840s. Why they did so is unclear, but certainly the Manichaean connection with the Sogdians and their international trading networks—especially with the West—played a role. It is also possible that the West Uyghur elite—who were of the pro-Manichaean Ädiz clan—wanted to promote their lineage's legitimacy through its connections with the Uyghur steppe empire and its Manichaeism. The Ganzhou Uyghurs, who were descendants of the anti-Manichaean Yaglakar clan (the original ruling lineage), had no such compulsion and became Buddhist as soon as they started interacting with the Guiyijun culture of Dunhuang, where they also became avid patrons of Buddhist art.[34]

The ruling elite of the West Uyghur Kingdom, however, continued to support the Manichaean community for some time. They even used Manichaean priests as envoys to the courts of China.[35] Gradually, this started to change. Beginning in the middle of the tenth century, Chinese court records note that the tribute missions from the West Uyghurs did not include Manichaean priests, but rather Buddhist monks bringing relics and texts.[36] In a memoir that describes the destruction of a Manichaean temple in 983, it is clear that the Uyghur elite were moving away from their old faith.[37] They painted over old Manichaean cave temples with Buddhist iconography and converted Manichaean temples into Buddhist ones.[38] As part of the purification and commemoration rituals, they drove inscribed stakes into the ground heralding this transformation (see fig. 1.6).

As the Buddhist turn progressed, the Manichaeans lost their royal support and had to accommodate themselves to the new Buddhist culture developing among the Uyghurs.[39] By the late tenth century, for example, they had moved the annual Bema festival—the biggest event in the Manichaean calendar—back a month so that it would not interfere with a celebration of the Buddha's renouncement of worldly life on the eighth day of the second month (see fig. 1.7).[40]

To stem the tide of this religio-cultural transformation, the Manichaeans tried to ingratiate themselves with the nobility by writing ever more panegyric paeans to the Uyghur ruler. In 1019, for example, a grieving father commissioned a Manichaean book for his dead son in which he also lauded the Uyghur ruler.[41] Yet it was all to no avail. The last dated Manichaean text—a Uyghur text translated from Sogdian for the purpose of fixing festival days—is from 1025.[42]

As Buddhist life and culture were burgeoning, so too was the economic and political power of the West Uyghur Kingdom. In the early decades of the eleventh century, they took nominal control of Dunhuang.[43] In recognition of these developments and their century-long alliance, the Khitan court invited the Uyghurs to join their diplomatic mission of 1026, which aimed to establish

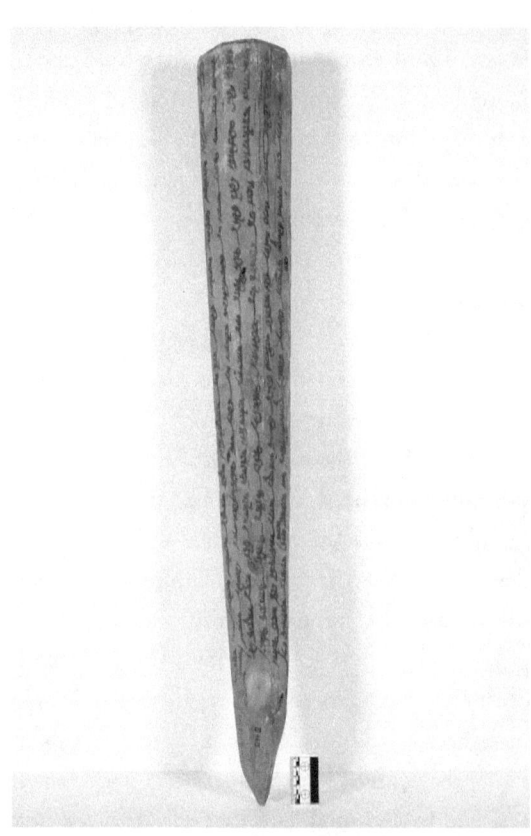

1.6 Stake inscription for a Buddhist monastery built in 1008

(Inv. No. III 4672). © Staatliche Museen zu Berlin, Museum für Asiatische Kunst

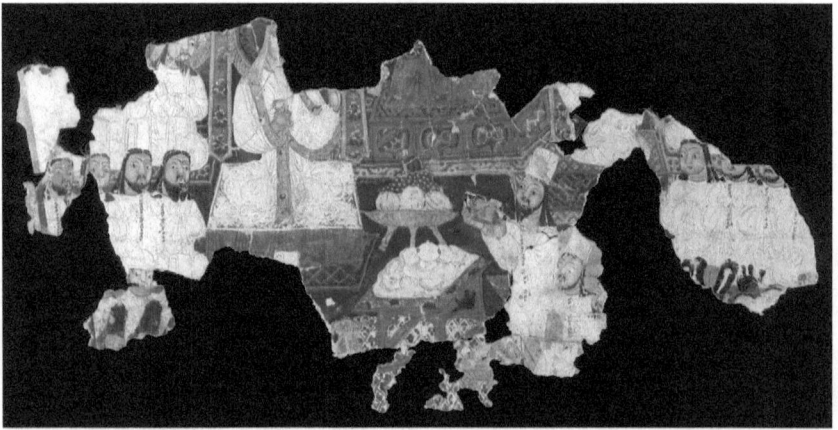

1.7 Bema Scene, full-page book painting shown from picture-viewing direction (H: 12.4 cm, W: 25.2 cm)

Fragment of a Turfan Manichaen Illuminated Codex (Inv. No. III 4979 verso). © Staatliche Museen zu Berlin, Museum für Asiatische Kunst

relations with Mahmud of Ghazna in what is now Afghanistan. The Uyghurs, however, were still threatened by the Tanguts, who by the mid-eleventh century had recaptured Dunhuang.[44]

THE GRADUAL EMBRACE OF BUDDHISM

As the condensed history above makes clear, the Uyghur conversion to Buddhism was not a single momentous event but a process that unfolded over time. It was also a dynamic process that involved numerous Buddhist communities. An array of Buddhists lived in the territory the Uyghurs ruled: Chinese Buddhists, Khotanese Buddhists, Sogdian Buddhists, Tokharian Buddhists, Tibetan Buddhists, and others. Christians, too, became subjects of the West Uyghur Kingdom.[45] In trying to conceptualize the process by which the Uyghurs became Buddhist, it is important to keep in mind that they were a minority elite ruling a predominantly Buddhist population. Consider, for example, this chapter's epigraph: a Song dynasty envoy notes fifty Buddhist monasteries in the Uyghur capital city of Qocho. The Tang dynasty tablets and the Chinese books he found in these monasteries make it clear that many of them were Chinese monasteries.

Although Manichaeism remained the state ideology and the favored tradition of the Uyghur nobility for more than a century, there is a good amount of evidence that some of these elites had become Buddhist. Some early evidence comes from the earliest extant Uyghur text, a ninth-century trilingual document written in Sanskrit, Tokharian, and Uyghur, in Brāhmī script. It describes the vows a Buddhist layman is expected to uphold (see fig. 1.8).[46]

This manuscript confirms that Uyghurs were using the Uyghur language in relation to the Buddhist faith. Other evidence shows that they used other local languages and scripts as well to access the Dharma. For example, they were able to read and write Buddhist texts in Sanskrit and Tokharian in Brāhmī and Uyghur script,[47] and they wrote Buddhist texts in both the Tokharian language and Brāhmī script, as well as in Sogdian language and script.[48] They also used the Tibetan script to write Buddhist texts in Uyghur, as evidenced in the so-called "Buddhist catechism" preserved in Paris (see fig. 1.9).[49]

The Uyghurs also used the Tibetan script to phonetically transcribe Chinese Buddhist texts.[50] Even those who could not read Chinese characters would still

1.8 Early trilingual Sanskrit, Tokharian, and Uyghur text in Brāhmī script. IOL Toch 81
Courtesy of the International Dunhuang Project

be able to recite the scriptures. In one illuminated manuscript, the "colophon goes on to list a dozen or so Buddhist texts (mostly by their Chinese titles) that the scribe has copied and then recited in a single day as an offering to 'the buddha, the gods and *nāgas* of the eight quarters, and the protectors of the four directions.' By the merit of this, he hopes that one day he will be able to return to his own country, and that after he dies, he will be born free of suffering, not in hell, and preferably in the god realms."[51]

The linguistic complexity of this particular Sino-Tibetan work also makes clear that Uyghurs were accessing the Dharma directly through Chinese sources.[52] Despite all the evidence of multilingual engagement with the Dharma during the ninth and tenth centuries, it is hard to gauge how widespread interest in Buddhism was among the Uyghur elite at this time; especially since the state religion continued to be Manichaeism.

Eventually, however, the Uyghurs began translating both Tokharian and Chinese Buddhist works into their own language and script, and this development marks the broader—or full—conversion of the Uyghur elite to Buddhism around the turn of the millennium. Two important sources document this decisive shift. The first is the memoir noted above, written by a Uyghur Manichean named Käd Ogul Xoštir, who laments the destruction of a Manichaean temple and its replacement by a Buddhist one in 983:

1.9 A Uyghur "Buddhist Catechism" containing questions and answers about the Dharma in Tibetan script. Pelliot tibétain 1292

Courtesy of the Bibliotheque nationale de France

> In the year of the sheep and of the element *kuu*, under the planet Saturn, by command of the "Lancer" Khan, Arslan Bilgä Tängri Ellig the Fourth, my Divine One, the Royal Princess, had the Buddhist monastery with three wheels that was built in the eastern part of the old inner city moved. In the time of the Teacher, Astūd Frazend, they tore down the Manistan and erected the Buddhist monastery. O, alas! They also pulled down and took the decorations of the interior part of the Manistan, and they carried them away and put them up in the Buddhist monastery, and they took the red brocade canopy and glazed and painted statue that were within the great chamber of this sacred and great Manistan and had the Buddhist monastery decorated with them.[53]

The other is the stake inscription noted above from the year 1008 (figure 1.6), which celebrates the founding of a Buddhist monastery on the ruins of a Manichaean temple.[54] Both of these documents show that the Uyghur elite were not only abandoning Manichaeism in favor of Buddhism but also actively destroying the Manichean church, and that this radical transformation happened around the year 1000. Why then?

DID UYGHURS CONVERT TO BUDDHISM AS A DEFENSE AGAINST A QARAKHANID THREAT?

One of the two main explanations scholars have postulated about the shift to Buddhism is that the Uyghur elite was, through conversion, attempting to unify the majority Buddhist kingdom against the expanding power of the Islamic Qarakhanids in the West. Based on the historical evidence, however, this seems unlikely.

The Qarakhanids were one of the original Nine Tribes of the Turk empires on the Mongolian plateau that had moved west when these empires collapsed.[55] They became one of several groups that jockeyed for power in Central Asia when the Abbasid caliphate waned in the ninth century. The most important and powerful of these new local dynasties was the Persian dynasty of the Samanids centered in Bukhara (in today's Uzbekistan). In the tenth century the Samanids ruled over the wealthiest and most advanced region of the Muslim world. Turks in the surrounding steppe areas were impressed by the Samanids' wealth and power and gradually started to become Muslim. Islam for the first time began to move beyond the urban confines of Central Asia and to acquire converts among the nomads of the steppe. Yet because the nomads always held a military advantage, these conversions were a double-edged sword for the Samanids. Turkic slaves made up the Samanid army, and although the practice of manning Muslim armies with Turkic slaves, acquired through either raids or the Inner Asian slave trade, had worked well for centuries, the system had begun to break down when the Turks themselves became Muslim. Fired up with the zeal of the newly converted, the Turks started not only to challenge their erstwhile Persian rulers in Central Asia but also to move militarily against the Abbasid caliphate itself.

The military slaves of the Samanid dynasty established themselves as the Ghaznavid dynasty (994–1186 CE) in the area of what is now Afghanistan and Pakistan (see fig. 1.10).[56]

Similarly, by the middle of the tenth century the Qarakhanids had converted to Islam and started to expand their domain south and eastward into the Tarim

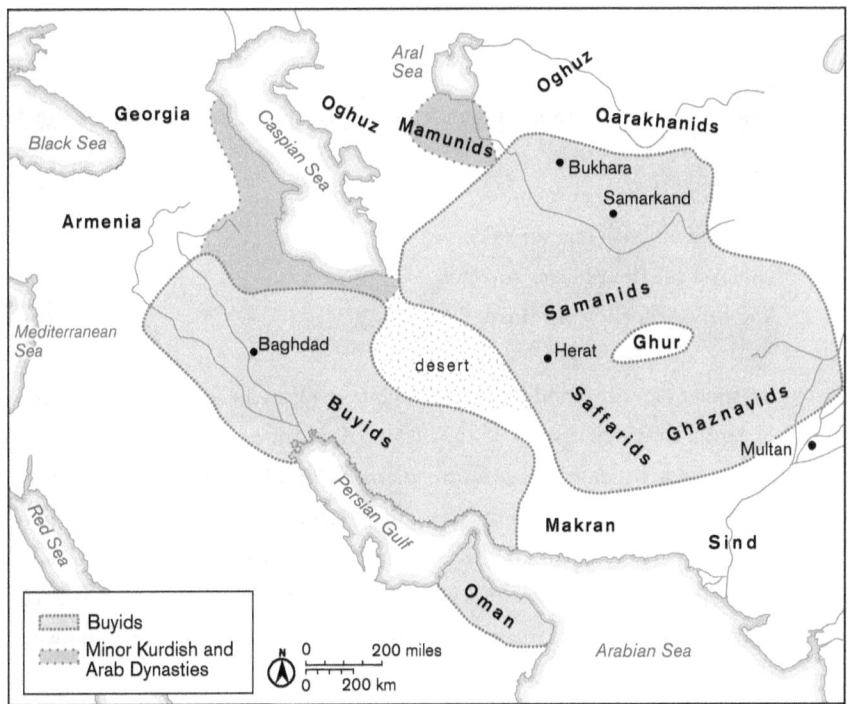

1.10 Post-Abbasid Central Asia

Basin. By 966 they had captured Kashgar, and in 1006 they captured the ancient Buddhist city-state of Khotan. A folkloric verse immortalized this Qarakhanid Islamic conquest:

> We came down on them like a flood,
> We went out among their cities,
> We tore down the idol-temples,
> We shat on the Buddha's head![57]

Such Qarakhanid attacks did not only threaten the Buddhist Khotanese. Kashgari's *Divan Lugat al-Turk*—an Arabic encyclopedia of Turkic languages from the 1070s—provides evidence that the Qarakhanids also threatened the Uyghurs:

> We boarded the boat,
> And crossed the Ila [River];
> Then we headed toward the Uighur
> And conquered Minlaq.[58]

Kashgari records yet another poetic verse referring to this campaign:

> We attacked them at night;
> We lay in ambush on every side;
> Then we cut their horses' forelocks,
> And killed the men of Minlaq.[59]

Based on such evidence, modern scholars have suggested that it was this Qarakhanid Islamic threat that spurred the Uyghur Buddhist conversion.

Although such a scenario is certainly plausible and fits our stereotype of the meeting of Buddhism and Islam in Asian history, it seems unlikely.[60] First, there is no corroborating evidence to validate such a claim. Aside from these ambiguous folkloric verses there is no historical evidence that the Qarakhanids actually threatened, much less attacked the Uyghurs. Moreover, the Uyghurs were both militarily powerful and backed by the imperial juggernaut of the Khitan Liao. But more importantly, the historical record makes clear that the Qarakhanids were more focused on conquering the riches of Central Asia than on expanding into Inner Asia. To explain this requires a brief excursus into Central Asian history.

When the Samanid state had begun to weaken, the Qarakhanids conquered their territory in Central Asia, which subsequently brought them into conflict with the Ghaznavids. Their disputes enabled yet another group of Turks, the Seljuk, to take advantage of the situation and expand their own state.[61] By 1040 the Seljuk had defeated the Ghaznavids near Merv (in today's Turkmenistan) and, rather than stay in Central Asia, they kept marching west, conquering Baghdad in 1055.[62] After proclaiming themselves a sultanate, they marched farther west and took Anatolia from the Byzantine Empire in 1071.[63] When the Seljuk realized they could not defeat Byzantium, a feat only the Ottoman Turks would achieve four centuries later, they returned to Central Asia, where in short order they defeated and expelled the Qarakhanids to the east. The Qarakhanids therefore took control of the area that is now the western part of Xinjiang province in China. The Seljuks eventually defeated that group as well in 1103.

Nevertheless, as was often the case with nomadic Inner Asian empires, the death of the great Seljuk Sultan Malikshah resulted in family feuds and competing claims to the throne.[64] Even though Malikshah's son was eventually able to take control, the infighting had weakened the state. The Qarakhanids saw this as an opportunity and revolted. Sultan Sanjar was able to suppress the uprising, yet at great cost, and in this weakened state he came up against and lost to the Qara Khitai—the Western Liao—at the Battle of Qatwan on September 9, 1141 (see fig. 1.11).

Much more can, of course, be said about this period of Central Asian history, but I have recounted these interactions to cast doubt on the claim that the Qarakhanids wanted to attack or conquer the Buddhist Uyghurs. Rather, they and the other medieval Turkic Muslim states were interested in the riches and wealth of knowledge found in Central Asia and the Islamic heartland. The Uyghurs were irrelevant. Marvazi's description of how Mahmud of Ghazna responded to the Khitan and Uyghur attempt to establish trade relations in 1026 captures this sentiment well:

[When] he saw what stupidity [the letter] contained, moved as he was by strong belief in Islam, he did not find it possible to grant what was requested with regard to the establishment of sincere relations and correspondence, and he dismissed the envoys, saying to them: "Peace and truce are possible

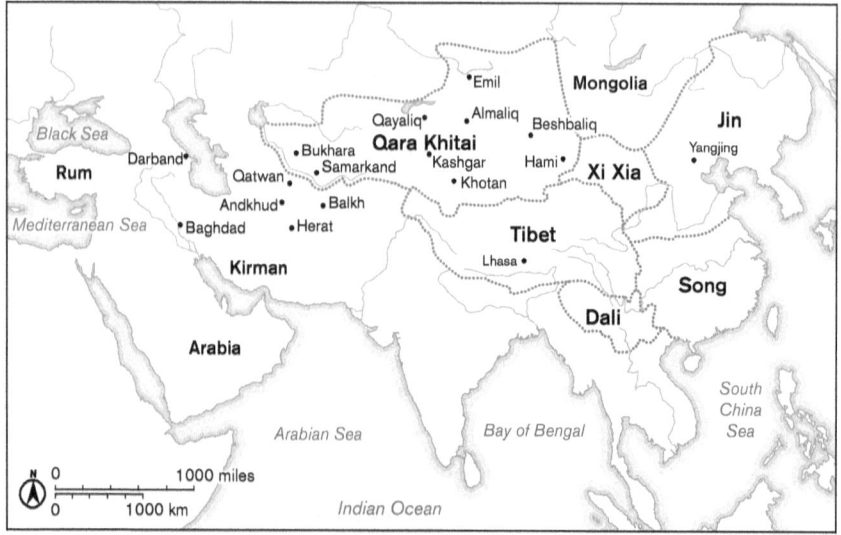

1.11 The Qara Khitai's Western Liao

only so far as to prevent war and fighting. There is no faith uniting us that we should be in close relations. Great distance creates security for both of us against any perfidy. I have no need of close relations with you until you accept Islam. And that is all."[65]

In short, the notion that the Uyghurs converted to Buddhism as a hedge against an expanding Islam seems doubtful. If anything, the Uyghurs probably had more to fear from the expansionist Buddhist Tanguts.

WHY DID UYGHURS REJECT MANICHAEISM?

The second explanation that scholars offer for the Uyghur conversion to Buddhism is that Manichaeism had failed them. Manichaeism was founded by the Iranian prophet Mani (216-274/276 CE) in the third century, and like the other major axial age religions—Buddhism, Hinduism, and Jainism—it sought salvation of the soul through transcendence of the material world.[66] Mani proclaimed that in the beginning there had been a cosmic world soul that had fractured, and particles of this primordial unity of goodness and light had become trapped in the darkness of the material world. In Mani's understanding a piece of this cosmic soul animates each of us, and when we die, this shard of the cosmic primordial reality is recycled into a new form. As a result, the cosmic soul remains splintered and mired in the debased and sinful material world. For Mani, the ultimate aim was to bring back together all of these cosmic soul particles, whereby the endless cycle of reincarnation within the material world of darkness and evil would be overcome. The question, of course, as with all religions, was how this ultimate transcendence of the debased material world would be achieved.

Mani followed other religions in establishing a social model comprising a renouncing religious elite supported by a laity active in the material world. The Manichaean renouncers, known as the Elect, observed five strictures—they were forbidden to lie, kill, eat flesh or drink alcohol, have sex, or accumulate personal possessions—and spent their days focused on prayer and hymns.[67] At night they gathered for the main ritual of the Manichean tradition, the "Table of God," a cultic meal the lay members of the community offered to the Elect. Throughout the year the Elect also did several rounds of fasting and partook in the confession of sins with the laity.[68]

The role of the laity, also known as Auditors, was to support these religious specialists through working in the material world—preferably in such occupations as trade and finance—and giving a portion of their income to the church. Auditors also had many other religious commitments. They followed ten rules: renunciation of idolatry, lying, greed, killing, fornication, theft, teaching of sorcery, slackness and negligence of work, and standing in two opinions (regarding religion).[69] The Auditors confessed their sins every Monday, and like in later Islamic practice, had four daily prayers devoted to the four aspects of the Father of Greatness (God, Light, Power, Wisdom), as well as a Ramadan-like thirty days of fasting with a break after sunset that was meant to remind them of Mani's passion after twenty-six days of imprisonment. In addition, the Auditors had to fast on fifty Sundays, as well as for two consecutive days at five other times of the year. In total, they were to fast for almost ninety days of the year.[70]

The Manichaeans focused on fasting and called their daily ritual the "Table of God" because Mani believed that only by eating properly could a person liberate their soul particle. As such, "Mani . . . breathed the intellectual atmosphere of his time," that is, a Stoic preoccupation with "the positive and negative effects of food" and an "international obsession with dietetics in the Hellenistic and

Late Antique times."[71] The fasting and healthy eating he advocated for the Auditors took on much deeper cosmological and salvific functions in relation to the Elect. Their strictly regimented lives and diet became the means by which the cosmic particles of light were liberated from gross and debased bodies. One scholar of Manichaeism explains this alimentary model of salvation as follows: "For the ordinary human, digestion is a crucial part of exporting soul to the surrounding world.... But for the reformed, perfected bodies of the Manichaean Elect, metabolism does not end in reproduction or in deeds inflicted on surrounding things; instead it is redirected and becomes a totally different sort of export, namely, the ascension of soul back to the realm of light."[72] In short, transcendence of the material world and its sufferings and a return to the primordial unity of the cosmic soul depends on how and what we eat.

Mani fused this Stoic obsession with the body to his larger cosmological and mythological conceptualization of how the universe functioned. As a result, Manichaeism provided answers that resonated in the age of Late Antiquity and thereby became what we now call a "world religion," practiced by an array of peoples stretching from Africa to China. Yet the very reasons it became popular presented problems when new ideas about the body and the cosmos appeared. For the great Neo-Platonist Augustine of Hippo (345–430 CE), who had been a Manichaean before becoming Christian, the teachings of Mani "represented quite simply the last gasp of a bygone era."[73]

Some scholars have suggested that the Uyghurs turned away from Manichaeism and toward Buddhism because the community was becoming too wealthy and thereby not living up to its ascetic values, but to me this explanation is simplistic.[74] Claims of religious hypocrisy are common among followers of ancient Buddhism as well as contemporary Christianity, yet rarely is hypocrisy proven to lead to the rejection of a tradition. Rather, the Uyghur abandonment of Manichaeism—like Augustine's—had deeper intellectual roots. New Indic and Chinese ideas about the body and the cosmos found in Buddhism, which was then becoming the dominant mode of thought across East Asia, were challenging the Manichaean tradition fundamentally. Buddhist doctors—deemed to be better—were being placed in the Manichaean temple in Qocho.[75] This is a strong indication that the seven-hundred-year-old ideas enshrined in the teachings of Mani about the body and salvation were being put to the test.

Such questioning, however, was probably not simply about cosmological and physiological matters but also about the viability and practicality of maintaining

Manichaean ritual mandates. For example, Manichaean rules took no notice of climatic variation: "Elects were supposed to drink only rainwater which was collected in a vessel as it fell. They were forbidden to drink water from the ground (wells, springs, rivers), which was regarded as contaminated. Since there is virtually no rainfall in the Turfan Basin, blocks of glacial ice had to be brought from the high mountains along the northern rim of the Tarim and then chipped into ice chunks to melt as drinking water for them."[76] An extant fragmentary document alludes to this process of ice collection from the Tianshan mountains: "[The request?] of the [(male) Presbyter] and of the Lady Presbyter [is that?] they [shall] cut and [] the ice into [five] blocks."[77]

Even though Uyghur elites had been dabbling in the Dharma for more than a century, Manichaeism continued as a viable tradition among the Uyghurs for several decades into the eleventh century. Therefore, it is not surprising that the traditions influenced each other. Manichaeism influenced Buddhist art and literature,[78] and Buddhism influenced Manichaean thought and practice.[79] But eventually Buddhism won out, and the remaining Manichaeans either converted or sought refuge elsewhere among the Qarakhanids.[80]

THE ASIA-WIDE TURN TOWARD BUDDHISM

The decisive turn to Buddhism around the year 1000 was shaped by one further major factor: everyone else was doing it. All of the peoples and states across East Asia—the Khitan Liao dynasty, the Chinese Song dynasty, the Tai Dali kingdom,[81] the Hexi Tibetans' Tsongkha kingdom, the Tangut Xixia dynasty, Korea's Koryo,[82] and Japan's Heian[83]—were becoming Buddhist (see fig. 1.12). The Uyghur conversion to Buddhism was thus part and parcel of an Asia-wide turn to the Dharma.

Throughout the tenth century, both the neighboring Tsongkha (Tibetan) and the Xixia (Tangut) were developing a sophisticated fusion of religious and political power that foreshadowed the so-called Tibetan Renaissance.[84] Yet the most influential actor in this tenth-century turn to the Dharma was the Song emperor Taizu (927-976), who used Buddhism as an ideological tool of state consolidation in the formation of the Song dynasty.[85] In particular, he had witnessed the upheavals and dislocations the Shizong emperor's (r. 954-958) massive purge of Buddhism had caused, resulting in the closing of more than thirty thousand

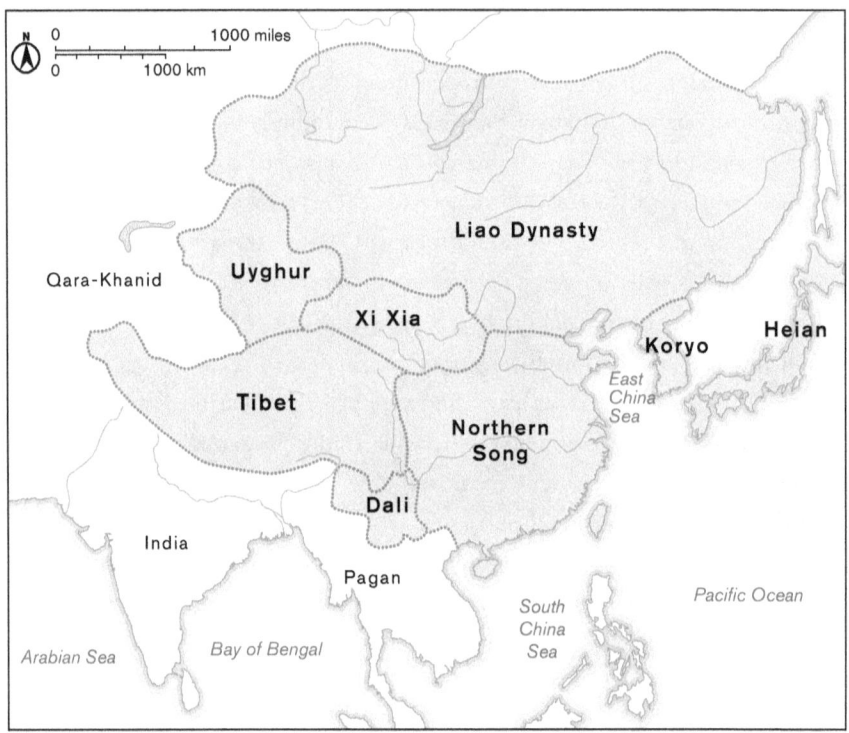

1.12 Buddhist Asia

monasteries. In contradistinction to such destruction, the Taizu emperor aimed to use Buddhism as both a vehicle of governance and a means of promulgating morality. To this end he launched a monumental project: creating a printed version of the Chinese Buddhist canon. It began in 971 and took twelve years to carve the 130,000 blocks that comprised what came to be known as the Kaibao canon. As Jiang Wu, Lucille Chia, and Chen Zhichao explain, the canon was created

> to serve different purposes of the newly established Song dynasty. First, it represented a new state attitude toward Buddhism, one that looked favorably on Buddhism and intended to revive it after the recent persecution under Shizong in the Late Zhou. Second, Kaibao canon served as a powerful diplomatic tool, especially in light of the Song failure to subjugate militarily the various states, such as the Khitan Liao and the Tangut Xi

Xia, that challenged its supremacy in East and Inner Asia. Third, the early Song emperors, starting with Taizong, envisioned Buddhist texts as integral to their aim of connecting their dynasty to the cultural and literary accomplishments of past regimes, and of reuniting the scholarship of north and south, which had been separated in the late Tang and Five Dynasties.[86]

First the Song court needed to make sure that they actually had all the texts needed to compile the Buddhist canon. Thus 300 monks were sent west in 964, and a second group of 157 monks were sent to India in 966 to bring back any holy scriptures not found in China. The importance of this initiative resulted in 57 further trips between 966 and 1078, either Chinese monks going to India or Indian monks coming to China.[87] And because these missions passed through the West Uyghur Kingdom, Uyghurs were necessarily becoming aware of the Song dynasty's turn toward the Dharma. This again is why, beginning in the 960s, Uyghurs started sending Buddhist monks instead of Manichean priests with their tribute missions to the Song court.

The Uyghurs, however, also had strong political and economic ties with the Khitan Liao. There are nine records of the Uyghurs sending envoys to the Liao court between 933 and 1005, and twelve between 1041 and 1073. Contact was so regular that the Liao established a "colony for Uighur envoys and traders in their upper capital (Shangjing Linhuangfu)," and Lu Tao, a Song envoy to the Liao, claimed that Uyghurs not only traded with "but were also engaged in espionage" on behalf of the Liao.[88] Whether this is true is unknown, but during this period of much fighting among the Song, Liao, and Xixia, the Uyghurs may well have functioned as intelligence operatives under the guise of merchants or Buddhist pilgrims.[89]

Whatever the case may have been, in the three-way struggle for supremacy in Buddhist East Asia among the Song, Liao, and Xixia, the Khitan Liao finally prevailed after a full-scale invasion of the Song in 1004. The resulting Chanyuan Treaty defined the political and economic relations between the Northern and Southern dynasties until Khubilai Khan finally conquered the Song in 1279. In the first decade of the eleventh century, however, the Song defeat and the Chanyuan Treaty shifted the balance of power toward the Khitan, who then became the major political and economic power at the time.[90] And with the Dharma the central feature of the Khitan state, Buddhism

1.13 The Phoenix Temple in Kyoto, Japan
Wikimedia Commons

became not only a political and economic unifier across East Asia but also a cultural and artistic one.

A well-known example of this Khitan influence is the Phoenix Temple in Kyoto. Built in 1053, it has long been held up as a classic example of sui generis Japaneseness (see fig. 1.13).

But the architectural style of this temple is actually based upon Liao dynasty precedent, and some of its artistic elements can even be traced back to art found at Dunhuang in Inner Asia.[91] The Phoenix Temple is thus more a monument to the interconnectedness of the Khitan Buddhist world that stretched from Inner Asia to Japan.

Uyghurs became Buddhist amid this interconnected world. They had a great deal of contact with the Song court, so much that in 1031 they received a copy of the Kaibao canon. But there is little evidence that "Song Buddhism" as such greatly influenced the development of early Uyghur Buddhism. In contrast, Liao Buddhism clearly did exercise considerable influence. The Uyghurs used the Khitan canon (based on the Kaibao canon and completed in 1068; see fig. 1.14) as the source for the translation of works into Uyghur.[92]

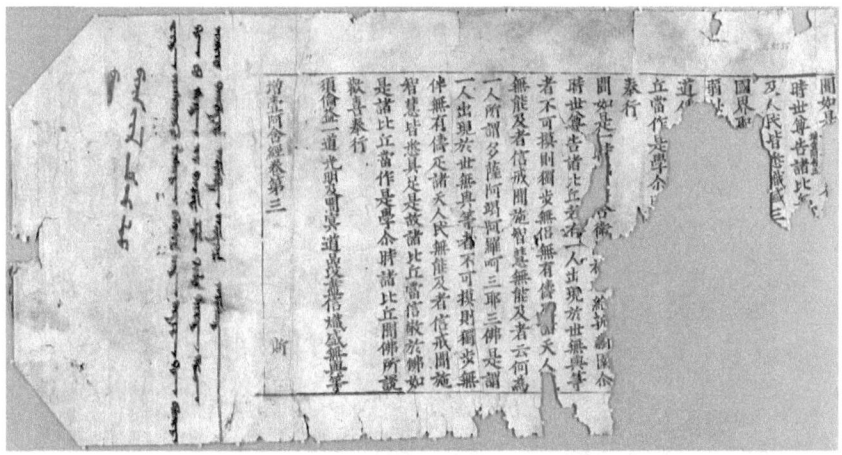

1.14 Page of the Khitan canon with a Uyghur inscription. Ch 5555
Courtesy of the collection at the Berlin-Brandenburchische Akademie der Wissenschaften in der Staatsbibliotek zu Berlin–Preußischer Kulturbesitz, Orientabteilung

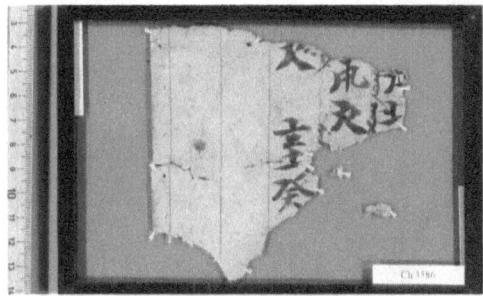

1.15 Khitan big-script manuscript with Uyghur interlinear glosses. Ch 3586

Courtesy of the collection at the Berlin-Brandenburchische Akademie der Wissenschaften in der Staatsbibliotek zu Berlin–Preußischer Kulturbesitz, Orientabteilung

The Khitan influence on the Uyghurs can be seen in their transliteration of the word "nirvana" (Ch. *niepan* 涅盤), based on the characters used in the Khitan canon, which unlike in other Chinese works uses the character *pan* with a blood radical (血 - 盤) instead of the wood radical (木 - 槃).[93] Further evidence of this religio-cultural and linguistic exchange is found in a text written in the Khitan's so-called "big script" that contains Uyghur interlinear glosses (see fig. 1.15).[94]

Still, the clearest confirmation of the Uyghur engagement with Liao Buddhism is the doctrinal orientation of the early Uyghur corpus of Buddhist literature, which conforms with what has been called the "north Chinese Buddhist complex" that fused together Huayan Buddhism, Chan Buddhism, and tantric

1.16 The *praṇidhi* scene No. 1 in Cave 20, Bezeklik, Xinjiang, China

After Albert von Le Coq, *Chotscho: Facsimile-Wiedergaben der wichtigeren Funde der ersten Königlich Preussischen Expedition nach Turfan in Ost-Turkistan* (Berlin: Dietrich Reimer, 1913)

1.17 The *praṇidhi* scene No. 14 in Cave 20, Bezeklik, Xinjiang, China

After Albert von Le Coq, *Chotscho: Facsimile-Wiedergaben der wichtigeren Funde der ersten Königlich Preussischen Expedition nach Turfan in Ost-Turkistan* (Berlin: Dietrich Reimer, 1913)

Buddhism.⁹⁵ Simply put, the Khitan were not just a source for the development of Uyghur Buddhism; their devotion was also an inspiration for the Uyghurs' own conversion. During this Asia-wide turn to Buddhism, adopting the Dharma made good political and economic sense, and the Uyghur were expanding their political and economic engagement not only with Dunhuang but also with the Liao and Song courts.

Yet the Uyghur conversion could not only have been about external geopolitical concerns. Recall that the Uyghurs were a minority ruling over a populace that was in the majority Tokharian and Chinese, both of whom were Buddhist.

1.18 Bezeklik murals in Berlin's Museum für Völkerkunde before the building was bombed during World War II

(Inv. No. Streseman X). © Staatliche Museen zu Berlin, Museum für Asiatische Kunst. Photograph by Max Krajewski

Becoming Buddhist 35

Although the Uyghur strategy of maintaining Manichaeism as the state religion may have worked to perpetuate both the glories of the Ädiz clan and their imperial legacy, it may also have distanced them from their subjects.

Of course, we have no historical records mapping out the decision-making process of the Uyghurs' conversion to Buddhism, but we know of their strong ties with the Liao, and the same strong connections were likely with the local Chinese and Tokharian Buddhists. One piece of evidence confirming Uyghur engagement with and recognition of these communities within their realm is found in the famous murals of Cave 20 at Bezeklik. This cave complex outside the capital city of Qocho—the construction of which was paid for by Uyghur elites—is best known for its fifteen monumental murals depicting the Buddha giving predictions of future buddhahood to various disciples through time (see figs. 1.16 and 1.17).

1.19 State Hermitage *praṇidhi* scene from the Bezeklik caves, Xinjiang, China, TU-775

Courtesy of the Hermitage Museum, St. Petersburg (https://hermitagemuseum.org/wps/portal/hermitage/digital-collection/25/.+archaeological+artifacts/178668)

Bezeklik Cave Temples Restoration Exhibit

1.20 Bezeklik Cave Temple Restoration Project, Ryukoku Museum
https://museum.ryukoku.ac.jp/en/bezeklik/

The figures were in fact so awe-inspiring that the German explorers who discovered them decided to dismantle them and send them back to Berlin, where they were eventually displayed at the Museum für Völkerkunde (see fig. 1.18).[96]

Sadly, all except one of these murals were destroyed during the Allied bombing in the Second World War.[97] The sole surviving mural was taken by the retreating Soviet army and is now on display at the Hermitage in St. Petersburg (see fig. 1.19).

More recently, in celebration of this spectacular monument of Buddhist art a digital re-creation of a parallel set of paintings from Cave 15 at Bezeklik has recently been built at the Ryukoku Museum in Japan (see fig. 1.20).[98]

Beyond these remarkable Buddha images, many other important images were found in Cave 20, including representations of the Chinese and Tokharian monastic communities (see figs. 1.21 and 1.22).

These murals therefore confirm that for the recently converted Uyghur elite the two communities were important actors in the Buddhist community of the

1.21 Tokharian monks in Cave 20, Bezeklik, Xinjiang, China

After Albert von Le Coq, *Chotscho: Facsimile-Wiedergaben der wichtigeren Funde der ersten Königlich Preussischen Expedition nach Turfan in Ost-Turkistan* (Berlin: Dietrich Reimer, 1913)

1.22 Chinese monks in Cave 20, Bezeklik, Xinjiang, China

After Albert von Le Coq, *Chotscho: Facsimile-Wiedergaben der wichtigeren Funde der ersten Königlich Preussischen Expedition nach Turfan in Ost-Turkistan* (Berlin: Dietrich Reimer, 1913)

West Uyghur Kingdom.⁹⁹ Their importance in forming early Uyghur Buddhism is also confirmed by the fact that the earliest translations into Uyghur were based on Tokharian and Chinese sources.¹⁰⁰ The earliest Uyghur translation of a Chinese text, for example, was the apocryphal *Eight Yang Sutra*,¹⁰¹ which was followed by numerous other works then popular at Dunhuang, such as the *Lotus Sutra*, the *Sukhāvatīvyūha Sutra*, and the *Ten King Sutra*.¹⁰² There are also five known Uyghur translations from Tokharian, including the *Araṇemi Jātaka*, the *Daśakarmapathāvadānamālā*, and the *Maitrisimit* about the future Buddha Maitreya.¹⁰³

In summary, the Uyghur conversion to Buddhism was a drawn-out process that involved many strains of inspiration and influence, shaped by political, economic, and religious factors.

CHAPTER 2

Buddhist Politics

Buddhism has no tie with any sort of "social" movement, nor did it run parallel with such, and it had established no "social-political goal."

—Max Weber, *The Religion of India*

Early Buddhism was a political failure.[1] Max Weber, however, was incorrect in his judgment that Buddhism was "apolitical" and "otherworldly." Rather, throughout its history—and especially in East Asia—Buddhism has always been intimately tied to political power.[2] Indeed, from the story of the Buddha's relics being divided among the eight rulers of ancient India to the legends of the Buddhist ruler Aśoka, it is clear that early Buddhists well understood that the success of their tradition depended on relations with the state. And the spread of Buddhism across the length and breadth of Asia confirms that this relationship worked. As numerous scholars have shown, the Dharma not only provides various models and theories that can be mobilized for political legitimacy but also, and perhaps more importantly, offers spiritual powers that can be used to maintain and project political power. It was precisely these attributes that helped drive the tenth- and eleventh-century adoption of Buddhism as part of the project of state consolidation throughout East Asia. The Song, Liao, Koryo, Heian, Tsongkha, Dali, and Tibet—all of these states used the Dharma, its socioeconomic structures, political theories, and magical powers, to build, maintain, and expand their empires.

Uyghur rulers might also have used all that Buddhism offered to secure their fledgling state against expansionist neighbors such as the Buddhist Tanguts.[3] But they did not. There is no monumental Buddhist project—artistic, architectural, or textual—that reflects a Uyghur ruler's involvement. The Uyghurs maintained the traditional model of Turkic rule by divine right—whereby the ruling lineage was blessed by Heaven—as well as Manichean titles from the imperial period, throughout the time when Buddhist art, culture, and thought were becoming dominant.[4] In other Buddhist realms rulers are incessantly praised in texts, inscriptions, and colophons as paragons of the Dharma and Buddhist rule.[5] But based on the available evidence, it was only ever the elite of the West Uyghur Kingdom who adopted Buddhism. Uyghur Buddhism was therefore never anything like a "state religion."

BUDDHISM BEYOND THE STATE

Buddhism nonetheless became a vehicle of both political dialogue and economic exchange for the Uyghurs as it had for the Song, Khitan Liao, Tangut Xixia, and Korean Koryo. As discussed in chapter 1, the Dharma mediated Uyghur relations with the Cao family in Dunhuang as well as the kingdom of Khotan in the west.[6] Moreover, the Uyghurs, aware of the Dharmic shifts taking place in mid-tenth-century China, stopped sending Manichaean priests to the Song and Liao courts and instead sent monks bearing Buddhist gifts. In 965, for example, the Uyghurs sent a monk named Fayuan to the Song court to present a tooth relic of the Buddha along with a glass vessel and an amber bowl. In 1003 a Uyghur monk named Yixiu took to the Song court Buddhist scriptures in Sanskrit, a rosary engraved with the Bodhi symbol, and several other Buddhist relics. And the following year a Uyghur monk visited the Song court and claimed to be able to make it rain:

> On Renyin Day, an ambassador sent by the Xizhou Uyghurs came to offer a tribute of local products.... On Jichou Day the emperor said to the court: "The sun has been shining excessively lately. There is a non-Chinese Buddhist monk who has come to Our Court in the Xizhou Uyghur embassy, who boasts of being able to summon a dragon to make rain fall. We got him to show this art in the temple and there actually was a response. Even if something like this is not in the Confucian scriptures, there should be nothing to be avoided in order to protect the people from the blazing sun."[7]

The Uyghur thaumaturge was apparently successful, and a few years later another monk sent by the Uyghur court presented the Song court with forty-six pounds of amber and forty-six pounds of brass. Such offerings were not unidirectional, though they were often presented as such in Chinese sources on account of the traditional tribute system model whereby trade with foreign countries was an elaborate part of the imperial ideology of China as the center of the universe. Trade was represented as if it were tribute presented to the Chinese emperor by subjects from afar, and the Chinese goods sold in return were represented as the magnanimous gift of the Chinese sovereign. Regardless of the performative elements of this exchange, these examples show that the presence of Buddhists within these Uyghur missions to the Song court was advantageous for them both politically and economically.

The same was true of the Uyghur relations with the Khitan Liao. As we saw in chapter 1, the Uyghur were much closer to the Liao than to the Song. Uyghur clothing even followed Khitan fashions.[8] But, as with the Song, relations were mediated through the Dharma. For example, in 1001, the Uyghurs sent Indian monks and skilled doctors as a gift to the Liao. Moreover, the *Records of the History of the Liao Dynasty* (*Liao shi jishi benmo* 遼史紀事本末) notes that Uyghur monks were involved with the compilation and study of the *Hand Mirror of the Dragon Niche* (*Longkan shoujian* 龍龕手鑑), a dictionary of Chinese characters found in the Buddhist canon.[9]

The Uyghurs also carried out such Buddhist politics with their immediate neighbors, the Tangut, with whom relations were sometimes troubled. In 1001 the Uyghurs requested military assistance from the Song to repel Tangut advances,[10] and during the first half of the eleventh century the Tangut not only annihilated the Ganzhou Uyghurs but also took Dunhuang from the West Uyghur Kingdom. Once the Uyghurs became Buddhist these relations began to change, and on account of their linguistic dexterity the Uyghurs were invited to the Xixia court to translate Buddhist scriptures into Tangut:

> Nanxiao [the Tangut emperor Jingzong (r. 1038–1048)] was born on the fifth day of the fifth month and he established this day as a day of celebration. The original custom was to celebrate the winter solstice. Nangxiao determined that the first week of every season should be a sacred holiday, so that officials and common people should revere the Buddha and pray for happiness to him. For this, at a distance of fifteen li from Zhongxing [the Tangut capital], corvée laborers built many pagodas, all as tall as fifteen *zhang*, as

well as the Gaotai Temple ... where the Great Collection of Sutras [i.e., Tripitaka], presented by the Middle Kingdom, was preserved. He invited many Uyghur monks to dwell there, explain the texts of the scriptures and render them with the Tangut writing.[11]

As with the Song and Liao, such interactions were not simply a one-way affair. The Tangut influenced Uyghur Buddhist art and practice, and Tangut texts were translated into Uyghur.[12]

Being Buddhist therefore had both political and economic consequences, and it brought with it more intangible assets such as "superior powers of healing, prognostication, and protection."[13] Based on the available evidence, we know that the Uyghurs were especially drawn to medicine and the astral sciences.[14] They translated Indian medical treatises as well as ritual texts for health and safety into Uyghur.[15] They also translated various Chinese divinatory texts like the *Book of Changes* (Ch. *Yijing* 易經) and the *Records of the Jade Casket* (Ch. *Yuxiaji* 玉匣記).[16] A major factor for many in the decision to adopt the Dharma was the protective power that Buddhism provided from misfortune.[17] As one scholar has put it: "Certainly the most important *function* of the clerical and Buddhist arm of the ... governing apparatus from its beginning was precisely apotropaic—protection of the state."[18]

It is therefore not surprising that many early Uyghur Buddhist texts and artworks invoked the Dharma as a protective shield. Two Buddhist works widely reproduced by the Uyghurs were the *Lotus Sutra* and the *Golden Light Sutra*. Unsurprisingly, these had also been an integral part of the imperial consolidation of Buddhist Japan. In 741 the Japanese ruler advocated the building of one monastery and one nunnery in each province, each of which would house ten copies each of the *Lotus Sutra* and the *Golden Light Sutra*. Their purpose as provincial state temples was "to provide prayers and other services directed to 'protection and stabilization of the nation.'"[19] "The *Golden Light Sutra* provided a spiritual and ideological antidote for the constant threat of [indigenous non-Japanese] Emishi attack or sabotage: the Shi Tenno [four heavenly kings]. According to the sutra, the four heavenly kings would materialize to defend and protect righteous Buddhist rulers in times of crisis."[20] Even though Uyghur Buddhism never became a state religion, the kingdom was situated at a frontier, and thus the protection afforded by the Dharma was important.[21] Uyghur art features iconographic representations of guardian deities like Vaiśravaṇa (see fig. 2.1).[22]

2.1 Mural with *Vaiśravaṇa* from the Bezeklik Caves, Xinjiang, China

After Albert von Le Coq, *Chotscho: Facsimile-Wiedergaben der wichtigeren Funde der ersten Königlich Preussischen Expedition nach Turfan in Ost-Turkistan* (Berlin: Dietrich Reimer, 1913)

Uyghurs also came to draw upon the full arsenal of Dharmic power made available to them through their expansive Buddhist network, as Denise Leidy explains:

> Small banner paintings preserved from Dunhuang, such as two examples discussed above, and various sites in Turfan depicting the protector [Vaiśravaṇa] either individually or accompanied by elite worshippers, indicate that he was often the focus of personal devotion by members of the ruling class.... The prominence awarded Vaiśravaṇa at Bezeklik [also] suggests that the Uighurs expanded an existing cult to this guardian in order to position themselves as the new, true protectors of the faith.[23]

It was not only the worship of Vaiśravaṇa that the Uyghurs adopted from Dunhuang. They also took up the cult of the thousand-armed Avalokiteśvara, which was strongly connected with rituals for protecting the state (see fig. 2.2).[24] Leidy continues:

> Avalokiteśvara with 1000 hands and 1000 eyes was particularly popular in the northwest regions of China and in Turfan. Over forty-five murals and banner paintings from Dunhuang dating from the late 8th to the 13th century are extant. Examples from the Uighur period include paintings found at Kharakhoja and in Temple α in Turfan and the mural in cave 39 at Yulinku near Dunhuang.... It seems likely that the importance awarded to Avalokiteśvara's more powerful manifestations at Bezeklik also reflects his ability—shared by Vaiśravaṇa—to protect the state from invaders and other disasters.[25]

To augment this Buddhist arsenal, the Uyghurs acquired from the Khitans ritual practices such as a powerful mantra that secured the "protection of the state" (Ch. *huguo* 護國),[26] as well as the ritual complex focused on the esoteric Buddhist divinity Tejaprabha, known as the "Lord of Constellations" because he protected against "cosmic calamities"[27] (see fig. 2.3).

Protecting the state through the power of the Dharma was a fundamental element of the Asia-wide Buddhist turn around the year 1000, but not the only one. Key Buddhist scriptures—such as the *Lotus Sutra* and the *Golden Light Sutra*—were another because they underpinned this turn, providing teachings that

2.2 Avalokiteśvara with a thousand hands and a thousand eyes from Dunhuang
Courtesy of the Hermitage, St. Petersburg

2.3 Buddha Tejaprabha's Paradise, Bezeklik, Xinjiang, China
After Albert von Le Coq, "Die Buddhistische Spätantike in Mittelasien Ergebnisse der Kgl. preussischen Turfan-Expeditionen," NII "Digital Silk Road" / Toyo Bunko. doi:10.20676/00000040

resonated with the times. The *Golden Light Sutra* is known for its focus on repentance and confession. The title comes from the fourth chapter, "The Dream of the Golden Drum of Penitence":

> The bodhisattva Ruciraketu dreams one night of a golden drum that lights up the sky like the "circle of the sun." A holy man materializes to beat the drum, and it sounds the need for confession and repentance as articles of faith. The theme of repentance, linked to penitence and the accumulation of merit, is a pivotal teaching of the sutra and subtends its imagery of golden light.... He copies and celebrates the sutra, obeys its precepts, lives a

penitent and circumspect life based on its teachings, and enjoins his people to do the same; as a result he flourishes, his domain prospers, there is no sickness or calamity, no enemies, no armies to vanquish.[28]

And at this time Buddhists across Asia took seriously the call for acts of repentance. In Song dynasty China, for example, rituals of redemption for the extirpation of sin became ubiquitous.[29] In Japan, aristocratic men wrote in their diaries that "they are sinners and transgressors, commission good works in penitence, and become preoccupied with pollutions and personal endangerments."[30] The same sentiments are found in Uyghur materials, especially the confession of sins, which became a foundational part of their Buddhist practice.

The *Lotus Sutra*, in contrast, encourages virtue (Skt. *guṇa*) as a way to accumulate spiritual merit, and the visual arts were the best way to articulate such virtue. With regard to twelfth-century Japan, Mimi Yiengpruksawan writes: "By sponsoring temples and art to celebrate Buddha and Buddhist teachings, and by copying sutras, the virtuous person earns merit toward desired goals, be it health and wealth or rebirth in a pure land. Art, whether in the commissioning, collection, or connoisseurship of objects, became an antidote to the free-floating anxieties endemic to a world in transition."[31] This same dynamic unfolded among the Uyghurs, where becoming Buddhist brought an explosion of art and literature alongside political and economic calculations.[32] Yiengpruksawan explains: "The physical pleasure of objects was in many senses the counterpart in the world of cultural production of physical violence in the world of politics. Temples, and the collections of sculptures, paintings, and sutras they housed, were used by members of the imperial household and their associates as tax shelters through the commendation of lands to their upkeep. On the intangible plane of spiritual comfort, however, the production of such artifacts offered an ostentatious but effective means of shoring up the self in an age of anxiety."[33] Both in Japan and among the Uyghurs the pending fear of a rapidly changing world created "an emergent interest in portraiture and 'true likeness,'" as evidenced in temple banners from Turfan that represented donors instead of Buddhist deities (see fig. 2.4).

Why were the Japanese and the Uyghurs both beset by the "idea of annihilation" and the need for "shoring up the self in an age of anxiety"? One reason was persistent warfare or the threat thereof. In the case of the Uyghurs, this fear is found in extant letters from the late tenth and early eleventh centuries that

2.4 Portrait of Uyghur donor Kara Totok represented as the main figure in a temple banner

(Inv. III 4524) © Staatliche Museen zu Berlin, Museum für Asiatische Kunst. Photograph by Dietmar Katz

warn of military confrontations and the need to defend the roads.[34] And one of the extant Manichaean benedictions, meant to be recited at new year celebrations to laud the ruler and realm, alludes to the violence then raging:

Our Devout One, who shines [like] the Sun [God]: for the sake of his (i.e., Mani's) doctrine on the inside and for the sake of his entire realm on the outside, he let his bejeweled and enlightened body suffer ... in the service of the realm ... [when] all of the bush and field crops, and the fruit plants and trees got scorched. Because of that, the guardian and tutelary spirits of the twenty-two cities of the Kočo country [praised] the great glory of our wonderful Devout One.[35]

The *Old Uyghur Annals* also warn that enemies and other dangers threatened the realm.[36] But for the Uyghurs—as for the other Buddhist peoples and states at the turn of the millennium—there was a further and more profound existential factor: the end of the Dharma and the coming of Maitreya, the Buddha of the Future.

THE BUDDHA MAITREYA

Buddhism is anchored by two myths. The first is that the Dharma is so profound and human ignorance and greed are so vast that the comprehension and practice of Buddhism will be lost and disappear. The second myth, however, tempers this claim by asserting that a new buddha will appear in the world and teach the Dharma anew, and the cycle of rise and decline will be set in motion again. Early Buddhist texts claim that seven buddhas have appeared through history: Vipaśyin, Śikhin, Viśvabhu, Krakucchanda, Kanakamuni, Kāśyapa, and Śākyamuni (the Buddha of the contemporary era, on whom the clock is ticking). When Buddhism will actually end has animated Buddhist thought for two millennia,[37] and it has also driven Buddhists across Asia to transform both their religious tradition and its political realities.[38] In China, for example, fears about the "end of the Dharma" were instrumental in the development of both the Zen and Pure Land traditions and in various millenarian political movements over the centuries.[39]

Central to many of these movements, and indeed the entire apocalyptic narrative of the Dharma, is the myth of the Buddha Maitreya. Buddhist texts tell us that he currently resides in Tuṣita heaven and will, messiah-like, eventually return when the Dharma has been totally forgotten to revive the Buddhist dispensation.[40] For Buddhists, of course, the question has always been when this would actually happen. For those partaking in the East Asia-wide Buddhist turn in the tenth and eleventh centuries, the answer was that the end times would start in 1052 CE.[41]

Why and how this date was determined is unclear, but it has been suggested that the advance of Islam into Buddhist India and especially the fall of Khotan to the Qarakhanids may have been a factor.[42] These events had given rise to the myth of Shambhala among Buddhists in what is now northwest India and Pakistan. Shambhala is first found in the early eleventh-century *Kālacakratantra*, which prophesies a world where the Dharma is under relentless assault. In particular, it claims that Buddhism will be threatened in the future by Muslims, and the final eschatological battle will take place between them and the twenty-fifth (and final) ruler of Shambhala, Kulika Rudracakrin, who will ride forth with his Buddhist army from the hidden realm, annihilate the Muslims, and usher in a new golden age of the Dharma.

Although this myth was animated by real-world events, it also drew upon the Buddhist tradition's deep well of apocalyptic narratives concerning the rise and fall of the Dharma. It became a readily accepted model to explain the contemporary world for Buddhists in northwest India, and through the burgeoning relations between India and China and the Song dynasty's Kaibao Buddhist canon project, made its way east as well. One such conduit was the Kashmiri monk Devaśāntika (Ch. Tianxizai 天息災, d. 1000), who translated a text into Chinese detailing such apocalyptic language and visions.[43] This work was followed by others, such as the *Essential Readings for Buddhists* (Ch. *Shishi yaolan* 釋氏要覽), a dictionary compiled in 1019 by the monk Daocheng that included timetables for the end times.[44]

Chinese concern about the Dharma's demise and Maitreya worship spread to Japan on account of the interconnected Khitan Liao Buddhist world. Ten catastrophic outbreaks of smallpox, measles, influenza, and plague between 995 and 1030 had occurred in Japan, fueling the apocalyptic vision. In addition, "the appearance of SN 1006 on Kyoto's southern horizon in May of 1006—the largest supernova in history—contributed to the growing sense of doom."[45] The supernova was followed by meteor showers in 1007; a triple conjunction of Jupiter and Saturn in 1007-8; the Kamo river flooding in 1017; a Jurchen fleet attacking Hakata in 1019; typhoons in 1028 and 1034; and the main sanctuary at Toyouke Shrine in Ise collapsing in heavy wind in 1040 and the palace burning down a month later.[46] With such a concatenation of catastrophes, the Japanese practiced ritual actions such as placing scriptures—most often the *Lotus Sutra*—in caskets and then burying them in mounds. As D. Max Moerman explains:

> The process required that sutras be transcribed according to strict ritual protocols, enclosed within reliquary-shaped containers, and buried underground

to protect and preserve the teachings until the arrival of the next Buddha, Miroku (Skt. Maitreya), some 5.67 billion years in the future.... The primary motivation was the concern to preserve the sutras throughout the age of mappo [the end times] until the coming of Miroku, who will use the buried sutras in his three inaugural sermons beneath the Dragon Flower Tree. The location of the major sutra mounds—such as the mountains of Hiei, Koya, and Kinpusen—were, like Hiko, believed to be the sites of Miroku's future descent.[47]

The Japanese were not the only ones to take ritual action to deal with the end times and the coming of Maitreya. The Khitan Liao, for example, revived the cutting of the Buddhist canon into stone at Yunju monastery on Fang Mountain near Beijing. The cutting had been initiated by the monk Jingwan in the seventh century when the fear of the Dharma's demise was also rampant. By the end of the eighth century the project had faltered, and in 964-965 it was revived under Liao patronage. Mimi Yiengpruksawan describes the new project:

> Extant stone tablets were reorganized, and subsequent carving went forward based on the Liao edition of the canon. It was a massive project, eventually yielding thousands of tablets, whose impetus clearly lay in Jingwan's pledge. Indeed, his vow to preserve the Buddhist scriptures is echoed in the inscription by a Liao official and his monastic advisor on a stele commemorating the restoration of Yanjunsi in 965. They seek, through the durability of stone, to safeguard Buddha's teachings in the many worlds and ages that lie ahead. In 1005 the stele was recut and another inscription added, which states that through the medium of stone the teachings will be preserved until the coming of Maitreya—that is, Future Buddha who appears after the eschaton.[48]

The Khitan also rebuilt the northern pagoda at Chaoyang, and when they installed relics inside it, they memorialized them with an inscription: "deposited at noon of the 8th day of the 4th moon of the 12th year of the Chongxi reign (May 19, 1043) of the Great Khitan State, with eight years remaining of *Xiangfa* (Semblance Dharma) followed by entry into *Mofa* (Latter Dharma)." Moreover, as Youn-mi Kim has shown, "these relics and texts suggest that the upper cella was intended to function as a 'miniature ritual altar related to the Buddhist incantation known as *Uṣṇīṣavijayā dhāraṇī* (Superlative Spell of the Buddha's

Crown),' which would generate protective powers of the spell in perpetuity. By 1052 there were five Chinese versions of the dharani in circulation... [that] explained its efficacy during the Semblance and Latter Dharma."[49] Such texts and ideas made their way to Dunhuang, where in the tenth century "the most grandiose and important restoration project" was the repair of Cave 130, which featured a large statue of Maitreya Buddha as its main icon.[50]

The worship of Maitreya and its links with an "age of anxiety" was pervasive across Asia around the time of the Uyghur conversion, and the cult of Maitreya became the most important element of early Uyghur Buddhism. Yet unlike the Japanese and Khitan, who had only recently adopted this tradition from the Chinese, the Uyghurs had long been involved with the worship of Maitreya on account of their engagement with the Tokharians.[51] The Tokharians focused on Maitreya and had already in the fifth century begun representing the so-called *praṇidhi* scene—the prediction of future buddhahood—in their artwork (see figs. 2.5 and 2.6). This scene would become central to early Uyghur Buddhist art.[52]

The earliest extant Uyghur text—the trilingual one discussed in chapter 1—mentions Maitreya. Another important and early Uyghur text, the *Maitrisimit*,

2.5 Fifth-century Tokharian mural of king presenting an umbrella to the Buddha, Kizil Cave 38

After Tan Shutong and An Chunyang, *Shinkyō no hekiga—Kijirusenbutsudō (Murals of Xinjiang: The Thousand Buddha Caves at Kizil)*, 2 vols. (Beijing: Zhongguo waiwen chubanshe, 1981), I, fig. 123

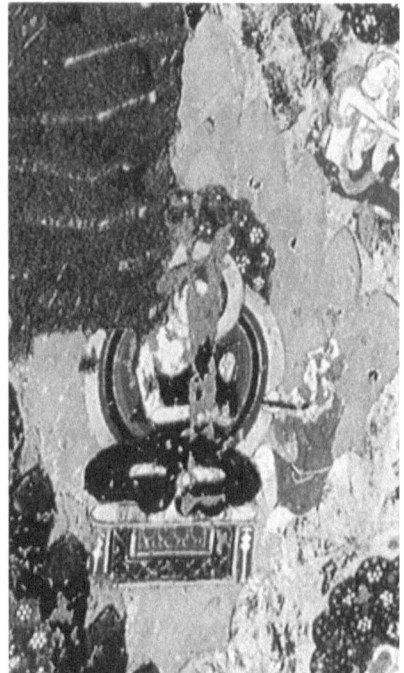

2.6 Fifth-century Tokharian mural of merchant presenting treasures to the Buddha, Kizil Cave 38

After Tan Shutong and An Chunyang, *Shinkyō no hekiga—Kijirusenbutsudō (Murals of Xinjiang: The Thousand Buddha Caves at Kizil)*, 2 vols. (Beijing: Zhongguo waiwen chubanshe, 1981), I, fig. 114

which was translated from a Tokharian original and probably dates to the second half of the tenth century, is a twenty-seven-chapter teaching about Maitreya.[53] In the colophon of the earliest version of the *Maitrisimit*, the lay brother Boz Bay Tirāk and lay sister Yidläk, who commissioned the work, state their wish: "Later may it happen that we meet Buddha Maitreya, attain the blessing of Buddhahood and ... Buddhahood."[54] Similarly, in another version from 1067, the colophon records: "In order that ... I, lay brother [Čuu] Taš Yegän Totok, who believes in the Three Jewels, and [my wife] Tözün will meet the coming Buddha Maitreya, we have arranged for the painting of this image of Maitreya and the copying of the *Maitrisimit Sutra*."[55]

Central to the Uyghur cult of Maitreya was the desire to be reborn at the time of the future Buddha—or in Tuṣita heaven—in order to receive a blessing or prophecy of future buddhahood. In a stake inscription commemorating the founding of a Buddhist monastery in 1019, for example, the two donors express their hope for such a prediction from Maitreya.[56] From the Sanskrit inscriptions that top the Uyghur *praṇidhi* scenes in the Bezeklik caves, we know that the mythology of this tradition goes back to the *Mahāvastu*, which claims that there were actually fourteen (not six) buddhas between Dīpaṃkara and Kāśyapa.[57] With the addition then of the present Buddha, Śākyamuni, the *praṇidhi* murals in caves 20 and 15 at Bezeklik together depict fifteen buddhas, each of which iconographically confirms that in times of trouble the best hope for future buddhahood is not one's effort in this life but being reborn at the time of a future buddha so as to acquire both the merit and the prophecy needed for salvation.

This desire to be reborn at the time of Maitreya's earthly descent is found in the earliest texts of the so-called Nikāya schools. This was the tradition that the Tokharians followed and transmitted to the Uyghurs. Yet on account of the Maitreya fever in the tenth and eleventh centuries, new ideas and rituals relating to the future buddha were developing in other Buddhist traditions. In China, for example, the Yogācāra school had long promoted not simply waiting for Maitreya to be reborn on earth but praying to be reborn directly into Tuṣita heaven, where Maitreya now resides.[58] Leading Buddhists such as the pilgrim and translator Xuanzang promoted this idea. In the tenth century the Yogācāra Faxiang school, which was then growing in popularity both in the Liao dynasty and in Dunhuang, revived it, and the Uyghurs subsequently adopted the tradition.[59] They not only adopted its new ideas and rituals but also fused them with the original Tokharian practices to create a distinctive new ritual repertoire.[60] One such practice was asking Maitreya directly to "eradicate ailments and the sufferings of the Uyghur people in the realm of Kocho."[61] Jens Wilkens describes another text that includes "a diagnosis of the present situation" as one of "degeneration, depravity and impurity, in which the Uyghur nobility tirelessly work to rebuild a thriving Buddhist community." In these works the nobility are represented as the "'charisma of the realm of Kočo' (OU *kočo ulušnung kuṭı kıvı*), a term reminiscent of the protective deities guarding the land of the Uyghurs."[62]

The worship of Maitreya among the Uyghurs thus worked on multiple levels. By promoting the cult through textual and artistic production—including representations of themselves—the Uyghur elite were "shoring up the self in an age of anxiety" and grappling with the "idea of annihilation" (see figs. 2.7 and 2.8).

Yet unlike all the other surrounding polities, even amid fear and upheaval, the Uyghur ruler himself did not take up these issues. He never claimed to be a cakravartin, a bodhisattva, a new Aśoka, or any of the other standard ideological models available for Buddhist rulers.[63] Rather, the Uyghur nobility were the

2.7 Portrait of male Uyghur donor from Bezeklik Caves, Xinjiang, China

After Albert von Le Coq, *Chotscho: Facsimile-Wiedergaben der wichtigeren Funde der ersten Königlich Preussischen Expedition nach Turfan in Ost-Turkistan* (Berlin: Dietrich Reimer, 1913)

"charisma of the realm of Kočo." Their support of the Dharma was both protecting the Uyghur state and making salvation possible.

THE IMPORTANCE OF NOT BEING BUDDHIST

We know that the West Uyghur Kingdom was ethnically, linguistically, and religiously diverse from Arabic sources and letters preserved in Cave 17 from Dunhuang.[64] They make it clear that trade and business involved Manichaeans, Christians, and Buddhists of various ethno-linguistic groups.[65] Perhaps the Uyghur ruler avoided embracing the Dharma to keep from upsetting this

2.8 Portrait of a female Uyghur donor from Bezeklik Caves, Xinjiang, China

After Albert von Le Coq, *Chotscho: Facsimile-Wiedergaben der wichtigeren Funde der ersten Königlich Preussischen Expedition nach Turfan in Ost-Turkistan* (Berlin: Dietrich Reimer, 1913)

equilibrium. The ongoing wars among the Buddhist realms of the Song, Liao, and Xixia may have been reason enough to avoid taking a strict ideological stand, which could have drawn the West Uyghur Kingdom into the conflicts. He may also have been cautious about what embracing Buddhism might do to the lucrative trade between the Islamic west and the Buddhist east, which the Uyghurs facilitated. Evidence shows that even the Buddhist establishment was apparently divided on the issue; one Uyghur text promotes the conversion of the royal house[66] while another warns against it.[67] Whether this later argument actually won the day or not, the Uyghur rulers never did adopt the accoutrements and language of Buddhist rule. Instead, throughout the eleventh and twelfth centuries, they kept their Turkic and Manichaean royal titles and their inherent linkages to the glories of the ancient steppe empire.

The Uyghur perpetuation of their former culture may have circumvented both multiconfessional and intra-Buddhist disputes around religious authority and political legitimacy. By maintaining their older ideological models, the Uyghur rulers were able to stay above the fray of contemporary conflicts. To this end they not only kept their titles from the imperial period but also avoided any mention of Buddhism in their royal history.[68] Instead, the royal narrative focused on the history of Huaixin, the grand minister who became khan, revived Manichaeism, and brought the Ädiz clan into power.[69] They also maintained this legacy through their self-identification as the Ten Uyghur—the ten tribes that composed the original Toguz Oguz confederation of the Turk empire[70]—and their imperial seal that features the weighty title "The Blessed Great Uyghur State."[71]

Notably, none of this imperial history or its accoutrements draws any connection to Buddhism. During the Mongol empire period, however, when Buddhism was more like a state religion, the Uyghur telling of their history began to change. It became expressly Buddhist. In one such story, for example, the primordial Uyghur ruler descends from Tuṣita heaven and is identified with Maitreya.[72] In another thirteenth-century story this same ruler converts after Buddhist monks defeat shamans in a debate.[73] Yet such retellings are later, Mongol-era Buddhicized versions of Uyghur history. The earlier ones maintain the historical Uyghur connection with Manichaeism. Moreover, unlike the later Mongol-period Uyghur Buddhist histories, which reflect the universalist dispensation of the Dharma found in Tibeto-Mongol sources of the Yuan dynasty period and thus begin with the history of India and the Buddha, the earliest Uyghur histories focus solely on the Uyghur ruling lineage.[74]

One reason that the Uyghur ruling house promoted this particular history during this transitional period is that it worked on multiple levels and for various audiences. One such level was the theory of "two realms"—the religious and the political—that characterized both Manichaean and Buddhist political ideologies. In the case of Buddhism this theory of rule drew upon Buddhist political thought and held that the secular and religious realms are represented, respectively, by a ruler and the Buddhist monastic community, who in symbiotic relationship oversee the proper functioning of a Buddhist state.[75] A similar theory of "two realms" is also foundational to the Manichaean tradition. This fact has led one scholar to claim that "it was probably within the Manichaean community that the notion of the 'two laws' or 'two orders' (*iki törlüg*), the spiritual and the political order of life, both sustaining each other, was first conceived.... The Buddhists were to take up the formula, for we find it in Buddhist texts as well."[76] Manichaean colophons, for example, contain such passages: "From the Four Light Kingly Gods may there come protection for the inner side, the religion, and on the outer side, protection for our Sage and Wise King! May the two kinds of orders be strong!" Or: "(May there be a blessing...) on the inner side upon the fivefold pure and clean religion, and on the outer side upon the whole blessed Ten Uyghur realm."[77] In Buddhist texts, such as the early bilingual Sanskrit-Uyghur translation of the *Āṭānāṭikasūtra*, we find similar phrasing: "May all hostile evil (men) who think bad and evil against the realm and the law of the Blessed Ten Uyghur be humiliated!... On the inner side (may there be) the pure teaching and discipline, on the outer side may the realm and the law triumph!"[78] And in the colophon to a Buddhist confession text, we read: "May (the gods and ghosts) protect and guard on the inner side the teaching and discipline, and on the outer side the realm and country!"[79]

The concept of two realms was therefore an ideological model that worked for both religious communities, and the Manichaean benedictions for the Uyghur ruler recited at the annual new year celebration came to include both Buddhists and Christians:

> It will be that [] will be the ones who [prop up] and hold him in their tight grip. My divine Khan! Should he ascend to the beyond (i.e., die), [], the [twenty-]two cities of the divinely blessed Kočo country, and inside, the pure Elects who [] the doctrine and precepts, and outside, [his realm] and both [Buddhist] monks and Christian [], and its notables and distinguished ones, its elite and nobility [] with upright thoughts and single-mindedness...[80]

Indeed, the religious diversity of the Uyghur realm encouraged ideological and institutional fluidity; as a result, the Uyghur ruler did not need to promote himself specifically as a *Buddhist* ruler.

A DISTINCTIVE BUDDHIST REALM

The Uyghur ruler, however, is rarely present but not wholly absent from Buddhist sources. He is mentioned in the Buddhist stake inscriptions noted in chapter 1 and in colophons to three Buddhist translations. In the colophon to one confession text, the donors hope that the merit generated by this pious deed of writing out the text will "be transferred to the Majesty Prince Kutlug Bars!"[81] Similarly, the donors of the eleventh-century *Maitrisimit* hope that the merit of this deed will go toward "the majesty of our Heavenly Uigur Prince Tängri Bögü El Bilgä Arslan: May he together with the realm of the Ten Uyghur, the thirty princely sons, the nine envoys and wise men, thousand servants, ten thousand inner servants for thousand and ten thousand years graciously rule the realm!"[82] Even in these explicitly Buddhist contexts the Uyghur rulers are not presented in any kind of Buddhist guise.[83] Moreover, the fact that the Uyghur ruler is mentioned in only three colophons bears out the "two realms" theory: the political and spiritual orders were separate.

Buddhism also did not figure centrally in other functions of the state. Other realms at this time were preserving the Dharma in the face of the end times by producing editions of the Buddhist canon, but this never happened among the Uyghurs. There is no Uyghur Buddhist canon.[84] Similarly, we know that the Uyghur state appointed monks to act as mediators between the court and Buddhist monasteries, but there is no evidence that the court became entangled in monastic or Dharmic disputes. In fact, these mediator monks were appointed on the basis of their "ethnic" origin and not in relation to their religious affiliation. The Chinese community of monks was headed by a *dutong* (a Tang dynasty title for the leader of a Buddhist community), the leader of the Tokharian monks was entitled *käši ačari*, and the head of the Uyghur community was given the title *šazin ayguči*, "minister of the religion."[85] Moreover, there is no evidence in the extant civil documents that these officials—or Buddhism in general—had any impact on state policies or legal practices.

One consequence of this laissez faire approach to the Dharma among the Uyghurs was that a distinctive from of Buddhism developed. Much as in the modern West, where Buddhism is also not connected to political power, there developed a freewheeling attitude among the Uyghurs. In both cases the lack of political involvement with—or oversight of—the Dharma creates a situation where Uyghurs (or contemporary Westerners) are free to do what they want with the tradition.

In the case of the Uyghurs, for example, scholars have long noted their individualistic approach to both Buddhist art and literature. One scholar has remarked that Uyghur Buddhists had a "self-confident attitude to traditional Buddhist literature."[86] To put it another way, they had no qualms mixing and matching texts from diverse Buddhist schools of thought and practice into distinctive new texts.[87] In one manuscript, the *Aranemi Jataka*—a story about one of the Buddha's previous lives—was paired with a confession text, and in another excerpts from the Buddha's early teachings in the *Saṃyukta-Āgama* were joined with passages from the Mahāyāna *Lotus Sutra*.[88] Similarly, the so-called Uyghur "Lehrtext" is a collection of disparate Yogācāra texts,[89] and the *Abitaki Sūtra* is a wholly unique collection of Pure Land texts.[90]

Beyond this mixing and matching, the best example of the Uyghurs' freewheeling textual practices is how they translated scriptures. As Peter Zieme has described them, they are better understood as "'adoptions' rather than translations."[91] The Uyghur translation of Shenxiu's Chan text *Treatise on Contemplating the Mind* (*Guanxin lun* 觀心論 T. 2009 and 2833), for example, "has copious additions and alterations when compared with the Chinese original."[92] Similarly, the Uyghur translators of such iconic works as the *Golden Light Sutra* and *Lotus Sutra* felt no qualms about inserting explanatory commentaries from other texts—or their own interpretations—into these scriptures.[93] In the case of the *Golden Light Sutra*, for example, the translator inserted the following personal plea: "O Lord, how can I alone, with only myself and my one tongue ... praise thee in perfect manner? Now I, oh incomparable Lord ... direct my supplications and prayers to thee. May all the good deeds I have done serve to bring me gain in finding Buddhahood quickly ... I would bring gain and profit to the living beings, I would redeem and save them all from bitter suffering."[94] In the case of the *Biography of Xuanzang*, the translator added material focusing on the worship of Maitreya not found in the original.[95] In other cases the Uyghurs created new texts out of a pastiche of other works, like a commentary on the *Vimalakīrti Sūtra*,[96] or made up wholly new texts, such as the Zen-inspired work *The Sūtra That Teaches the Mind Essence*.[97] They also embellished Buddhist narrative literature with contemporary people and events in order to create their own "sermons."[98]

The lack of a political authority defining the Dharma made this freedom possible. The Uyghurs created their own distinctive Buddhist texts and by extension their own form of Buddhism. Indeed, this freedom is probably why the Uyghurs never translated the monastic code.[99] It also may explain why in Uyghur Buddhist literature the founding of the nun order is presented in a positive light, which goes against the entire Buddhist tradition since the Buddha decreed that the creation of the nun order would cut the length of the Dharma from 5,000 to 2,500 years.[100] Whether this radical reinterpretation was done in recognition of the fact that Uyghur women were prominent donors of the Buddhist community is unknown, but it confirms the Uyghurs' "individualistic" and "self-confident" approach to the Dharma.

The same creativity can be seen in the Uyghur approach to language. In other Buddhist societies, on account of the Dharma's connection to political authority, the tradition had one language and one script, but such was not the case with the Uyghurs. Rather, from the very beginning of their involvement with Buddhism they approached it through multiple languages and scripts.[101] Even as late as the Yuan dynasty, for example, the Uyghurs revived the Brāhmī script that had first been used in the ninth and tenth centuries.[102]

Over time, however, the multilingualism of early Uyghur Buddhism faded and the main source language came to be Chinese. Uyghur elites were increasingly engaged politically and economically with not just Dunhuang and the Liao and Song dynasties but also the Xixia and Jin dynasties, and this informed how they came to practice the Dharma. It also changed the medium through which Uyghurs both accessed and performed the Dharma when they developed a systematized form of transcribing spoken Chinese. Chinese envoys in the twelfth century recorded that Uyghur monks performed their ritual services in Chinese. As in other Sinographic Buddhist cultures, like Korea and Japan, the Uyghurs likely read Chinese texts in their own inherited form of pronunciation. The Japanese have the so-called "Kan-on" system (Ch. *Hanyin*—Chinese pronunciation), which was introduced from Chang'an in the seventh and eighth centuries and became the inherited Japanese pronunciation of Chinese. For the Uyghurs this happened later. Their inherited form of pronunciation is based on a northwest form of Middle Chinese spoken in Dunhuang during the early Song period,[103] as is reflected in the phonetic transcription and parallel translation of the *One Thousand Character Classic* (Ch. *Qianziwen* 千字文).[104] For example, the four-character line 鳥官人皇—pronounced *niao guan ren huang* in modern Chinese—is transcribed in Uyghur script as *tev qan žen xo*, which parallels the Japanese reading of the same line as *teu kwan jin kwau*.

Having established this systematized form of transcribing spoken Chinese, a group of Uyghur elites thereby produced a whole host of Chinese texts in Uyghur script that could be read in ritual services. This included Uyghur transcriptions of the Chinese *Lotus Sutra*, the *Mañjuśrīnāmasaṃgīti*, the *Brahmajāla Sūtra* (*Fangwang jing* 梵網經), the *Ekottarāgama* (*Zengyi Ahan jing* 增一阿含經), the *Āgama Sutra* (*Ahan jing* 阿含經), and confession texts like the *Book for the Redemptions of Sins* (*Cibei daochang chanfa* 慈悲道場懺法) (see fig. 2.9).

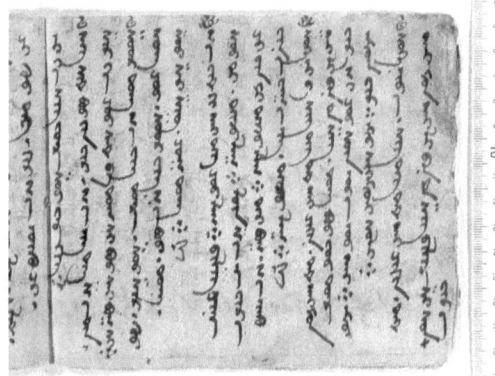

2.9 Uyghur transcription of a Chinese sutra, U5335, p. 24

Courtesy of the collection at the Berlin-Brandenburchische Akademie der Wissenschaften in der Staatsbibliotek zu Berlin–Preußischer Kulturbesitz, Orientabteilung

2.10 Uyghur text with Chinese characters, 1935.52.0011 recto
Courtesy of the Etnografiska Museet, Stockholm

Whether the Uyghurs created such texts to avoid having to read the complicated and difficult Chinese characters or simply because they did not know how to read the characters that well is not known. However, the fact that in other Buddhist texts Chinese characters were incorporated into the Uyghur versions indicates that their knowledge of Chinese was rather sophisticated (see fig. 2.10). Even more surprising is that where Uyghurs used characters, they did not read them in Chinese but in Uyghur.[105]

One text, for example, contains the passage "bir 時-nüng qolunung eniš čöpdikingä ikinti ärsär 佛-sïz ödkä qoluqa tušušmaq üzä 三-ünč 者 nizvani qïlïnčning aïrïnga bu tušta 佛 qutïnga alqïš alu umadïlar ärsär" (First, when you encounter the evil world in the course of time; second, when you encounter the time without a buddha; third, when you encounter suffering by the pain of the deed of illusion, in these times, if you could not accept the prophecy of becoming a buddha). This text is interesting because it involves the worship of Maitreya and the wish for future buddhahood, as described above, but it begins with the compound 時-nüng, the Chinese character for "time" (時, pronounced *shi*), combined with the Uyghur genitive case ending (*nüng*). A Uyghur may have read this character-case ending combination in Sino-Uyghur as *ši-nüng*. The problem with such a supposition, however, is that like other Turkic languages, Uyghur has vowel harmony. Thus if a Uyghur read the character in Chinese as *ši*, the case ending would have to be *ning*, per the rules of vowel harmony. Thus the case ending *nüng* reveals that 時-*nüng* was not read in Chinese but rather in Uyghur, as *öd-nüng*.[106]

The same phenomenon of reading Chinese characters in Uyghur is also found in a short poem:

> 子-larï ögindä qangïnda
> ušaq kičig bolup qalsar yämä
> 大 atalarï täg ök qatïglanu tavranu
> uqušsuz taqï artuqraq bay boldïlar

Uyghur poetry is based on alliteration, and in this case the head rhyme is based on the vowels *o* and *u*.[107] If the characters were read in the inherited Uyghur pronunciation of Chinese, the first character 子 (Ch. *zi*, "child"), would be read *sï*, which does not rhyme with *ušaq*. Similarly, the character 大—pronounced *da* and meaning "big"—does not rhyme with either *ušaq* or *uqušsuz*. Uyghurs therefore read these two characters in their own language as *oglan* ("son") and *ulug* ("great"), which creates the necessary alliteration:

> oglan-larï ögindä qangïnda
> ušaq kičig bolup qalsar yämä
> ulug atalarï täg ök qatïglanu tavranu
> uqušsuz taqï artuqraq bay boldïlar

In other cases, however, the Uyghurs used transcription to represent the sounds of Chinese characters without the actual characters. To make clear that this was how it was to be read, the word *tegmä* (meaning "called, named") would be inserted into the text.

> Müni yänä *var ćun ši* tegmä säkiz türlüg vibakdïlarining
> arasïnda bešinč tïn vibakdï üzä *luγ li qab šig* tegmä altï türlüg
>   adïra qabšuru yörgülük samazlarnïng arasïnda ärkä tayaqlïγ temištäki
>   nïng samaz üzä yörmiš kärgäk tep

Masahiro Shōgaito explains: "The three Chinese characters (*aṣṭa vibhaktayaḥ*) are transcribed as *var ćun ši* in the Uighur alphabet, which is followed by its Uighur translation *säkiz türlüg vibakdïlari-ning*, headed by *tegmä*. Likewise, (*saṭ samāsāḥ*), transcribed as *luγ li qab šig* in the Uighur alphabet, is translated as *altï türlüg adïra qabšuru yörgülük samazlar-nïng*, headed by *tegmä*."[108]

These examples help to characterize the distinctive nature of the Uyghur engagement with the Dharma and its literary heritage and to demonstrate how the lack of political control over Buddhism enabled Uyghurs to develop it in a distinctive fashion not tied to projects of state power or questions of political legitimacy.

CHAPTER 3

Buddhist Economics

Wealth is desirable. . . . Sloth and non-exertion is an obstacle to wealth . . . Monks, by increasing in ten growths the Aryan disciple grows in the Aryan growth, takes hold of the essential, takes hold of the best for his person. What ten? He grows in landed property, in wealth and granary, in child and wife, in slaves and folk who work for him, in four-footed beasts, he grows in faith and virtue, generosity and wisdom.

—Anguttara Nikāya[1]

As the preceding two chapters have shown, the Buddhist conversion of the Uyghurs was not a "top-down" affair as was so often the case across Asia. Rather than the ruler adopting the Dharma for political consolidation, spiritual power, or access to the new technologies that Buddhists brought with them, the Uyghur nobility and merchant elite drove the adoption of Buddhism and sustained the tradition over the centuries. This chapter considers how wealth and status figured into the Uyghur turn toward Buddhism.[2]

BUDDHISM AND WEALTH

Max Weber famously argued that Protestant theology—especially the uncertainty inherent in John Calvin's theory of predestination—drove northern Europeans to develop modern capitalism and use it in their effort to conquer the world.³ In making his argument, Weber had to show that other world religions lacked the specific attributes of Protestant Christianity. He claimed that Buddhism was "apolitical" and "otherworldly," but also—the focus of this chapter—that Buddhism lacked "economic rationalism and rational life methodology."⁴ Unfortunately, the Weberian view of Buddhism corresponds to much popular understanding of the Dharma.⁵ Indeed, Buddhism's presumed disinterest in material power and wealth production is why many consider it a "good" religion.⁶

However, as one scholar has succinctly put it, Weber was "ludicrously wrong."⁷ Since the 1956 publication of Jacques Gernet's groundbreaking *Buddhism in Chinese Society: An Economic History from the Fifth to the Tenth Centuries*, scholars of Buddhism have explored the deep interconnections between the Dharma, economic expansion, and integration across Asia.⁸ Today, these interconnections are fundamental to the scholarly understanding of how Buddhism came to be such a successful missionary religion.⁹

To understand the Dharma and economic expansion in Asia, we need to recall the context in which the Dharma developed.¹⁰ Based on the possible range of the Buddha's lifetime (600–300 BCE), we know that the Dharma came together during the so-called axial age, when India was undergoing enormous political, economic, cultural, and technological changes.¹¹ These intertwined developments had a profound impact not only on the structure and nature of Indian society but also on how people understood themselves and the world around them. The Buddha and others like him, such as the Hindu Upanisadic thinkers and the Jains, were trying to answer big questions about the meaning of life.

The Buddha's fundamental idea that everything is impermanent captured the tenor of the times. One significant change going on around him involved political structures. India was at the time divided into small lineage-based republics, like his father's kingdom (see fig. 3.1).¹² These small republics were gradually being absorbed into more complex kingdoms. Although families still ruled their own smaller kingdoms, the larger entities that absorbed them inevitably became more genealogically diffuse. These new proto-states required more abstract ideologies of legitimacy than the earlier clan-based political structures.¹³ To maintain their power, the ruling elites needed not only ideological innovations but also a greater resource base with which to finance the structures that sustained them, such as burgeoning bureaucracies and armies.

68 Buddhist Economics

3.1 Republics of Early India

Changing political configurations coincided with the introduction of iron technology into India, which fueled two major innovations: the iron plow and improved weaponry. The plow allowed for expanded rice cultivation, which in turn propelled a shift from nomadic pastoralism to settled farming. Settled farming led to population growth and the rise of cities.[14] Urbanization brought other large-scale changes, including the expansion of trade, a merchant class, and a stratified social structure. These new cities and complex economies required protection as well as administration, which fostered the development of centralizing states. On account of agricultural surplus and increasing financial transactions, states established a regular system of taxation that could in turn pay for both an educated bureaucracy and a standing army. Iron, of course, made far better weapons.[15] These intertwined technological, social, economic, and political developments came together during the formation of the Nanda Kingdom (345–321 BCE) and then the Mauryan Empire (322–185 BCE), which controlled the largest territorial expanse of India until the British Empire colonized the entire subcontinent (fig. 3.2).

3.2 The Mauryan Empire

Forging such an empire required the creation and circulation of wealth in the form of money. Wherever it occurs, monetization profoundly affects a society, well beyond matters of trade, because it puts everything, whether a food item, a day's labor, or a person, on the same plane and makes them comparable. Money also introduces new levels of abstraction, especially through usury, that fundamentally transform the human perception of the world. As a result, people search for explanations. It is not a coincidence that Greek philosophy flourished shortly after the minting of coins in the Mediterranean.[16] Nor is it surprising that, as historian Jonathan Berkey has noted, "two of the more memorable episodes from the accounts of Jesus' life—his encounter with the moneychangers in the Jerusalem temple, and his remark about rendering unto Caesar that which was Caesar's—involved coins."[17] The leveling and abstraction that come with the introduction of money reformulate the concepts and moral values that undergird the existing social order, and Buddhism was formulated amid these profound disruptions.

The Dharma not only reflected but also interpreted these transformations. The Buddha has often been imagined as a "radical" or a "progressive" who criticized the caste system or anticipated Marxism. I agree that he was a radical and a progressive, but in a much different way. The Buddha supported the new market economy and what it entailed: urbanization, trade, wealth production, familial reordering, individualism, free will, and new political structures. Rather than appeal to an idealized or romantic notion of the past, he urged his followers to move forward and embrace the new economic and social transformations, even though this meant giving up familiar nomadic pastoralism.[18] According to the Buddha, the best plan was to leave the farm, the family, and the old traditions behind; move into the city and create a new religious identity within the world of commerce. That was his radical progressivism.

The Dharma thrived within the urban world of trade, and the Buddha's teachings are filled with references to such commerce. Early Buddhist scriptures contain rates of currency conversion,[19] and debt and trade appear throughout as similes and as the basis of parables about spiritual obstacles. Because wealth was considered a sign of goodness and poverty a sign of moral failure,[20] Buddhist texts feature rapt descriptions of the laity's wealth and ostentatious possessions, such as: "A wealthy businessman or his son has a house with a gabled roof, plastered inside and outside with well-fitting doors and casements. Therein a couch is spread with a costly skin of antelope, having a canopy overhead and a scarlet cushion at each end. Here is a lamp burning and four wives wait upon him with all their charms."[21] Making money and being rich was not a problem for the Buddha—quite the opposite—and the production of wealth came to fundamentally shape Buddhist doctrine and practice.

The new world of trade that flourished during the monetized Mauryan Empire appears throughout Buddhist literature and art as well. For example, the Buddha had originally decreed that all monks must stay in one place during the rainy season, which gave rise to the monastic institution. However, he later allowed monks to violate this rule if they traveled with a merchant caravan or trading vessel.[22] Over time the Buddha himself came to be portrayed in art and literature as a merchant caravaneer.[23] Stories abound of him saving merchants lost at sea or in the desert.[24] These stories and many others make clear that the Buddha (or, more precisely, the disciples who later codified his teachings) was acutely aware of the socioeconomic changes unfolding at the time.

In this regard the Buddha differed importantly from other thinkers of the axial age. Hindu philosophers in India and the Confucians in China, for example, were both profoundly wary of a monetized economy and its social implications, and they wanted to prevent the massive social transformations it would inevitably bring. Both Hinduism and Confucianism clung conservatively to the past, fearing that new developments threatened the moral order of well-established social hierarchies. Confucian thinkers created an idealized fourfold hierarchy of society with merchants at the bottom.[25] Hindu law codes did the same. The Brahmans condemned activities essential for business, such as international travel, and strictly regulated the new merchant class. For good measure, Hindu codes grouped businessmen along with drunkards, sadists, and lepers.[26]

The Dharma took a different view. Although it ultimately presents a critique of the material world, it also recognizes that the world of trade and money—or, as Gustavo Benavides puts it, "the processes that underlie need and desire, production and work, giving and taking, hierarchy and equality, coming into being and dissolution"—cannot be entirely rejected.[27] The Buddha and his disciples realized that a monetized economy and its new business elite were the future. The story of Trapusa and Bhallika, the Buddha's first lay disciples, makes this clear.[28] Unlike the Buddha's former mendicant colleagues, who upon hearing his first sermon decided to become monks, Trapusa and Bhallika were businessmen, and they did not want to give up the comforts of everyday life or their families. So, in return for a donation, the Buddha offered them a list of deities to pray to for protection while traveling on business. This exchange established the social and ritual dynamic between the monastics and the laity that is central to the Buddhist community even today.

The Buddha went even further and incorporated wealth creation into Buddhist doctrine and practice. In his view the best way to generate positive karma was through the production of wealth, since it could be used to support the Dharma and to generate merit. Making money is nothing to be ashamed of, as it is essential to creating merit and thus a fundamental part of being Buddhist.[29] The *Milindapañhā*, a Buddhist text from the first centuries of the Common Era, recounts a dialogue between the Buddhist sage Nāgasena and the Indo-Greek king Menander. It includes the story of a prostitute who has acquired so much merit, and thus power, that she can make the Ganges River flow backward. The famous Buddhist king Aśoka is so astounded at this display that he wants to know how it was done. She explains that it was through the transmutation of wealth into merit, but the most remarkable detail of the story is how she earned her wealth. As she tells Aśoka: "Whoever, sire, gives me wealth, whether he be a noble or a Brahman or a merchant or a worker or anyone else, I minister to each in the same manner not thinking there is any special elegance in a noble or anything contemptible in a worker. I serve each lord of wealth without approval or repugnance."[30] She treated all her customers the same, regardless of caste or class. With this story, the Dharma is challenging the caste system on economic, not moral grounds, as is often claimed: "receiving services is not conditioned by one's position in the status hierarchy, but on one's ability to pay for services."[31] The story expresses the Buddha's regard for social mobility in the market economy of early India, where one's position in the world was no longer predetermined. Indeed, in Buddhist Asia social status came to be defined solely by wealth.

Even though the Dharma might be seen as an early form of prosperity theology, it also recognizes the harsh realities that a market economy unleashes. Early Buddhist texts depict not only the realities of economic specialization but also the inevitable disparities in wealth they generated.[32] The early Buddhist canon recognizes six classes of financial being: very wealthy, wealthy, faring well, faring poorly, poor, and destitute,[33] and the Dharma addresses these inequalities and the suffering the system created. Still, the Buddha recognized that material wealth was a necessary evil until the final utopia of universal nirvana could be achieved. Wealth played a crucial role in Buddhism, as the laity took on the duty of acquiring it in order to support the nonproductive monks and nuns.

This practice of giving (*dāna*) between the monastics and the laity was not purely financial. The relationship was governed by the logic referred to in Buddhist sources as "field of merit." By living according to the strict rules of the *Vinaya*, the monastic code, monks not only became suitable recipients of donations but also functioned as vehicles for the production of merit, or good karma. By following the *Vinaya*, monks became individuals with spiritual—or, more specifically, karmic—power. By supporting them, laypeople ensure not only that monks can do the hard work of achieving enlightenment but also that they themselves can receive karmic blessings from the monks. This means in theory that giving money to a leper would not be equivalent, karmically, to giving money to a monk because the leper is not a field of merit. Only monks, who adhere to the monastic code and live like the Buddha, can be mediums of karmic transference. The importance of this relationship to Buddhist communities across Asia cannot be underestimated.

Because this relationship is the cornerstone of the ritualized social structure, it is essential that both monks and the laity properly fulfill their roles. To that end, the main ritual of monastic life, the *poṣadha* ceremony, ensures that monks are living righteously and deserve lay donations. The *poṣadha* involves the monastic community reciting the key regulations of the monastic code publicly every two weeks and the monks confessing any transgressions they may have committed.[34] The ritual not only publicly ensures the moral rectitude of the community but also confirms that the monks are indeed a "field of merit" and thereby worthy of receiving offerings. Only by demonstrating moral purity can the monastic community operate as a field of merit that generates karma for the lay donors.

Of course, in order for this system to work the laity needed to create excess wealth, and the Buddha instructed both his lay followers and the monastics to acquire it.[35] Wealth is said to indicate moral standing and good karma, and poverty indicates moral failure and bad karma.[36] This distinction applies not solely to the laity but also to the monastics, since monasteries become fields of merit only by being wealthy.[37] Giving to a wealthy monastery earns more karmic return, and thus the economic cycle feeds itself.

Because of this emphasis, the monastic code came to regulate a wide range of monastic economic activity, such as landholding, lending and borrowing on credit, investment of perpetual endowments, dealing in commodities, and the ownership of servants and slaves as well as "goods and objects of extraordinary value ... such as ships, dams, irrigation tanks, parks and fields."[38] Buddhist monasteries became incredibly wealthy and "one of the most powerful economic forces in society."[39] On account of the Dharma's prosperity theology, the Buddhist laity also sought wealth and many became very rich, and their wealth flowed into Buddhist monasteries in the form of gifts. As one Chinese source records, the wealthy gave to Buddhist monks "as generously as if they were slipping shoes off their feet. The people and wealthy families parted with their treasure as easily as with forgotten rubbish. As a result, Buddhist temples were built side by side, and stupas rose up in row and row."[40]

In sum, the Dharma finessed the legitimacy of wealth creation. As a result, the teachings of the Buddha came to resonate with merchant classes across Asia, including among the Uyghur. Some of the earliest Buddhist texts translated into Uyghur involve the ritual protection of merchants,[41] and the most widely reproduced early Uyghur Buddhist text promises wealth. The Buddha says that

> any being, if he thinks thoughts of building, constructing a town, country, or house and home, must first of all read this sutra at the site three times. Then he must start the construction work immediately, digging the ground, putting up the walls, and kneading the mud. Then he must without any doubts build the house.
>
> In the southern quarter a summer room, on the north side a winter dwelling, on both sides, in the eastern quarter and the western quarter, a corridor, as well as a kitchen, a guest hall, large and small gates, a well, a fireplace, a stone mortar, a hand mill, storerooms, and a stable for livestock through to a lavatory for people must all be constructed completely. Then, at that time, those below the ground, the powerful, the terrible, the slayers, and the tormentors will all disappear ... all demons, spirits, and divisive ones will all hide and vanish. They will vacate the site and flee faraway, they will depart without form and shadow, and they will be unable to cause hazards.
>
> Happiness will come to the master of the new house, and he will be with blessings. Throughout the year he will be in a state of continuously being in happiness. His wealth will accumulate without his especially trying and he will become well-to-do and his earnings will accumulate without making much effort. ...

If one reads this sutra and acts [accordingly], until the seventh generation all will be blessed and prosper.[42]

EURASIAN TRADE

Although the teachings of the Buddha sanctioned the production of wealth and provided rituals to that end, it is quite another thing for a practitioner to actually do it. Obviously, not all followers of prosperity theologies become rich. Many factors come into play in most economic success stories. In a Uyghur story about a poor man wanting to join a caravan of rich merchants heading to Byzantium, to be successful requires not wealth and capital but rather faith in the Dharma.[43] Regardless, the available evidence confirms that Uyghur Buddhists were prosperous.

One factor in that economic success was a functioning state that provided not only security through its own military power and shrewd geopolitical alliances but also a formalized system of rules and regulations. Although the Uyghur ruler claimed legitimacy through the age-old steppe imperial model of a heaven-blessed ruler and maintained some traditional Turkic elements in the organization of his government, the entire regulatory system of the West Uyghur Kingdom was based on Chinese precedent. Its administrative and taxation systems, as well as its legal system of private contract, all derived from Tang dynasty precedents.[44] This uniformity of government regulations enhanced the power of the state and fostered an environment suitable for economic development.

One measure of this successful regulatory unification was the standardization of written Uyghur in the early eleventh century. Although we may marvel at the linguistic diversity and multi-script nature of the Uyghurs' early involvement with Buddhism, such multilingualism is complicated; having one language and one script is far more efficient.[45] That the West Uyghur Kingdom instituted the vertical Uyghur script as the standard across all media—from legal documents to scriptures and political inscriptions to account books—confirms both the "legibility" and the effectiveness of the state at this time.[46] These two factors helped to create the space wherein the Uyghur economy could develop.

The Uyghur economy was also premised on political and economic alliances with other states. The Uyghurs maintained such relations with all the major powers of East Asia, which enhanced the health and wealth of the state and its allied business elite. The main alliance, with the Khitan Liao, brought them increased security under the umbrella of a powerful nomadic Inner Asian steppe empire. It also made the Uyghurs—situated as they were on the Silk Road's chokepoint—the key middlemen of East-West trade.[47] This position was of great benefit to the Uyghur realm in the tenth century but became crucial in the wake of the Chanyuan Treaty of 1005.[48] The Chanyuan Treaty was ratified between the Song and Liao dynasties after the Khitan had launched a devastating invasion of China in 1004. The Song and Liao had been jockeying for dominance throughout the tenth century, but neither had fully gained the upper hand. With the Khitan victory, the power dynamic between these two states changed dramatically. The Chanyuan Treaty confirmed that the Song were the inferior power and required them to pay a huge annual indemnity of silver and silk to the Liao court. This arrangement greatly increased Liao income and, as Michal Biran explains, "by dint of these revenues Liao was able to export many Chinese goods, which were produced either locally or in Song, and to import luxury goods. These developments coincided with the burgeoning of the Qarakhanid dynasty, which was apparently Liao's principal Muslim trading partner."[49]

The Uyghurs handled this burgeoning trade in luxury goods between the Muslim West and the Buddhist East.[50] From the West they brought an array of gems (amber, jade, coral, pearls), animal products (kingfisher feathers, elephant tusks, rhinoceros horns), and, most important, Islamic glass vessels. From the East they brought an array of Chinese goods as well as musk from the Khitan's homeland in Manchuria. But they were far more than just middlemen. They also created new products that became wildly popular, such as the "cloth of gold and silk" (Ar. *nasīj al-dhahab al-ḥarīr*), which became one of the most highly prized commodities in medieval Eurasia (see fig. 3.3).[51]

They also developed new financial institutions, such as the *ortoq*, which involved several businessmen joining together in a partnership to conduct long-distance trade.[52] With the *ortoq* they created their own "commercial network [that] covered North and Central China, Manchuria, Mongolia, the Hexi corridor, Tibet, and Khotan from the tenth century to Mongol times."[53] One extant Uyghur document records how this entrepreneurial spirit paid off:

> My father, Basa Togrıl, without leaving a single *bakır* of debt (unpaid) left everything, vineyard, landed property, house and household goods, and went to Tangut. The next year, as a result of trading, he sent from Kucha half a

3.3 Cloth of gold with winged lions and griffins (ca. 1225-1275). Central Asia. Silk and gold thread: lampas; overall: 124 x 48.8 cm (48 13/16 x 19 3/16 in.); mounted: 135.6 x 59.4 cm (53 3/8 x 23 3/8 in.)
The Cleveland Museum of Art, 1989.50. Open access: www.clevelandart.org

yastuk [= 4½ pounds] in weighed coin and sixty head of horses as a gift. Then he sent seven pieces of brocade as a gift from a shelter at Babak. From Burqanlig Sumitu he sent 1 *yastuk* of weighed coin as a gift.[54]

The full scale of this economic boom is hard to deduce from the fragmentary historical record, but this newfound wealth both helped the Uyghur state to consolidate its power and enabled the financing and building of new Buddhist institutions.

As in any period of explosive growth, new social mores about wealth and status developed. Extravagance became more common. Uyghur merchants, for example, who were the leaders in moving high-end pearls from the Persian Gulf to China, became obsessed with wearing ever more elaborate pearl earrings.[55] The new economy and its tandem status anxiety are perhaps best captured in one merchant's catalogue of what he needed to buy for his daughter's wedding:

Periodical (?) report of... I received 2 *yastuk*, 35 *sitir*[56] (in cash) (to spend as a dowry). I bought a... for 27 *sitir* in cash. I bought white pearls from Kočo for 12 *sitir*, pearls on a... chain (?) for 9 *sitir*, 5 1, and a local sack for the... from the Buddhist monk of... for 1 *sitir*, 2 *bakır*. For... *sitir*, 3 *bakır* I bought eight (pieces of) cornelian. I bought amber for 1 *sitir*, I bought four beads for 1 *sitir*, 7 *bakır*. I bought two copper... for 2 *sitir*, 6 *bakır*. I bought a big mirror for 3 *sitir*, 8 *bakır*. I bought a small mirror for 1 *sitir*. I bought a scarlet brocade with gold for 7 *sitir*. For 5 *sitir*, 5 *bakır* I bought a... For 2 *sitir*, 3 *bakır* I bought... For 6 *sitir* I bought a... breastplate, for 12 *sitir* I bought leather for a padded coat. I bought purple brocade with gold for a... garment for 4 *sitir*. I bought home-procured brocade for a... padded coat for 1½ *sitir*. For 6 *sitir* I bought a Byzantine... I bought home produced brocade for a silk garment for 1½ *sitir*. I bought a horse blanket for... *sitir*. I bought a... purple bag for the household blanket(s) for 2 *sitir*... *bakır*. I bought a red gold-shot brocade (to cover) a pillow for 1 *sitir*. For 1 *sitir* I bought a silk dust cover (?). I bought for 1½ *sitir* two pieces of brown raw hide (and?) for 3 *sitir* a striped blanket of... fathoms length. I bought 5 thin (pieces of brocade?) for 4 *sitir*. I bought two (or twelve?)... combs (?) for 4 *sitir*. I bought two steel knives for 2 *bakır*. I bought two packets of packing needles for 1 *sitir*. I bought two packets of awls (?) and one rectangular packet of packing needles (?) for 1 *sitir*. I bought one half load of... [cotton?] for stuffing pillows for 3 *bakır*. I bought two lengths of colored silk fabric for bandages (?) of which one was a... for injuries (?) and other a saddle-gall dressing for open wounds. I bought one silk handkerchief with a border (?) to be carried in the sleeve (?) and a purple bag for 4 *bakır*. I bought for 7 *bakır* a breastplate (?). For 5 *bakır* I bought tinder. For 5 *bakır* I bought a sable skin. For 8 *bakır* I bought (a pair of) leather boots, and for 1 *sitir* a red bag in woven material. For 4 *bakır* I bought two branches of *batu* (?). I bought four branches of coral for 2 *bakır*. I bought white coral for 3 *bakır*. I bought two silk... for 6 *sitir* in cash, and a... mattress for the stomach for... For sheep for the wedding feast, I bought three sheep from Taman the son of Ali the butcher for 6 *sitir*, 5 *bakır*. I bought a horse for 2 *sitir* from M... For 1½ *sitir* I bought wine. I bought one *Shi* of grain for 2½ *sitir*. Analyzing the dowry of 2 *yastuk*, 35 *sitir*, the amount provided by the family was 31 *sitir*. In addition to this my younger brother, including me in the transaction, gave the girl a slave, and an excellent weaver, able to weave Byzantine (?) cotton cloth, and a young man aged 25 called Sevdi.[57]

This remarkable list suggests not only the wealth of one Uyghur family but also the conspicuous consumption needed to maintain one's status in the community. In another entry, however, this same father laments the high cost of "keeping up appearances" and that he had taken out a loan of three *yastuk*, which at 30 percent annual interest (the standard rate in China and the Uyghur realm at the time), actually ended up costing him fourteen *yastuk*, since it took him twenty-three years to pay it back.[58]

Uyghur merchants could therefore certainly generate wealth, but keeping it and their status in the community was not always easy. Nor was being on the road to do business; thus some sought the solace of women (see fig. 3.4). As the document records: "This is Tämär Quš: [obscene portrait] Madam Yimkičor went, and Tämär Quš too. Thus he desired a (carnal) desire: 'May she go without delay!' He gave her four pieces of wool cloth."[59]

These members of the Uyghur elite were those who supported the Dharma. They raised the capital to fund the *ortoq* merchant trading networks that flourished across Eurasia in the eleventh and twelfth centuries. As such, they fit into our romantic view of Silk Road trade full of plucky merchants plodding through the desert with camels weighed down with precious commodities. However, as recent research has shown, much of Silk Road trade was dominated by less exalted goods and was locally oriented.[60] The case of the Uyghur economy bears this out: the bulk of their trade was in horses and cotton.[61]

The main market for horses was China, where the soil lacks selenium, a vital mineral for the raising of strong horses. Throughout history Chinese dynasties had been dependent on Inner Asian peoples and states to provide them horses, and for the Song dynasty, in particular, this situation was acute. They had lost control of all the horse-breeding territories on their northern border to the

3.4 Prostitution contract. Or.8210S/S.1360

After Nicholas Sims-Williams and James Hamilton, *Turco-Sogdian Documents from 9th–10th century Dunhuang* (London: Corpus Inscriptionum Iranicum and School of Oriental and African Studies, 2015), pl. 17

Khitan or the Tangut, with whom they were in continual conflict and unable to trade this vital military asset. The Song, who annually needed approximately 22,000 horses, had to find new markets, which they did with their allies the Tsongkha Tibetans.⁶² The Tsongkha bred and sold their own horses to the Song, but they also brought to market the horses of the Amdo Tibetans and the Uyghurs (see fig. 3.5).

The middlemen in these transactions, serving as the bridge across the Sino-Tibetan cultural and linguistic divide, were Uyghur merchants. As one Chinese observer of these business deals claimed: "Whenever Tibetans and Chinese trade, if there is no [Uighur merchant] serving as middleman (*kuai*), they cannot complete the transaction."⁶³

The success of Uyghur merchants in the horse trade depended not only on their business acumen and large commercial networks but also on the size and

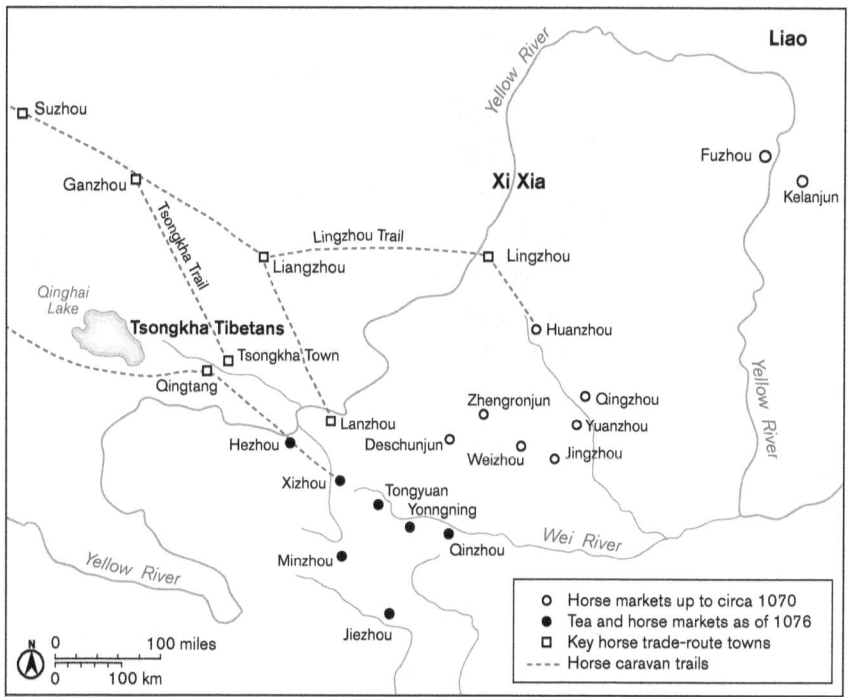

3.5 Horse Markets in the Northern Song
After Paul J. Smith, *Taxing Heaven's Storehouse: Horses, Bureaucrats, and the Destruction of the Sichuan Tea Industry, 1074–1224* (Cambridge, MA: Harvard Council on East Asian Studies, 1991)

ecological variation in the West Uyghur Kingdom. Their territory stretched from the Zünghar basin north of the Tianshan range to the oasis cities of the Turfan basin. They maintained two seasonal capitals: Beshbaliq on the steppe during the hot summer months and Qocho in the Turfan basin during the winter.[64] In the lush pastures of the Zünghar basin the Uyghurs managed their horse enterprises, and in the irrigated oasis cities of the Turfan basin they produced cotton.

Cotton, specifically the African-Asian species *Gossypium herbaceum*, had been cultivated in this region for more than a millennium when the Uyghurs became involved in the industry.[65] Although they had no new techniques for the growing, harvesting, or cleaning of cotton, they had both the capital to invest and an Asia-wide trading network for its distribution. They also happened to get into the business just as the Song dynasty had legalized the sale of cotton in China for the first time. Previously, the Chinese state, at the request of the "silk lobby," had kept cotton from competing in the Chinese textile market. This governmental decision was not based solely on fears of free market competition. Chinese society was highly stratified, and sartorial regulations, reserving silk for the elite and hemp for the masses, helped to maintain social distinctions. Successive dynasties from the Han (202 BCE--220 CE) up through the Tang (618-907) feared that the introduction of cotton would threaten the preservation of these social status markers. Moreover, both silk and hemp had monetary use in the payment of taxes; thus the financial authorities viewed cotton as a potentially destabilizing element in the fiscal regime.[66] As a result, Central Asian cotton had never developed into a valuable commodity. When the Song changed these policies, the situation was transformed, and the Uyghurs were able to take advantage of it.

Another boon for the Uyghurs was the changing climate.[67] Most importantly, a centuries-long dry spell came to an end in the ninth century, and wetter conditions enabled an unprecedented expansion of agricultural lands in the Turfan region.[68] Of course, when the climate changed again in the thirteenth century to drier conditions, the Uyghur economy suffered. Drier grasslands could not sustain large herds of horses, and a drier Tarim basin would not allow the growing of a water-intensive crop such as cotton. The simultaneous upheavals of the Mongol conquest and subsequent civil wars exacerbated these later environmental transformations. Moreover, the Mongols greatly promoted the cultivation of cotton in China during the Yuan dynasty, thereby further weakening the Uyghur economy.[69]

Before then, however, the Uyghurs had benefited from a surprising concatenation of forces that enabled their realm not only to survive but to thrive. Not even the fall of their powerful ally the Liao dynasty in the early twelfth century seemed to affect the Uyghurs; they simply continued to recognize the Khitan as their patrons in their new guise as the Qara Khitai—or Western Liao—in Central Asia. And as the East-West trade revived under the shrewd political rule of the Qara Khitai, the Uyghurs were once again perfectly situated to act at the transit point for this exchange.[70] This middleman position was further enhanced when in the mid-twelfth century the Tanguts promulgated a new legal code that instituted a 10 percent tax on all goods transported through their territory.[71] This inadvertently benefited the West Uyghur Kingdom because merchants avoided Tangut territory and went instead through Turfan and across the Mongolian plateau directly into the territory of the Jurchen Jin dynasty (1115–1234 CE).[72] Whether the Uyghurs also taxed these merchants—perhaps at a lower level than the Tanguts—is unknown; however, the influx of people and goods via the new trade route certainly boosted the larger economy.[73]

During the eleventh and twelfth centuries, the Uyghur economy boomed coterminous with the Uyghur conversion to Buddhism. Being Buddhist helped grease the wheels of business across East Asia, and flaunting wealth through patronage of the Dharma not only advanced one's spiritual ambitions but also confirmed one's status within the community. It was not only the Uyghur elite who benefited; so too did Buddhist institutions.

THE MONASTIC ECONOMY

As the Uyghur economy prospered during the eleventh and twelfth century under the Khitan security umbrella, so too did the wealth of Buddhist institutions. For the sake of salvation the laity routinely offered donations for the performance of rituals and for the production of Buddhist texts and artwork, but they also sometimes offered monasteries money and land as well as other financial assets such as slaves. Monasteries could put these resources to work through leasing or moneylending to generate even more wealth. It was this economic boom with its attendant ritualization through the theories of "giving" and "field of merit" that made Uyghur Buddhism possible.

The full details of this dynamic are unfortunately lost from the historical record. For example, we have no evidence telling us how much it would have cost to have a Uyghur monk perform a funeral, recite a protective spell, or do an astrological reading. Based on contemporary Chinese sources from Dunhuang, we can postulate that such ritual performances may have been rather lucrative. In one tenth-century legal case, a nun named Jingjin had by the time of her death accumulated enough money from ritual performances to buy nine houses in Dunhuang.[74] Whether monastics in the West Uyghur Kingdom could make as much as their brothers and sisters in the Buddhist realm of Guiyijun is unknown; however, all the evidence together shows that the foundational aim of making merit through giving was central to Uyghur Buddhism.[75]

All the colophons of Buddhist texts make clear that the donor paid for the work to be produced in order to generate merit that could help their own spiritual path or be transferred to deceased and living family and friends. A laywoman had a text for the confession of sins prepared so as to produce merit for herself: "I, the lay sister Üträt, who has firm and pure faith in the three jewels, have thought of the Buddhas and have realized and understood that this our body is transient and that only one gain remains, and that there is no indestructible possession apart from meritorious deeds. I have therefore had this jewel of a confessional text, which cleanses one from all evil deeds, respectfully copied."[76] In another colophon, a family of donors hopes their meritorious deed will help their deceased relatives:

> The lay brothers and lay sisters faithful to the teachings of the Buddha, our mother Baz Ädgü, our father Bägräk Tutung, our wife Okšagu, our daughters Mängi Silig, Mänglig Silig, Är Kutlug Silig, Ana Ögi, Öz Yaruk, our fathers... Yüz Čor... Even if their souls should be born again in hell, among the *pretas* [hungry ghosts], or in an animal existence, may this merit, the good deed [of producing this sutra], reach them all, and may they be reborn in Heaven![77]

Similarly, the inscriptions related to the building of a Buddhist monastery express hope that the merit will ensure the karmic future of not only family and friends but everyone:

> Tarduš Tapmiš Yayatgar Čangši Yälü Qaya, the layman with ////// pure and faithful heart for the three Jewels, together with my dear wife, the laywoman, Tängrikän Körtlä Qatun Tängrim, our dear daughter, Yügätmiš Qatun Tängrim, and our son, ////
>
> We had heard and understood the great merit of building a monastery preached by the wise God of Gods Buddha in the sutra about a Brahman called Cadiski, and had thought of the emptiness and vacuity of these bodies and of the transitoriness of all obtained goods,
>
> And then having hoped 'May it become an advantage to let us bring from lower existence to higher existence' as well as 'May we be reborn in the Gods' Land (in the way) to Buddhahood,'
>
> We agreed to make a statue of Maitreya and the Buddhist monastery named /////// Candradas for the well-behaved monks coming and going from the four directions.

The persons who are going to rejoice in accordance with this virtuous work of ours are as follows: Our elder sister... Our elder brother... Our elder sister-in-law... our Younger sisters... our sons-in-law... our younger brothers... our father-in-law... our maternal uncles... the sons of our younger sisters or daughters...

Furthermore //// we transfer /// the merit of this meritorious and good deed to our /// deceased parents... who had shown us this bright earthly world, as well as to the deceased relatives, nephews, uncles. Let some share of this merit reach everywhere all the living beings in the Four Births and the Five Ways of Existence. May all the human beings get into the eternal peace above in the gods' Land and further in Nirvana. Let's become Buddha![78]

The same ideas also animated the desire to produce Buddhist works of art; doing so was a powerful means of generating merit, as seen in this inscription from a temple banner:

Now, at a good chosen time, on a desirable day, in a blessed month, i.e. on the 13th day of the 3rd month of the fortunate Mouse year, I, Nam Čor, the layman with a very firm heart for the Three Jewels, together with my wife Kiu Šun, we have thought day and night as follows: "The body is transitory, and the movable property will decay. We may not adhere to the transitory body nor to the decaying goods. So let us think [of our?] soul. May we not obtain a human body again!

We have humbly ventured to have the image of Cakravarti-Cintamani Bodhisattva (= Skt. Cintamanicakra Avalokitesvara = Ch. Ru-yi-lun Guan-yin) painted. May this meritorious and good deed yield fruits. We two and our dear children, i.e. Qutlug Sïngqur, Ädgü Sïngqur, Ogul Sïngqur, Qutadmïš Alp Sïngqur, and our elder brother Alp Yegän, and our daughter-in-law Yumšaq and so on, all of us shall be joyful, and free from illness and disease, from pain and danger in this present world. Furthermore, we transfer this meritorious and good deed to our deceased parents. And whoever of the relative groups, beginning with son and daughter till the seven degrees, may they be saved from the evil ways of existence (animal, hungry ghost, hell) /// and be reborn above in the Tusita heaven. And let us see in the future time Maitreya Buddha by the strength of this meritorious and good deed. [Let us decorate] Maitreya Buddha's graceful body with the Jambu-river gold. When

86 Buddhist Economics

3.6 Male donor portraits from the Bezeklik caves, Xinjiang, China

After Albert von Le Coq, *Chotscho: Facsimile-Wiedergaben der wichtigeren Funde der ersten Königlich Preussischen Expedition nach Turfan in Ost-Turkistan* (Berlin: Dietrich Reimer, 1913)

our strength goes away (= we die), then we want to be saved from this [awful] samsara! [May] all sufferings in the five ways of existence disappear!"[79]

Having one's portrait and name included in even grander works of art—such as cave temples—also garnered a great amount of merit, and clearly confirmed one's social status and economic wherewithal (see figs. 3.6 and 3.7). Not all donations were so grandiose. Monastic account books from Turfan duly record small cash donations presented by local parishioners.[80]

Some evidence suggests that monastics might have exploited this system, such as this Uyghur letter, which shames a donor about sending along Buddhist statues:

3.7 Female donor portraits from the Bezeklik caves, Xinjiang, China
After Albert von Le Coq, *Chotscho: Facsimile-Wiedergaben der wichtigeren Funde der ersten Königlich Preussischen Expedition nach Turfan in Ost-Turkistan* (Berlin: Dietrich Reimer, 1913)

To Toyïn: from me, Samzun, from the illustrious Samgharama with relics.

Many times asking for bliss and partnership, I send this message.
Again my word: Send me on request one statue of Vajravidāraṇa, then one model [mould?] of the Bhrum Bhrum Vajrapāṇi as well as one statue of it, one figure of Mārīcī, then a bell and vajra, these six ritual utensils as it may be.
Is merit not necessary to you and me? To achieve merit one should send me what I wished. Do not be sluggish!
Again (to?) Sävinč Qaya: I, Samzun, send this message from the relic place, many times asking for bliss and partnership. You promised to send me

jewels. You did not send. Why did you not send? Is your heart not touched?[81]

Whether such pleas were common among the Uyghurs is unknown, but this suggests how the ritual logic of Buddhism could lend itself to financial conniving. However, Buddhist monks are not likely to have done so routinely since, by the system the Dharma set up, they were already guaranteed a steady flow of income by carrying out an array of merit-making activities.

Moreover, Buddhist monastics had even further means of producing wealth, one of the most important of which was the control of land.[82] Donors gave land to generate merit—or to avoid taxes.[83] Either way, these properties became an important means for monasteries to generate further wealth; as in many Buddhist cultures, the landholdings were substantial. During the Wei dynasty (386–534 CE) in North China, for example, the Buddhist monasteries around the capital city of Luoyang owned up to two-thirds of the available land.[84] In medieval Korea the samgha controlled one-sixth of the arable land.[85] In Burma the samgha controlled 370,500 acres of land during the Pagan period (849–1297).[86] Similarly, in coastal China from the tenth to early twelfth centuries, Michael Walshe has shown,

> Buddhist monasteries controlled anywhere from one third to one half of all common land. In Fuzhou, the average ratio of monks to land was one monk owning 160 *mu* of land [26.5 acres], whereas in the same geographical area, one peasant owned on average 14.5 *mu* [2.4 acres]. Buddhists controlled high-quality (cultivable) land in this region. By the late twelfth to the thirteenth century, although Buddhist monasteries had lost some of their land—particularly coastal land—to merchants and officials, they still controlled about one fifth of the common land. Moreover, this did not include mountain or forest land, which would raise the amount to at least almost one fourth of the total land available.[87]

In thirteenth-century Quanzhou the samgha held almost a quarter of the land, which meant that seventeen laypeople sustained themselves on fifteen acres of land, while each member of the monastic community had access to the produce of one and a half times that area.[88] Whether Uyghur monastic landholdings ever reached such remarkable levels is unknown, but numerous contracts and other documents prove that they were given and did own a lot of land.

Upon that land were many vineyards. According to the monastic code, Buddhist monks and nuns are not supposed to drink alcohol; however, such regulations have often been ignored.[89] In India's northwest region of Gandhara, which had come under Hellenistic influences, for example, Buddhists had long been involved in the production and consumption of wine.[90] And as Martha Carter has found, other religious communities in the region also produced wine: "Nestorian Christian communities spread viticulture with their monastic communities in Iran and Central Asia far exceeding their needs for liturgical wine, and to the Manichaeans the grape was 'a fruit of light' fit for consumption by the elect."[91] Thus by the time the Uyghurs adopted Buddhism wine production had long been established in the Turfan region, and as monasteries acquired land they simply took over the industry.[92]

The monastic code also forbids Buddhist monks and nuns from farming. To be more precise, monastics are not allowed to appear in public as menial laborers—or even to engage in menial labor out of public view—because that would diminish their "field of merit" status and thus the moral standing of the monastic community within the broader lay community.[93] Uyghur Buddhist monks therefore needed to find other people to work their land holdings. Slavery had been a foundational element of Inner Asian societies for centuries,[94] and Uyghur monks followed other Buddhist institutions across Asia in buying and selling slaves for agricultural labor.[95] Based on extant legal documents, Buddhist monastic institutions also hired workers from the general population.[96]

On account of all of these various economic activities, Uyghur Buddhist monasteries became not just wealthy but also part of the economic lifeblood of the West Uyghur Kingdom. As in other parts of the Buddhist world, Uyghur monasteries, and even individual monks, came to function as banks.[97] They used their accumulated capital to offer loans, as seen in one contract:

Pig year, second month, on the twenty-sixth.
    Since I, Sivsadu Tutung, needed silver, I received ten *stater* silver from the monk Sinsun. On the tenth of the tenth month, I will return it properly.
    If I should flee before I give it, my younger brother Ozmiš Togrıl should correctly return it.

The witness is Arqagur Inal, the witness is Sarig Toyin, the witness is Öküz Togrıl, the witness is Känt Qaya, the witness is Artï Inal.

This seal is both of us.

I, Sivsadu Tutung, wrote it according to dictation.[98]

While such loans may have been beneficial for the borrowers, they also helped the bottom line of the monasteries. In one fragmentary letter, we learn that one Buddhist institution offered a substantial loan whereby "the property belonging to the monastery became rich again."[99] Such loans between monastics and the general populace were not in all cases simple financial transactions. The following contract involves a father giving his son to a monk for three years in exchange for ten silver coins.

Pig year, first month, on the tenth.

Since I, Qaytso Tutung, needed silver coins to buy things, I gave my own son named Titso to the monk Čintso as a deposit for three years. We have agreed on the silver coins for the deposit as follows. I gave the son as pledge for 10 *stater* silver coins. I, Qaytso Tutung, received these 10 *stater* silver coins fully weighed on the day the contract was made out. I, the monk Čintso, gave these coins without one missing.

In the first year I will give this son one pair of pants and one shirt, one pair of shoes, one pair of felt boots; in the second year, one cotton shirt; and in three years, one fur.

If the son goes with those in the house of the monk Čintso and should commit theft and trickery, or if he should lose things that have been taken, it is my responsibility, the monk Čintso.

If he goes alone and should commit theft and trickery, and if he should steal things, it is my responsibility, Qaytso Tutung.

When he falls ill, I, the monk Čintso, will give him soup and food for seven days. When the illness exceeds seven days, it is I, Qaytso Tutung, who will take care of him, and correctly give what he lacks every day.

If he falls ill and dies, half of his possessions will go the monk and the other half to me, Qaytso Tutung.

Until three years have passed, I, the monk, will not give the son back to Qaytso Tutung. But if I [Qaytso Tutung] do say "Hand him over," I will have to return the silver coins with interest from the day they were handed over.

The witness is Qutd(a)miš Qaya, the witness is Sangicun.
This seal is mine, Qaytso Tutung.
I, Buyan Qaya, wrote it.[100]

Whether this contract was an anomaly or common practice is unknown, but it further reveals the centrality of monasteries in the economic and social life of the West Uyghur Kingdom.

Although it was economically beneficial for monasteries to become such important financial institutions, doing so brought risk. As we will see in chapter 5, when the Mongol civil war ravaged the Uyghur economy, this accumulated wealth led to uprisings and violence against Buddhist monasteries.[101] Even before that, the monks were aware of their wealth's potential to generate animosity. They therefore produced texts that explicated the future horrors of hell awaiting those who stole "the fields, vegetable gardens, vineyards, trees and fruit stocks belonging to the monastery and give them to strangers, to lay people, or take all of this for yourself, eat and consume them."[102] This same text proclaims that if anyone were to steal from a monastery they would be reborn in hell with the body of a vegetable garden that would continuously be showered with fiery boulders. Whether such karmic threats held the laity in check is not known. This text confirms monastic recognition of the double-edged nature of wealth accumulation.

Monastics, of course, did not make money simply for rapacious, proto-capitalist aims. Buddhist institutions used their wealth not only to promote and perpetuate the Dharma but also to help the broader community. Evidence shows that Buddhist institutions helped those in need.[103] And, on account of their financial resources, Buddhist monks sometimes released slaves from servitude.[104] Regardless of the range of motivations for accumulating wealth, the wide-ranging nature of the Buddhist economy kept the Dharma in business.

CHAPTER 4

Uyghur Buddhisms

The Uyghurs eagerly believe in Buddhism. They have a temple together with a statue of the Buddha made from plaster. During every service, they sacrifice a sheep and engage in hard drinking. Dipping their fingers into the blood of the sheep, they spread it on the Buddha's lips. They hold up the Buddha's foot and wail at it. They call this practice "intimate worship." When chanting, they clothe themselves in ceremonial robes and chant in Indian language.

—Hong Hao 洪皓, *Report on Songmo* (松漠紀聞, ca. 1150)[1]

Hong Hao (1088–1155) was the Song dynasty's ambassador to the Jurchen Jin court in the Songmo region of north China for fifteen years. Upon his return, he wrote a report that chronicled his experiences there and included in it the above description of Uyghur Buddhist practice. It is well known that Uyghur envoys and merchants were resident at the Jin court, but how accurate is this description of Uyghur Buddhism? Drinking, animal sacrifice, and wailing do not fit our contemporary understanding of Buddhism, but wearing ceremonial robes and chanting in an Indic language do. If Hong Hao made up or embellished his description, he may have wanted to denigrate the "barbarians" with their undignified non-Chinese Buddhist practices. But if Hong Hao has given an accurate description of Uyghur Buddhist practice, we may need to rethink our understanding.

Reconceptualizing Buddhism beyond the nineteenth-century construct of "modern Buddhism" has been a focus of scholarship for more than thirty years.[2] Such work has documented how this modern Buddhism came about and challenged many of the popular (mis)conceptions about Buddhism that it set in motion. All of this has done little to change popular perceptions of Buddhism, so, to many, Hong Hao's description of Uyghur Buddhism will seem quite strange or even improbable. But, for example, according to the vows of both Buddhist monastics and the laity, one is not supposed to drink alcohol. Yet, as noted in chapter 3, Buddhist monasteries in Gandhara produced wine, and alcohol played a role in the Buddhist world of Dunhuang. Similarly, in a Uyghur ritual text for a good harvest an offering of wheat beer is presented to Kubera, the god of wealth.[3] Moreover, from pilgrim inscriptions we know that Uyghurs presented alcohol as part of their ritual offerings to monks and monasteries.[4] Might some Uyghurs have gone further, drinking alcohol while on pilgrimage or during a ritual celebration? Other than Hong Hao's brief report, we have no evidence on this matter.

There is more evidence for the Uyghur custom of sacrificing or offering sheep to the Buddha. One ritual, for example, calls for "the sacrifice of a he-goat and a pig in order to prepare a banquet. The goal of the rituals referred to in the text is to produce an outstanding crop yield."[5] Marco Polo, who passed through Turfan in the late thirteenth century, wrote that Uyghur Buddhists offered sheep in exchange for blessings for their children: "[They] will feed up a sheep in honor of the idol, and at the New Year, or on the day of the idol's feast, they will take their children and the sheep along with them into the presence of the idol with great ceremony. Then they will have the sheep slaughtered and cooked, and again present it before the idol with like reverence, and leave it there before him, whilst they are reciting the offices of their worships and their prayers for the idol's blessing on their children."[6] This ritual is more of a food offering than a blood offering, but Polo's description of the Uyghurs offering a slaughtered sheep suggests that Hong's overall description may be accurate. But it certainly shows, once again, that there are many ways of being Buddhist. This chapter therefore explores not only how everyday lived Buddhism was practiced among the Uyghurs but also how it changed from the freewheeling early days to the golden age of the Mongol empire period.

A DISTINCTIVE BUDDHISM

The Buddhist tradition is incredibly diverse in its doctrines and practices.[7] Some scholars contend that we should speak of "Buddhisms" rather than a unified

"Buddhism."[8] Yet, as with Christianity, most assume that Buddhism is one religion organized into three main traditions that all trace their origins back to one founder—in this case, Śākyamuni Buddha. According to conventional understanding, these three traditions—called *yānas* or "vehicles"—are the Hīnayāna (the Small Vehicle, better known today as the Nikāya, or mainstream Buddhism), the Mahāyāna (the Great Vehicle), and the Vajrayāna (the Diamond Vehicle, or Tantric Buddhism). Within each school further divisions are drawn based on different interpretations of the Dharma. The Nikāya tradition, for example, developed into sixteen distinct schools of thought and practice, only one of which, the Theravāda, survives today, the dominant form of Buddhism in Southeast Asia. The Mahayana tradition, which developed centuries after the passing of the Buddha and is the dominant form in East Asia, comprises numerous schools such as Chan (or Zen), Pure Land, Huayan, and Tiantai. And Tantric Buddhism, codified more than a millennium after the Buddha's death, shows up in distinctive schools of thought such as Shingon in East Asia and the various schools of Tibetan Buddhism.

Modern scholars with their "Protestant presuppositions" have amply documented how and why all of these different doctrinal interpretations developed over the course of time.[9] Such scholarly doxographies have value but do not tell us much about what Buddhists across Asia actually believed or how they practiced Buddhism, especially outside the rarefied realm of the monastery. The laity were not engaged in thorny theological debates about the nature of the Buddha; they were interested in generating good karma for themselves and their family members through ritual performances, artistic and textual production, pilgrimage, and the confession of sins. Such practices make up everyday, lived Buddhism, which focuses less on doctrinal minutiae and more on rituals securing blessings for money and health. By exploring the everyday practices of Uyghur Buddhists, we can better understand what Uyghur Buddhism actually was.

The extant historical record from the first three hundred years of Uyghur Buddhist history provides ample evidence for this everyday type of practice among the Uyghurs but little related to Uyghur monastics. We do not even know which *Vinaya* the monastic community used, and we lack extensive scholarly treatises revealing the philosophical debates that animated Uyghur monastics during this time. We have plenty of evidence that there were Buddhist monasteries in the West Uyghur Kingdom: records of land grants for the establishment of monasteries as well as monastic account books. Monastics and the field of merit they provide for the laity is the *sine qua non* of any Buddhist society. We have the texts that the Uyghur monastics chose to translate, with the financial support of the laity, and they give us some inkling of the nature of early Uyghur Buddhism.[10] Together, these documents challenge conventional categories for classifying schools of Buddhism.

The textual evidence provides an intriguing look at the distinctive character of Uyghur Buddhism, and this section examines the most compelling. First, however, it is important to recall the historical context in which it was produced. Uyghur Buddhists understood the tenth and eleventh centuries to be a period of upheaval and even quite possibly the end of the Dharma. As we saw in chapter 2, Uyghur Buddhist practice revolved around shoring up one's karmic register and the cult of Maitreya.[11] In particular, as represented in the murals from the Bezeklik caves, the myth of the Buddha Maitreya involved professing the desire to be reborn at the time of his return so as to secure future buddhahood. Some of the earliest works translated into Uyghur—the *Garland of Legends Pertaining to the Ten Courses of Action* (*Daśakarmapathāvadānamālā*) and the *Maitrisimit*—focused on these ideas. The *Garland of Legends* is a cycle of stories written in a vivid and popular style arranged according to the ten so-called "courses of action" (*karmapatha*). In each chapter a teacher draws upon the *jataka* and *avadāna* literature (stories about the Buddha's previous lives) to explain to a pupil the dire consequences of choosing one of the evil paths (see fig. 4.1).

The *Maitrisimit* also draws extensively upon the *jataka* and *avadāna* literature, but it centers on the Buddha preaching to his disciples, Śāriputra and Ānanda, about the life of the future Buddha Maitreya. Both texts are thus squarely focused on the issues of the day: karmic consequences and the coming of Maitreya.

Both of these important texts were translated from Tokharian, which has led many scholars to assume that they represent an early Nikāya Buddhism that the Chinese Mahāyāna tradition later supplanted once the Uyghurs started to draw their inspiration from Dunhuang and the Khitans. Scholars have further speculated that when the Uyghurs became part of the Mongol empire in the thirteenth century, they adopted Tibetan Buddhism. This is how the history of Uyghur Buddhism is conventionally presented: an early Tokharian Nikāya phase, then a Chinese Mahāyāna Buddhist phase, and finally a Tantric Buddhist phase before the Uyghurs converted to Islam.

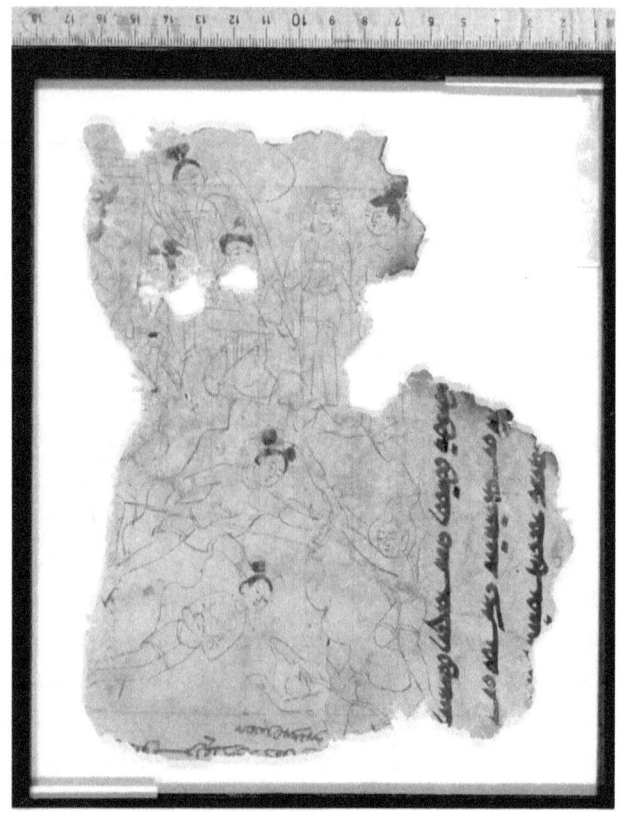

4.1 Illustrated *Daśakarmapathāvadānamālā*. U 1041 recto
Courtesy of the collection at the Berlin-Brandenburchische Akademie der Wissenschaften in der Staatsbibliotek zu Berlin–Preußischer Kulturbesitz, Orientabteilung

Although presenting Uyghur Buddhist history in this way has some heuristic value, it contains some underlying "Protestant presuppositions" and obscures the fact that the Uyghurs did not maintain sharp divisions between different Buddhist traditions.[12] Unlike Christianity, with its hard doctrinal boundaries between different denominations, Buddhism is more fluid. In Southeast Asia, for example, Theravada monks used tantric meditation techniques.[13] In the Uyghur case, in addition to the two Tokharian texts discussed above, another popular tenth-century work was the apocryphal Chinese tantric ritual purification text the *Eight Yang Sutra* (*Bayang jing* 八陽經 T. 2897). And, as discussed in chapter 2, the most reproduced text of the time was the Uyghur translation of the Chinese *Golden Light Sutra* (which focuses on karmic consequences, confession, and the protection of a Buddhist state).[14] Finally, a colophon to a Mahāyāna Buddhist commentary translated from Tokharian reveals that the Tokharians were not purely followers of the Nikaya tradition as generally assumed.[15] They translated and engaged with Mahāyāna texts and practices as well, as did the Uyghurs.

This mixing of traditions can also be found in texts that discuss the confession of sins. The Uyghur adoption of this practice presumably drew inspiration from the *Golden Light Sutra*, which was translated very early and includes this well-known section on confession:

> And whatever evil, cruel act was done by me previously, I will confess it all before the Buddhas. Whatever evil I have done by not attending to my parents, by neglecting the Buddhas, by neglecting the good; whatever evil I have done by being drunk with the intoxication of authority or with the intoxication of high birth or by being drunk with the intoxication of tender age; whatever evil I have done, bad thought, bad word, by an act badly done (or) by not perceiving a mishap; whatever evil I have done by the application of foolish reasoning, by a mind dark with ignorance, under the influence of an evil friend or by a mind distracted by impurities, under the compulsion of sport (or) enjoyment, or through the influence of anxiety (or) anger, (or) through the fault of unsatisfied wealth; whatever evil I have done by my association with ignoble people, by reason of envy (and) greed, (or) by the fault of guile (or) wretchedness; whatever evil I have done through failure to gain the mastery over my desires by reason of fear at the time of approaching troubles; whatever evil I have done through my influence of a flighty mind or through the influence of passion (and) anger (or) through being oppressed by hunger and thirst; whatever evil I have done for the sake of drink and food, for the sake of clothing, for a reason involving women, through the various afflictions of impurities; whatever evil of body, speech and mind, bad action accumulated in threefold manner, I have done, together with similar things, I confess it all. Whatever disrespect I may have shown to Buddhas, doctrines, likewise to Sravakas, I confess it all. Whatever disrespect I may have shown towards Pratyekabuddhas or towards Bodhisattvas, I confess it all. If I have shown disrespect towards those who preach the Good Law or towards meritorious beings, I confess it all. If I have unawares continually rejected the

Good Law (or shown) disrespect to my parents, I confess it all. (Whatever evil I have done) through stupidity or from folly or through being full of pride and arrogance, through passion, hatred or delusion, I confess it all.[16]

The chapter of the *Golden Light Sutra* that contains this passage circulated among the Uyghurs as an independent text in versified form.[17] Other Uyghur confession texts were also in circulation.[18] In the early eleventh century a Uyghur translation of the *Book for the Redemptions of Sins* (*Cibei daochang chanfa* 慈悲道場 懺法), better known as the *Precious Confession of Emperor Liang* (*Lianghuang baochan* 梁皇寶懺 T. 1909), was prepared.[19] This Chinese work was supposedly composed at the request of Emperor Wu of the Liang dynasty (464–549), who hoped to absolve the sins of his evil wife after she was reincarnated as a snake.[20] The *Book for the Redemptions of Sins* draws upon ideas that had become widely influential in Chinese Buddhism during the fourth and fifth centuries and became a key ritual practice among the Buddhists of the Song and Liao dynasties. From this world the Buddhism of the West Uyghur Kingdom was largely derived.

One of the ideas in the *Book for the Redemptions of Sins* is *chanhui* 懺悔, meaning "to remorsefully apologize for transgressions so as to thereby request mercy."[21] Eric M. Greene explains the meaning and development of this particular Chinese Buddhist practice:

First ... [*chanhui*] is not primarily a matter of *confession*, if by this word we mean the revelation of specific, hitherto hidden transgressions. The scripts that Chinese Buddhists used (and to this day still use) to conduct *chanhui* rituals usually do consist of sins, but the lists are almost always formulaic and inclusive; what they enumerate are not the specific deeds that the ritualist is conscious of having committed but all possible transgressions that one might be guilty of in this or even previous lifetimes. Indeed, it is the nonspecific nature of such a script that allows it to be used as a communal liturgy ... Second, *chanhui* is not a purely internal act, as the word "repentance"... might suggest. Rather, to engage in *chanhui* is in some manner to *express* one's remorse to another person or to a divine presence. It is, accordingly, a necessarily social and ritual act ... Third, and most important ... one who repents the named transgressions typically goes on to request that their negative effects, in the form of bad karma, be eliminated.[22]

The *chanhui* ritual differs from conventional Christian notions about confessing one's sins in that it is both communal and public.[23] As David Chappell explains: "Kinship lay at the heart of everything in traditional China. Misfortune arose not only from individual misdeeds, but from wrongs by family members of neighbors or from deceased relatives in distress. Recovery was also collective. Repentance could relieve the suffering for any and all relatives in visible and invisible worlds as well as bring about individual transformation and salvation.... What was new for Chinese Buddhists was the notion that individual misdeeds could result in collective punishment and that salvation for the dead was possible if sincere repentance, pleas, and vows were made by the living."[24] After the *Book for the Redemptions of Sins* was translated into Uyghur, such ideas became part of Uyghurs' Buddhist practice.[25] They even used the text when they celebrated the Ghost Festival, the most important Chinese Buddhist festival, during which merit is transferred to one's deceased ancestors.[26]

However, the Uyghur confession texts are not simply duplicates or direct translations and copies of the Chinese original. When they translated, the Uyghurs had no qualms about meddling with the source text. They readily deleted passages, added explanatory passages, and changed verse to prose or vice versa. In the translation of the *Book for the Redemptions of Sins*, for example, the confession texts are specifically focused on the individual who paid for the text or had the ritual performed, in contrast to the Chinese text, where the terms for "I so-and-so" (*Wo moujia* 我某甲 or *moujia* 某甲) are glossed over and understood in a communal context. The Uyghur shift from communal to private is evidenced in the practice of writing the names of the people who paid for the translation—typically a high-status married couple—directly into the text (and often in a different hand), as in this example:

> May they all equally know and see (it) through their pure wisdom, through their true bright eyes, through their true evidence, through attaining true equability. Now, we, <u>Käd Bars and Abitu</u>, since we are alive, we raise hope and support; in front of all Buddhas we completely confess, admit, disclose and publish all our bad deeds we have done before and we do not hide and conceal them. Confessing and admitting our bad deeds we have carried out and earned before we venture to ask for *kṣānti* (taking from us our sins).[27]

For the Uyghur elite, the confession of sins was a far more individualistic practice than was the case in the Chinese tradition.

This insertion of oneself into the text also appears in the other major confession text that circulated among the Uyghurs, *The Performing Confession Scripture,* which has been the subject of much scholarly debate. This text, for which no known Buddhist original text exists, consists of four parts: an introduction emphasizing the seriousness of evil deeds with examples of past acts of repentance by well-known Buddhist figures; a selection of sins, each followed by a formulaic expression of repentance and hope for absolution; a closing section warning of the danger of hell and expressing the hope for rebirth on earth during the time of the Buddha Maitreya; and a transfer of merit section, in which the merit resulting from having the text copied is transferred to various persons living and dead.[28] Because it has some similarities with Manichaean confession texts, some scholars have suggested that the Manichean texts influenced the Buddhist ones, and others have argued the opposite. As Jens Wilkens notes in his detailed study of this long-running debate, the evidence points in both directions. Regardless, even if the tradition of Manichean confession "primed" the Uyghurs to adopt Buddhist confession practices, the Uyghur confession rituals were part and parcel of Chinese Buddhist practice.[29] And the explosion of Chinese confession rituals at this time was related to the commercialization of the Song economy and the merchant classes' fear of punishment for dubious moral practices, as noted by economic historian Richard von Glahn; the same concerns no doubt also motivated the Uyghur Buddhist merchant elite.[30]

Thus, despite the individual orientation of the confession texts—a possible mark of acculturation to local values—the bulk of Uyghur Buddhist material reflects what one scholar has called the "north Chinese Buddhist complex."[31] Developing in the late Tang and the Five Dynasties period, the fusion of Huayan, Chan, and esoteric Buddhism became the de facto Buddhism of the Liao and is called the "Perfect Teaching" (*yuanjiao* 圓教). This school traced its origins not to the standard Huayan teachings of Yunhua Zhiyan (雲華智儼, 602-668) and Fazang (法藏, 643-712) but to Qingliang Chengguan (清涼澄觀, 737-838) and the works of his disciple Guifeng Zongmi (圭峰宗密, 780-841). Liao Buddhism combined Huayan Buddhism with tantric practices related to Vairocana Buddha and Samantabhadra as well as with the scholarly and gradualist Chan schools that were opposed to the Tiantai-oriented and "sudden enlightenment" traditions then popular in the Song dynasty.[32] "The major premise of this system was that since all Buddhist doctrinal teachings and practices originate from and converge upon the 'one-mind,' their totality can be organized into a comprehensive system accommodating all 'practical' dimensions... [and that] each dharma realm represents one specific expression of the crucial Huayan concept of the 'one true mind.'"³³

In creating and promoting this new interpretation of the Dharma, the scholars of the Perfect Teaching drew upon a range of texts that included works such as the *Avataṃsaka Sutra* (*Huayan jing* 華嚴經 T. 279), the *Diamond Sutra*, the *Golden Light Sutra*, the twenty-fifth chapter of the *Lotus Sutra* (known as the *Avalokiteśvara Sūtra*), the *Vow of Samantabhadra* (*Puxian xingyuan* 普賢行願), the *Amitābha Sūtra* (*Amituo jing* 阿彌陀經 T. 366), the *Perfect Enlightenment Sutra* (*Yuanjue jing* 圓覺經 T. 842), and the *Sutra on Maitreya's Ascent to Tuṣita* (*Guan Mile shangsheng Doushuai tian jing* 觀彌勒上生兜率天經 T. 452).³⁴

That the Uyghurs translated all of these texts confirms that the "north Chinese Buddhist complex" was central to the development of early Uyghur Buddhism. Further evidence is in fragments found in Turfan of the *Xu Yiqiejing yinyi* (續一切經音義, a phonetic dictionary of Chinese characters in Buddhist scriptures) edited by the Liao monk Xilin, as well as commentaries by the Liao monk Quanming 詮明 (ca. 930–982). The Uyghurs were keenly aware of developments happening within Khitan Buddhism, including a revived interest in the Faxiang school—or the Yogācāra "mind-only" school.³⁵ An original Uyghur text on Buddhist thought, for example, explicates the "Five States" based upon one of the fundamental treatises of the Faxiang Yogācāra school, the *Discourse on the Perfection of Consciousness-Only* (*Cheng Weishi Lun* 成唯識論 T. 1585).³⁶ The Uyghur embrace of the "mind-only" school of thought is also reflected in the fact that when they translated texts not aligned with Yogācāra, they inserted "mind-only" interpretations into the Uyghur version. In his translation of the *Golden Light Sutra*, for example, the early eleventh-century Uyghur translator Šingko Šäli Tutung "tried to explain the ten pāramitās on the basis of the teaching" of the mind-only school.³⁷

A more audacious example of this insertion of Yogācāra thought is the Uyghur translation of a commentary on the famous *Vimalakīrti Sūtra*, which focuses on the religious practices of a layman.³⁸ Thus, although the Uyghur commentary is ostensibly based on the Tiantai scholar Daoye's *Collected Commentaries on the Vimalakīrti Sūtra from "Inside the Passes"* (Ch. *Jingmingjing jijie guanzhongshu* 淨名經集解關中疏 T. 2777), the Uyghur translator(s) purposely edited out the

Tiantai commentary. In its stead the "translator" inserted Yogācāra thought, including a detailed study of the eighth consciousness, *ālaya-vijñāna*,[39] a notion that is not even found in Tiantai thought.[40] And in a comparison of the four wisdoms with the Buddha's three bodies, the translator/editor included in the Uyghur commentary a Chan interpretation unknown in the Yogācāra tradition.[41]

The addition of a Chan interpretation may simply reflect the Perfect Teaching, which included Chan thought, but this Uyghur innovation might have been based on a broader engagement with Chan Buddhism. This Uyghur engagement with Chan can be seen in their commentaries on the *Perfect Enlightenment Sutra* (*Yuanjue jing* 圓覺經 T. 842),[42] translations of the *Treatise on the Contemplation of the Mind* (*Guanxin lun* 觀心論 T. 2833),[43] and the *Inquiry Into Divine Thinking* (*Siyi fantian suowen jing* 思益梵天所問經 T. 586),[44] as well as distinctive Chan poems on the "Night Watches."[45] Similarly, the Uyghur translation of all the major texts related to Pure Land Buddhism could have been part of the Perfect Teaching, or an independent and broader engagement with this particular tradition focused on the worship of Amitābha Buddha.[46] The same question can also be asked about the extensive Uyghur translations of the *Diamond Sutra*, related commentaries, and miracle tales: is it all simply a manifestation of the Perfect Teaching, or something else?[47]

Although it is clear that the Liao dynasty's Perfect Teaching profoundly influenced the development of Uyghur Buddhism, the Uyghurs felt free to adopt any and all forms of Buddhism regardless of whether they fit within the paradigm of the Perfect Teaching. To expect otherwise is symptomatic of the "Protestant presupposition" problem and the penchant to map Buddhist thought and practice into clear and distinct traditions. Such simplifying models miss the trees for the forest. Trying to fit Uyghur Buddhism into today's taxonomies also ignores the distinctiveness that this book has been highlighting: a freer approach to the Dharma fostered by Uyghur Buddhism's disconnect from centralizing political power. With no authority defining what was to be normative, much less what should be translated and put into a hypothetical canon, Uyghur Buddhists could readily draw from the widest array of Buddhist thought and practice.

In addition to all the texts related to the Perfect Teaching, the Uyghurs translated a vast array of stories about the Buddha's past lives, as well as several biographies of the Buddha including the *Araṇemi Jātaka*, the *Viśvantara Jātaka*, stories from the *Jātakamālā* of Haribhaṭṭa and Ārya Śūra, the *Śārdūlakarṇāvadāna*, and

4.2 Illustrated *Viśvantara Jātaka*. Ink on Paper, 44 x 17.5 cm. U 3904
Courtesy of the collection at the Berlin-Brandenburchische Akademie der Wissenschaften in der Staatsbibliotek zu Berlin–Preußischer Kulturbesitz, Orientabteilung

the *Buddhacarita* (see fig. 4.2).[48] They also translated the popular "transformation texts" (*bianwen*) from Dunhuang, such as the story of Maudgalyāyana saving his mother from hell.[49]

A recent discovery—a Tangut blockprint excavated from the ruins of Kharakhoto in Inner Mongolia—perhaps best highlights the Uyghurs' eclectic approach to the Dharma. The Tangut blockprint is a version of a text written by the Northern Song Tiantai priest Ciyun Zunshi (慈雲遵式, 964–1032), *Illustration of the Ten Realms of Mind Contemplation in the Perfect and Immediate Teaching* (*Yuandun Guanxin Shifajietu* 元頓觀心十法界圖) (see fig. 4.3).

Zunshi had included a maṇḍala that represented the ten realms with the heart character (*xin* 心) at its center, for use in visualization practice. Zunshi's work was eventually lost in China, but before that it had been sent to Japan, where it became the source for the *Visualization Maṇḍala of the Heart and Ten Worlds of Kumano* (*Kumano Kanjin Jikkai Mandara*), which depicts the stages of life from old age to death; the possible fates after death in hell or other realms of existence; and the means of salvation through birth in a Pure Land.

The rediscovered Tangut blockprint bears a detailed inscription that parallels the explanatory text in Zunshi's *Illustration of the Ten Realms*, confirming that Zunshi's work also made it to the Tangut realm. Based on this new information, Kitsudō Kōichi and Arakawa Shintarō have argued that one of the iconic but fragmentary Uyghur wall paintings now on display in the Humboldt Forum in

4.3 Twelfth-century Tangut blockprint, 62.5 x 42 cm. X-2538

State Hermitage Museum. After Kitsudō Kōichi and Shintarō Arakawa, "New Research on the *Guanxin Shijietu* (*Illustration of the Ten Realms of Mind Contemplation*)," (2018), fig. 5.5

Berlin is actually a representation of Zunshi's maṇḍala (see fig. 4.4).[50] In particular, they claim that the central dais depicted in the Uyghur wall painting was not, as earlier scholars have speculated, for a buddha or bodhisattva, but rather the heart character 心, as in the blockprint and the *Kumano Kanjin Jikkai Mandara*.

This interpretation has a number of implications for our understanding of Uyghur Buddhism. It not only once again confirms the Buddhist relations maintained between the Uyghurs and the Song court as well as the Tanguts but also, and more importantly, reveals that the Uyghurs adopted an expressly Northern Song Tiantai Buddhist practice in contrast to the commentary discussed above, which was systematically purged of any Tiantai interpretations. This curious twist again shows how willing Uyghurs were to incorporate all forms of Buddhist thought and practices into their own distinctive form of Buddhism.

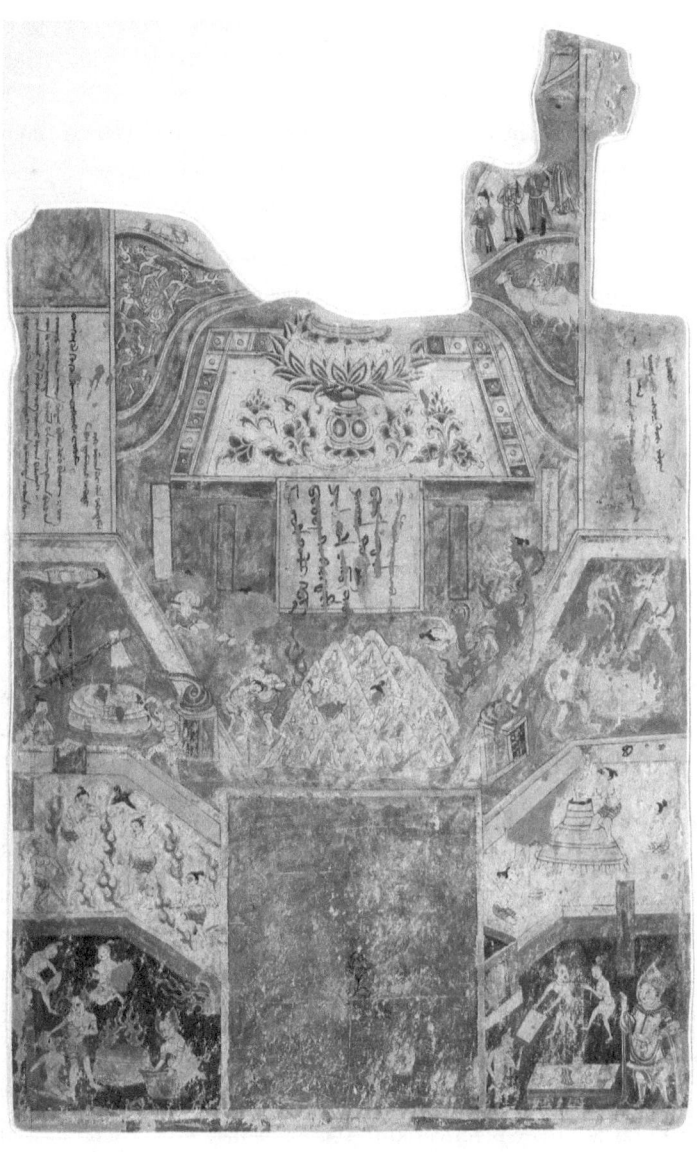

4.4 Uyghur wall painting with hell realms and dais
(III 8453). © Staatliche Museen zu Berlin, Museum für Asiatische Kunst

MATERIAL BUDDHISM

Such questions about the differences between Huayan and Tiantai thought—as well as Yogācāra notions about the six forms of consciousness—were presumably largely the domain of the monastic elite and quite possibly some of the educated laity. To look deeper into everyday Buddhism among the Uyghurs, beyond questions of texts and doctrines, I turn to how Uyghur Buddhism was materialized in objects—art, texts, and temples—produced as part of Buddhist practices.[51]

Although much attention has been paid to the Uyghurs' liberal approach to the art of translation—the willingness to edit freely, add and delete material, or simply create whole new texts—little has been said about the actual practice of preparing these translations. In part, this is because little is known. We know the names of only a handful of translators, and it is unclear if they worked in teams (as was the case in China) or individually.[52] The early eleventh-century Uyghur translation of the ten-volume *Biography of Xuanzang* is usually attributed to Šingko Šäli Tutung but actually appears to be the work of several translators.[53] In the typical Chinese case, a final editing process would have standardized the work of the various translators, but that does not appear to have been done for the *Biography of Xuanzang*. Chinese terms were translated differently from chapter to chapter, and the quality of the translation differs between chapters as well.

The *Biography of Xuanzang* may, however, be an anomaly. Most Uyghur translations of Buddhist texts are well done even if certain liberties may have been taken in the process. The Uyghurs were interested in having the "best" version of the text, and they not only revised their translations over time but also adopted something like critical methods in their translation practices.[54] If they were translating a Chinese text, for example, they would consult the Tibetan version(s) in order to ensure the proper reading. Sometimes they even consulted the Sanskrit original.[55] This desire for accuracy is reflected in the following letter wherein a translator requests copies of texts be sent to him so that he can prepare proper translations—or versified forms of them—to be presented to the Uyghur ruler:

> To my teacher. My, Kinsudu's letter.
>
> > If I am to show this dhyāna-book to the Uighur ruler (Iduq-qut), I would have written all of them in verses. I cannot think of it, nor can I improve my work. My message is this:

> May someone send me a complete version of the dhyāna-book of Vajrasattva, and also the complete dhyāna-book of Śrī Cakrasaṃvara, and also a complete dhyāna-book of Mahākāla, and then may he send them to me. My message is like this.
>
> May someone make complete copies of these three dhyāna-books into one book, and may he send it to me.[56]

Such concern for accuracy and completeness was not only reserved for the Uyghur ruler. Uyghur translators understood that many Buddhist texts—especially those written in Literary Sinitic—were incredibly dense and required explication. In one case, the Uyghur translator dealing with the terse sentence "The samādhi is three samādhis" (三昧三三昧) (from the *Commentary on the Vimalakīrti Sūtra* by Kumārajīva) considered it necessary to explain the meaning of this passage.[57] He wrote: "Samādhi is Indian. In Uyghur, on the other hand, one calls it meditation. Furthermore, there are three types of meditation: first, emptiness samādhi [Śūnyatā-samādhi], second, the intangible, formless unmarked samādhi [Ānimitta-samādhi], third, desireless samādhi [Apraṇihita-samādhi]."[58]

Based on this example, we can see that Uyghur translators were conscientious in their work and tried to make the Dharma comprehensible. At the same time, we do not know how texts were chosen for translation because the extant colophons refer not to intellectual motivation, only to the generation of merit. The economics of this process are clear. As discussed in chapter 3, the laity paid translators—presumably monks—to prepare these works so that they could produce good karma for themselves and others and to confirm their social status. But we do not know the specifics: how much it cost to produce such a manuscript, how long it took, or what was done with it when completed. Did the laity take the manuscript home and read it, use it in ritual performances, or simply put it on their shrine as part of the "cult of the book" that was so prevalent across the Buddhist world?[59]

Such details around translation lie beyond our grasp, but we do know more about the materiality of Uyghur manuscripts.[60] Most of the early manuscripts were written in black ink—with red ink for ornamentation—with a reed pen on paper.[61] Many are in the distinctive long and narrow *pustaka* format based on palm leaf manuscripts that were popular in the Tarim Basin (see fig. 4.5).

Some of these manuscripts are also illustrated (see fig. 4.6).

108 *Uyghur Buddhisms*

4.5 Uyghur pothi manuscript. U 3909 recto.
Courtesy of the collection at the Berlin-Brandenburchische Akademie der Wissenschaften in der Staatsbibliotek zu Berlin–Preußischer Kulturbesitz, Orientabteilung

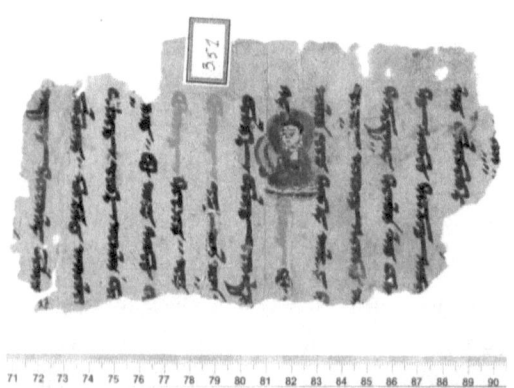

4.6 Illustrated *Säkiz Yükmäk Yaruk Sutra*. U 7123 recto
Courtesy of the collection at the Berlin-Brandenburchische Akademie der Wissenschaften in der Staatsbibliotek zu Berlin–Preußischer Kulturbesitz, Orientabteilung

Other manuscripts follow Chinese conventions and thus use either the long scroll or concertina format (see figs. 4.7 and 4.8).

Some are also written with a brush instead of a reed pen. There are also texts in the codex format (see fig. 4.9).

The diversity of format and style is wide, but one consistent factor throughout the history of the West Uyghur Kingdom is the apparent shortage of paper. We know that the Uyghurs imported paper from Dunhuang.[62] They also dealt with the shortage by trying to make paper locally out of cotton.[63] Yet more often

4.7 Uyghur scroll manuscript, U4921 verso
Courtesy of the collection at the Berlin-Brandenburchische Akademie der Wissenschaften in der Staatsbibliotek zu Berlin–Preußischer Kulturbesitz, Orientabteilung

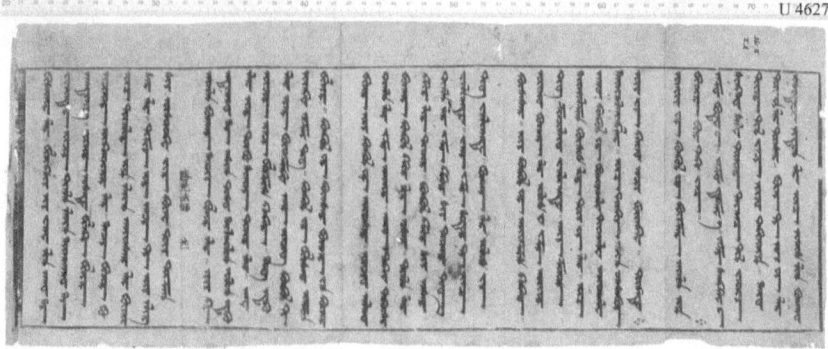

4.8 Uyghur concertina manuscript, U4627
Courtesy of the collection at the Berlin-Brandenburchische Akademie der Wissenschaften in der Staatsbibliotek zu Berlin–Preußischer Kulturbesitz, Orientabteilung

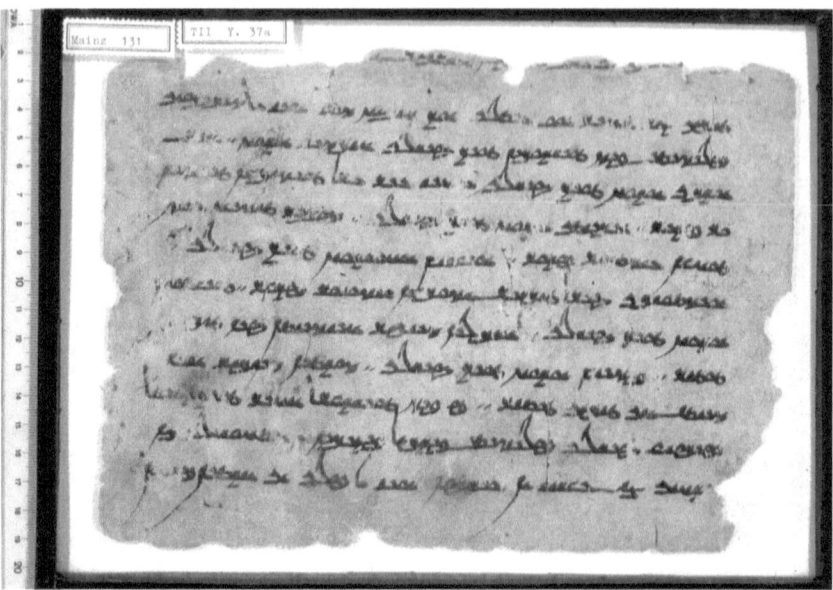

4.9 Uyghur codex manuscript, Mainz 131
Courtesy of the collection at the Berlin-Brandenburchische Akademie der Wissenschaften in der Staatsbibliotek zu Berlin–Preußischer Kulturbesitz, Orientabteilung

than not the Uyghurs reused Chinese documents that were written or printed on only one side, writing their own texts on the blank side.

Whether this recycling of Chinese Buddhist texts played a role in shaping Uyghur Buddhism is unclear; however, it is certain that the Chinese Buddhism of Dunhuang informed Uyghur practices. Uyghurs therefore adopted talismans used for health and protection found in such works as the *Sūtra of the Divine Talismans of the Seven Thousand Buddhas to Increase the Account* (七千佛神符益算經 T. 2904) (see fig. 4.10).[64]

They also adopted the worship of Guanyin, the Bodhisattva of Compassion, who, if prayed to, could save one in times of need.[65] In some cases this borrowing even included the wholesale copying of the Chinese original (see figs. 4.11 and 4.12).[66]

Such aesthetic and ritual appropriation is also reflected in the Uyghur versions of the *Scripture on the Ten Kings*. Composed in the late Tang dynasty (618–907), this text describes the Ten Kings of purgatory, who judge the actions of a deceased person in order to determine his or her status of rebirth. It was used

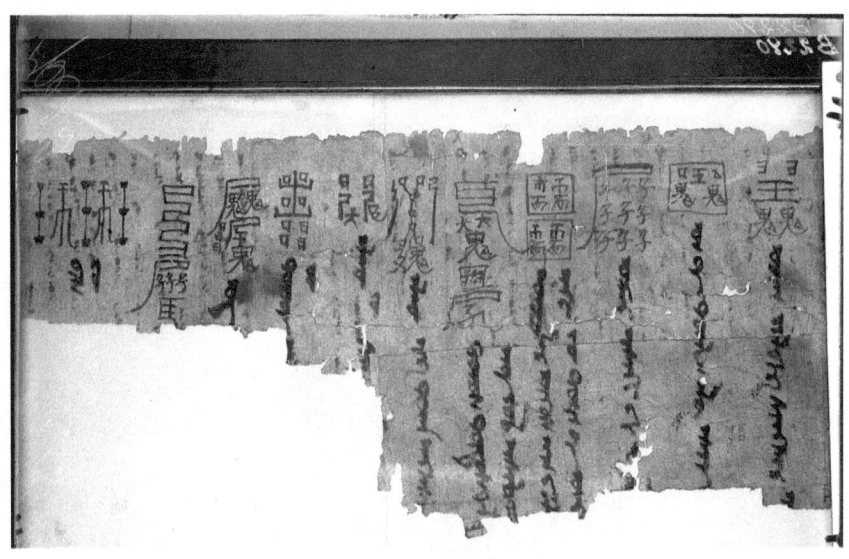

4.10 Uyghur text with Chinese amulets
(Inv. No. B 2290) © Staatliche Museen zu Berlin, Museum für Asiatische Kunst

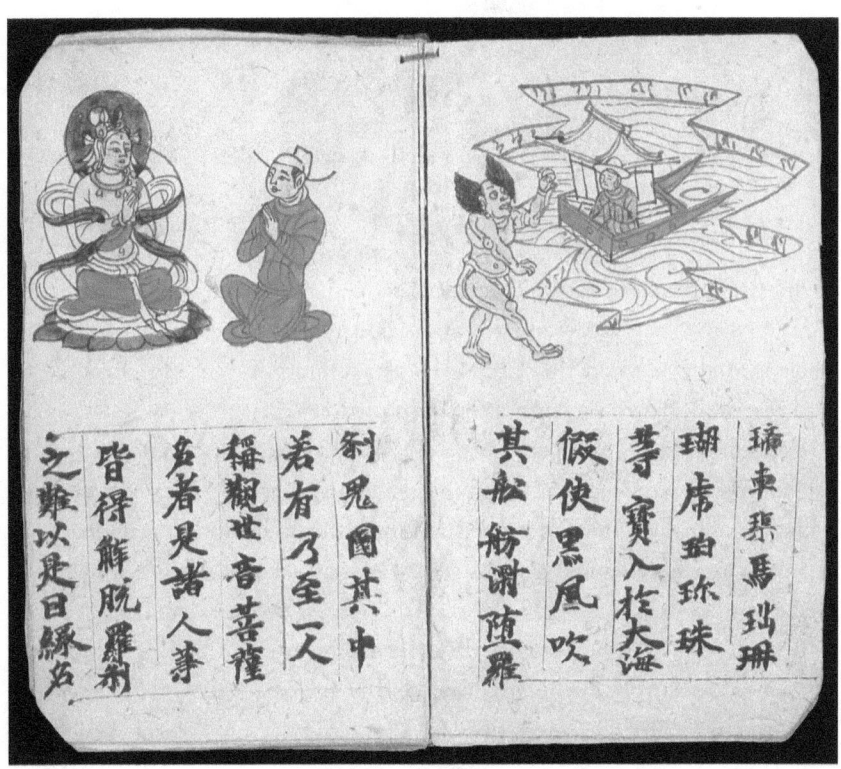

4.11 Chinese version of *Guanyin Sutra*. Or.8210/S.6983
Courtesy of the International Dunhuang Project

4.12 Uyghur translation of *Guanyin Sutra*. SI 5846
After Institute of Oriental Manuscripts, Russian Academy of Sciences, and the Toyo Bunko, eds., *Catalogue of the Old Uyghur Manuscripts and Blockprints in the Serindia Collection of the Institute of Oriental Manuscripts, RAS*, vol. 1 (Tokyo: The Toyo Bunko, 2021), pl. 1

during death rituals to ensure that a deceased individual would pass through the bureaucracy of purgatory and secure a good rebirth. The Uyghurs not only wholeheartedly adopted this Chinese funerary practice but also emulated its aesthetic in their own versions of the scripture (see fig. 4.13).

Concerns about death and karma are also reflected in the large corpus of Uyghur material related to the Bodhisattva Kṣitigarbha (Ch. Dizang 地藏), who is known for his two vows: to take responsibility for all beings between the death of Śākyamuni Buddha and the return of Maitreya; and to release all beings in the hell realms (see fig. 4.14).[67]

In one extant Uyghur text of this corpus, for example, the practitioner is advised to worship Kṣitigarbha/Dizang on the eighteenth day of the month in order to counteract the forces of King Yama, the Lord of Death: "(The eighteenth) day is the day that King Yama (walks around) the world. Who, on that day, chants the name of Dizang Bodhisattva one thousand times, he will not fall

4.13 Fragment of the *Scripture on the Ten Kings*: the court of one of the Ten Kings (Inv. No. III 2). © Staatliche Museen zu Berlin, Museum für Asiatische Kunst

into the hell where tongues are ripped out when he passes away."[68] The cult of Dizang arose in medieval China at a time of anxiety about the end of the Dharma similar to the situation at the turn of the millennium, which no doubt played a role in his popularity among the Uyghurs.[69]

Uyghur interest in the ritual practices then popular in Dunhuang did not always result in a translation. The Uyghurs either simply read the texts in Chinese or transcribed them phonetically in the Uyghur script, as seen in chapter 2. In other cases the Uyghurs commissioned works that were aesthetically and visually in the "Chinese style," like this painting of Guanyin from Dunhuang (see fig. 4.15). In a Chinese style, it also contains Uyghur elements that confirm that its patron was a Uyghur noblewoman.[70]

Although these examples show that the Chinese influence on Uyghur Buddhism and its material and visual culture was profound, it was not the only influence.[71] The artworks found at the two major cave complexes built by the Uyghurs at the summer capital of Beshbaliq, and at Bezeklik outside the winter

4.14 Kṣitigarbha and the Ten Kings, tenth to eleventh century, Qocho. 101 x 94 cm. (Inv. No. III 4782). © Staatliche Museen zu Berlin, Museum für Asiatische Kunst

4.15 Veneration of Guanyin. First half of the tenth century. Central Asia, Dunhuang, Mogao Caves. Painting on silk, 96.8 x 65 cm. EO1175
Musée des Arts Asiatiques-Guimet. @ RMN-Grand Palais/Art Resource, NY

116 *Uyghur Buddhisms*

4.16 Buddhist cave temple complex at Beshbaliq

After Zhongguo Shehui Kexueyuan Yanjiusiu, *Beiting Gaochang Huihu Fosi Yizhi* (*Remains of a Uygur Monastery Gaochang-Beiting*) (Shenyang: Liaoning meishu chubanshe, 1991), color plate 1

4.17 Bezeklik Caves outside Qocho (Gaochang)
Photo by author

capital in Qocho (see figs. 4.16 and 4.17), are especially rich examples of the many other influences.

But the Uyghurs also developed a style wholly their own, as evidenced in the iconic cave murals at Bezeklik presented in chapters 1 and 2; moreover, the murals at Beshbaliq reflect a different style altogether, one that drew inspiration from Buddhist art in both Afghanistan and China.[72] Thus while the caves at Beshbaliq exhibit the standard motif of the Thousand Buddhas found in cave temples along the Silk Road, they also include distinctive donor portraits and historical murals in this unique Uyghur style (see figs. 4.18 and 4.19).[73]

Similarly, while Tokharian and Chinese influences are evident in the murals of Bezeklik, there are other artworks that reflect a distinctive Uyghur style. This is most notable in the numerous mixed-medium temple banners now housed in Berlin, as well as a banner now in the Hermitage that renders the Lotus Sūtra with explanatory textual citations among the images.[74]

The production of such stunning works of art was a key component of Buddhist practice but was invariably the preserve of an elite few. Pilgrimage, however, was available to all.[75] More than 300 extant Uyghur pilgrim inscriptions make clear that this way of merit making was avidly practiced.[76] The inscriptions also give a better sense of what Uyghurs actually did in their everyday lives as Buddhists. Going on pilgrimage to worship was a means to achieve a better rebirth. One reads: "Since I usually climb to the Amitābha Cave Temple and worship there, I have enriched my life so as to ascend to Tuṣita heaven and be reborn there. Thus writing this on this sacred Chinese scroll, I, the Buddha's servant Yaqšidu Tutung wrote these two lines as a memento."[77] This sentiment is also reflected in an inscription from the Yulin caves: "On the 28th day of the 9th month of the fortunate Horse Year [1390 or 1402], we, Öljäy Tömur and Darm-a Siri came from Shazhou to this sacred mountain temple in order to worship. After having worshipped, as returning [I] Kackur Kiya, have humbly written [this text]. As the fruit of our merits from this worship may our bad karma of the present as well as the past and future existences be cleaned, and, together with all sentient beings, may we attain Buddhahood quickly! Sadhu, sadhu may it be!"[78]

Praying for a better rebirth was not the only thing these pilgrims did when they visited temples and pagodas across north China.[79] They also recited the rosary over long periods: "In the dog year, in the middle of the fifth month, I came here. Having counted the prayer beads on a rosary for one month, I come into existence."[80] Another inscription tells of being in meditation for a month: "In the horse year, I, Toyincuq Tutung, having climbed up [to this cave?], ventured to descend into meditation. In the 7th month, [I spent] one month."[81] Another records a seven-month retreat at a mountain hermitage: "It has been three years since I, Buyan-Qaya, came here from the city of Suzhou [modern Jiuquan], but I did not leave. Staying in a mountain hermitage for about seven

4.18 Uyghur donor of cave temple in the underground south entry to the cave temple complex at Beshbaliq

After Zhongguo Shehui Kexueyuan Yanjiusiu, *Beiting Gaochang Huihu Fosi Yizhi* (*Remains of a Uygur Monastery Gaochang-Beiting*) (Shenyang: Liaoning meishu chubanshe, 1991), color plate 10

4.19 Mounted figures attacking a city with donors below. West wall of south chamber 105, Beshbaliq

After Zhongguo Shehui Kexueyuan Yanjiusiu, *Beiting Gaochang Huihu Fosi Yizhi* (*Remains of a Uygur Monastery Gaochang-Beiting*) (Shenyang: Liaoning meishu chubanshe, 1991), color plate 10

months, I wrote this inscription. 'May it be a memory for others to see!'"[82] Other inscriptions show that pilgrimages and related activities were not necessarily individual affairs:

> Who are the people standing (here)? We are the 30 people under the leadership of Lüsün Zhanglao, Padmaśrī Diyanči, Kuyšidu, Buddhakīrti Šila, Suda Šila, and Prajñaśri. They stayed to practice the good deeds in this monastery for three months. During the time when we went to practice meditation and to complete the number of service, I completed the number of my service, and I ventured to write. Let there be witness [religious] brothers in the future... Considering writing... the servant... considering them to be new students, considering "may they read the dharani correctly like this," I, Tolun Tämür, the servant, ventured to write, considering "may there be witness in the future!"[83]

Some have asked why pilgrims bothered to write down their thoughts and descriptions. Why did they want someone in the future to witness their righteous activities? With regard to a similar practice, autographic rock graffiti in premodern Korea, Maya Stiller has suggested that it was a means for the elite to demonstrate their social status: "Such travel practices show how social competition emerged in the spatial context of a landscape."[84] This may have been the case with the Uyghurs since much of Buddhist merit making—such as commissioning artwork or texts—costs money and thus by extension confirms social status.

Yet while such striving may have played a role in creating the texts and artworks that we can now admire and study, the majority of Buddhist acts—done by people across the social spectrum—have left no record. Nevertheless, based on the extant material it is clear that the eclecticism of early Uyghur Buddhism was shaped by similar concerns the world over: health, wealth, and prosperity in the here and now and hereafter.

THE GOLDEN AGE OF UYGHUR BUDDHISM

The West Uyghur Kingdom had been allied with the Khitan Liao dynasty since shortly after its founding. The alliance had served both well economically, militarily, politically, and religiously. In the early twelfth century, however, the power and success of the Khitans waned, and they were eventually conquered by the Jurchen, who founded the Jin dynasty in north China (1115–1234 CE). The Khitans fled to the Mongolian plateau, where they regrouped. After acquiring numerous Turkic and Mongol followers, the Khitans—renamed Qara Khitai ("Black Chinese")—moved into Central Asia and founded the Western Liao empire (1124–1218). The Uyghur ruler duly submitted to this new state, which included sending several of his relatives as hostages to the Western Liao court and sending Uyghur elites to tutor the Qara Khitai leaders. Much as before, this alliance served the Uyghurs well, as the security umbrella of the Western Liao enabled them to thrive on account of their pivotal position in the East-West trade network.[85]

This amicable relationship, however, came to an end at the beginning of the thirteenth century. The split arose around a Qara Khitai tax representative sent to the Uyghur court. This official, a Buddhist monk, was so aggressive in his duties that a century later the historian of the Mongols, Rashid al-Din, wrote: "When he took power, he extended the hand of tyranny over the Iduq-qut, the amirs and the Uighur tribes. He demanded unreasonable taxes and they [the Uyghurs] came to loathe him."[86] In 1209 the Uyghur ruler Barchug Art Tegin, in consultation with the chief minister Bilgä Bukha, had the Buddhist tax collector killed and sent an envoy to the Qara Khitai court explaining what they had done.

The Uyghur ruler clearly knew that by killing a representative of the Qara Khitai state he was ending an alliance of more than two hundred years. But recent events had told him that the power of the Western Liao was waning and a new power was rising. The surrounding nomadic empires had long employed Uyghurs in their governments due to their sophistication and cosmopolitanism, and one of these individuals was the erudite Tatar Tongga, whom the Naimans on the Mongolian plateau employed as a tax collector. When Chinggis Khan attacked the Naimans and Tatar Tongga tried to flee with the important government seals, he was captured. According to *History of the Yuan Dynasty*, Tatar Tongga explained the value of seals for a functioning government to Chinggis Khan, who then commissioned him to develop a writing system for Mongolian (see fig. 4.20).[87]

When Mongol envoys came to Qocho shortly after Barchug Art Tegin had killed the Qara Khitai tax collector in 1209, the Uyghur ruler readily submitted

4.20 The early Uyghur-based Mongol script as used on Guyuk Khan's imperial seal (r. 1246–1248)

After Čolmon, *Mongyol tamay-a seyilümel* (Hohhot: Öbör mongyol-un suryan kümüjil-ün keblel-ün qoriy-a, 1996), 6

to Chinggis Khan. Later that same year, Barchug Art Tegin confirmed his loyalty to the Mongols by rebuffing a group of Merkits who sought refuge in the West Uyghur Kingdom after Chinggis Khan attacked them. This pleased Chinggis Khan, who shortly thereafter established a garrison in the West Uyghur Kingdom that would become an important military post in the Mongol campaigns against the Tanguts. (Barchug Art Tegin would not actually meet Chinggis Khan until 1211 when he was campaigning against the Tanguts.) Because of this early and unstinting support of the Mongols, Chinggis Khan later proclaimed that Barchug Art Tegin was "to be [his] fifth son, to be bound as a brother with the emperor's sons" and given a royal princess in marriage. The Uyghurs thus began their long career as the "steppe intelligentsia" of the Mongol empire and became permanently linked with Chinggis Khan.[88]

How this relationship developed and came to shape Uyghur Buddhist history over the course of the Mongol empire (including its collapse) is the topic of the next chapter.[89] Here I focus on how the Mongol involvement with Buddhism came to influence Uyghur Buddhism during the thirteenth and fourteenth centuries.[90] In brief, this period saw a retreat from the freewheeling and eclectic nature of Uyghur Buddhism. When Buddhism became a part of the Mongol state apparatus, Uyghur Buddhism became yoked to an imperial project and with that, came to be defined by developments in the metropole.

For example, whereas in the West Uyghur Kingdom period rulers had not been eulogized in colophons as paragons of Buddhist piety or righteous Dharmic rule, in the Mongol period this form of praise became de rigeur. Take for example this colophon to a translation, one of many from the Yuan period:[91]

> From [sunset] to (sun)rise, may your fortunate name be heard!
> May your ... army march and conquer countries!
> In the land of ..., may you find wealth, and may disaster never befall (you)!
> May the Lord of All, our brave father, live for a thousand (years and) ten thousand days!
> In the seven climates, may your good name waft like incense!
> May the Best of the Best, the Lord of Lords, join and come together (with all the people)!
> May the ... Uyghur realm (be) well ...!
> May the Lord of the World, our Emperor, live a thousand (years), ten thousand days!
> May the countries [of the Chinese], Tangut, Persians [remain far away]!
> May the ... goods increase and ...!
> May ... the large sea ... make!
> May the Lord of the Universe, our Emperor, live a thousand years, ten thousand days!
> Where he walks, may the way of our Khan be enjoyable!
> May destructive weather not occur, may the cattle become as many as the stars!
> ... may the Uyghur realm coagulate like yogurt! [meaning "become strong"]
> May the Ruler of the ..., our [Uyghur] Idukkut Khan, live a thousand years, ten thousand days![92]

Such grandiose paeans to Mongol and Uyghur Buddhist rulers were not only incorporated into major translation projects. In a colophon to a translation of the *Avalokiteśvara Sūtra* commissioned by the laywoman Šaraki, the Mongol ruler Tugh Temür (r. 1329-1332) and his wife are praised thus: "May the emperor and empress who belong to the lineage of the bodhisattvas live many tens of thousands of years!"[93] Even in a simple Uyghur Buddhist refuge formula, the Mongol ruler is also mentioned: "A second time, by striving for the good, so that the lives of the former and later kings and rulers beginning with the Emperor and the imperial princes may be long, and through my oath for the highest and best Buddhahood [I take refuge] in the Buddha."[94]

Uyghur Buddhism also changed when the Mongols turned toward Tibetan Buddhism.[95] Mongol engagement with Tantric Buddhism had begun through their relations with and eventual conquest of the Tanguts.[96] Tantric masters at the Tangut court had used ritual war magic related to the ferocious deity Mahākāla to successfully repel the Mongols, and the Mongols were so impressed that they eventually adopted Mahākāla as their patron deity and used his war magic in many of their military campaigns across Asia.[97] The Mongol connection with Tibetan Buddhism deepened after they set their sights on conquering Tibet.[98]

After some initial raids on the Tibetan plateau, the Mongol Prince Köden invited the leader of Sakya monastery, Sakya Pandita Kungga Gyeltsen (1182-1251), to Liangzhou. He and his nephew Pakpa Lama traveled to Liangzhou and met Prince Köden in 1247, and on the basis of that meeting, Sakya Pandita sent a manifesto to the political and ecclesiastical leaders of Tibet urging their acceptance of Mongol sovereignty with the Sakya as feudatory representatives. This agreement became moot when Güyük Khan abruptly died in 1248 and Möngke became Khan in 1251 (r. 1251-1259). Möngke shifted the Mongols' Tibet policy away from the Sakya and toward Karma Pakshi (1206-1283), the leader of a rival lineage, the Kagyü.[99] However, at the same time, Khubilai, then ruling north China, invited Pakpa Lama, who had since inherited his uncle Sakya Pandita's office, to his court. Pakpa arrived in 1253, and the following year Khubilai bestowed on him all the monasteries of Tibet's Tsang province. In 1258 Pakpa Lama initiated Khubilai into Buddhism.[100] After Möngke's death and a succession feud with his brother Ariq Böke, Khubilai took the Mongol throne in 1260 and Pakpa Lama became the main Tibetan Buddhist teacher at court. In 1264, Khubilai appointed him the National Preceptor (*Guoshi* 國師) and supreme head

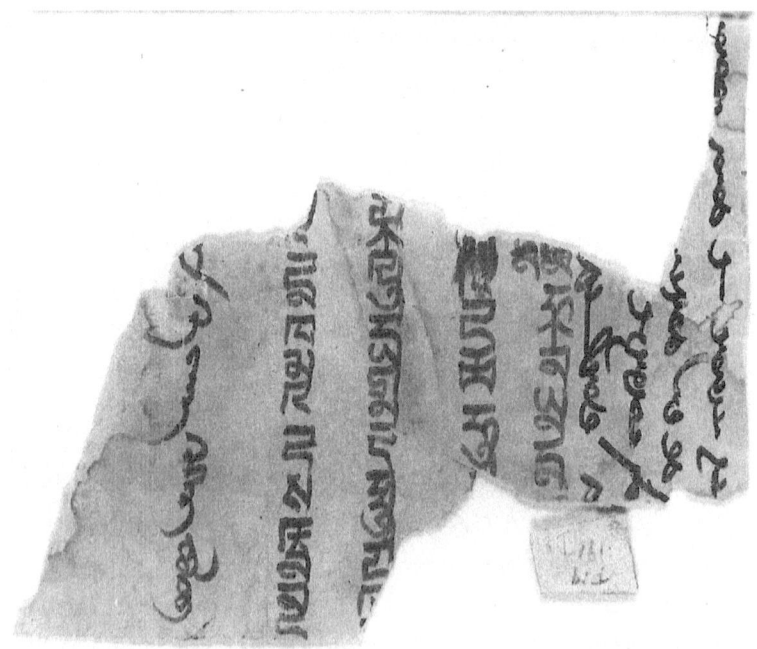

4.21 Uyghur in Pakpa script
(Inv. No. III 205). © Staatliche Museen zu Berlin, Museum für Asiatische Kunst

of the entire Tibetan clergy, whereupon he returned to Sakya monastery in Tibet. Shortly thereafter, the Drigungpa order, who opposed Sakya dominance, fomented widespread rebellion. Mongol forces quelled the revolt and evacuated Pakpa to the capital. During this time Khubilai commissioned Pakpa to devise an imperial script that could represent all languages within the empire. It was submitted and adopted by the court in 1269 and is now known as the Pakpa script (see fig. 4.21).[101]

Within a year Pakpa was granted the title Imperial Preceptor (*Dishi* 帝師). After traveling for several years, he renounced his title and returned to Tibet, arriving at Sakya in 1276. The following year he convened a general council that affirmed the ecclesiastical authority of the Sakya over Tibet.

After retiring to Sakya, Papka wrote his most important work, *What Is to Be Known* (*Shes bya rab gsal*), an introductory guidebook to Buddhism written for Khubilai Khan's heir apparent, Jinggim. The work featured the "two realms" model—the secular realm headed by the khan and the religious realm headed by the lama—that undergirds Mongol Buddhist political theory from the Yuan dynasty until the early twentieth century. Another Indo-Tibetan idea that the Mongols added to their arsenal of Buddhist political theory was that Mongol rulers were an emanation of Mañjuśri, the bodhisattva of wisdom.[102]

The worship and ritualization of Mañjuśri had a long history in China. Mañjuśri is said to reside on Five Peak Mountain (Wutai Shan 五台山) in north China's Shanxi province, and his worship has been intimately bound up with pilgrimage to this area. The worship of Mañjuśri as a significant component of political power was pervasive in China from the reign of Empress Wu in the Tang period, and the religio-political importance of this cult was so great that when access to Wutai Shan was restricted—as it was during the Song dynasty— the surrounding peoples such as the Khitan and Tangut made simulacra of the site in their own territory so that they could continue to worship.[103] Curiously, this practice was never adopted by the Uyghurs. They probably avoided the cult precisely because it was so intimately connected to political power.[104] Yet once the Mongols adopted the cult of Mañjuśri in the Yuan period, the Uyghurs followed suit and began translating texts related to his worship, as well as ones related to pilgrimage to Wutai Shan.[105] As a result, during the Mongol period Uyghurs began expressing their desire to go on pilgrimage to Wutai Shan.[106]

During the course of the thirteenth century Uyghur Buddhism adopted not only the Mongol dynasty's focus on Mañjuśri and Wutai Shan but also their devotion to Tantric Buddhism. Tantric, or esoteric Buddhist practices, had of course long been a part of Uyghur Buddhism, having been present in the Buddhism of both the Liao dynasty and Dunhuang (see fig. 4.22).[107]

But in the Mongol period the main source of tantric thought and practice among the Uyghurs came to be Tibetan.[108] They therefore translated works such as the *Guruyoga of Sakya Pandita*,[109] Pakpa Lama's explication of the *Śrīcakraśamvara* cycle of teachings,[110] Naropa's *Book of the Dead*,[111] and the *Tārā-Ekavimśatistotra* (*Praise of the Twenty-One Taras*),[112] as well as numerous *sadhana* texts focusing on the bodhisattvas Avalokiteśvara, Mañjuśrī, and Vajrapāṇi.[113]

Much of this new translation work was done in the Mongol capital of Daidu (today's Beijing), where leading Uyghur scholars had ready access to the resident Tibetan lamas.[114] Karunadaz (d. 1312), for example, who translated the foundational text for the worship of Mañjuśri, the *Mañjuśrīnāmasamgīti*, in 1302, had studied with Pakpa Lama.[115] The Uyghur translator Anzang worked at the court of Möngke Khan, and Ariq Böke ordered him to translate the *Avataṃsaka Sūtra*

4.22 Ḍākinī from Bezeklik caves

After Albert von Le Coq, *Chotscho: Facsimile-Wiedergaben der wichtigeren Funde der ersten Königlich Preussischen Expedition nach Turfan in Ost-Turkistan* (Berlin: Dietrich Reimer, 1913)

into Uyghur so as to promote Buddhist theories of political legitimacy, including the worship of Mañjuśrī and the cult of Wutai Shan.[116]

The multilingualism of the Uyghurs and their position at the Mongol court enabled them to undertake other translations as well. The Uyghur scholar Dhanyasena, for example, who was a member of the leading academic institution in China, the Hanlin Academy, translated an important work by Pakpa Lama into Chinese.[117] Dhanyasena also translated works that the Tibetans did not have, such as *The History of the Sandalwood Buddha Statue in China*, from Uyghur into Tibetan.[118] Other Uyghurs filled in other gaps by translating important Tangut Buddhist works into Uyghur, such as the *Avataṃsaka Repentance Ritual*.[119] The translation of this text and of the *Avataṃsaka Sūtra* itself shows that even though Uyghur Buddhism came to be influenced by Tibetan Buddhism at this time, and many texts were translated into Uyghur from Tibetan, it was never an exclusive engagement. Rather, like before, Uyghur Buddhism continued to absorb all kinds of Buddhist practices, only now it was under the influence of the Mongol imperial enterprise.

In the mid 1280s Khubilai Khan wanted to create a new and revised catalogue of the Chinese Buddhist canon, which, as evidenced in the Song-Liao-Xixia period, was a powerful symbol of Buddhist political power and legitimacy. To this end, he gathered together a multilingual team of twenty-nine scholars, including seven Uyghurs, to survey Buddhist texts in all the available languages (Chinese, Sanskrit, Tangut, Tibetan, Uyghur) and compile the most comprehensive Buddhist canon ever.[120] The project resulted in the *Zhiyuan fabao kantong zonglu* 至元法寶堪同總錄, a catalogue of 1,440 different texts in 5,586 chapters (Ch. *juan*).

Its preparation influenced Uyghur Buddhism by renewing interest in Sanskrit and Sanskrit texts. Uyghur scholars in Beijing translated the Sanskrit poetic work *Śatapañcāśatka*, among others, into Uyghur.[121] These Uyghur scholars also compared the Chinese and Tibetan versions of texts with the Sanskrit originals in order to prepare the best translations possible.[122] One scholar has commented: "'The [Uyghur translation of a Chinese *āgama*] shows considerable new lexemes, including Sanskrit words which are not yet attested in the known Old Uyghur texts...' and 'The Sanskrit words, including personal and place names, clearly imply that the translator had very good knowledge of Sanskrit, and perhaps constantly consulted the Sanskrit version of the text during the translation process.'"[123] Another notes: "'The utilization of Chinese *āgamas* by Uyghur

4.23 Uyghur text with embedded Brāhmī script. Mainz 713

Courtesy of the collection at the Berlin-Brandenburchische Akademie der Wissenschaften in der Staatsbibliotek zu Berlin–Preußischer Kulturbesitz, Orientabteilung

Buddhists points to a high degree of scholarly specialization of Uyghur Buddhist culture in the 13th and 14th century.'"[124]

The Mongol court also promoted the cross-fertilization of scholarship across and within religious traditions.[125] Thus although the Uyghurs had earlier engaged with a range of Buddhist works, such scholarly endeavors were taken to a whole new level in the Yuan period within the sophisticated Buddhist culture that the Mongol court promoted. For example, the Uyghurs utilized their new knowledge of Sanskrit to write texts in Sanskrit using the Uyghur script.[126] They also revived the use of Brāhmī script in order to better reflect the underlying Sanskrit terms and their pronunciation, which was often garbled when written in the Aramaic-derived Uyghur script. They embedded the Brāhmī characters into the vertical Uyghur script (see fig. 4.23) or added the Brāhmī gloss beside the term in question (fig. 4.24).[127]

This new scholarly orientation of the Yuan period is also reflected in the Uyghur interest in a range of new Buddhist literature. The Uyghurs tried not only to fill the gaps in their corpus of Buddhist literature but also to move away from the earlier freewheeling approach to the Dharma and become more

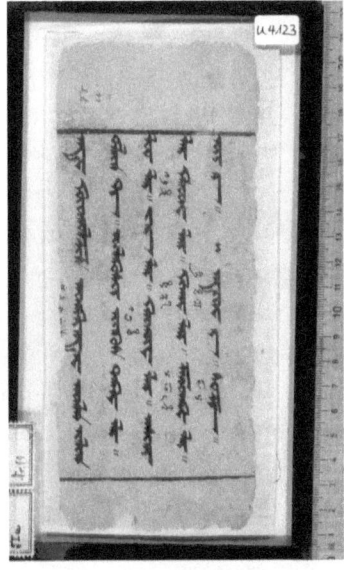

4.24 A printed fragment of the *Grahamātṛkādhāraṇī* with glosses in Brahmi Script. U 4123

Courtesy of the collection at the Berlin-Brandenburchische Akademie der Wissenschaften in der Staatsbibliotek zu Berlin–Preußischer Kulturbesitz, Orientabteilung

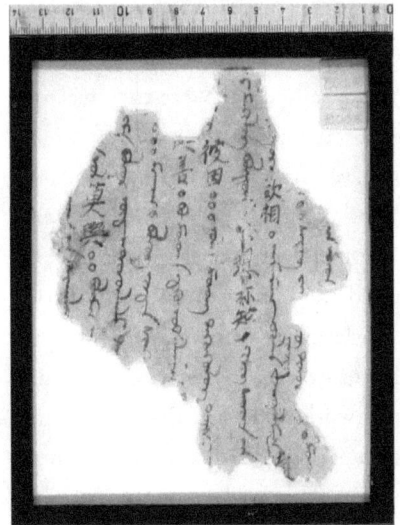

4.25 Uyghur translation of the *Madhyamāgama* (*Zhong ahanjing* 中阿含經 T. 26) with quoted Chinese passages marked with characters and circles. Ch/U 7209 verso

Courtesy of the collection at the Berlin-Brandenburchische Akademie der Wissenschaften in der Staatsbibliotek zu Berlin–Preußischer Kulturbesitz, Orientabteilung

orthodox. An example is the decision to translate all five of the Chinese *āgamas*, which comprise all the teachings of early Buddhism, into Uyghur in the Yuan period (see fig. 4.25).[128]

Another example is the Uyghur decision to engage with the vast commentarial tradition of the abhidharma literature.[129] But the Uyghur translation of both the *āgamas* and the abhidharma literature was not done in a wholly systematic fashion. As the fragment of the *Madhyamāgama* in figure 4.25 reveals, the Uyghur translations include short passages from the Chinese text alongside the Uyghur versions. Each Chinese passage, however, is not complete, containing only a few characters, which makes identifying it virtually impossible if one does not already know the Chinese original. Thus, for example, in the Uyghur translation of the *Samyuktāgama* (T. 100) the Chinese passage 王者繫縛人 以鐵木 繩及繩 is abbreviated to simply the first five characters 王者繫縛人. However, the Uyghur translation includes the whole sentence: "If the kings suppress and lock up people with ankles or wooden collars etc." Why the translations were done in this way is unclear; however, as was the case with the earlier Uyghur translations, the translator(s) tried to make them as coherent as possible. Here, for example, the translator "seemed to be unsure of his interpretation of the three characters *tie* 鐵 'iron,' *mu* 木 'wood,' and *sheng* 繩 'rope,' and so immediately after this translation, he gave an alternative for the second half of the sentence. It begins with the Chinese character *you* 又 'or' then the Uyghur (*urug ymä ter*) 'with strings and hooks.'"[130]

Regardless of this attempt at coherency or comprehensiveness in translation, it is not entirely clear how these texts were actually used. Were they teaching aids, mnemonic devices, or a way to teach students how to translate from Chinese into Uyghur? Even though we do not have answers, Uyghur engagement with the *āgama* literature was certainly part and parcel of the scholarly turn that the Yuan court promoted. The same is true for the Uyghur engagement with the abhidharma literature, in which they adopted the same truncated translation style as used for the *āgamas* (and made the translations even more problematic by omitting crucial sections of the text).[131] Take for example the Uyghur version of the *Abhidharmakośa-bhāṣya*. When writing this work in the fourth–fifth century, the Indian scholar Vasubandhu utilized a two-part framework: first he summarized the Sarvāstivādin school's interpretation of a particular point of Buddhist thought in about 600 verses; then he critiqued each one from the perspective of the Sautrāntika school in prose.[132] The Uyghur versions, however, preserve only one side of the intellectual debate by completely omitting the initial summary and including only the commentary.[133]

Such selective editing had long been a part of Uyghur Buddhist practice, and the case of the *Abhidharmakośa-bhāṣya* may just have been the latest manifestation of this textual approach. Either way, the fact that the Uyghurs were

4.26 Uyghur monks wearing Tokharian style robes, from a mural at Beshbaliq
After *Beiting Gaochang Huihu Fosi Yizhi*, color plate 21

engaging with the abhidharma material at all was part and parcel of the scholarly turn of the Mongol period. Another part of Uyghur scholarly focus was engagement with the monastic code (*Vinaya*). As noted in chapter 1, although the *Vinaya* is the foundation of any Buddhist community, we have no evidence it was ever translated into Uyghur during the West Uyghur Kingdom and therefore do not know which *Vinaya* the monastic community used. There are only a few bilingual fragments of such literature extant from this early period, and they have led most scholars to assume that the Uyghurs used the *Vinaya* of the Tokharians. The Uyghur practice of wearing the same robes as those worn by Tokharian monks further supports this theory, since robe style was an important aspect of the monastic regulations (see fig. 4.26).[134]

Even if they did initially use the Tokharian monastic code, it is unclear if the Uyghurs continued to use it throughout the eleventh and twelfth centuries, when their knowledge of Tokharian would presumably have waned. Indeed, it is likely that at some time in the centuries prior to the Mongol conquests the Uyghurs had started to use the Chinese *Vinaya* for both procedural and ritual matters.

Regardless, we have no evidence from this early period that the Uyghurs were actively engaged with the *Vinaya* in their own language. This changed during the Mongol period when Uyghurs in the imperial capital came to believe that it was necessary for the proper functioning of any Buddhist community to have its own *Vinaya*. Thus we know that they created their own original versions of the *pravāraṇā* ceremony, which was performed by monks in India on the last day of the rainy season retreat during which they publicly confessed their sins and repented their errors.¹³⁵ In making these new works the Uyghurs incorporated passages from the *Dharmaguptaka Vinaya*, which suggests that they were following the monastic rules of Chinese Buddhists and not those of the Tibetans, who follow the *Mūlasarvāstivādin Vinaya*.¹³⁶

Questions about monastic rules and these new scholarly pursuits carried out by monks in the imperial capital were presumably of little interest to the average Uyghur layperson, whose practice of everyday lived Buddhism had other priorities. Nevertheless, on account of the economic expansion made possible by the *pax mongolica*, the Uyghur laity were able to continue their support of the Dharma by paying for translations, the building of Buddhist temples, and the making of ritual objects (see fig. 4.27).¹³⁷

They similarly continued with their rituals regarding health, prosperity, and merit making, as captured in a colophon to a 1308 blockprint:

> I, the layman Buyančog Bagši with sincere belief in the Three Jewels, firstly thinking and reflecting on the virtues of the Buddhas; secondly that the merit may reach both of my blessed ones, my mother and my father; and thirdly with the thought that all of my wishes for welfare in the present time may be fulfilled and that later I will escape from the sufferings of samsara through the vehicle of Buddhahood; have thus ordered to print on the posatha fasting day—the eighth of the six month of the year of Ape-Wu of the shigan cycle—these sutra jewels of the Tripiṭaka: *Dabanruojing, Huayanjing, Fahuajing, Sosingki* (?), *Cibeichan, Jin'gangjing* from the printing blocks of the monastery called Hongfasi in the city of Zhongdu [presumably Beijing].
>
> By the power of this meritorious deed may my father, the teacher and sage Toyinčog Tutung Beg and my mother Ogul Yitmiš Tngrim be born in very good places and immediately obtain Buddhahood! I, Buyančog Bagši, may all my wishes for welfare in the present time be fulfilled, and later I want to obtain Buddhahood! May the wishes of my beloved elder brothers, younger brothers, elder sisters, younger sisters, wives, sons, daughters, offspring and family members for the present time be fulfilled, and later may my beloved acquaintances of the five *gati* obtain Buddhahood and be born in good places!

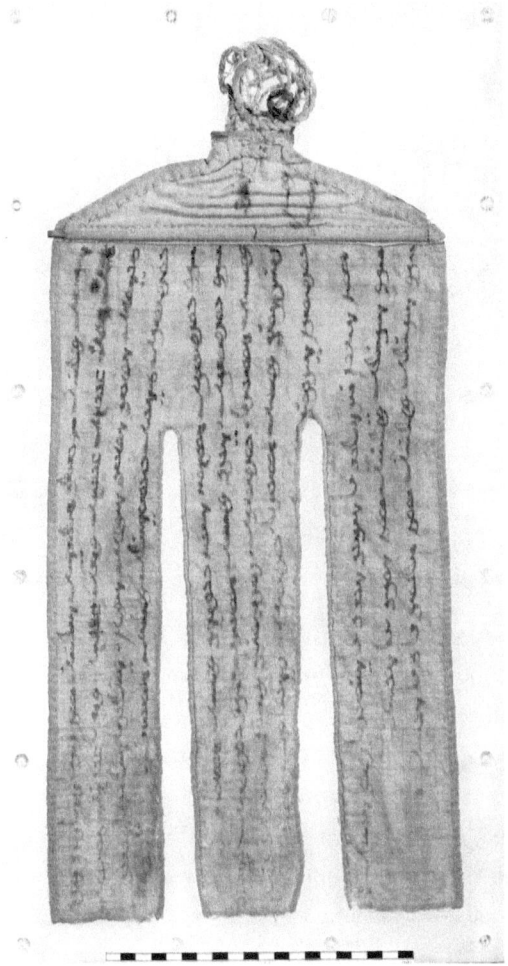

4.27 Temple banner dedicated to Vairocana Buddha
(Inv. No. III 7309). © Staatliche Museen zu Berlin, Museum für Asiatische Kunst

May the holy ones who will recite the dharma, persist in goodness and in full mind! I, sādhu, well!¹³⁸

As this example shows, the interests of the laity were much the same as before, but Mongol rule brought with it a new technology—block printing—that transformed the lay practices of the Uyghur elite (see fig. 4.28).

Printing had developed centuries earlier in China, and Buddhists had been at the forefront of adopting the technology because the production of texts generated good karma.¹³⁹ Yet curiously, the Uyghurs did not use printing during the

4.28 Uyghur blockprint of *The Big Dipper Sutra*
Courtesy of the collection at the Berlin-Brandenburchische Akademie der Wissenschaften in der Staatsbibliotek zu Berlin–Preußischer Kulturbesitz, Orientabteilung

West Uyghur Kingdom. Only during the Yuan period, when there was an empire-wide push to organize and print Buddhist canons in Chinese, Tibetan, and Tangut—and the financial resources to do so—did the Uyghurs follow suit.[140] Although they still did not produce a printed Uyghur Buddhist canon, individual Uyghurs requested the printing of texts for their own karmic ends.[141] The range of texts that they commissioned was remarkably broad: Mahāyāna sutras, tantric texts, Chinese apocrypha, commentaries, *jātakas*, calendars, and ritual texts.[142] Moreover, as specified in the extant colophons of these works, the number of copies that these individuals had printed at one time could range from 100 to as high as 10,000. In many cases, however, the printing of texts was connected to the enthronement of a new Khan or military victory celebrations, which shows that printing itself was also intimately connected with Mongol state power.[143]

The influence of the Mongol empire on the development and nature of Uyghur Buddhism during the Yuan period was immense. It included the extensive adoption of Tibetan Buddhism, more scholarly pursuits, and the use of block-printing technology. Undergirding these new developments was the economic expansion made possible by the *pax mongolica*, from which the Uyghurs benefited handsomely. Because of that economic growth, Uyghurs were able to support these new ideas and practices and to foster a golden age of Uyghur Buddhism. But as the Mongol empire began to falter, so too did this largesse.

CHAPTER 5

Becoming Muslim

(Dharma is) in the power of meritorious deeds,
In these words of the former masters,
In the reward for previous good deeds,
Even if they were the work of Muslim Tajiks.

—Uyghur Buddhist Poem[1]

While the Mongol empire fostered the golden age of Uyghur Buddhism, it also sowed the seeds of its destruction. And it was within this larger historical context that Uyghur Buddhists came to engage with Central Asian Muslims, which ultimately led to the Uyghurs abandoning the Dharma and becoming Muslims. The story of the Uyghur conversion fits well the common story line of the green wave of Islam crashing over the poor defenseless Buddhists, seeming to confirm all the popular stereotypes about these two religions. One is synonymous with peace, tranquility, and introspection, the other with violence, chaos, and blind faith. One conjures up images of Himalayan hermitages and Japanese rock gardens, the other scenes of primitive and dirty villages with burqa-clad women. In more recent years this narrative has been problematized by the reality of Buddhist ethnic cleansing and the genocide of Muslims in Sri Lanka and Myanmar.[2] Yet the meeting between Buddhists and Muslims has never simply been a confrontation. Rather, the interaction of these two religions has also involved much else, including artistic, cultural, and intellectual exchange.

The case of the Uyghurs was no different. As the steppe intelligentsia of the Mongol empire, as well as powerful merchants across Eurasia, they played an important role in pushing Buddhism into the heart of the Muslim world.³ This development profoundly transformed Islam in everything from aesthetics to political ideology to theology. Indeed, this impact presumably played a role in fostering the Tibetan belief that the Uyghur kingdom was Shambhala.⁴

Yet for a host of reasons—from the Mongol legacy to economics and geopolitics—the Muslim advance into northwest China continued. The Moghuls, the erstwhile rulers of the Uyghur homeland, converted to Islam in 1354. Even so, the Uyghurs remained Buddhist, and exchanges between the two religions continued as they had during the Mongol empire period.

The Mongol empire, however, had not only enabled a florescence of Uyghur Buddhism and Buddhist-Muslim exchange but also maintained its power through endless wars and succession feuds. In these battles the Uyghur kingdom was often on the front lines, and its agricultural and economic systems started to fray. This crisis was further exacerbated by major geopolitical shifts in both China and Central Asia. All of these factors ultimately led the Uyghurs to slowly convert to Islam.

BUDDHISTS AND MUSLIMS IN MONGOL EURASIA

While the West Uyghur Kingdom flourished in the twelfth century under the protection of the Western Liao, their immediate neighbors to the west were largely Muslim and also subjects of the Qara Khitai. This was the first time in Islamic history that Muslims were under the rule of a non-Muslim state. It might have been an untenable situation, but the Western Liao were able to leverage their nomadic and Chinese backgrounds to maintain power. As Michal Biran explains: "Their dual identity as Chinese and nomads, combined with the broad religious tolerance they gave their subjects, enabled them to gain legitimacy among their Muslim subjects despite their 'infidelity.'"⁵

One element of this success was premised on the fact that Muslims knew very little about contemporary China. Since the time of the Tang dynasty, Muslim interaction with China had been minimal and as a result, Muslim knowledge of China was frozen in time. China had grown into something of a fantasy: a rational, materialist utopia; a land of bureaucratic order, education, sumptuous wealth, and technological wizardry.⁶ This common view was so favorable that Central Asian Muslims remembered their time as subjects of the Tang dynasty wistfully.⁷ This vision helped the Qara Khitai's project of legitimating themselves even though they were non-Muslim.

The Muslims of Central Asia accepted Qara Khitai rule most fundamentally because they brought order and a measure of prosperity to their subjects. Muslim jurists judged that the Western Liao, although infidels, formed a righteous government. This was feasible because, since the eleventh century, Muslim political theory had been based on the principle of justice. The importance of justice came to be encapsulated in a phrase attributed to the Prophet Muhammad—"A just infidel is preferable to an unjust Muslim ruler."⁸ The Qara Khitai had brought order and reinvigorated the Eurasian economy, and for a people who had suffered nearly a century of continuous political and economic upheaval at the hands of various ineffectual Muslim rulers, such "infidel" rule was welcome.

Muslim scholars also depicted the Qara Khitai as "a mighty wall or dam that protected Islam from its eastern enemies."⁹ Who would these enemies have been? At the time, this image of a protective wall or dam was largely figurative, likely derived from the Alexander Romance (the Macedonian general had supposedly built a wall in Inner Asia to keep out the evil forces of Gog and Magog). In reality, the Western Liao were no wall at all. Rather, it was precisely the porousness of their borders that enabled East-West trade to revive across Inner Asia—and made their rule so effective. Muslim traders were heavily involved in this revived economy, especially with the nomads of the Mongolian plateau,¹⁰ so the claim that the Western Liao were a bulwark against the infidel hordes of the East was more of a literary trope, which burnished the Qara Khitai's reputation and fostered their claims of legitimacy.

But when the power of the Western Liao began to weaken in the late twelfth century, the previously unspecified infidel enemies came to be identified as Buddhists. This shift began with Güchlüg Khan, a powerful leader on the Mongolian plateau who had tried to resist Chinggis Khan but failed and took refuge in the territory of the Western Liao. When the Western Liao weakened, Güchlüg eventually took over as ruler (r. 1211-1218) and then very publicly converted to Buddhism.¹¹ This was a dramatic break from the Qara Khitai policy of studiously avoiding identification with the Dharma and the practice of something like religious tolerance. As both political and economic circumstances deteriorated under Güchlüg's reign, Muslims prayed for infidel rule to come to an end, and their prayers were answered when Chinggis Khan launched his first campaign into the West. He did so, however, not to save the Muslims but to exterminate the threat Güchlüg Khan posed to his own claims of dominance on the Mongolian plateau. In 1218 he put an end to Güchlüg Khan and the Qara Khitai, and later Muslim historians (who worked for the Mongols) would use his story to portray the Mongols as the liberators of the Islamic world.¹²

Muslim authors also began describing the Buddhist persecution of Islam.¹³ The Persian historian Juvaini, for example, wrote about a Buddhist massacre of Muslims that supposedly took place among the Uyghurs.¹⁴ Juvaini claimed that "none [are] more bigoted than the idolaters of the East, and none more hostile to Islam," and offered a harrowing account of how Güchlüg Khan had an imam in Khotan crucified on the door of his own madrasa.¹⁵ Although there is no corroborating evidence to confirm or contest Juvaini's claims, the Franciscan friar William of Rubruck also noted the tension between Buddhists and Muslims in the Uyghur realm. He claimed that Muslims "shun [Buddhists] to the point that they are unwilling even to talk about them. Consequently, whenever I asked the Saracens about these people's religion, they were scandalized."¹⁶

These tensions were likely exacerbated by the Mongol policy of population transfers, whereby Muslims were forcibly moved into Buddhist areas. One Muslim source records that by the mid-thirteenth century fifty thousand Muslims had been moved to Beshbaliq, the Uyghur summer capital.¹⁷ How did they react to their forced move? And what did the Uyghur Buddhists think about being inundated with Central Asian Muslims? We do not know, but some dialogue must have occurred since Juvaini also offers an informed description of Buddhism.¹⁸ Although not an elaborate exploration of the Dharma, it does reveal that Buddhist-Muslim interaction was not quite as hostile as the testimony described above would lead us to believe. Some form of dialogue not only was possible but actually took place.

Such exchange was made possible by the Mongols' open religious policy.¹⁹ Although there may have been tensions between Buddhists and Muslims in Central Asia, the Mongol rulers relied on both to run their expanding empire. Chinggis Khan, for example, employed both Buddhist and Muslim advisers.²⁰ His successor Ögedei (r. 1229-1241) followed suit by building Buddhist monuments in the imperial capital and introducing tax farming to north China upon the recommendation of his Muslim advisers.²¹ Similarly, Möngke Khan both received tantric initiation from Karma Pakshi and respected Islamic practices.²² Khubilai Khan also received tantric initiation and actively supported not only the promotion of Muslim administrators in China but also the importation of people and ideas from the Islamic world.²³ To this end he established numerous institutes for the Islamic intellectual elite in Yuan dynasty China, such as the Muslim Medical Office (established in 1270), a Directorate of Muslim Astronomy (1271),[24] and a Muslim School for the Sons of the State that taught Persian (1289). And it was the same in the Muslim world, as evidenced in the case of Hülegü, the founder of the Il-khanid realm in Iran.

Like his brother Khubilai, Hülegü was both a devotee of Buddhism and an avid supporter of Muslim science. His relationship with Persian polymath Nasir al-Din Tusi and his building of a state-of-the-art observatory near present-day Tabriz have received much attention,[25] his affiliation with Buddhism less. During the Mongol conquest of Tibet, Hülegü had already established relations with the Kagyü suborders of the Drigungpa and Pakmo Drukpa in western Tibet. In the mid-1250s he had started to financially support their monasteries,[26] and the Il-khanid court maintained these relations throughout the thirteenth century by having an official stationed in Tibet.[27] Hülegü also built three Buddhist temples: one at his summer pastures in the mountains of Armenia and two in Iran at Khoy and Maragha.[28] Three of his successors—Abaqa (r. 1265-1282), Arghun (r. 1284-1291), and Gaikhatu (r. 1291-1295)—also supported the Dharma.[29] Arghun held debates at his court that pitted Buddhists against local Muslim scholars such as 'Ala' ad-Dawla as-Simnani; and Gaikhatu's investiture ceremony included a tantric initiation during which he received the Tibetan name Rinchen Dorjé in 1291.[30] Arghun also wanted his son, the future Ghazan Khan, to be trained in the faith, as noted by Rashid al-Din's *Compendium of Chronicles*: "When Abaqa Khan passed away and [Ghazan's] father Arghun Khan sent him to Khurasan as governor and commander of the army, he built major temples in Khabushan, and he spent most of his time conversing, eating, and drinking with the *bakshis* in those temples. The belief he had for that sect and the worship he performed of the idols were beyond description."[31] Ghazan, however, would convert to Islam in June 1295.[32]

The common scholarly consensus is that Ghazan converted for political reasons.[33] The economy was in tatters, local powerful Muslim rulers were rebelling, and most of his leading Mongol and Turk generals had already converted. To prove his zeal, he issued an order to destroy all Buddhist monasteries and convert all Buddhists in the Ilkhanid realm to Islam.[34] Doubt remains as to whether this was actually carried out. Issuing such an order and claiming that one has killed infidels is a standard component of Islamic conversion stories and does not mean that it actually took place.[35] And the same sources that tell of these anti-Buddhist actions also show that Buddhists continued to be active in Iran for years after the purported purge. It seems likely that Ghazan's turn against Buddhism was based more on financial considerations than religious ones. The Il-khanids were in dire straits after the profligacy of his predecessor Gaikhatu,³⁶ and, as had happened repeatedly throughout history, Buddhist temples were ransacked for their wealth in order to fix the economy.³⁷ Once the monasteries had been divested of their assets, however, they were allowed to continue practicing their faith, as had happened elsewhere in Buddhist Asia. In the case of the Il-khans, Buddhists tried to convert Ghazan's successor, Öljeitü Khan (r. 1305-1316), back to the Dharma.³⁸ Although the attempt failed, it shows that Buddhists remained active in the Il-khanid domains for more than fifty years. During this time Buddhists not only received the support and largesse of the Mongol court but also established temples across the Il-khanid realm "between the Black Sea and the area south of the Caspian Sea, along the routes that linked Anatolia to the Indus River"³⁹ (see fig. 5.1).

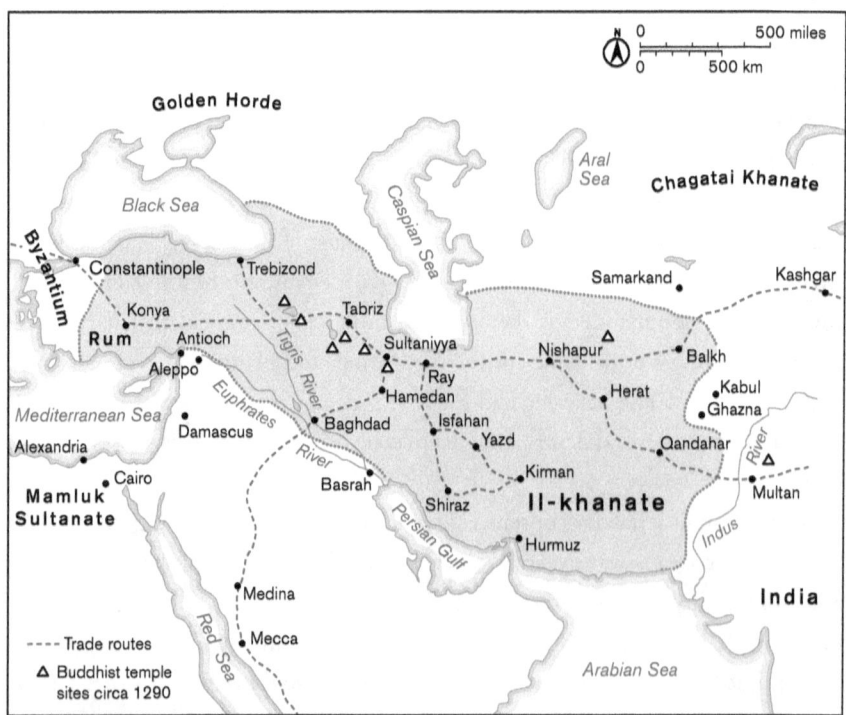

5.1 Buddhist sites in the Il-khanid realm
Courtesy of Roxann Prazniak

This powerful Buddhist presence in the Islamic heartland led later Muslim historians to be "mortified into silence" about it, and our knowledge of this period has long remained limited.[40] In recent years, however, numerous scholars have gone back to Il-khanid sources and uncovered the profound impact that these Buddhists had on Il-khanid culture and early modern Islam more broadly. Buddhist art, for example, changed the aesthetics, form, and style of Islamic art.[41] Moreover, intellectual engagement with Buddhism influenced Islamic thought. Muslim intellectuals, for example, countered Buddhist political theories of the *cakravartin*—the wheel-turning world conqueror—with the messianic idea of the "Lord of Auspicious Conjunction" (*ṣāḥibqirān*), which later became central to Timurid and Mughal conceptions of universal sovereignty.[42] Similarly, the Tibetan Buddhist idea of bodily reincarnations—such as the Karmapa Lama or the Dalai Lama—enabled Sufi masters to proclaim that Öljeitü Khan was a manifestation of Ali.[43] In this world Muslim scholars such as Ala al-Dawla Simnani and Rashid al-Din—author of the first-ever world history, the *Jami' al-tawarikh*, or *Compendium of Chronicles*—could seriously and sympathetically engage with the Dharma.

It has been more difficult to identify precisely which groups of Buddhists were involved in this intellectual exchange. Persian sources, for example, note that Kashmiri and Chinese Buddhists were key interlocutors, but on account of the Il-khanid court's relations with Tibet, it is clear that Tibetans were also involved in this cross-cultural exchange. Evidence also shows Uyghur involvement. Rashid al-Din, for example, records a story about the Buddha's previous lives. The Buddha appears as a merchant traveling by ship, and when a sea monster seizes the hull, he prays, "*Namo buddhayah*." Upon hearing this phrase, the sea monster remembers his previous human birth and how he had said the same prayer. This memory fills the monster with compassion, and it lets go of the ship.[44] The prayer, *Namo buddhayah*, is a distinctive phrase found only in Central Asian Buddhism; its use in this context indicates that the Uyghurs transmitted the story.[45] Further evidence of Uyghur involvement in the intellectual and religious life of the Il-khanid realm is found in Rashid al-Din's *Tansuq Name*, a 1313 compilation of four Chinese medical texts translated into Persian (see figs. 5.2 and 5.3).[46]

One of the four texts in this compilation is Li Ziye's manual for pulse reading, the *Xifanzi maijue jijue* 唏范子脉訣集解. The peculiarities of the translation indicate Uyghur influence, as Dai Matsui explains:

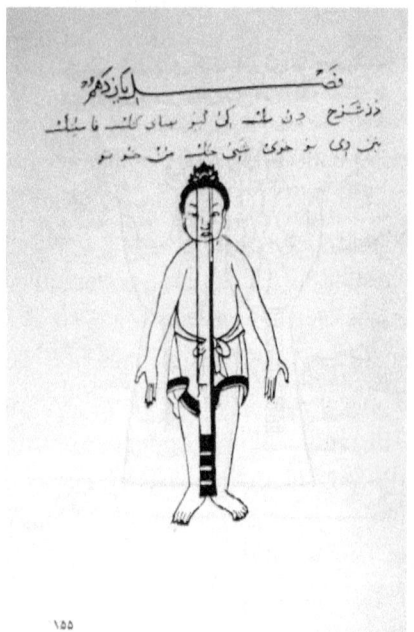

5.2 Body meridians in Rashid al-Din's *Tansuq Name*

After Mujtaba Minuvi's facsimile reproduction *Tanksūqnāmah yā Ṭibb-i Khatā* (Teheran, 1971)

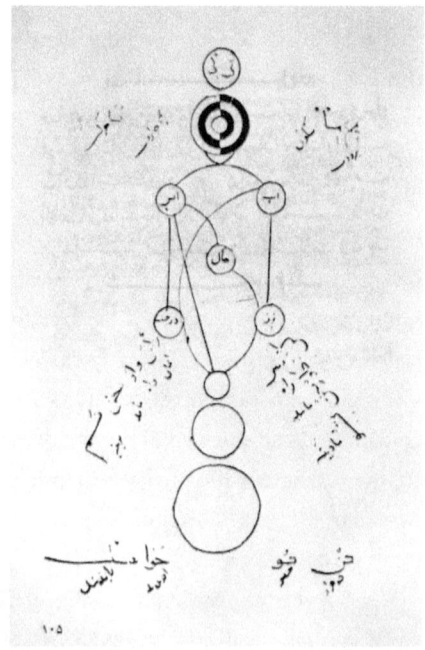

5.3 Zhou Dunyi's 周敦頤 "Diagram of the Supreme Polarity" (*Taijitu* 太極圖) in Rashid al-Din's *Tansuq Name*

After Mujtaba Minuvi's facsimile reproduction *Tanksūqnāmah yā Ṭibb-i Khatā* (Teheran, 1971)

[In] the Persian translation of the *Maijue*, the translator transcribed the whole Chinese passage in Arabic script—e.g. Ch. *An zhi bu zu ju zhi yu* > Pers. *Ān jī bu kīū tsīū jī yū*—then translated the text into Persian. Scholars have regarded this method as most curious: The Persian transcription itself does not seem to make any sense, for it is not accompanied by the original Chinese ideograms. However, it is remarkable that the Uigurs of East Turkestan had a similar method of translation of the Chinese texts: They first transcribed the pronunciation of the Chinese, and followed the translation of the Chinese text. For example, the Uigur version of the *Qian-zi-wen* 千子文, recently published by Shōgaito Masahiro, carries such a sentence: *yun ting ču yu säkridi yagmur yagdı, yun ting ču yu* (< Ch. *Yun teng zhi yu* 雲騰致雨) means "clouds leap and it rained." This method indicates that the Uigurs read aloud the text according to the Chinese pronounciation, and then learned the contents in Uigur. We can easily notice that this method is exactly the same as that adopted in the *Tansuq Name*, and we perceive some cultural influence of the Uigurs in the method of translation and the composition of the *Tansuq name* itself.[47]

From such evidence, it is reasonable to suppose that many of the Buddhist practices described in Persian sources actually came from the Uyghurs, not only because these practices are known to have been part of Uyghur Buddhism—such as the worship of Maitreya, Guanyin, Amitābha, and the Big Dipper[48]—but also because their linguistic representation in Persian reflects a Uyghur intermediary.[49] Therefore, the Uyghur role in shaping Il-khanid Buddhism and its impact on the Muslim world cannot be underestimated.[50]

THE MONGOL CIVIL WARS

As Buddhist Uyghurs in what is now Iran were influencing the Muslim world, their homeland was becoming the front line in a brutal Mongol civil war. The Mongol empire is commonly described as the "world's largest land empire in history" and readily represented on maps as a contiguous entity stretching from Korea to Poland, but it was never as unified as such depictions imply.[51] Legend has it that Chinggis Khan conquered the world and then divided it among his four sons into "Four Ulus" or Khanates. Jochi, the eldest, was given southern

144   Becoming Muslim

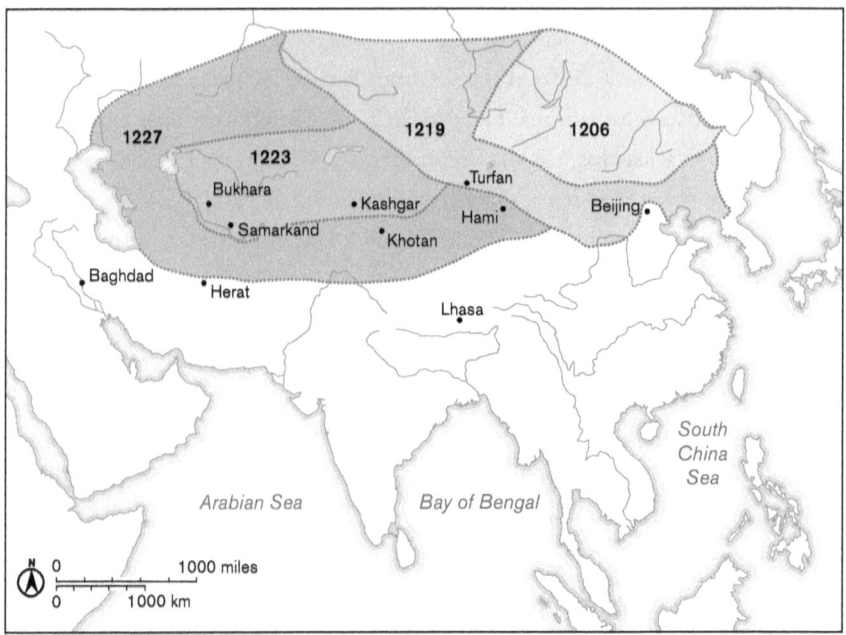

5.4 Chinggis Khan's Conquests at the Time of His Death

Russia; Chagatai, Central Asia; Ögedei, China; and Tolui, the youngest, Mongolia—the "hearth"—following Mongolian inheritance custom that gives the youngest the paternal homeland.[52] But this purported division was a grandiose fiction because Chinggis had not conquered all of this territory by the time he died in 1227 (see fig. 5.4).

The "Mongol empire" as it is commonly understood was actually formed during the campaigns of conquest carried out by Chinggis Khan's successors, especially Ögedei and Möngke (see fig. 5.5). In their wake the idea of the Four Ulus was put into practice, along with the notion that the three rulers of the "lesser" Ulus (the Chagataids in Central Asia, the Il-khans in the Middle East, and the Golden Horde in Russia) were subordinate to a "Great Khan" in China.

But even this system was just as much of a fantasy as the original story of Chinggis Khan divvying up the world and bequeathing it to his heirs. The Jochid Ulus (a.k.a. the Golden Horde) in southern Russia had virtually no relations with the "Great Khan" after their ruler, Batu Khan (ca. 1205-1255), refused to return to Mongolia to attend the *quriltai* that elected Ögedei as Great Khan in

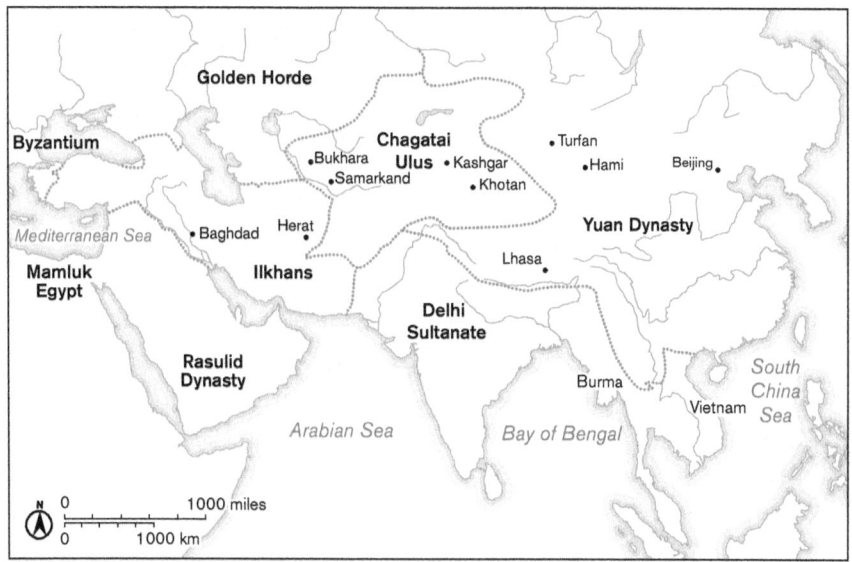

5.5 The Four Ulus of the Mongol Empire

1229. The Jochids were also the first Mongols to convert to Islam.[53] Because of their involvement with the slave trade that supplied soldiers to the Mamluks of Egypt, the Jochids were drawn more and more into the orbit of the Islamic world and moved further away from the Mongols in the East.[54] Their extensive financial dealings with the Mamluks also put them increasingly at odds with the Il-khans, who for decades fought the Mamluks over control of Syria and the Holy Land.[55]

The fighting that eventually erupted between the Il-khans and the Jochids was the opening salvo in the eventual disintegration of the Mongol empire into wholly separate entities, but there were other causes. Succession struggles had plagued the Mongols. Chinggis Khan chose his third son, Ögedei, to succeed him. His eldest son, Jochi, was out of the question because he was not Chinggis's own. During his rise to power his wife had been kidnapped and raped, and Jochi, which means "guest" in Mongolian, was the result. Chinggis Khan's second son, Chagatai, was his own, but he was erratic and a drunk to boot. Tolui was too young, so Ögedei was chosen. Ögedei's reign, however, was short and when he died with no clear successor, family feuds erupted. After years of contention, with powerful Mongol women working behind the scenes to push their children or husbands into the top position, Möngke, the eldest son of Tolui, finally became Khan in 1251. The lineage of Tolui had thus outmaneuvered the lineage of Ögedei, and after Möngke took the throne, he purged the lineages of Ögedei and Chagatai and their supporters in order to secure his power. When Möngke died in 1259, a succession struggle once again erupted, this time between two of Möngke's brothers, Ariq Böke and Khubilai. It took three years for Khubilai to defeat Ariq Böke because of the military backing his brother received from Qaidu (1230–1301), the grandson of their uncle Ögedei. Qaidu would subsequently wage a thirty-year war against the Toluids, trying to restore the lineages of Chinggis's other sons, Ögedei and Chagatai, in Central Asia.[56]

During the war between Qaidu and the Toluids, from roughly 1260 to 1301, the Uyghur homeland was caught between the Mongols of Central Asia (Qaidu) and the Yuan dynasty in China (the Toluids). But even before the chaos of the war, the Uyghurs' situation had begun to unravel. In 1253 Möngke Khan had the Uyghur ruler Sälindi put to death because he had supported Qaidu over Möngke to succeed Ögedei as Great Khan. Sälindi was publicly beheaded in Beshbaliq, with his brother and successor, Ögrünch, serving as executioner. Möngke also ordered his court historians to rewrite the history of the Mongols to justify the Toluid usurpation and even to remove Sälindi from the historical record.[57] This historiographical project also rewrote the story of Sälindi's father, the Uyghur ruler Barchug Art Tegin, who, as described in chapter 4, had submitted the Uyghurs to Chinggis Khan in 1209. As Christopher Atwood explains:

> In this subsequent version, attested in four independent citations, the events of Barchug Art Tegin's life were simplified both to remove the unfavoured line of his sons Kesmes and Sälindi and to remove the complex marital succession that they and their father Barchug Art engaged in with two Chinggisid princesses.... In return for the elimination of the 20 years of Uyghur history before 1251, the new version gave new polish to the story of Barchug Art Tegin's early submission [to Chinggis in 1209], eliminating his probationary period as a vanguard commander in the Mongol army, and having the princess El-Altun... bestowed on him immediately upon submission.[58]

By executing Sälindi and rewriting history in this way, Möngke Khan was putting the Uyghurs on notice, and soon thereafter a large Mongol garrison was set up in Beshbaliq.

In the succession struggles after Möngke's death, the Uyghurs were allied with Khubilai against Ariq Böke. Khubilai was supported by forces in Mongolia and north China, while Ariq Böke had the support of the Mongol rulers in Central Asia, specifically Algu, the ruler of the Chagatai Khanate, and his uncle Qaidu. When Ariq Böke conquered Gansu and made it the base of his operations, the Uyghurs were cut off from trading and interacting with China and for the first time—but not the last—they came under the control of a new Central Asian Mongol regime. The Uyghur postal relay requisition requests were now made in the name of Ariq Böke and not the "Great Khan" Khubilai.[59] Ariq Böke's power, however, quickly collapsed after Algu changed sides to ally with Khubilai; Ariq Böke surrendered in 1263. This victory, however, did not ease the pressure on the Uyghurs.

Qaidu took control of the Chagataid princes and launched a decades-long civil war against Khubilai's Yuan dynasty, and the Uyghurs were caught on its front lines.[60] The Uyghur economy collapsed, yet the Yuan demanded ever more taxes, even from the supposedly tax-exempt Buddhist monasteries.[61] Even in the face of such economic difficulties and Qaidu's rising power in Central Asia, the Uyghurs maintained their alliance with Khubilai. Although this Yuan-Uyghur alliance was thought to provide security to the Uyghurs, Khubilai had largely given up on defeating Qaidu and was instead focusing in the 1270s on defeating the Chinese Song dynasty. As a result, when two Chagataid princes, Duwa and Besma, besieged the Uyghur capital of Qocho, Qočqar, the son of Sälindi, whom Khubilai had appointed as ruler in 1266, was left to his own devices. He offered his daughter in marriage to Duwa, and the Chagataid forces retreated. Khubilai was pleased with this strategy and gave Qočqar a Mongol princess in marriage as well as a large infusion of paper money for the relief of his Uyghur subjects.

This introduction of paper money provided an economic lifeline for the Uyghurs, but it also bound them ever more tightly to the Yuan dynasty since it was the only Mongol regime that recognized the currency. The money was part and parcel of Khubilai's larger strategy of bringing the Uyghur realm firmly into the Yuan orbit, which would deprive Qaidu of the economic resources of this well-developed area. In 1278 Khubilai therefore re-manned the garrison at Beshbaliq, which the Uyghurs had abandoned a decade earlier on account of Qaidu's attacks. In 1281, to further bolster the Uyghur-Yuan alliance, Khubilai established twenty-two postal relay stations between Beshbaliq and Datong in northern Shanxi. And in 1283 and 1286 he built military agricultural colonies (Ch. *tuntian* 屯田) in Beshbaliq to feed the troops stationed there.

Khubilai also launched policies to integrate the Uyghurs into the Yuan administrative structure so as to rule them directly.⁶² In 1278 a Regional Supervision Bureau, charged with military and civilian rule over the entire Uyghur realm, was established; five years later this office was replaced by a Pacification Bureau that worked in coordination with the Beshbaliq Protectorate. Moreover, in 1276, an imperial edict was sent not only to the Uyghur ruler and the officials of all Uyghur cities but also to the Buddhist and Christian communities, ordering them to stop the practice of drowning unwanted female infants. In punishment, "Those caught committing such acts in the future would have one-half of their property confiscated. If a slave (*nu*) exposed the guilty party, he acquired 'hundred family' (*pai-hsing*) status, that is, became a freeman."⁶³

Thus by the late thirteenth century Uyghur Buddhists were no longer subject to the Chinese laws that had defined the West Uyghur Kingdom; they were now subject to Mongol law. This transformation is evident in Uyghur civil documents from this period that use the standard Mongol weights and measures and follow Yuan dynasty regulations regarding legal and tax matters. It is also evident in Uyghur pilgrim inscriptions, such as one that refers to the "whipping punishments" introduced by Khubilai: "I, . . . Qaya, shall go out from this underground cellar! Ah! This is true. If my words are false, I will receive the severe punishment of taking 57 whiplashes within the law."⁶⁴

But the Uyghurs never really got security in return. When Chagataid forces attacked once again, Qočqar fled to Hami. When his son Ne'üril Tegin petitioned Khubilai for more troops to defend the Uyghur realm, Khubilai declined and instead simply moved the ruling family to the walled city of Yongchang in Gansu. As a result, the Uyghur ruling family became virtually a government in exile that was wholly subsidized by the Yuan court and had very little influence in the homeland.⁶⁵

The main reason for this course of action was that Khubilai's strategy in Central Asia had largely failed. His attempt to economically weaken Qaidu had not hindered Qaidu's military advances and also led to agricultural breakdown and famine in the region throughout the 1280s. As the power of Qaidu and Duwa—whom Qaidu had made ruler of the Chagatai Khanate in 1282—was increasing, the Yuan dynasty was facing simultaneous rebellions in Tibet and Manchuria. In Tibet the Drigung order were rebelling against the control of the Mongol-allied

Sakya, and in Manchuria Nayan and other Mongol princes were rebelling against Khubilai's strengthening of Yuan authority, which threatened their autonomy. Both rebellions were put down, but this required moving troops out of Central Asia, which allowed Qaidu and Duwa to expand their power farther. They were able to take control over the Uyghur homeland, where they became the overlords and appointed a new Uyghur ruler in opposition to the Yuan-allied family in exile.[66]

When Khubilai died in 1294 Temür became emperor of the Yuan dynasty. He sought to solve the "Central Asia problem" once and for all. Temür stopped the campaigns against Japan and Southeast Asia and focused solely on defeating Qaidu and Duwa. In 1301 he sent out a massive army that met Qaidu in battle but was roundly defeated. As the Yuan army retreated to Qaraqorum in Mongolia, they burned all the grassland so Qaidu could not pursue them. But Qaidu died shortly thereafter, and to secure Qaidu's mantle for himself, Duwa sought peace with the Yuan dynasty. As Michael Biran explains:

> In his surrender to the Yuan, Du'a would seem at first to have been exchanging one master for another [Qaidu to Yuan], but here he built on his and Qaidu's achievements. In the early 14th century the position of the Khan in Central Asia and also in other areas of the empire was very different from Khubilai Khan's status when he rose to power. Du'a correctly calculated that recognizing the Khan's nominal supremacy would still allow him to maintain his autonomy. While Du'a's peace agreement is full of references to unity and to Mongol tradition, it may be possible to identify in it also a typical example of relations between Central Asia and China, with the nomad neighbors discovering the advantages of recognizing the nominal supremacy of the Chinese ruler and thus enjoying his gifts, free access to Chinese trade, and military assistance if required. The string of gifts received by Du'a's emissaries in the years after his surrender fits into this pattern.[67]

This peace deal and its economic rewards helped revive the fortunes of the Uyghurs, who once again served as the middlemen facilitating the trade for Central Asian agricultural products, animals, herbs, furs, wine, slaves, and so forth, as well as "a commercial infrastructure of loans, hospices, road maintenance, post stations and load animals for hire."[68] Unfortunately, the economic revival was brief.

When Duwa died he was succeeded by his son Könchek (r. 1307-1308), who continued his father's policies of expanding the Chagataid realm to the west and of weakening the Ögedeid heirs of Qaidu. When he passed away, his son Naliqo-a (r. 1308-1309) took the throne but was quickly executed on account of his pro-Muslim policies that alienated the Buddhist populace. Duwa's son Kebek therefore took over and engineered the submission of the last Ögedeid prince, Chapar, to the Yuan court, which in turn made Chapar Prince of Runing in Henan (far from Central Asia). Kebek then renounced the throne and gave it to his brother Esen Buqa (r. 1310-1320), who, to be confrontational, took over Chapar's grazing lands around Beshbaliq that were surrounded by Yuan military forces. After he set up his own garrisons directly across from those of the Yuan, tensions mounted and then escalated dramatically when the Yuan tried to limit the amount of trade allowed with China.

In response to this trade embargo Esen Buqa requested assistance from Özbek Khan (r. 1312-1342) of the Jochid, who declined and sided instead with the Yuan. Fearing an attack from both sides, Esen Buqa launched two first-strike offenses against the Yuan in 1314 but failed both times. He therefore retreated to join his brother Kebek, who recently had defeated the Il-khans in Iran. With Esen Buqa gone, the Yuan went on the offensive and marched all the way to today's Kirghizstan, destroying everything in their path. The Uyghur ruler, Ne'üril, helped push the Chagataid forces out of the Turfan basin, whereby the Mongol court gave him a new title, Prince of Qocho, which was then held by all his successors. On account of Ne'üril having "again established [Qocho] as a Uighur city" the Yuan made it their front line; as a result, it continued to be ravaged for the next decade.[69]

In 1323 Kebek Khan finally sued for peace with the Yuan, and the Uyghur realm reverted to the Chagataids. A Yuan dynasty map from 1331, for example, places the Uyghur realm in the territory of Döre Temür (r. 1330-1331) (see figs. 5.6 and 5.7).

Although the Uyghurs were no longer part of the Yuan dynasty, this did not hinder the re-establishment of trade relations between the two, which continued for decades. Kebek Khan helped this economic upswing by trying to restore the agricultural and urban life of the Uyghur realm that had been devastated during decades of civil war.

This revival included Buddhism. For example, a branch of the Chagataid nobility residing in Gansu province, the descendants of Algu, refurbished a

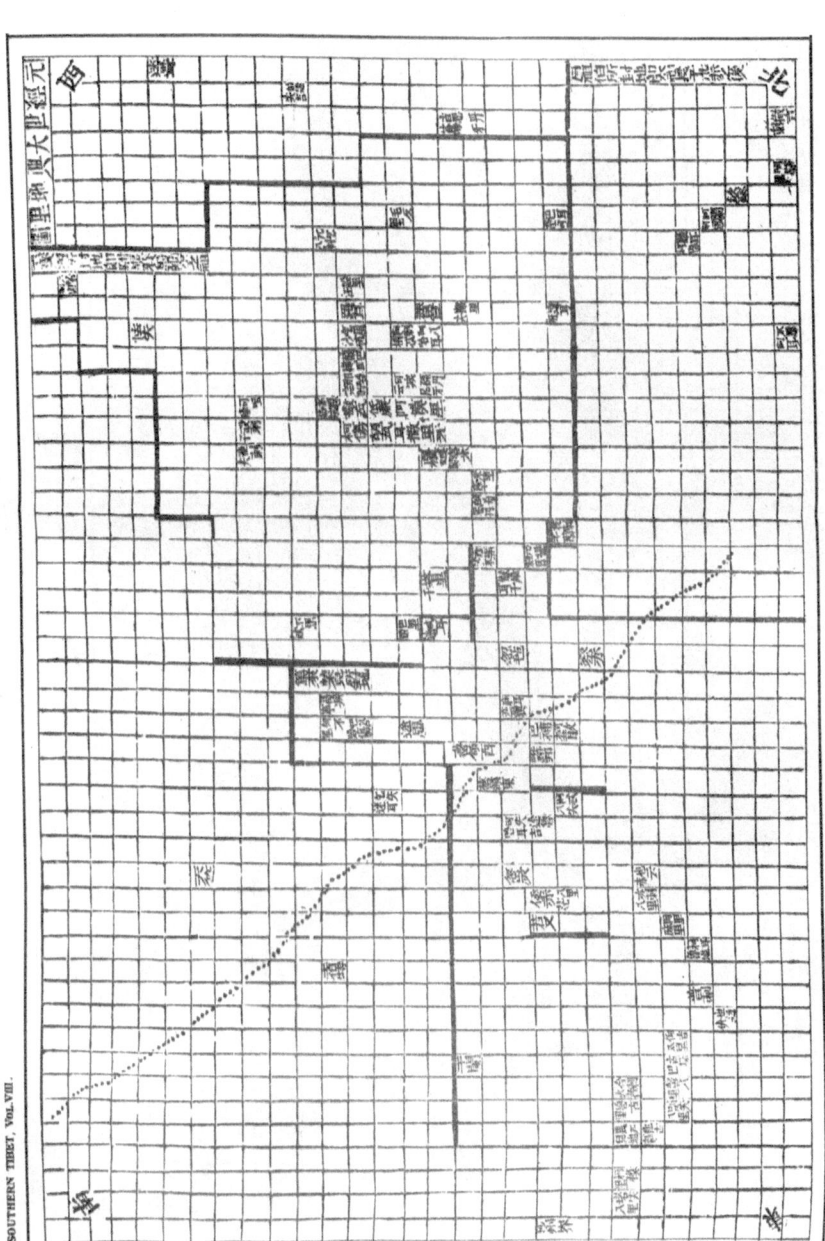

5.6 and 5.7 1331 Yuan dynasty map of Central Asia (*Yuan Jingshidadian Xibeibidili Tu* 元經世大典西北圖地里圖) After Sven Hedin, *Southern Tibet: Discoveries in Former Times Compared with My Own Researches in 1906–1908* (Stockholm: Lithographic Institute of the General Staff of the Swedish Army, 1922), vol. 8, plate 8

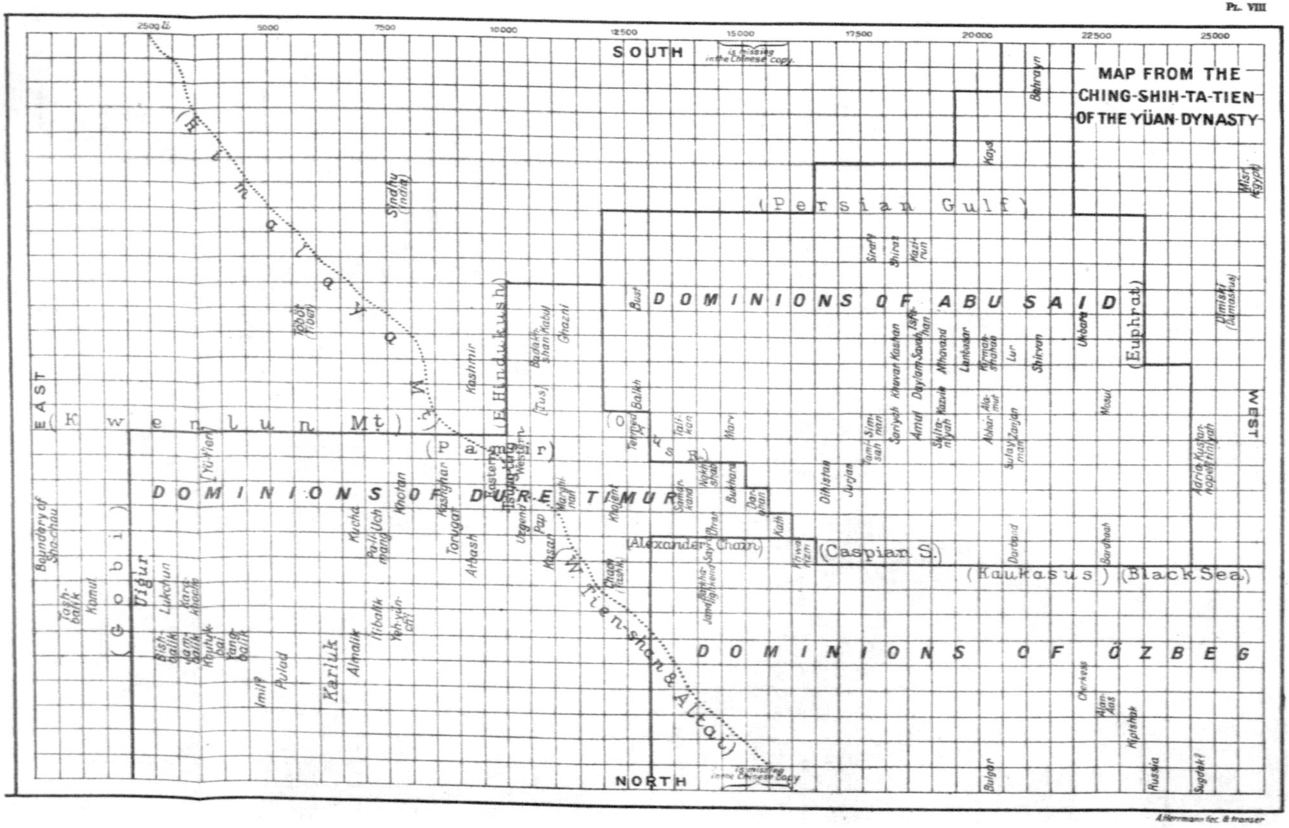

Pl. VIII

MAP FROM THE CHING-SHIH-TA-TIEN OF THE YÜAN DYNASTY

Buddhist monastery dedicated to Mañjuśrī and erected a stela proclaiming that all Chagataid rulers will go to Tuṣita Heaven, the abode of the Buddha Maitreya.

> Beginning with Algu until Nom Kulı
> The charismatic ones with ample punya,
> All Qans ascended the throne of Chagatay
> And ascended to the Tuṣita palace (after death).⁷⁰

Kebek's successor Eljigdai (1327-1330), who continued rebuilding the Central Asian and Uyghur economies by maintaining good relations with the Yuan court, followed this Chagataid support of the Dharma. His brother and successor Tarmashirin (r. 1331-1334), however, was a devout Muslim. He had raided Delhi and gathered huge spoils in India before returning to his base in Afghanistan, where he promoted Islam and advocated shifting the trading focus away from China and toward the Mamluks and the Delhi Sultanate. This did not sit well with the Buddhists in Central Asia—especially the Uyghurs—who had long traded with China.⁷¹ They rebelled, which led to a period of instability until a grandson of Duwa, Jankeshi (r. 1335-1337), took the Chagataid throne. According to Muslim sources, he was a devout Buddhist who not only built temples but also had Buddha statues placed in mosques, turning them into Buddhist temples.⁷²

Jankeshi, however, was killed by his brother Yisün Temür (r. 1337-1340), whom Muslim sources present as a madman who cut off his mother's breasts. That evidence aside, a well-known 1339 document from Turfan confirms not only that Yisün Temür wielded power successfully but also that he was involved in the protection of a Uyghur Buddhist monastery.

> (This is our word), (the word of) Yisün Temür.
>> To the Iduqud of Qočo. To Qulun Qaya and the other authorities.
>> To Buyan Qaya and the other officials.
>> This Temür came reporting. He complained that a man named Taibudu Tölemiš used force and took two orchards and vineyards from the fields and waters that belong to the Yogacarya-monastery, and would not give them back. Last year in the spring the owners received a document with a seal from here. But a person named Bulmıš used force and took that document with seal and again did not give them back the fields and waters of those

orchards and vineyards. Now we send this document with seal that the local authorities lawfully interrogate the persons involved and let them give back the orchards and vineyards together with the fields and waters. If unable to decide the matter there, the authorities should gather those people and send them here. Therefore we issued this document with seal. We wrote it in the year of the hare, in the mid-spring month, on the twenty-fourth day of the waning moon, when sojourning in Bulan.[73]

The dispute over meager resources described in this decree confirms the beleaguered state of the Uyghur economy at this time, but also that even after fifty years of warfare, Buddhism had survived. Another decree from this period shows that even with all the tensions they had had with the Yuan court, the Uyghurs were still able to support their monks in Beijing.[74]

Yisün Temür's reign, possibly weakened by the outbreak of bubonic plague in Isyk-Kul in today's Kirghizstan in 1338-1339,[75] came to an abrupt end when he was deposed by the Ögedeid ruler Ali Sultan, well known for being a fanatical Muslim who persecuted the Christians of Central Asia. Although the Chagataid princes quickly deposed Ali Sultan, the upheaval encouraged the Golden Horde to invade Central Asia until Özbek Khan died abruptly in 1342. A subsequent power struggle for the Chagataid throne ended with the splitting of the Chagatai Khanate into two. Timur (1336-1405) took over Central Asia and founded the Timurid dynasty,[76] while in the east, Tughluq Temür (r. 1347-1363) was put on the Moghul throne.[77] His heirs would rule Moghulistan—including the Uyghur homeland—until the late seventeenth century. Tughluq Temür would also convert to Islam in 1354, which began the slow process of Islamization among the Uyghurs.[78]

THE LONG, SLOW ROAD TO ISLAM

Because of stereotypes about Islam, the process of Islamization—especially in the Buddhist world—is often conceptualized as being both violent and quick. In most cases when a people, a culture, or a civilization, becomes Muslim, it has been a long and drawn-out process. After the Arab conquests in the seventh century, Muslim majorities in some parts of the Middle East were not achieved until the fourteenth century.[79] The Uyghurs similarly became Muslim over a long period of time. Although their ostensible rulers, the Moghuls, converted to Islam in the mid-fourteenth century, the Uyghurs continued being Buddhist for centuries thereafter. Two Uyghur manuscripts of the *Golden Light Sutra* from a Buddhist monastery near Suzhou in Gansu, dated 1687 and 1688, contain praise for their rulers: the Manchus of the Qing dynasty (1644-1912).[80] The Uyghur conversion to Islam was therefore anything but quick.

As a result, Buddhists engaged with Muslims for centuries, and at times this exchange was fruitful, as in the Il-khanid realm. At other times, however, there were tensions, especially when the power dynamics were flipped. In one Uyghur poem, for example, this tension shows in the author's attempt to refute Islamic teachings about creation:

> ... they say that God created ...
> the many trees, the mountains, the many creatures,
> and all things.
>
> When God created these things,
> Was there only emptiness before?
> Is it possible to beget false knowledge
> And to twist everything around?
>
> The Muslims themselves constantly say
> That there is no one who has ever seen
> The actual form of the Divine God
> Or his internal or external domicile.
>
> Without seeing the form of God,
> Who could truly hear these words of God?
> Are not the sayings of the prophets
> The only evidence of these words [of God]?
>
> Now, learn the [true] knowledge ...[81]

Another Uyghur poet had a more pessimistic perspective on the expanding political power of Islam and lamented a future without the Dharma:

Rasāyana will be lost.
Comrades in dharma and relatives will be dispersed.
Preacher masters will vanish.
The law without dharma will gain strength.
These places will not exist.
Buddha figures will not remain.
People will forget
the reason for doing puṇya.[82]

The same "end of the Dharma" sentiment in the face of encroaching Islam is also found in a famous Uyghur composition from the fourteenth century, the *Insadi Sutra*, but it also expresses the hope that Maitreya will return and extend his Buddhist dominion over both Baghdad and Byzantium.[83]

In approaching such materials and thinking about how the Uyghurs may have understood or imagined Islam, it is important to understand how the Buddhist tradition itself conceptualized Islam at the time. The most important source for the Buddhist view of Muslims during the Yuan dynasty is the *Kālacakratantra*, a treatise that had been complied in the early eleventh century in what is now northern Pakistan.[84] At that time the region was experiencing an influx of Muslims seeking refuge from persecution by the Abbasid caliphate, and Buddhism was in decline. The *Kālacakratantra*, as a result, is permeated with a sense of doom and expressly claims to be a hedge against the advance of Islam.[85] The very possibility of Islam taking over the world shapes the text's eschatology and soteriology, which is best encapsulated in the apocalyptic myth of Shambhala. The *Kālacakratantra* prophesies a future in which Islam takes over the world and the Buddhist savior, Kalkin Raudra Cakrin, rides forth with his army from the hidden kingdom of Shambhala, annihilates the Muslims, and ushers in a new golden age of pure Buddhism.

Even though this vision was a response to contemporary realities in northwest India, it defined Buddhist views of Islam for the next millennium—which is to say that Buddhists had a profoundly negative view of Islam. But Islamic sources from the Mongol period show that Buddhists were themselves also seen in a negative light. After all, the Buddhist Hülegü sacked Baghdad in 1258 CE and killed the caliph.[86] Muslim historians also fabricated stories of Buddhist persecution. Juzjani, a Muslim historian writing in India, told a story about how a miracle saved the Muslim world from the scheming Buddhists:

A fraternity of recluses and devotees of the infidels of Chin, and idol-worshippers of Tingit and Tamghaj, whom they style by the name of Tunian [*toyin* = monk], acquired ascendancy over Güyük. That faction constantly used to study persecuting Musulmans, and were wont to promote means of afflicting the people of Islam continually, in order that, mayhap, they might entirely uproot them, extirpate them completely, and eradicate both name and sign of the true believers from the pages of that country.

One of those [monks], who had a name and reputation in China and Turkestan, presented himself before Güyük and said: "If thou desirest that the sovereignty and throne of the Mughals should remain unto thee, of two things do one—either massacre the whole of the Musalmans, or put a stop to their generating and propagating." ... On account of the numerousness of the Musalmans in the countries of China, Turkestan, and Tingit, to massacre them would not be feasible, they [the monks] therefore came to this conclusion that it would be right that a mandate should be issued by Güyük, that all Musulmans should be emasculated and made eunuchs of, in order that their race might become extinct, and the empire of the Mughals be safe from their rebellion and sedition.

When such [like] tyranny and barbarity took root in the mind of Güyük, and his decision in this course was come to, he commanded that a mandate should be issued, to this effect, throughout all parts of the Mughal dominions.... Accordingly he delivered this mandate to [one of] those Mughal [monks], saying: "Do ye transmit this mandate into all parts of the empire, and use the utmost efforts in so doing."

When that accursed base one, who held that tyrannical mandate in his hand, was issuing from the place of audience in great glee and confidence, there was a dog which they used constantly to keep there, and which was wont to be near the throne, at the sides, and in the precincts of the dais, and the sovereign's exclusive seat; and on the animal's collar, studded with precious stones, was impressed a brand denoting its being royal property. It was a dog, which, in courage and fierceness, greatly exceeded and far surpassed a thousand roaring lions and howling tigers. This dog was in Güyük's place of audience, and, like unto a wolf upon a sheep, or fire among wild rue seeds, it seized hold of that impious monk, flung him to the ground, and then, with its teeth tore out that base creature's genitals from the roots; and by the Heavenly power and Divine help, at once, killed him, and the imprecation, according to the *hadith*, which Mustafa—on whom be peace!—had pronounced upon the son of Abu Lahb: "O God! Let one of thy dogs defile him!" was fulfilled upon that accursed wretch of a priest.

Such a miracle as this was vouchsafed in order that, under the shadow of the protection of the Most High God, the faith of Islam, the felicity of the Hanafi creed, the happiness of the Ahmadi belief, the prestige of the followers of the orthodox Muhammadi institutes, might continue safe from the malevolence of this accursed one.... Praise be to God for the triumph of Islam and the overthrow of idolatry![87]

In reality Güyük Khan favored Christianity, not Buddhism.[88] Juzjani's story nevertheless reveals how tensions boiled up to the surface as the Mongol empire forced Muslims and Buddhists not only to live together but also to confront one another in hostile military situations.

Within such encounters, it was not only Muslims who made up stories. Uyghur Buddhists went so far as to rewrite their history to say that when they established the West Uyghur Kingdom, they had subjugated the local Muslim population:

> All peoples living in the country of the Ten Uyghur,
> the son of our father Udan has grown up.
> They became very joyful and happy,
> saying "We will not experience the oppression by the foreign enemies in the ten directions!"

After he (i.e., the new king) attained the great throne, he himself gracefully carried out many deeds and actions.

To destroy the people of the Tarim (region), which had become enemies of the blessed Kočo Realm, he gracefully mounted the horses together with all his troops. After storming into Solmi City he with his worthy troops deigned to disperse and to scatter (the people), thus bringing his whole people upon the land (?) into peace and harmony. He deigned to march to the western (city) of Talas, and he deigned to cause more than ten city Lords beginning with the general Bagučak to appear (before him), sharpening and carving he deigned to take the city and the realm called Talas with its inner parts.

"To oppose the enemy standing in hard opposition by causing to enact hard commands and punishment—to show compassion and grace to those who bow and make kow- tow." (Following this rule) the jewel and ornament, the glance and brightness of the mighty and powerful kings and khans (i.e., our king) deigned to bring to memory the words of the rājaśāstra called 是, and instead of dispersing and destroying the people [aimed to satisfy them].

As soon as the people saw and heard this matter, they, the whole Čomak (= Muslim) people from afar and from near folded their hands in front of our holy Tängri and while greeting and bowing down, wondering and being surprised they spoke:

"As to the realm, it is the holy Uyghur Khan.
To have compassion on the people
which obeys the king—what is more than this?

As for the rulers, better than all is the holy Tängri Khan.
Did he not divide his property like a father?" Thus they spoke to each other.

Pressing their breasts and bowing down,
compressing their lips and bowing down,
they let fall a rain of blessings.

The people who heard this from afar said to each other:
"The holiest of realms is the realm of the Ten Uyghur.
This Tängri Khan has emanated as the most significant of rulers."[89]

These events did not happen either. As with Juzjani's story about the scheming Buddhists, this Uyghur reimagining of their past was a reflection of the new communal boundaries then being created in the Buddhist-Muslim interface of the Mongol empire.

The actual interactions between Muslims and Uyghur Buddhists appear to have been less hostile. For example, after his conversion to Islam, the Moghul ruler Tughluq Temür requested a Tibetan Buddhist teacher to come to his court.[90] He also allowed the Uyghurs to maintain their faith as long as they paid taxes to the Moghul state. The official scribe of a Timurid embassy from Shahrukh Khan sent to the Ming court in 1419 notes that the Uyghurs were still Buddhist: "By the end of Jumada II (July 11) they arrived at Turfan. Majority of the inhabitants of this town were unbelievers and worshipped idols. They had large idol-temples of superb beauty inside which there were many idols, some of them having been made newly and others old. In foreground of the platform there was a big image which was asserted by them to be the statue of Śākyamuni."[91] He also records that Buddhist monasteries and mosques stood side by side in the town of Hami:

> On the 21st of Rajab [August 2] they reached the town of Qamul [Hami]. In this town Amir Fakhru'd-Din had had built a magnificent mosque, facing which they had constructed a Buddhist temple of a very huge size, inside which there was set up a large idol. On the left and right sides of which there were considerable number of smaller idols. Just in front of the big idol there stood a copper image of a child of ten years of age of great artistic beauty and excellence. On the walls of the building there were frescoes of expert workmanship and exquisite colored paintings. At the gate of the temple there were statues of two demons which seemed ready to attack one another.[92]

The same situation was also recorded in Luo Yuejiong's *Record of Tribute Guests* (*Xian bin lü*), which notes: "In Lükchün [in Eastern Turkestan]... live two kinds of people: Muslims and Buddhists."[93] Nevertheless, while similarly noting the presence of Buddhists and Muslims in Uyghur territory, the Chinese envoy Chen Cheng (1365-1457) pointed out that they spoke the same language but "were distinguished from one another by religious and cultural markers: Uyghur men grew their hair long, while the Muslims shaved their heads; Uyghur women donned black veils, while Muslim women dressed in white."[94] And even though such distinctions may reflect potential tensions, there is no evidence the Moghals ever persecuted Buddhists or hindered their religious practices. In fact, in the 1360s, the Chagatai ruler issued a decree allowing a Tibetan lama, Dorjé Tashi Pelzangpo—the Yuan dynasty's National Preceptor at Qaraqorum—to visit his disciples among the Uyghurs.[95]

Such relations between the Uyghurs and Beijing continued even after the Mongols had been expelled by the Ming dynasty in 1368. In 1408, for example, the *Veritable Records of the Ming Dynasty* (*Ming shi lü* 明實錄) records that, "A priest in Turfan city, Kumaraširi, and others offered horses and products of the country to the Ming court. The Ming court deigned to reward them with 100 taels of silver, 700 strings of paper money, and seven sets of colored silk fabrics. And also, his disciples were rewarded with some paper money and presents according to their ranks."[96] Three years later the Buddhist monk Nandaśri led another Uyghur delegation that "offered horses and products of their country to the Ming court. Nandaśri and others were rewarded with some presents according to their ranks. The Board of rites by imperial edict gave Kumaraśri sixteen pieces of colored fabrics and three suits of clerical robes." And between 1426 and 1441 the "priest of Turfan," Paramartaśri, sent five missions. The last record of a Uyghur Buddhist monk at the Ming court was Piratyaśri in 1473, who was granted the rank of "Chief Officiant of the Buddhists."[97]

The ability of Uyghur Buddhists to visit the Ming court and continue their religious practices more than a century after their putative ruler's conversion to Islam confirms that, as elsewhere in the Muslim world, the collective conversion to Islam was a long and slow process. In fact, Uyghur Buddhists praised their Muslim rulers, as in this poem about Sulayman, the prince of Xining who ruled over the Uyghur homeland:

> On Prince Sulayman who is respectful, wise, and of heavy merit,
> On his special statements, which cannot be found in other people,
> And his superior works, which make in peace more than all words
> Let us tell more or less, just little by little.
>
> Guarding his ancestor's rules extremely skillfully
> Understanding the rules of other countries in detail
> One who keeps respecting all nations
> One did not exist before like this prince who is special and holy.
>
> Loathing drinking too much alcohol (and considering it) as poison
> And drinking a little in order to accomplish others' advantages
> One who never neglects beneficial deeds at all times
> Never existed one like this prince who is special and holy.[98]

Although this poem is fragmentary, it provides evidence of a time in which Buddhists and Muslims met openly and learned from one another. The Uyghur poem that serves as epigraph to this chapter recounts another instance, praises the Buddha, and notes that even Muslims can generate good karma.⁹⁹ The Buddhist Uyghurs were well aware of Islam without confrontation.

The possibilities of Buddhist-Muslim interaction in this period are well captured in the later history of Sulayman's family. One of his descendants, Prince Asuday, sponsored the translation into Uyghur of four Tibetan tantric works, including Naropa's *Book of the Dead*.¹⁰⁰ Asuday is also mentioned in two Chinese inscriptions at Dunhuang, one of which includes the Tibetan mantra *Om Mani Padme Hum* in six different scripts (Tibetan, Sanskrit, Uyghur, Pakpa, Tangut, and Chinese). Another example, in the opposite direction is the Arabic astronomical handbook (*zij*) that Khwaja Ghazi al-Sanjufini from Samarkand prepared in 1366 for Prince Radna, the Mongol viceroy of Tibet living in Hezhou in Gansu province. Although a Buddhist, he was interested in Islamic science. To better understand al-Sanjufini's work, Radna had parts of it translated into Mongolian and glossed in Chinese and Tibetan.¹⁰¹ Another fragmentary text has on one side "a divinatory tableau cast according to the principles of psammography or sand divination, a practice of Islamic geomancy," and on the other side "the colophon of a Vajrayana Buddhist treatise on the Path and Fruit (*mārgaphala*) doctrine, by its Tibetan name *lam-'bras* (Uigh. *lambïraz*)."¹⁰² This period of Buddhist-Muslim exchange lasted from the late thirteenth century until the early fifteenth century.

There were other geopolitical, economic, and religious changes that ultimately influenced the Uyghur adoption of Islam. When the Moghul ruler Tughluq Temür converted in 1354, he aligned himself not with a famous Central Asian Sufi lineage but with local Sufi masters from the town of Lop Katak.¹⁰³ Why he did so is not well understood,¹⁰⁴ but one factor was that the Kataki Sufis did not place stringent doctrinal demands on the Moghuls.¹⁰⁵ Instead the Kataki allowed the Moghuls to practice a form of "nomadic Islam" that was more eclectic and pluralistic. This allowed Buddhism to continue to flourish under Moghul rule. Making such an alliance with the Kataki and maintaining their nomadic traditions had numerous other intertwined political, economic, and religious consequences. Most notably, it further alienated the Moghuls from the Timurids, who were allied with the illustrious Central Asian Yasaviyya order.¹⁰⁶

Islam was not the only factor at play in the tensions between the Timurids and Moghuls. There was also the Mongol legacy that defined the post-Mongol world order. It required that all rulers be direct descendants of Chinggis Khan, and the Timurids were not Mongols: Timur was a Turk from the Barlas clan.

Even though he was indisputably the most powerful ruler in the world at the time, he could never proclaim himself "Khan." Doing so would have been too great a violation of the sacred Chinggisid principles, so to circumvent this problem, Timur married several Chagataid princesses and declared himself the "Imperial Son-in-Law." He also promoted himself as the great defender of Islam, such that Timurid legitimacy came to rest on the twin pillars of the Mongol legacy and Islam.[107] The later Timurid ruler Shahrukh, for example, would place a monument over Timur's burial site in 1420 that claimed not only that the legendary Mongol ancestor Alan Qoa was associated with the Virgin Mary and the Abrahamic Holy Spirit but also that Timur was a descendant of 'Ali, son-in-law of the Prophet Muhammad and first Shi'ite imam.[108] Shahrukh was boldly proclaiming the legitimacy of the Timurid dynasty largely on the basis of this dual heritage: Chinggisid and Islamic. Both of these genealogical claims were purely imaginary and capture the urgency the Timurids felt in trying to legitimate their rule in the shadow of the Mongol legacy and the Moghuls.

This problem came to the fore when a new Sufi order arose that challenged both Timurid claims. This was the Naqshbandiyya order founded by Baha ad-Din Naqshband (d. 1389), who rather ingeniously challenged the spiritual legitimacy of the Yasaviyya by claiming that he was restoring the mystical path of the Khwajagan ("Masters"), the real but secret lineage of Ahmad Yasavi's teacher, Abu Yusuf al-Hamadani (d. 1140).[109] As the Naqshbandi order later articulated, central to this claim was a secret initiation lineage that ran parallel to the conventional master-disciple transmission lineage (*silsila*) common to all schools of Sufism. Although theological innovation came to define the Naqshbandiyya, the key to their success was their decision to fuse the two major strands of post-Mongol Islamic thought. By coupling Naqshband's original mystical teachings with calls for reinstitution of the *shari'a*, Islamic law, the Naqshbandiyya challenged the twin pillars that upheld Timurid legitimacy, claiming the Timurids and their Yasaviyya enablers were not Muslim enough. Moreover, the very logic of *shari'aism* required the rejection of the Mongol legacy and its infidel customs in order to create a pure Muslim state. The quiet path of mystical introspection was replaced with *jihad* against the impious Timurids. When the Naqshbandiyya sought political and military support among the nomads in the east, they found a willing ally in the Moghul ruler Uways Khan (r. 1417–1429).

Timur had taken over half of the Chagataid Ulus, and the Moghuls and Timurids had been fighting ever since. Joining the Naqshbandiyya's campaign against the Timurids on one level simply made sense. But the Mongol legacy must also have been on the minds of both the Sufis and the Moghuls because the Moghuls, unlike the Timurids, were actual descendants of Chinggis Khan. Thus if they rejected the local Kataki Sufis, whom they had been following since Tughluq Temür, in favor of the Naqshbandiyya—a new Central Asian Sufi order with a legendary pedigree—they would be both the heirs of the Mongol legacy and the true rulers of Islam. A Moghul-Naqshbandiyya alliance was thus a winning proposition for both sides.

Not everyone won on account of this alliance. Because Naqshbandi *shari'aism* specifically advocated the "remov[al] of the evil customs of the strangers,"[110] the Uyghur Buddhists were now under threat within the Moghul domains. In addition, the fall of the Yuan dynasty in 1368 had caused major geopolitical reorientations to the east. In 1368 Zhu Yuanzhang expelled Toghan Temür and his Mongol followers from Beijing and founded the Ming dynasty (1368–1644). The Mongols fled north, but much to their surprise, the old Mongol capital of Qaraqorum was already occupied. Indeed, the entire Mongolian plateau, their ancestral "homeland," had been taken over by the Oirad (or Western Mongols). Believing it was not possible for his recently defeated army to wrest control away from the Oirad, Toghan Temür and the Mongols established themselves in the no-man's land between the Great Wall and the Gobi Desert, which today is the Inner Mongolian province of the People's Republic of China.[111] Two years after arriving as a refugee in this environmentally and politically marginal buffer zone, Toghan Temür died of dysentery.

Toghan Temür's ignominious death may symbolize the waning fortunes of the Mongols in the post-Yuan period, but such was not the view from China.[112] The Ming court continued to see the Mongols as a mortal threat and launched several campaigns against them. Yet, much to the anger and consternation of the court, the Mongols continued to elude defeat.[113] The ongoing Mongol-Ming struggle would change the power balance in the region.[114] Thus, although the Oirad controlled the "heartland" of the Mongolian plateau, they did not become a major power in the immediate post-Yuan period. To their west was the powerful Moghul ruler Tughluq Temür Khan and to their south were the Mongols, who, although weakened, were still a formidable force. Moreover, the Mongols and the Moghuls controlled the East-West trade, most importantly, the trade in Central Asian horses, which were essential for both the Ming military and its larger economy. Without them the Ming regime would quite literally grind to a halt. The immensity of this trade is reflected in the fact that annually the Ming bought nearly two million horses from the Mongols.[115] The post-Yuan Mongols may have been battered and defeated, but they still had the Ming over a barrel.

For the Ming court this situation was clearly intolerable, since in their view China's security was in the fickle hands of their barbarian enemies. The Ming adopted a two-pronged strategy to deal with the Mongols. The first was to find another source of horses, which they did by re-establishing the tea-for-horse trading network with Tibet.[116] (To show how enormously this trade expanded, a single transaction in 1435 involved the trade of 1,097,000 pounds of tea for 13,000 horses.)[117] The second was to maintain trade with the Mongols and Moghuls, but on their own terms by funneling all trade with Central Asia through the small independent city-state of Hami, which had been brought into the Ming system of frontier garrisons in 1406.[118] The Mongol khan Gülichi (1402–1408), however, did not agree and poisoned Engke Temür, the prince of Hami, who had initially made the deal with the Chinese. The Ming court was bewildered by this turn of events, but they still hoped to salvage the trade negotiations. However, when their envoys were also executed at the command of the new Mongol ruler Punyashri, the Ming finally decided to circumvent the Mongols entirely by negotiating with their archrival, the Oirad. The Ming then not only bestowed titles and privileges upon the Oirad ruler but also opened up direct trade relations. To repay the favor the Oirad ruler Mahmud (d. 1416) launched an assault on the Mongols in 1412, and after killing Punyashri, put his own son Delbeg (r. 1412–1414) on the Mongol throne. Thus, with the help of the Ming, the age of the Oirad had arrived (see fig. 5.8).

The Oirad ruler's name, Mahmud, is an Arabic name, and there is every reason to believe that many of the Oirad elite were at this time Muslim. Indeed, having been frozen out of relations with both the Mongols and the Ming, the Oirad had inevitably turned their attention toward the Moghuls and Timurids in the West.[119] This turn to the Muslim world may have begun as an economic decision, but it would also have religious implications. By aligning themselves with the West, the Oirad were drawn into the Islamic fold. Something similar was happening simultaneously in Southeast Asia.[120] When trade with China withered after the fall of the Yuan, both the Oirad and the Southeast Asian kingdoms linked up with Islamic trade networks, which inevitably brought Islamization.[121] But, unlike in Southeast Asia, the Oirad's

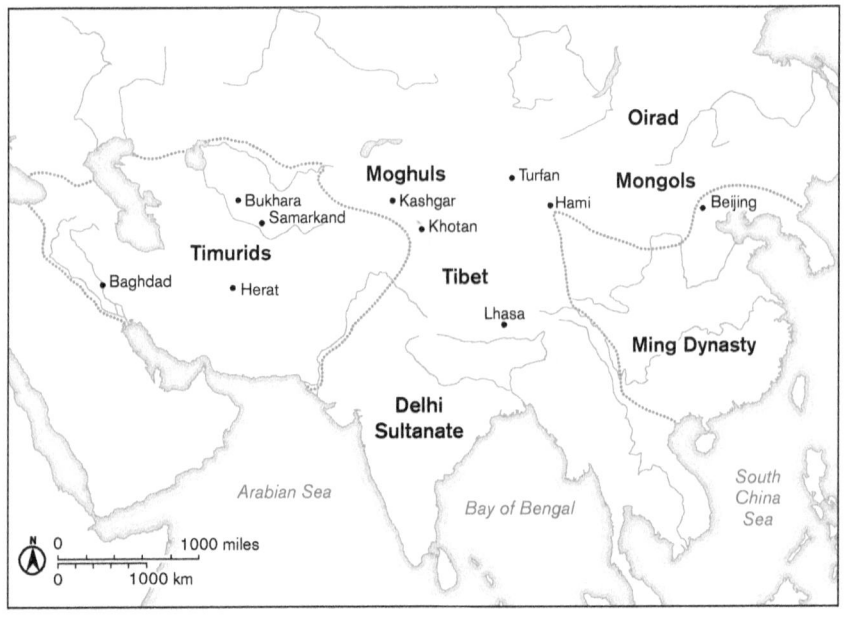

5.8 Fifteenth-Century Eurasia

conversion to Islam was short-lived, and only a few decades later the Oirad would become Buddhist.

The Oirad are one of the few peoples in the history of Islam to have given up the faith. Unlike in Spain and the Balkans, where the retreat of Islam was compelled by the use of brute force, the Buddhist conversion of the Muslim Oirads seems to have been a bloodless affair. Of course, the Oirad majority may not have been too devoted to Islam to begin with, and once trade with China opened up, they were no longer dependent on Islamic trade networks and being Muslim lost much of its value. In fact, being Muslim was probably a hindrance in dealing with China at this time.

After the Ming cut their relations with the Mongols and established direct economic ties with the Oirad, any power the Mongols had over the Ming evaporated, and their wealth and power rapidly collapsed. In their place rose the Oirad. That growing strength, however, not only affected the fortunes of the Mongols but also came to impinge upon the Moghuls. Uways Khan, for example, the erstwhile leader of the new Naqshabandi Muslim world and heir of Chinggis Khan, fought the Oirad twenty-one times and lost every battle but one. He was even taken hostage three times and had to give the Oirad ruler his sister as a wife to obtain his own release.[122] After the death of Uways Khan in 1429, the situation among the Moghuls only grew worse when a succession struggle erupted between his two sons, Yunus and Esen Buqa. But the collapsing Moghul economy was at the root of the crisis.

Even though the Ming emperor had abolished the horse trade with Central Asia in 1424, such trade continued surreptitiously through the city of Hami and kept the Moghul economy alive.[123] However, when the Oirad ruler Toghan (d. 1440) married into the Hami ruling family, he took control over this last entrepôt of Muslim trade with China, further squeezing the Moghuls. The final blow came when Toghan's son and successor Esen moved the horse trade away from Hami completely and established it in Datong near Beijing. The economic situation became so dire that Muslims started to flee the Moghul domains and became refugees in China.[124]

This economic blow also harmed the Uyghur Buddhists, who had thrived financially on the East-West trade for centuries. With animosities between the Moghuls and Timurids hindering trade with the West and the Oirads and Chinese choking off trade with the East, the Uyghurs were once again caught in the middle. Their situation worsened in 1449 when the Oirad ruler Esen annihilated a Chinese army and captured the Zhentong emperor at Tumu Fort (50 miles northwest of Beijing). This military defeat was pivotal in Chinese history because it changed the course and nature of the Ming dynasty.[125] Most significantly, it played a fundamental role in the subsequent Ming turn inward.[126] Ongoing troubles with the Mongols and Oirats also drove the Ming court to start building the Great Wall in earnest. Yet more damaging to the Uyghur economy—and support of Buddhism—was that international trade was beginning to go by sea.[127] The Silk Road trade that had sustained the Uyghur Buddhists for centuries was coming to an end.[128]

By the 1430s the city of Turfan was becoming predominantly Muslim.[129] In the 1450s Chinese envoys passing through Hami noted that the area was "dotted with mosques."[130] In response to these Muslim advances, some Uyghur Buddhists sought refuge in China. The monk noted above, Piratyaśri, the last on record to visit the Ming court, in 1473, did so to request asylum for 200 Uyghur Buddhists. Other Uyghur Buddhists presumably stayed.

While some may have succeeded in this new world, others might well have seen their deteriorating socioeconomic situation in religious terms as Muslims came to dominate the economy.[131] Islam challenged what had been the support system of Uyghur Buddhism for centuries. As Himanshu Ray explains:

> This support system worked at several levels: at the ideological level it influenced the accumulation and reinvestment of wealth in trading ventures by lay devotees; at the social level, donations to Buddhist monasteries provided status to traders and other occupational groups; at the economic level, Buddhist monasteries were repositories of information and essential skills such as those of writing; and at the community level, participation in the fortnightly *uposatha* ceremony instilled an identity among the lay worshippers.[132]

Islam, with its own prosperity theology, mosques, and larger trade networks across the entire Islamic world offered alternatives to all four of these structural components. Yet at what point did these alternatives and the "spiritual capital" of Islam finally outshine the Dharma?[133]

What would compel an individual Uyghur Buddhist to one day go to a mosque and profess the *shahāda*, the witness of faith: "There is no God but Allah, and Muhammad is His messenger"? According to one story, such decisions were the result of the late sixteenth-century Naqshabandi Sufi saint Ishaq Vali's miraculous powers:

> One of the saint's disciples led a trading mission from Yarkand to Suzhou [in Gansu], where he lodged with a local qadi (Islamic judge), Khoja Abdusattar, whose daughter was gravely ill. Through his disciple's entreaties, Ishaq Vali manifested himself from many miles away in Yarkand and miraculously cured the qadi's daughter. "At that time ... close to three thousand Uyghur infidels had gathered around Khoja [Abdusattar]. They all became Muslims, and secretly they became devotees of His Holiness [Ishaq Vali]."[134]

There were no doubt other, more worldly reasons an individual Buddhist became Muslim: the demeaning non-Muslim poll tax; the more burdensome 5 percent non-Muslim duty that cut into his trading profits; his family's shrinking social and economic standing in the community; the superior skills of Muslim physicians to heal his child (as earlier with Buddhist and Manichean doctors);[135] the difficulty of finding a suitable husband for his daughter. Or perhaps Islam had simply come to make more sense than the Dharma. Was it all of these factors or some others?[136]

Of course, it is on the macro level that historians and scholars of religion try to explain events and to paint a convincing portrait of what "actually happened" through a logical chain of cause and effect. Although such narratives are often admirable and useful, they also often lead to simplistic and monolithic explanations that obscure the very complexities they are trying to explain.

As noted at the beginning of this book, Peter Brown has warned against the dangers of offering such simple narratives of religious conversion. They result in a situation where "we are like little boys on the sea shore. We watch with fascinated delight as the tide sweeps in upon an intricate sandcastle. We note when each segment crumbles before the advancing waters."[137] Brown's image captures well the common story of the green wave of Islam crashing over the Uyghur Buddhists. Islamization, however, was a process no less complicated and drawn out than that of the Uyghurs' conversion to Buddhism. We therefore need to be wary of accounts that simplify the inordinately complex dynamics that shaped both of these conversions.

Conclusion

> *Having cleansed his pure spirit, and having freed him from faults, Almighty God decreed that Sultān Satuq Bughra Ghāzī be the eliminator of all heresies. He decreed that the Sultān be the one to make the Prophet's law radiant. It was the Sultān who made visible the rays of faith, and who killed all of the infidels and hypocrites.*
> —Legends of the Bughra Khans[1]

When Uyghur Buddhism came to an end is unknown. As noted in the previous chapter, all the evidence points to the fact that Uyghur Buddhism continued to thrive throughout the fifteenth century. The Ming dynasty continued to host Uyghur Buddhists at their court, and to facilitate this exchange maintained translation bureaus to make communication possible. In the early Ming period, for example, the scholar Tao Zongyi explained the workings of the alphabetic Uyghur script using the Pakpa script (see fig. Con.1). Later in the dynasty these translation bureaus produced Sino-Uyghur dictionaries with transcriptions and translations to facilitate dialogue (see fig. Con.2).

Not only the Chinese continued to engage with the Uyghurs and preserve their historical memory. On account of the legendary power of the Uyghur Buddhists during the Il-khanid period, their history was also remembered in the Muslim world, so much that in the famous *Miraj Name* manuscript produced in Herat, Afghanistan, in 1436, the painting of Muhammad is enframed by Uyghur script (albeit written sideways) (see fig. Con.3). Throughout the fifteenth century the surrounding peoples clearly had not forgotten about the Uyghurs and their Buddhism.

For the Uyghurs who converted to Islam, however, the situation was more fraught precisely because Uyghur identity and Buddhism were so intimately

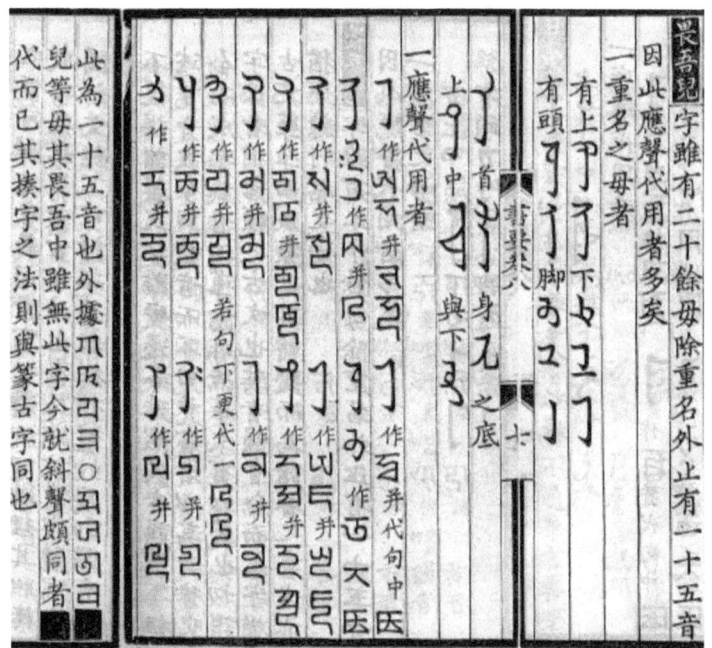

Con.1 Tao Zongyi's 陶宗儀 Shushi Huiyao 書史會要 vol. 8, folio 7a–8a
https://www.babelstone.co.uk/Phags-pa/Uighur.html

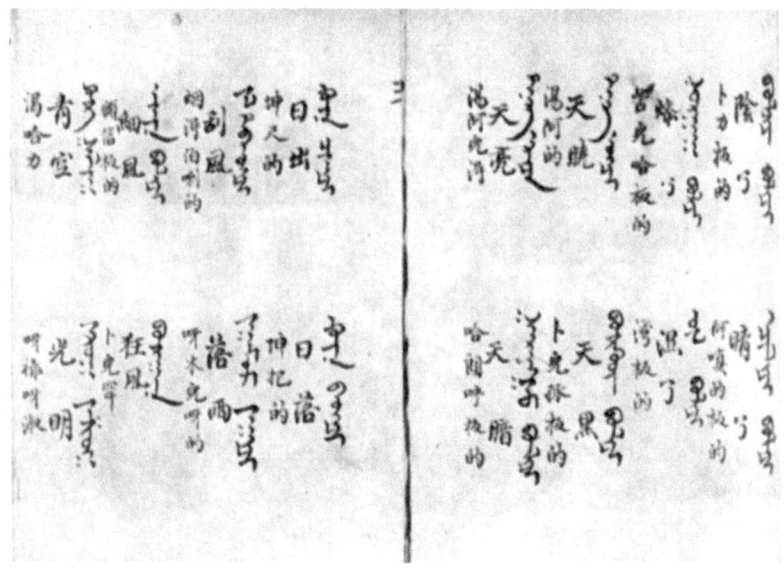

Con.2 Chinese-Uyghur dictionary

After Louis Ligeti, "Un vocabulaire Sino-ouigour des Ming: Le *Kao-tch'ang-kou an yi-chou* du Bureau des Traducteurs," *Acta Orientalia Academiai Scientiarum Hungaricae* 19, no. 3 (1966): 290

Con.3 Muhammad and the angel with seventy heads, from the *Miraj Name*, Herat, Afghanistan, 1436 CE (Manuscrit Supplément Turc 190, f. 19v)
Reproduced with permission of Bibliothèque nationale de France

Con.4 Pilgrims praying at the Imam Asim *mazar*
Photo by Rian Thum

intertwined. If one abandoned Buddhism for Islam, it was no longer possible for them to continue being Uyghur. As a result, unlike in many other conversion narratives that are linked to ethnogenesis, there is no Uyghur history of conversion to Islam. Not only the converts' Buddhist history was forgotten; so too was their Uyghur identity.

In its place these new Muslims created an entirely new historical narrative about themselves. It began with the Islamic conversion of the Qarakhanid ruler Satuq Bughra Khan in the tenth century and his people's destruction of the Buddhist kingdom of Khotan. In the same vein, they wrote numerous histories recounting how valiant Muslims were continuously victorious over various infidels, be they Kazakhs, Zünghars, or Manchus.[2] Most importantly, they developed stories about Sufi saints and their miraculous deeds, which became the basis for pilgrimages to sites around the Taklamakan desert. These sites came to tie the oasis-dwelling Muslims together as a people through sacred narratives and rituals (see fig. Con.4).[3]

As with the rest of Uyghur Buddhist history, the fact that many of these pilgrimage sites had originally been Buddhist was readily forgotten.[4] Yet, as noted in the introduction, this historical amnesia was beginning to be remedied through the scholarship of European orientalists. Their textual work gave the world glimpses of Uyghur Buddhism, and their insights came fully to light when the lost treasures of the Turfan basin were revealed in the early twentieth century. These discoveries not only fueled a century of scholarship on Uyghur Buddhism but also became fodder for the burgeoning nationalist movements in what these scholars called East Turkestan, the homeland of the Uyghurs.[5] The nationalists adopted the glories of Uyghur Buddhism in order to create a national history that would justify the claims of modern-day Uyghur Muslims on the territory of Xinjiang.[6]

The history of Uyghur Buddhism not only serves the interest of the contemporary Uyghur independence movement; it also forces us to rethink not only what it means to be Buddhist but also how we conceptualize the meeting of Buddhism and Islam. Moreover, this history makes clear that the Uyghurs were central figures in the long history of Buddhist Asia. Indeed, our understanding of both Asian and Buddhist history is woefully incomplete without an awareness of the Uyghurs. By being Buddhist for more than six hundred years, they changed not only the history of the Dharma but also the history of Eurasia.

Notes

INTRODUCTION

1. Ahmet Refik, *Büyük Tarih-i Umumi: IV Cilt* (Istanbul: Kitabhane-yi İslam ve Askeri, İbrahim Hilmi, 1328 [1912]), 277, quoted in "Buddha from Kashgar to Istanbul," https://blogs.bl.uk/asian-and-african/2019/11/buddha-from-kashgar-to-istanbul.html.
2. Sam van Schaik, "Fakes, Delusions, or the Real Thing? Albert Grünwedel's Maps of Shambhala," *Journal of the American Oriental Society* 140, no. 2 (2020): 273–286.
3. On the myth of Shambhala see Edwin Bernbaum, *The Way to Shambhala: A Search for the Mythical Kingdom Beyond the Himalayas* (Los Angeles: Jeremy P. Tarcher, 1980); and Lubos Belka, "The Myth of Shambhala: Visions, Visualizations, and the Myth's Resurrection in the Twentieth Century in Buryatia," *Archiv Orientální* 71, no. 3 (2003): 247–262.
4. On the continued—albeit unclear—use of the ethnonym Uyghur in the Turfan region through the eighteenth century see Hans van Ess, "Der Name der Uiguren," in *Über den Alltag hinaus: Festschrift für Thomas O. Höllmann zum 65. Geburtstag*, ed. Shing Müller and Armin Selbitschka (Wiesbaden: Harrassowitz, 2017), 253–266.
5. On Muslim identities in Qing-period Xinjiang see Rian Thum, *The Sacred Routes of Uyghur History* (Cambridge, MA: Harvard University Press, 2014); Eric Schluessel, *Land of Strangers: The Civilizing Project in Qing Central Asia* (New York: Columbia University Press, 2020).
6. Stanislas Julien, "Concordance sinico-sanskrite d'un nombre considerable de titres d'ouvrages bouddhiques recueillé dans un catalogue chinois de l'an 1306," *Journal asiatique* 14 (1849): 366–367.
7. On these expeditions see, for example, Ch. Trümpler, *Das große Spiel: Archäologie und Politik zur Zeit des Kolonialism (1860–1940)* (Essen/Köln: Dumont, 2008); I. F. Popova, *Russian Expeditions to Central Asia at the Turn of the 20th Century* (St. Petersburg: Slavia Publishers, 2008); Franziska Torma, *Turkestan-Expeditionen. Zur Kulturgeschichte deutscher Forschungsreisen nach Mittelasien (1890–1930)* (Bielefeld: Transcript, 2011); Simone-Christiane Raschmann, "S. F. Oldenburg's Cooperation with German Scholars and Explorers of Central Asia at the Beginning of the 20th C. and the Significance of His

Finds for the Uighur Studies," in *Sergei Fedorovic Oldenburg*, ed. I. F. Popova (Moscow: Nauka, 2016), 285-305.

8. On the development of the idea of the "Silk Road" see Daniel Waugh, "Richthofen's 'Silk Roads': Toward the Archaeology of a Concept," *The Silk Road* 5, no. 1 (2007): 1–10; Tamara Chin, "The Invention of the Silk Road, 1877," *Critical Inquiry* 40, no. 1 (2013): 194-219.

9. For earlier studies on the history and culture of Uyghur Buddhism see Annemarie von Gabain, *Das Leben im uigurischen Königreich von Qočo: (850–1250)* (Wiesbaden: Harrassowitz, 1973); Peter Zieme, *Religion und Gesellschaft im Uigurischen Königreich von Qočo* (Opladen: Westdeutscher Verlag 1992); Fu Ma 付马, *Sichouzhilu shang xizhou huihu wangchao: 9–13 shiji zhongya dongbu lishi yanjiu* 絲綢之路上的西州回鶻王朝：9–13世紀中亞東部歷史研究 [The West Uyghur Kingdom on the Silk Road: Study on the history of Eastern Central Asia during the 9th–13th centuries] (Beijing: Social Science Academic Press, 2019).

10. On the historiography of this meeting see Johan Elverskog, *Buddhism and Islam on the Silk Road* (Philadelphia: University of Pennsylvania Press, 2010), 1–11.

11. Peter Brown, *Authority and the Sacred: Aspects of Christianization of the Roman World* (New York: Cambridge University Press, 1995), x.

12. The seminal text that ushered in a wave of postcolonial Buddhist studies scholarship was Donald S. Lopez, Jr., *Curators of the Buddha: The Study of Buddhism under Colonialism* (Chicago: University of Chicago Press, 1995).

13. On meditation see, for example, Robert Sharf, "Buddhist Modernism and the Rhetoric of Meditative Experience," *Numen* 32, no. 3 (1995): 228-283; Joanna Cook, *Meditation in Modern Buddhism: Renunciation and Change in Thai Monastic Life* (New York: Cambridge University Press, 2010); and Erik Braun, *The Birth of Insight: Meditation, Modern Buddhism, and the Burmese Monk Ledi Sayadaw* (Chicago: University of Chicago Press, 2013). On ritual see, for example, John S. Strong, *Relics of the Buddha* (Princeton, NJ: Princeton University Press, 2004); Toni Huber, *The Holy Land Reborn: Pilgrimage and the Tibetan Reinvention of Buddhist India* (Chicago: University of Chicago Press, 2008); Mark Rowe, *Bonds of the Dead: Temples, Burials, and the Transformation of Contemporary Japanese Buddhism* (Chicago: University of Chicago Press, 2011).

14. Lopez, *Curators of the Buddha*, 8. On the trepidation of non-Buddhologists dealing with Buddhist materials, see also Stephen Teiser's comments on the "fear" of Sinological readings of the *Heart Sutra* ("Perspectives on Readings of the Heart Sutra: The Perfection of Wisdom and the Fear of Buddhism," in *Ways with Words: Writing about Reading Texts from Early China*, ed. Pauline Yu et al. [Berkeley: University of California Press, 2000], 131). For a valuable overview of the *sui generis* study of Buddhism and its implications, see Richard Cohen, "Why Study Indian Buddhism?" in *The Invention of Religion: Rethinking Belief in Politics and History*, ed. Derek R. Peterson and Darren R. Walhof (New Brunswick, NJ: Rutgers University Press, 2002), 19–36.

15. On Buddhism as the "first pan-Asian faith," see Arthur Cotterell, *Asia: A Concise History* (Singapore: Wiley, 2011), 126–135.

16. As the noted scholar of Indian Buddhism Gregory Schopen has argued, scholars of Buddhism need to take history—"including documents, decrees, edicts, ordinances, law

codes... and the economy"—seriously if Buddhist studies "is ever to be anything other than the intellectual backwater that it now seems to be." Gregory Schopen, "The Cheshire Cat, the Queen of Hearts, and New Directions in Buddhist Studies," Keynote Lecture at the 2012 Graduate Student Conference in Buddhist Studies, University of Virginia, accessed April 15, 2013, https://www.youtube.com/watch?v=6JRz2a0lzDM.

1. BECOMING BUDDHIST

1. D. Sinor, Geng Shimin, and Y. I. Kychanov, "The Uighurs, the Kyrgyz and the Tangut (eighth to the thirteenth century)," in *History of Civilizations of Central Asia*, volume 4, ed. I. Iskender-Mochiri (Paris: UNESCO, 1998), 203.
2. Gérard Fussman, "Upāya-kauśalya: l'implantation du bouddhisme au Gandhāra," in *Bouddhisme et cultures local. Quelques cas de réciproques adaptations*, ed. Fukui Fumimasa and Gérard Fussman (Paris: École Française d'Extrême-Orient, 1994), 17-51.
3. Jens Wilkens, "Buddhismus bei den türkischen Völkern in Zentralasien," in *Der Buddhismus II: Theravāda-Buddhismus und Tibetischer Buddhismus*, ed. Manfred Hutter (Stuttgart: Kohlhammer 2016), 470.
4. On these two scholarly suppositions see Johan Elverskog, *Uygur Buddhist Literature* (Turnhout: Brepols, 1997), 8-9; Takao Moriyasu, *Die Geschichte des uigurischen Manichäismus an der Seidenstraße: Forschungen zu manichäischen Quellen und ihrem geschichtlichen Hintergrund*, trans. Christian Steineck (Wiesbaden: Harrassowitz, 2004), 149-192.
5. What is actually meant by "the language of the Turks [Ch. Tujue]" has been much debated; if such a translation was actually prepared it was probably done in Sogdian, the lingua franca of Inner Asia and the Silk Road. Liu Mau-Tsai, *Die chinesischen Nachrichten zur Geschichte der Ost-Türken (T'u-Küe)*, 2 vols. (Wiesbaden: Harrassowitz, 1958), 34.
6. Edouard Chavannes, *Documents sur les Tou-kiue (Turcs) occidentaux* (Saint Petersburg: Academie Imperiale des Sciences, 1903), 301.
7. Annemarie von Gabain, "Buddhistische Türkenmission," in *Asiatica: Festschrift Friedrich Weller zum 65. Geburtstag*, ed. J. Schubert and U. Schneider (Leipzig: Harrassowitz, 1954), 161-173; Hilda Ecsedy, "Trade-and-War Relations between the Turks and China in the Second Half of the 6th Century," *Acta Orientalia Academiae Scientiarum Hungaricae* 21 (1968): 131-180; Peter Zieme, *Religion und Gesellschaft im Uigurischen Königreich* (Opladen: Westdeutscher Verlag, 1992), 10-12.
8. Hao Chen, *A History of the Second Türk Empire (ca. 682–745A.D.)* (Leiden: Brill, 2021).
9. Walther Fuchs, "Huei-ch'ao's Pilgerreise durch Nordwest-Indien und Zentral-Asien um 726," *Sitzungsberichte der Preußischen Akademie der Wissenschaften* 30 (1938): 30.
10. On the importance of ruling Ötükän for Inner Asian steppe empires see Thomas T. Allsen, "Spiritual Geography and Political Legitimacy in the Eastern Steppe," in *Ideology and the Formation of Early States*, ed. H.J. M. Claessen and J. G. Oosten (Leiden: Brill, 1996), 116-135; Jens Wilkens, "Ein Bildnis der Göttin Ötükän," in *Studies in Turkic Philology: Festschrift in Honour of the 80th Birthday of Professor Geng Shimin*, ed. Zhang Dingjing and Abdurishid Yakup (Beijing: China Minzu University Press, 2009), 449-461.
11. Tayeb El-Hibri, *Reinterpreting Islamic Historiography: Harun al-Rashid and the Narrative of the 'Abbasid Caliphate* (New York: Cambridge University Press, 1999), 8.

1. Becoming Buddhist

12. Nicola Di Cosmo, "Maligned Exchanges: The Uyghur-Tang Trade in the Light of Climate Data," in *Texts and Transformations: Essays in Honor of the 75th Birthday of Victor H. Mair*, ed. Haun Saussy (Amherst, MA: Cambria Press, 2018), 117-136.
13. Christopher I. Beckwith, "The Impact of the Horse and Silk Trade on the Economies of Tang China and the Uighur Empire: On the Importance of International Commerce in the Early Middle Ages," *Journal of the Economic and Social History of the Orient* 34 (1991): 183-198.
14. Larry V. Clark, "The Conversion of Bügü Khan to Manichaism," in *Studia Manichaica. IV*, ed. R. E. Emmerick, W. Sunderman, and P. Zieme (Berlin: Berlin-Brandenburgische Akademie der Wissenschaften, 2000), 82-123.
15. Xavier Tremblay, *Pour une histoire de la Sérinde. Le manichéisme parmi les peuples et religions d'Asie Centrale d'après les sources primaires* (Wien: Verlag der Österreichischen Akademie der Wissenschaften, 2001), 116.
16. Gustavo Benavides, "Buddhism, Manichaeism, Markets and Empires," in *Hellenisation, Empire, and Globalisation: Lessons from Antiquity*, ed. Luther H. Martin and Panayotis Pachis (Thessaloniki: Vanias Publications, 2004), 34.
17. Étienne de la Vaissière, *Sogdian Traders: A History*, trans. James Ward (Leiden: Brill, 2005).
18. This is, of course, the interpretation found in Manichean sources and is also echoed in later Muslim sources (see, for example, 'Ala-ad-Din 'Ata-Malik Juvaini, *The History of the World Conqueror*, trans. John A. Boyle [Manchester: Manchester University Press, 1958], vol. 1, 58). On Külüg Bilga Khan's conversion, including an important re-evaluation of its history, see Clark, "The Conversion of Bügü Khan," 82-123.
19. Colin Mackerras, *The Uighur Empire according to the T'ang Dynastic Histories: A Study in Sino-Uighur Relations 744–840* (Columbia: University of South Carolina Press, 1972), 10.
20. Takao Moriyasu, "Introduction à l'histoire de Ouïghours et de leurs relations avec le Manichéisme et le Bouddhisme," in *Shiruku Rōdo to sekaishe* [World history reconsidered through the Silk Road] (Osaka: Osaka University, 2003), 24-38.
21. Morris Rossabi, "The Silk Trade in China and Central Asia," in *When Silk Was Gold: Central Asian and Chinese Textiles*, ed. James C.Y. Watt and Anne E. Wardwell (New York: The Metropolitan Museum of Art, 1997), 9.
22. In 821-22 the Tibetans and Tang made an alliance, which is known from a stela in Lhasa. János Szerb, "A Note on the Tibetan-Uigur Treaty of 822/23 A.D," in *Contributions on Tibetan Language, History and Culture*, ed. E. Steinkellner (Wien: Arbeitskreis für Tibetische und Buddhistische Studien, 1983), 375-386.
23. Philip Jenkins, "Climate Shocks and the Fate of Empires (and of World Religions)," https://patheos.com/blogs/anxiousbench/2022/-2/climate-shocks-and-the-fate-of-empires-and-of-world-religions/.
24. On this group of Uyghurs see Michael R. Drompp, "The Uighur-Chinese Conflict of 840-848," in *Warfare in Inner Asian History (500–1800)*, ed. Nicola Di Cosmo (Leiden: Brill, 2002), 73-104; Michael R. Drompp, *Tang China and the Collapse of the Uighur Empire: A Documentary History* (Leiden: Brill, 2005). See also Christopher P. Atwood, "The Notion of Tribe in Medieval China: Ouyang Xiu and the Shatou Dynastic Myth," in

Miscellanea Asiatica: Festschrift in Honour of Françoise Aubin, ed. Denise Aigle et al. (Sankt Augustin: Steyler Verlag, 2010), 593-621.
25. On this group of Uyghurs see Elisabeth Pinks, Die Uiguren von Kan-chou in der frühen Sung-Zeit (960–1028) (Wiesbaden: Otto Harrassowitz, 1968).
26. Takao Moriyasu, "Qui des Ouigours ou des Tibétaines ont gagné en 789-792 à Bešbalïq?" Journal asiatique 269, no. 1-2 (1981): 193-205.
27. Nicholas Sims-Williams and James Hamilton, Turco-Sogdian Documents from 9th–10th century Dunhuang (London: Corpus Inscriptionum Iranicum and School of Oriental and African Studies, 2015), 75-76.
28. Arthur Waley, A Catalogue of Paintings Recovered from Tun-huang by Sir Aurel Stein, K.C.I.E. Preserved in the Sub-Department of Oriental Prints and Drawings in the British Museum, and in the Museum of Central Asian Antiquities, Delhi (London: Trustees of the British Museum, 1931), 317.
29. Rong Xinjiang. "The Relationship of Dunhuang with the Uighur Kingdom in the Tenth Century," in De Dunhuang à Istanbul: Hommage à James Russell Hamilton, ed. L. Bazin and P. Zieme (Turnhout: Brepols, 2001), 276.
30. For a list of the tribute missions sent by Guiyijun to Song and Liao between 924 and 1023 see Fujieda Akira, "Sha-shū Kigi-gun setsudoshi shimatsu," Tōhō Gakuhō 13 (1942): 48-51.
31. On the Tsongkha see Tsutomu Iwasaki, "The Tibetan Tribes of Ho-hsi and Buddhism during the Northern Sung Period," Acta Asiatica 64 (1993): 17-37; Bianca Horlemann, Aufsteig und Niedergang der Tsong Kha-Stammeskonföderation im 11./12. Jahrhundert an der Schnittstelle von Tibet, China, und Zentralasien (Frankfurt: Peter Lang, 2004); Bianca Horlemann, "The Relations of the Eleventh-Century Tsong Kha Tribal Confederation to Its Neighbour States on the Silk Road," in Contributions to the Early History of Tibet, ed. M. T. Kapstein and B. Dotson (Leiden: Brill, 2007), 83-106.
32. Saguchi Tōru, "Historical Development of the Sarïgh Uyghurs," Memoirs of the Research Department of the Toyo Bunko 44 (1986): 1-21; Larry V. Clark, "The Early Turkic and Sarig Yugur Counting Systems," in Turfan, Khotan und Dunhuang, ed. R. E. Emmerick et al. (Berlin: BBAW Akademie Verlag, 1996), 18-49.
33. Michal Biran, The Empire of the Qara Khitai in Eurasian History: Between China and the Islamic World (New York: Cambridge University Press, 2005), 15.
34. Yukiyo Kasai, "Uyghur Legitimation and the Role of Buddhism," in Buddhism in Central Asia I: Patronage, Legitimation, Sacred Space, and Pilgrimage, ed. C. Meinert and H. H. Sørensen (Leiden: Brill, 2020), 61-90; Lilla Russell-Smith, Uygur Patronage in Dunhuang: Regional Art Centres on the Northern Silk Road in the Tenth and Eleventh Centuries (Leiden: Brill, 2005).
35. According to Chinese sources, in 934 eight Manichaean priests came to the court with goods; in 951 Manichaean priests came with jade and cotton; moreover, in "the second month of the first year of the Guangshun Era, [951], of the Zhou Dynasty, the Uyghurs dispatched an ambassador and a Manichaean priest with a tribute of 77 uncut blocks of jade, white cotton cloth, marten furs, yak tails and medicines" (Moriyasu, Die Geschichte des uigurischen Manichäismus, 185).
36. In 965 a Uyghur Buddhist monk presented a tooth relic of the Buddha to the Song court (Pinks, Die Uiguren von Kan-chou, 123-124).

180   1. Becoming Buddhist

37. Larry V. Clark, *Uygur Manichaean Texts: Texts, Translations, Commentary* vol. III (Turnhout: Brepols, 2017), 362.
38. "Several surviving caves in Turfan, including cave 38 at Bezeklik, bear witness to this shift: close examination of the cave walls shows that the caves had two layers, often a Manichaean layer (not always visible) lies beneath a Buddhist layer" (Werner Sundermann, "Completion and Correction of Archaeological Work by Philological Means: The Case of the Turfan Texts," in *Histoire et cultes de l'Asie centrale préislamique*, ed. Paul Bernard and Frantz Grenet (Paris: Editions du Centre National de la Recherche Scientifique, 1991), 283-289; Moriyasu, *Die Geschichte des uigurischen Manichäismus*, 1-38; Zsuzsanna Gulásci, *Mani's Pictures: The Didactic Images of the Manichaeans from Sasanian Mesopotamia to Uygur Central Asia and Tang-Ming China* (Leiden: Brill, 2015), 229-233.
39. As Matsui has noted in his study of a temple's account book, by the end of the tenth century one Manichaean temple housed 46 Manichaeans and 100 Buddhist monks. Moreover, not only did the Manichaeans not get the "King's donation" (*ilig labï*), but while the Buddhists received 500 *quanpu* as a donation, the Manichaeans only received 90. Dai Matsui, "An Old Uigur Account Book for Manichaean and Buddhist Monasteries from Temple α in Qočo," in *Zur lichten Heimat: Studien zu Manichäismus, Iranistik und Zentralasienkunder im Gedenken an Werner Sundermann*, ed. Team Turfanforschung (Wiesbaden: Harrassowitz, 2017), 409-419.
40. Werner Sundermann, "A Manichaean Liturgical Instruction on the Act of Almsgiving," in *The Light and the Darkness: Studies in Manichaeism and Its World*, ed. P. Mirecki and J. BeDuhn (Leiden: Brill, 2001), 200-208. On the specifically Dunhuang celebration of the Buddha's renouncement of worldly life on the eighth day of the second month see: Éric Trombert, "La fête du 8ème jour du 2ème mois à Dunhuang a'après les comptes de monastères," in *De Dunhuang au Japon: Etudes chinoises et bouddhiques offertes à M. Soymié*, ed. J.-P. Drège (Genève: Droz, 2000), 25-72; F. Wang-Toutain, "Le sacre du printemps: les cérémonies bouddhiques de 8e du 2e mois," in *De Dunhuang au Japon: Etudes chinoises et bouddhiques offertes à M. Soymié*, ed. J.-P. Drège (Genève: Droz, 2000), 25-72.
41. Clark, *Uygur Manichaean Texts*, 109.
42. Larry V. Clark, "The Manichean Pothi-Book," *Altorientalische Forschungen* 9 (1982): 159.
43. The nature of the West Uyghur Kingdom's control of Dunhuang is debated; while Chinese scholars claim that the Uyghurs fully controlled Dunhuang, Takao Moriyasu argues it was not direct control ("The Sha-chou Uighurs and the West Uighur Kingdom," *Acta Asiatica* 78 [2000]: 28-48).
44. Gabain, *Das Leben im uigurischen Königreich*, 19.
45. The question of the Sogdian influence on early Uyghur Buddhism has been much debated. For a summary of the Laut-Moriyasu debate about this issue see Xavier Tremblay, "The Spread of Buddhism in Serindia—Buddhism among Iranians, Tocharians and Turks before the 13th century," in *The Spread of Buddhism*, ed. Ann Heirman and Stephan Peter Bumbacher (Leiden: Brill, 2007), 75-130. More recently the general consensus has it that there was a Sogdian influence in terms of language and especially art. Jens Wilkens, "Buddhism in the West Uyghur Kingdom and Beyond," in *Transfer of Buddhism across Central Asian Networks (7th to 13th Centuries)*, ed. Carmen Meinart (Leiden: Brill, 2016), 207.

46. Dieter Maue, "Three Languages on One Leaf: On IOL Toch 81 with Special Regard to the Turkic Part," *Bulletin of the School of Oriental and African Studies* 71, no. 1 (2008): 59-73.
47. J. U. Hartmann, K. Wille, and P. Zieme, "Indrasenas Beichte: Ein Sanskrit-Texte in uigurischer Schrift aus Turfan," *Berliner Indologische Studien* 9/10 (1996): 203-216; Niu Ruji and Peter Zieme, "The Buddhist Refuge Formula: An Uigur Manuscript from Dunhuang," *Türk Dilleri Araştırmaları* 6 (1996): 41-56; Dieter Maue, "The Equanimity of the Tathāgata," in *Aspects of Research into Central Asian Buddhism: In Memoriam Kogi Kudara*, ed. Peter Zieme (Turnout: Brepols, 2008), 179-190; Dieter Maue, "Uigurisches in Brāhmī in nicht-uigurischen Brāhmī-Handschriften," *Acta Orientalia Academiae Scientiarum Hungaricae* 62, no. 1 (2009): 1-36; Dieter Maue, "Uigurisches in Brāhmī in nicht-uigurischen Brāhmī-Handschriften Teil II," *Acta Orientalia Academiae Scientiarum Hungaricae* 63, no. 3 (2011): 319-361; Dieter Maue and Niu Ruji, "80 TBI 774 b: A Sanskrit-Uigur Bilingual Text from Bezeklik," *Studies on the Inner Asian Languages* 27 (2012): 43-92.
48. Durdu Fedakar, "Das Alttürkische in sogdischer Schrift: Textmaterial und Orthographie (Teil I)," *Ural-Altaische Jahrbücher* NF 10 (1991): 85-98; Durdu Fedakar, "Das Alttürkische in sogdischer Schrift: Textmaterial und Orthographie (Teil II)," *Ural-Altaische Jahrbücher* NF 13 (1991): 133-157; Z. Özertural and M. Knüppel, "Die uigurischen Texte in sogdischer Schrift und die Vermittlung der sogdischen Schreibkultur an die Uiguren," *Ural-Altaische Jahrbücher* NF 18 (2003/4): 148-160; Yutaka Yoshida, "Die buddhistischen sogdischen Texte in der Berliner Turfansammlung und die Herkunft des buddhistischen sogdischen Wortes für Bodhisattva," *Acta Orientalia Academiae Scientiarum Hungaricae* 61, no. 3 (2008): 325-358; Yutaka Yoshida, "Turco-Sogdian Features," *Iranica* 17 (2009): 571-586; Georges-Jean Pinault, "Le tokharien pratiqué par les Ouïgours. À propos d'un fragment en tokharien A du Musée Guimet," in *Études de Dunhuang et Turfan*, ed. Jean-Pierre Drège and Olivier Venture (Genève: Droz, 2007), 327-366; Michaël Peyrot, Georges-Jean Pinault, and Jens Wilkens, "Vernaculars of the Silk Road—A Tocharian B-Old Uyghur Bilingual," *Journal Asiatique* 301, no. 1 (2019): 65-90.
49. D. Maue and K. Röhrborn, "Ein buddhistischer Katechismus in alttürkischer Sprache und tibetischer Schrift (Teil I)," *Zeitschrift der Deutschen Morgenländischen Gesellschaft* 134 (1984): 286-313; D. Maue and K. Röhrborn, "Ein buddhistischer Katechismus in alttürkischer Sprache und tibetischer Schrift (Teil II)," *Zeitschrift der Deutschen Morgenländischen Gesellschaft* 135 (1985): 68-91; T. Moriyasu, "Étude sur un catéchisme boudhique ouigour en écriture tibétaine (P.t. 1292)," *Memoirs of the Faculty of Letters, Osaka University* 25 (1985): 1-85; Dieter Maue, *Alttürkische Handschriften Teil 1: Dokumente in Brāhmī und Tibetischer Schrift* (Stuttgart: Franz Steiner Verlag, 1996).
50. On the use of Tibetan as a lingua franca in the Tarim Basin until the beginning of the eleventh century see Géza Uray, "L'emploi du tibétain dans les chancelleries des états du Kan-sou et de Khotan postérieurs à la domination tibétaine," *Journal asiatique* 269 (1981): 81-90; Tsuguhito Takeuchi, "Sociolinguistic Implications of the Use of Tibetan in East Turkestan from the End of Tibetan Domination through the Tangut Period (9th-12th c.)," in *Turfan Revisited: The First Century of Research into the Arts and Cultures of*

the Silk Road, ed. D. Durkin-Meistererernst et al. (Berlin: Dietrich Reimer Verlag, 2004), 341-348.
51. Sam van Schaik, "Tibetan Buddhism in Central Asia: Geopolitics and Group Dynamics," in *Transfer of Buddhism Across Central Asian Networks (7th to 13th Centuries)*, ed. Carmen Meinert (Leiden: Brill, 2016), 72-73. See also F. W. Thomas and G. L. M. Clauson, "A Second Chinese Buddhist Text in Tibetan Characters," *Journal of the Royal Asiatic Society* 2 (1927): 281-306.
52. On the manuscript evidence of Uyghurs using the Chinese language see Imre Galambos, "Non-Chinese Influence in Medieval Chinese Manuscript Culture," in *Frontiers and Boundaries: Encounters on China's Margins*, ed. Zsombor Rajkai and Ildikó Bellér-Hann (Wiesbaden: Harrassowitz Verlag, 2012), 72-86.
53. Clark, *Uygur Manichaean Texts*, 362.
54. Takao Moriyasu, "Uighur Buddhist Stake Inscriptions from Turfan," in *De Dunhuang à Istanbul: Hommage à James Russell Hamilton*, ed. Louis Bazin and Peter Zieme (Turnhout: Brepols, 2001), 162-164.
55. On the history of the Qarakhanids see Peter B. Golden, "The Karakhanids and Early Islam," in *The Cambridge History of Early Inner Asia*, ed. Denis Sinor (New York: Cambridge University Press, 1990), 343-370; E. O. Davidovich, "The Karakhanids," in *History of Civilizations of Central Asia, vol. IV: The Age of Achievement: AD 750 to the end of the fifteenth century*, ed. M. S. Asimov and C. E. Bosworth (Paris: UNESCO, 1998), 119-144; Jeff Eden, *Warrior Saints of the Silk Road: Legends of the Qarakhanids* (Leiden: Brill, 2019), 1-19.
56. C. E. Bosworth, *The Ghaznavids: Their Empire in Afghanistan and Eastern Iran 994–1040* (Edinburgh: Edinburgh University Press, 1963), 4-23.
57. Maḥmūd al-Kāšγarī, *Compendium of the Turkic Languages (Diwan Lugat at-Turk) Volume 1*, ed. and trans. Robert Dankoff and James Kelly (Cambridge, MA: Harvard University Press, 1982), 270. Although this poem describes an attack on the Uyghurs, it most likely actually refers to the Qarakhanid conquest of Khotan; see Robert Dankoff, "Three Turkic Verse Cycles Relating to Inner Asian Warfare," *Harvard Ukranian Studies* 3-4, no. 1 (1979-80): 161.
58. al-Kāšγarī, *Compendium of the Turkic Languages*, vol. 2, 271-272.
59. al-Kāšγarī, *Compendium of the Turkic Languages*, vol. 1, 327.
60. On the stereotype of Buddhist-Muslim interaction as solely involving the Muslim destruction of Buddhism—and its historiographical implications—see Johan Elverskog, *Buddhism and Islam on the Silk Road* (Philadelphia: University of Pennsylvania Press, 2010), 1-11.
61. Peter B. Golden, "The Migrations of the *Oguz*," *Archivum Ottomanicum* 4 (1972): 78-80.
62. On the Islamic response to this Turkic invasion see David Cook, *Studies in Muslim Apocalyptic* (Princeton, NJ: The Darwin Press, 2002), 84-91.
63. S. Vryonis, Jr., *The Decline of Medieval Hellenism in Asia Minor and the Process of Islamization from the Eleventh through the Fifteenth Century* (Berkeley: University of California Press, 1971), 70-120.
64. The classic treatment of this phenomenon is Joseph Fletcher, "Turco-Mongolian Monarchic Tradition in the Ottoman Empire," in *Eucharisterion: Essays Presented to*

Omeljan Pritsak, ed. I. Sevcenko and F. E. Sysyn (Cambridge, MA: Ukrainian Research Institute, 1979-1980), 237-242.
65. Vladimir Minorsky, *Sharaf al-Zaman Tahir Marvazi on China, the Turks and India* (London: The Royal Asiatic Society, 1942), 20-21.
66. On the history of Manichaeism see Samuel N.C. Lieu, *Manichaeism in the Later Roman Empire and Medieval China* (Tübingen: J. C. B. Mohr, 1992). On Manichean religious practices see Jason BeDuhn, *The Manichaean Body: In Discipline and Ritual* (Baltimore: Johns Hopkins University Press, 2000).
67. Nicholas Sims-Williams, "The Manichaean Commandments: A Survey of the Sources," in *Papers in Honour of Professor Mary Boyce* (Acta Iranica 25) (Leiden: E. J. Brill, 1985), 573-582.
68. Iris Colditz, "Manichaean Time-Management: Laymen between Religious and Secular Duties," in *New Light on Manichaeism: Papers from the Sixth International Congress on Manichaeism*, ed. Jason D. BeDuhn (Leiden: Brill, 2009), 73-99.
69. Gulácsi, *Mani's Pictures*, 166.
70. Colditz, "Manichaean Time-Management," 81-88.
71. Jason BeDuhn, "The Metabolism of Salvation: Manichaean Concepts of Human Physiology," in *The Light and the Darkness: Studies in Manichaeism and Its World*, ed. P. Mirecki and J. BeDuhn (Leiden: Brill, 2001), 36, 15.
72. BeDuhn, "The Metabolism of Salvation," 17.
73. BeDuhn, "The Metabolism of Salvation," 34.
74. "High priests... lived in luxury. They owned land with peasantry, held servants or slaves, used expensive carpets and furniture, wore luxurious clothes, kept private rooms, and took sumptuous meals.... Their lifestyle was far different from what is prescribed in the 'Compendium of the Doctrine and Styles of Mani, the Prophet of Light.'" Takao Moriyasu, "The West Uighur Kingdom and Tun-huang around the 10th-11th Centuries." *Berichte und Abhandlungen: Berlin-Brandenburgische Akademie der Wissenschaften* 8 (2000): 346-347.
75. Moriyasu, *Die Geschichte des uigurischen Manichäismus*, 51, 117-118.
76. Clark, *Uygur Manichaean Texts*, 348.
77. Clark, *Uygur Manichaean Texts*, 398.
78. Zsuzsanna Gulácsi, "The Manichaean Roots of a Pure Land Banner from Kocho (III 4524) in the Asian Art Museum, Berlin," in *Language, Society, and Religion in the World of the Turks: Festschrift for Larry Clark at Seventy-Five*, ed. Zsuzsanna Gulácsi (Turnhout: Brepols, 2018), 187-204; Juten Oda, "On Manichaean Expressions in the *Säkiz yükmäk yaruq*," in *Splitter aus der Gegend Turfan: Festschrift für Peter Zieme anläßlich seines 60. Geburtstags*, ed. Mehmet Ölmez and Simone-Christiane Raschmann (Istanbul: Şafak Matbaacilik, 2002), 179-198.
79. Werner Sunderman, "Manichaeism Meets Buddhism: The Problem of Buddhist Influence on Manichaeism," in *Bauddhavidyāsudhākarah: Studies in Honour of H. Bechert on the Occasion of His 65th Birthday*, ed. P. Kieffer-Pülz and J.-U. Hartmann (Swisttal-Odendorf, 1997), 647-656. See also Claudia Weber, *Buddhistische Beichten in Indien und bei den Uiguren* (Wiesbaden: Harrassowitz Verlag, 1999); Aloïs van Tongerloo, "The Buddha's First Encounter in a Manichaean Old Turkic Text," in *Il Manicheismo Nuove Prospettive Della*

Rechercha: Dipartimento Di Studi Asiatica Università Degli Studi Di Napoli "L'Orientale." Napoli, 2–8 Settembre 2001, ed. Aloïs van Tongerloo and Luigi Cirillo (Turnhout: Brepols, 2005), 385-396.

80. Among the Qarakhanids the Manicheans' literacy enabled them to establish a Sogdian-based chancellery before the court fully adopted the Arabic script for the writing of Turkic. Larry V. Clark, "The Turkic Script and the *Kutadgu Bilig*," in *Turkologie in Mainz*, ed. H Boeschoten and J. Rentzsch (Wiesbaden: Harrassowitz, 2010), 89-106.

81. Megan Bryson, "The Great Kingdom of Eternal Peace: Buddhist Kingship in Tenth-Century Dali," *Asia Major* 32, no. 1 (2019): 87-111.

82. Sem Vermeersch, "Buddhism and State-Building in Song China and Goryeo Korea," *Asia Pacific Perspectives* 1, no. 1 (2004): 4-11.

83. Mikael S. Adolphson, *The Gates of Power: Monks, Courtiers, and Warriors in Premodern Japan* (Honolulu: University of Hawai'i Press, 2000).

84. Ronald M. Davidson, *Tibetan Renaissance: Tantric Buddhism in the Rebirth of Tibetan Culture* (New York: Columbia University Press, 2005), 86-92.

85. Huang Chi-Chiang, "Imperial Rulership and Buddhism in the Early Northern Song," in *Imperial Rulership and Cultural Change in Traditional China*, ed. F. P. Brandauer and Chun-Chieh Huang (Seattle: University of Washington Press, 1994), 144-187.

86. Jiang Wu, Lucille Chia, and Chen Zhichao, "The Birth of the First Printed Canon: The Kaibao Edition and Its Impact," in *Spreading Buddha's Word in East Asia: The Formation and Transformation of the Chinese Buddhist Canon*, ed. Jiang Wu and Lucille Chia (New York: Columbia University Press, 2016), 170.

87. Jan Yün-hua, "Buddhist Relations between India and Sung China," *History of Religions* 6, no. 1 (1966): 24-42; 6, no. 2 (1966): 135-168. See also Rong Xinjiang, "Cultural Contacts between China and India from the Late Tang to the Early Song in Light of the Dunhuang Manuscripts," in *The Silk Road and Cultural Exchanges between East and West*, ed. Sally K. Church (Leiden: Brill, 2022), 152-186.

88. Kōichi Kitsudō, "Liao Influence on Uigur Buddhism," in *Studies in Chinese Manuscripts: From the Warring States to the 20th Century*, ed. Imre Galambos (Budapest: Institute of East Asian Studies, Eotvos Lorand University, 2013), 243.

89. On Uyghur pilgrimages to the renowned pagodas built by the Khitans see Simone-Christiane Raschmann, "Pilgrims in Old Uyghur Inscriptions: A Glimpse Behind the Records," in *Buddhism in Central Asia I: Patronage, Legitimation, Sacred Space, and Pilgrimage*, ed. C. Meinert and H. H. Sørensen (Leiden: Brill, 2020), 211. On the Khitan pagodas see Nancy S. Steinhardt, *Liao Architecture* (Honolulu: University of Hawai'i Press, 1997).

90. See the essays collected in the special issue "Perspectives on the Liao," ed. Valerie Hansen, François Louis, and Daniel Kane, *Journal of Song-Yuan Studies* 43 (2013): 1-412.

91. Mimi Yiengpruksawan, "A Pavilion for Amitabha: Yorimichi's Phoenix Hall in Transcultural Perspective," in *Buddhist Transformations and Interactions: Essays in Honor of Antonino Forte*, ed. Victor H. Mair (Amherst, MA: Cambria Press, 2017), 401-516.

92. Masahiro Shōgaito, *The Uighur Abhidharmakośabhāṣya preserved at the Museum of Ethnography in Stockholm* (Wiesbaden: Harrassowitz, 2014), 27.

93. Kitsudō, "Liao Influence on Uigur Buddhism," 240-245.

94. Ding Wang, "Ch 3586—ein khitanisches Fragment mit uigurischen Glossen in der Berlin Turfansammlung," in *Turfan Revisited: The First Century of Research into the Arts and Cultures of the Silk Road*, ed. D. Durkin-Meistererernst et al. (Berlin: Dietrich Reimer Verlag, 2004), 371-379.
95. Kirill J. Solonin, "The Glimpses of Tangut Buddhism," *Central Asiatic Journal* 52, no. 1 (2008): 64-127, 70. On Liao Buddhism see Henrik H. Sørensen, "Esoteric Buddhism Under the Liao," in *Esoteric Buddhism and the Tantras in East Asia*, ed. C. D. Orzech et al. (Leiden: Brill, 2011), 456-464; Kirill J. Solonin, "Buddhist Connections between the Liao and Xixia: Preliminary Considerations," *Journal of Song-Yuan Studies* 43 (2013): 171-219.
96. Susan Whitfield, "A Place of Safekeeping? The Vicissitudes of the Bezeklik Murals," in *Conservation of the Ancient Sites on the Silk Road*, ed. Neville Agnew (Los Angeles: Getty Conservation Institute, 2010), 95-106.
97. Fortunately, before these murals were destroyed they were photographed and published in large folio format in A. von Le Coq's *Chotscho: Facsimile-Wiedergaben der wichtigeren Funde der ersten Königlich Preussischen Expedition nach Turfan in Ost-Turkistan* (Berlin: Dietrich Reimer, 1913).
98. Y. Okada and S. Sakamoto, "Virtual reconstruction of the Bezeklik Wall Paintings," in *Rongshe yu chuangxin: Guoji Dunhuang xiangmu di liu cihui yilun wenji (Tradition and Innovation: Proceedings of the 6th IDP Conservation Conference)*, ed. Shitian Lin and A. Morrison (Beijing: Beijing tushuguan chubanshe, 2007), 259-263.
99. Kōichi Kitsudō, "Historical Significance of Bezeklik cave 20 in the Uygur Buddhism," in *Buddhism and Art in Turfan: From the Perspective of Uyghur Buddhism*, ed. Irisawa Takashi (Kyoto: Research Center for Buddhist Culture in Asia Ryukoku University, 2012), 141-152.
100. Takao Moriyasu, "L'origine du bouddhisme chez les Turcs et l'apparition des textes bouddhiques en turc ancient," in *Documents et archives provenant de l'Asie Centrale. Actes du Colloque Franco-Japonais*, ed. Akira Haneda (Kyoto: Dohosha, 1990), 150-151.
101. Juten Oda, *A Study of the Buddhist Sutra Säkiz Yükmäk Yaruq or Säkiz Törlügin Yarumïš Yaltrïmïš in Old Turkic* (Turnhout: Brepols, 2015).
102. On these three works see Elverskog, *Uygur Buddhist Literature*, Nos. 34, 36, 58; and more recently Peter Zieme, "Old Turkish Versions of the 'Scripture on the Ten Kings,'" in *Proceedings of the 38th PIAC, Kawasaki, Japan: August 7–12, 1995*, ed. Giovanni Stary (Wiesbaden: Harrassowitz, 1996), 401-425; Simone-Christiane Raschmann, "The Old Turkish Fragments of the Scripture on the Ten Kings (Shiwangjing) in the Collection of the Institute of Oriental Manuscripts, RAS," in *Dunhuang Studies: Prospects for the Coming Second Century of Research*, ed. I. F. Popova and Liu Yi (St. Petersburg: Slavia, 2012), 209-216.
103. On these three works see Elverskog, *Uygur Buddhist Literature*, Nos. 13, 23, 81. The other two texts are an unidentified commentarial text (Yukiyo Kasai, "Ein Kommentar zu einem unbekannten uigurisch-buddhistischen Text, der aus dem Tocharischen übersetzt wurde," *Studies on the Inner Asian Languages* 21 [2006]: 21-47), and the so-called "Idiyut Text," which is a conversation between a master and a pupil about the unworthiness of worldly affairs and possessions and the importance of striving for buddhahood.

Peter Zieme, "An Old Uigur Idiyut Text," in *The History behind the Languages: Essays of Turfan Forum on Old Languages of the Silk Road*, ed. Academia Turfanica (Shanghai: Shanghai Guji Chubanshe, 2000), 1–12.

2. BUDDHIST POLITICS

1. Sheldon Pollock, "Axialism and Empire," in *Axial Civilizations and World History*, ed. Johann P. Arnason, S. N. Eisenstadt, and Björn Wittrock (Leiden: Brill, 2005), 400. Some of this failure can no doubt be attributed to the fact that the Buddha, or at least the early corpus of Buddhist texts, does not engage with any of the political theories that animated axial age India. George Erdosy, "City States of North India and Pakistan at the Time of the Buddha," in *The Archaeology of Early Historic South Asia: The Emergence of Cities and States*, ed. F. R. Allchin (New York: Cambridge University Press, 1995), 116. On the non-Buddhist orientation of the Śungas, Satavahanas, and Kushans see Kathleen D. Morrison, "Trade, Urbanism, and Agricultural Expansion: Buddhist Monastic Institutions and the State in Early Historic Western Deccan," *World Archaeology* 27, no. 2 (1995): 203–221; and Gérard Fussman, "Kushan Power and the Expansion of Buddhism Beyond the Soleiman Mountains," in *Kushan Histories: Literary Sources and Selected Papers from a Symposium at Berlin, December 5 to 7, 2013*, ed. Harry Falk (Bremen: Hempen Verlag, 2015), 153–202. Moreover, on the important question of whether the legendary "*cakravartin*" Aśoka was even a Buddhist, see Patrick Olivelle, "Aśoka's Inscriptions as Text and Ideology," in *Reimagining Aśoka: Memory and History*, ed. P. Olivelle, J. Leoshko, and H. P. Ray (Delhi: Oxford University Press, 2012), 157–183. For a different take—namely, that Aśoka did actually convert to Buddhism—see Nayanjot Lahiri, *Ashoka in Ancient India* (Cambridge, MA: Harvard University Press, 2015), 132–140.

2. See, for example, Heinz Bechert, *Buddhismus, Staat und Gesellschaft in den Ländern des Theravada Buddhismus* (Frankfurt: A. Metzner [vol. 1, 1966]; Wiesbaden: Harrassowitz [vol. 2, 1967; vol. 3, 1973]); Stanley J. Tambiah, *World Conqueror and World Renouncer: A Study of Buddhism and Polity in Thailand* (New York: Cambridge University Press, 1976); Antonino Forte, *Mingtang and Buddhist Utopias in the History of the Astronomical Clock: The Tower, Statue and Armillary Sphere Constructed by Empress Wu* (Rome: École Française d'Extreme-Orient, 1988); Joan Piggott, *Emergence of Japanese Kingship* (Stanford, CA: Stanford University Press, 1997); Charles D. Orzech, *Politics and Transcendent Wisdom: The Scripture of the Humane King in the Creation of Chinese Buddhism* (University Park: Pennsylvania State University Press, 1998); Craig J. Reynolds, "Power," in *Critical Terms for the Study of Buddhism*, ed. Donald S. Lopez Jr. (Chicago: University of Chicago Press, 2005), 211–228; Ian Harris, *Buddhism, Power and Political Order* (New York: Routledge, 2007); Michael L. Walter, *Buddhism and Empire: The Political and Religious Culture of Early Tibet* (Leiden: Brill, 2009); Thomas Jülch, *The Middle Kingdom and the Dharma Wheel: Aspects of the Relationship Between the Buddhist Samgha and the State in Chinese History* (Leiden: Brill, 2016); April D. Hughes, *Worldly Saviors and Imperial Authority in Medieval Chinese Buddhism* (Honolulu: University of Hawai'i Press, 2021).

3. On possible Qarakhanid attacks against the Uyghurs see Kim Hodong, "The Cult of Saints in Eastern Turkestan: The Case of Alp Ata in Turfan," in *Proceedings of the*

35th Permanent International Altaistic Conference, ed. Chieh-hsien Chen (Taipei: National Taiwan University, 1993), 209.

4. On the Turkic imperial model of a ruler being blessed by heaven see Peter B. Golden, "Imperial Ideology and the Sources of Political Unity amongst the pre-Chinggisid Nomads of Western Eurasia," *Archivum Eurasiae Medii Aevi* 2 (1982), 37-77; Peter B. Golden, "The Türk Imperial Traditional in the Pre-Chinggisid Era," in *Imperial Statecraft: Political Forms and Techniques of Governance in Inner Asia, 6th–20th Centuries*, ed. D. Sneath (Bellingham: Western Washington University Press, 2006), 42-44.

5. In fact, the Uyghur ruler is only mentioned obliquely in three extant colophons (see below).

6. On the Uyghur relations with Khotan see, for example, H. W. Bailey, "A Turkish-Khotanese Vocabulary," *Bulletin of the School of Oriental and African Studies* 11 (1944): 290-296; Valerie Hansen, "The Tribute Trade with Khotan in Light of Materials Found at the Dunhuang Library Cave," *Bulletin of the Asia Institute* 19 (2005): 37-46.

7. Renyin Day is the fifth month of the first year of the Jingde era (1004). Jichou Day is the seventh month. Takao Moriyasu, *Die Geschichte des uigurischen Manichäismus an der Seidenstraße: Forschungen zu manichäischen Quellen und ihrem geschichtlichen Hintergrund*, trans. Christian Steineck (Wiesbaden: Harrassowitz Verlag, 2004), 186-187.

8. Mariachiara Gasparini, *Transcending Patterns: Silk Road Cultural and Artistic Interactions through Central Asian Textile Images* (Honolulu: University of Hawai'i Press, 2020), 98-99.

9. Kōichi Kitsudō, "Liao Influence on Uigur Buddhism," in *Studies in Chinese Manuscripts: From the Warring States to the 20th Century*, ed. Imre Galambos (Budapest: Institute of East Asian Studies, Eotvos Lorand University, 2013), 227.

10. Annemarie von Gabain, *Das Leben im uigurischen Konigreich von Qočo: (850–1250)* (Wiesbaden: Harrassowitz, 1973), 19.

11. Kirill Solonin, "The Formation of Tangut Ideology: Buddhism and Confucianism," in *Buddhism in Central Asia I: Patronage, Legitimation, Sacred Space, and Pilgrimage*, ed. Carmen Meinert and Henrik H. Sørensen (Leiden: Brill, 2020), 132. On the Uyghur influence on Tangut Buddhism and visual culture see also Yang Fuxue 楊福學, *Huihu wenxian yu huihu wenhua* 回鶻文獻與回鶻文化 (*Uyghur Literature and Uyghur Culture*) (Beijing: Minzu chubanshe, 2003), 476; Shi-Shan Susan Huang, "Reassessing Printed Buddhist Frontispieces from Xi Xia," *Zhejiang University Journal of Art and Archaeology* 1 (2014): 140.

12. Kōichi Kitsudō and Peter Zieme, "The *Jin'gangjing zuan* in Old Uighur with Parallels in Tangut and Chinese," *Written Monuments of the Orient* 2 (2017): 43-87; Dai Matsui, "Uighur Scribble Attached to a Tangut Buddhist Fragment from Dunhuang," in *Tanguty v Czentral'noj Azii: Sbornik statej v chest' 80-letija professor E. I. Kychanova*, ed. Rossiskaja Akademija Nauk Institut Vostochnykh Rukopisej (Moscow: Rossiskaja Akademija Nauk Institut, 2012), 238-243.

13. Orzech, *Politics and Transcendent Wisdom*, 116.

14. Lilla Russell-Smith, "Stars and Planets in Chinese and Central Asian Buddhist Art in the Ninth to Fifteenth Centuries," *Culture and Cosmos* 10, no. 1-2 (2006): 99-124.

15. "Indian medicine exerted the greatest influence on the development of Old Uigur medicine. Many standard works like the *Yogaśataka* and the *Siddhasāra* were translated

into Old Uigur, either in bi-lingual [Sanskrit/Uighur in Brahmi script] editions or in Uigur alone.... As demonstrated recently by Dieter Maue, Vāgbhaṭa's *Aṣṭāṅgahṛdayasa mhitā* is attested in Old Uigur translation." Peter Zieme, "Notes on Uighur Medicine, Especially on the Uighur Siddhasāra Tradition," *Asian Medicine* 3 (2007): 309. See also Dieter Maue, "An Uighur Version of Vāgbhaṭa's *Aṣṭāṅgahṛdayasaṃhitā*," *Asian Medicine* 4 (2008): 113-173.

16. Willi Bang and Annemarie von Gabain, "Türkische Turfan-Texte I: Bruchstücke eines Wahrsagebuches," *Sitzungsberichte der Preußischen Akademie der Wissenschaften* (1929): 241- 268. On the distinctive nature of the Uyghur translation of the *Yijing* see Peter Zieme, "Chinese Classical Works in Uighur Tradition," in *Tulufan xue yanjiu: di san jie Tulufan xueji Ou-Ya youmu minzu de qiyuan yu qianxi guoji xueshu yantao huilun wenji* (Shanghai: Shanghai Guji Chubanshe, 2010), 465. For more on the Uyghur use of Chinese divinatory texts see Dai Matsui, "Uighur Almanac Divination Fragments from Dunhuang," in *Dunhuang Studies: Prospects and Problems for the Coming Second Century of Research*, ed. I Popova and Liu Yi (St. Petersburg: Slavia, 2012), 154-166; Abdurishid Yakup, "An Old Uyghur Fragment of an Astrological Treatise Kept in the Beijing National Library," in *Zur Lichten Heimat: Studien zu Manichäismus, Iranistik und Zentralasienkunde im Gedenken an Werner Sundermann*, ed. Team Turfanforschung (Wiesbaden: Harrassowitz Verlag, 2017), 711-718.

17. On "state-protecting Buddhism" see the essays in Stephanie Balkwill and James A. Benn, *Buddhism and Statecraft in East Asia* (Leiden: Brill, 2022).

18. Ruth Dunnell, "Esoteric Buddhism Under the Xixia (1038-1227)," in *Esoteric Buddhism and the Tantras in East Asia*, ed. C. D. Orzech et al. (Leiden: Brill, 2011), 468. On the importance of state protection in the Tangut realm see also Rob Linrothe, "Xia Renzong and the Patronage of Tangut Buddhist Art: The Stupa and Ushnīshavijayā Cult," *Journal of Song-Yuan Studies* 28 (1998): 91-121.

19. Mimi Hall Yiengpruksawan, *Hiraizumi: Buddhist Art and Regional Politics in Twelfth-Century Japan* (Cambridge, MA: Harvard University Asia Center, 1998), 23.

20. Yiengpruksawan, *Hiraizumi*, 24.

21. In the introductory chapter of the *Maitrisimit*, for example, the protective spirit of the realm of Qocho is mentioned together with pan-Indian deities. J. P. Laut, "Gedanken zum alttürkischen Stabreim," in *Splitter aus der Gegend von Turfan: Festschrift für Peter Zieme*, ed. Mehmet Ölmez and S. C. Raschmann (Istanbul: Ölmez, 2002), 134-135.

22. Kōichi Kitsudō, "Historical Significance of Bezeklik cave 20 in the Uygur Buddhism," in *Buddhism and Art in Turfan: From the Perspective of Uyghur Buddhism*, ed. Irisawa Takashi (Kyoto: Research Center for Buddhist Culture in Asia Ryukoku University, 2012), 148.

23. Denise P. Leidy, "Bezeklik Temple 20 and Early Esoteric Buddhism," *Silk Road Art and Archaeology* 7 (2001): 205.

24. On the cult of Avalokiteśvara among the Uyghurs see Chen Aifeng 陈爱峰, 高昌回鹘时期吐鲁番观音图研究 (*Study on Turpan Avalokiteśvara Paintings of the Qočo Uighur Period*) (Shanghai: Shanghai Guji Chubanshe, 2020); Yukiyo Kasai, "The Avalokiteśvara Cult in Turfan and Dunhuang in the Pre-Mongolian Period," in *Buddhist Rituals in Central Asia II: Practices and Rituals, Visual and Material Transfer*, ed. Yukiyo Kasai and Henrik H. Sørensen (Leiden: Brill, 2022), 246-271; Peter Zieme, György Kara, and Liliya Tugusheva,

Avalokiteśvara-Sūtras: Edition altuigurischer Übersetzungen nach Fragmenten aus Turfan und Dunhuang (Turnhout: Brepols, 2022).

25. Leidy, "Bezeklik Temple 20," 207.
26. Henrik H. Sørensen, "Esoteric Buddhism Under the Liao," in *Esoteric Buddhism and the Tantras in East Asia*, ed. C. D. Orzech et al. (Leiden: Brill, 2011), 460. This text is also found in Uyghur translation and is based on Vajrabodhi's translation, *Cuṇḍīdevīdhāraṇī* (*Foshuo qi ju di fo mu zhun ti da ming tuoluoni jing*, T. 1075), see Peter Zieme, *Magische Texte des uigurischen Buddhismus* (Turnhout: Brepols, 2005), 65-79.
27. Henrik H. Sørensen, "Astrology and the Worship of the Planets in Esoteric Buddhism of the Tang," in *Esoteric Buddhism and the Tantras in East Asia*, ed. C. D. Orzech et al. (Leiden: Brill, 2011), 239. The Tejaprabha ritual text was also translated into Uyghur (Zieme, *Magische Texte*, 81-88).
28. Yiengpruksawan, *Hiraizumi*, 167.
29. Richard von Glahn, *The Sinister Way: The Divine and the Demonic in Chinese Religious Culture* (Berkeley: University of California Press, 2004), 139-141.
30. Yiengpruksawan, *Hiraizumi*, 57.
31. Yiengpruksawan, *Hiraizumi*, 52.
32. The same artistic efflorescence is also seen in the caves excavated and refurbished at Dunhuang and Yulin in the tenth century. See, for example, Dorothy C. Wong, "A Reassessment of the Representation of Mt. Wutai from Dunhuang Cave 61," *Archives of Asian Art* 46 (1993): 27-28; Sonya S. Lee, "Repository of Ingenuity: Cave 61 and Artistic Appropriation in Tenth-Century Dunhuang," *Art Bulletin* 94, no. 2 (2012): 199-200.
33. Yiengpruksawan, *Hiraizumi*, 92.
34. L. Ju. Tuguseva, "Three Letters of Uighur Princes from the MS Collection of the Leningrad Section of the Institute of Oriental Studies," *Acta Orientalia Academiae Scientiarum Hungaricae* 24, no. 2 (1971): 173-187.
35. Larry V. Clark, *Uygur Manichaean Texts: Texts, Translations, Commentary, vol. III* (Turnhout: Brepols, 2017), 231.
36. Zhang Tieshan and Peter Zieme, "A Further Fragment of Old Uighur Annals," *Acta Orientalia Academiae Scientiarum Hungaricae* 66, no. 4 (2013): 397-410.
37. Jan Nattier, *Once Upon a Future Time: Studies in a Buddhist Prophecy of Decline* (Berkeley, CA: Asian Humanities Press, 1991), 27-63.
38. Anne M. Blackburn, "Buddhist Technologies of Statecraft and Millennial Moments," *History and Theory* 56, no. 1 (2017): 71-79, 74. On the influence of the Buddha's dispensation supposedly reaching its two-thousand-year mark in driving the large-scale transregional Buddhist projects in the Indian Ocean world during the fifteenth century see Tilman Frasch, "The Theravāda Buddhist Ecumene in the Fifteenth Century: Intellectual Foundations and Material Representations," in *Buddhism across Asia: Networks of Material, Intellectual, and Cultural Exchange, vol. 1*, ed. Tansen Sen (Singapore: Institute for Southeast Asian Studies, 2014), 347-368.
39. Maria Hsia Chang, *Falun Gong: The End of Days* (New Haven, CT: Yale University Press, 2004), 32-59; Hughes, *Worldly Saviors and Imperial Authority in Medieval Chinese Buddhism*, 35-56.

40. Alan Sponberg and Helen Hardacre, *Maitreya: The Future Buddha* (New York: Cambridge University Press, 1988).
41. James B. Apple, "Eschatology and World Order in Buddhist Formations," *Religious Studies and Theology* 29, no. 1 (2010): 118.
42. Mimi Yiengpruksawan, "A Pavilion for Amitabha: Yorimichi's Phoenix Hall in Transcultural Perspective," in *Buddhist Transformations and Interactions: Essays in Honor of Antonino Forte*, ed. Victor H. Mair (Amherst, MA: Cambria Press, 2017), 422.
43. The work in question was the *The Primary Ritual Ordinance of Mañjuśrī* (Skt. *Mañjuśrīmulakalpa*, Ch. *Wenshushili genben yigui jing*, T 1191). On the apocalyptic language of this work see Glenn Wallis, *Mediating the Power of Buddhas: Ritual in the Manjusrimulakalpa* (Albany: State University of New York Press, 2002), 106-109.
44. Mimi Yiengpruksawan, "Countdown to 1051: Some Preliminary Thoughts on the Periodization of the Buddhist Eschaton in Heian and Liao," in *Texts and Transformations: Essays in Honor of the 75th Birthday of Victor H. Mair*, ed. Haun Saussy (Amherst, MA: Cambria Press, 2018), 377.
45. Yiengpruksawan, "Countdown to 1051," 376
46. Yiengpruksawan, "A Pavilion for Amitabha," 425.
47. D. Max Moerman, "The Archaeology of Anxiety: An Underground History of Heian Religion," in *Heian Japan, Centers and Peripheries*, ed. M. Adolphson, E. Kamens, and S. Matsumoto (Honolulu: University of Hawai'i Press, 2007), 245, 260. For more on this practice and its use of Chinese products, reflecting connections across Liao-Song-Japan, see Yiwen Li, "Chinese Objects Recovered from Sutra Mounds in Japan, 1000–1300," in *Visual and Material Cultures in Middle Period China*, ed. P. B. Buckley and S. S. S. Huang (Leiden: Brill, 2017), 284-317.
48. Yiengpruksawan, "Countdown to 1051," 379.
49. Yiengpruksawan, "Countdown to 1051," 387.
50. Henrik H. Sørensen, "The Life and Times of Daozhen—A Saṃgha Leader and Monk Official in Dunhuang During the 10th Century," *Buddhist Road Papers* 5, no. 3 (2020): 10.
51. Takao Moriyasu has suggested that the Buddhist Uyghur adoption of the Maitreya cult arose from the presence of Maitreya worship in Manichaeism. I thank Yukiyo Kasai for bringing this argument to my attention.
52. On the development of the *praṇidhi* scene and its transmission to the Uyghurs see Ines Konczak, "Origin, Development and Meaning of the *Praṇidhi* Paintings on the Northern Silk Road," in *Buddhism and Art in Turfan: From the Perspective of Uyghur Buddhism*, ed. Irisawa Takashi (Kyoto: Research Center for Buddhist Culture in Asia Ryukoku University, 2012), 43-55; Ines Konczak-Nagel, *Praṇidhi-Darstellungen an der Nördlichen Seidenstraße: Das Bildmotiv der Prophezeiung der Buddhaschaft Śākyamunis in den Malereien Xinjiang* (unpublished diss., Ludwig-Maximilians-Universität, 2014).
53. Jens Peter Laut and Jens Wilkens, *Alttürkische Handschriften Teil 3: Die Handschriftenfragmente der Maitrisimit aus Sängrim und Murtuk in der Berliner Turfansammlung* (Stuttgart: Franz Steiner Verlag, 2015). For an updated bibliography of studies on the *Maitrisimit* see Jens Peter Laut, "Göttingen Üniversitesindeki Maitrisimit Projesi Üzerine," in *Beşbalıkı Şingko Şeli Tutung anısına uluslararası eski Uygurca çalıştayı bildirleri, 4–6 Haziran 2011* (Ankara: Türk Dil Kurumu, 2022), 15-18.

54. Konczak, "Origin, Development and Meaning of the Praṇidhi Paintings," 50.
55. Konczak, "Origin, Development and Meaning of the Praṇidhi Paintings," 52.
56. Moriyasu, *Die Geschichte des uigurischen Manichäismus*, 202.
57. J. J. Jones, *The Mahāvastu, vol. 3* (London: Luzac & Co., 1956), 224-250.
58. Jan Nattier, "The Meanings of the Maitreya Myth: A Typological Analysis," in *Maitreya: The Future Buddha*, ed. A. Sponberg and H. Hardacre (New York: Cambridge University Press, 1988), 29.
59. On the influence of the Faxiang school on Uyghur Buddhism at this time see Yukiyo Kasai, *Der alttürkische Kommentar zum Vimalakīrtinirdeśa-Sūtra* (Turnhout: Brepols, 2011).
60. Yukiyo Kasai, "Der Ursprung des alttürkischen Maitreya-Kults," in *Die Erforschung des Tocharischen und die alttürkische Maitrisimit*, ed. Y. Kasai, A. Yakup, D. Durkin-Meisterernst (Turnhout: Brepols, 2013), 71. See also Peter Zieme, "Zum Maitreya-Kult in uigurischen Kolophonen," *Rocznik Orientalistyczny* 49 (1994): 536-549.
61. Jens Wilkens, "Sacred Space in Uyghur Buddhism," in *Buddhism in Central Asia: Patronage, Legitimation, Sacred Space and Pilgrimage*, ed. C. Meinert and H. H. Sørensen (Leiden: Brill, 2020), 201.
62. Wilkens, "Sacred Space," 192-193.
63. In the case of China, and East Asia more broadly, there are generally six types of Buddhist legitimating strategies: 1) the ruler is hailed as a buddha; 2) the ruler is identified as a *Cakravartin*, a Wheel-Turning King of Buddhist political theory whereby legitimacy is based on promoting the Dharma; 3) drawing upon the deep well of apocalyptic thinking in the Buddhist tradition, a particular period is framed as the end times and the ruler is presented as a savior and guardian of Dharma when monks have become corrupt; 4) using the same end-times rhetoric, the ruler is identified with Maitreya, the Buddha of the Future, who will restore order; 5) building on the idea of the state as a field of Buddhist practice and salvation, the ruler is identified with the Bodhisattva Mañjuśrī; 6) in the same framework, the ruler is identified with the Bodhisattva Avalokiteśvara. Sem Vermeersch, "Who is Legitimating Whom? On Justifying Buddhism's Place in the Body Politic," in *Buddhism in Central Asia I: Patronage, Legitimation, Sacred Space, and Pilgrimage*, ed. C. Meinert and H. H. Sørensen (Leiden: Brill, 2020), 16.
64. "The Toguz Oguz Xaqan traditionally belongs to the Manichaean sect. There are, however, within his metropolis and dominions Christians, as well as Dualists (i.e., Zoroastrians [actually Manichaeans]), and Buddhists. He has nine ministers." A. P. Martinez, "Gardīzī's Two Chapters on the Turks," *Archivum Eurasiae Medii Aevi* 2 (1982): 134.
65. On the interaction among these various groups see James Hamilton, *Manuscrits ouïgours du Ix–X siècle de Touen-Houang*, Volume 1 (Paris: Peeters, 1986), 175-177.
66. Regarding a text that seems to be about the conversion of a laywoman (A. Yakup, "An Old Uyghur Appeal to T[ä]ngrikän Tegin T[ä]ngrim to Renounce Secular Life," *Turkic Languages* 23 [2019]: 6-30), Peter Zieme has instead argued that it actually is "a kind of religious memorandum, which was intended to encourage the royal house to turn to Buddhism" ("Die Lehre des Buddha und das Königshaus des Westuigurischen Reichs: Die vier Begegnungen," *Journal of Old Turkic Studies* 4, no. 2 [2020]: 546).

67. Peter Zieme, "An Old Uigur Idiyut Text," In *The History behind the Languages: Essays of Turfan Forum on Old Languages of the Silk Road*, ed. Academia Turfanica (Shanghai: Shanghai Guji Chubanshe, 2000), 8-10.
68. John A. Boyle, *Genghis Khan: The History of the World Conqueror by Ata-Malik Juvaini* (Seattle: University of Washington Press, 1997), 54-59. For a careful study of this story in relation to Mongol imperial ideology see Christopher P. Atwood, "The Uyghur Stone: Archaeological Revelations in the Mongol Empire," in *The Steppe Lands and the World Beyond Them: Studies in honor of Victor Spinei on his 70th Birthday*, ed. F. Curta and B. P. Maleon (Iasi: Editura Universitatii, 2013), 315-344.
69. Yukiyo Kasai, "Ein Kolophon um die Legende von Bokug Kagan," *Studies on the Inner Asian Languages* 19 (2004): 1-25. On this story see also Larry V. Clark, "Manichaeism among the Uygurs: The Uygur Khan of the Bokug Clan," in *New Light on Manichaeism: Papers from the Sixth International Congress on Manichaeism*, ed. Jason D. BeDuhn (Leiden: Brill, 2009), 61-71.
70. James Hamilton, "Toquz-Oguz et On-Uygur," *Journal asiatique* 250 (1962): 23-64.
71. The inscription reads *da fu da huihu guo* 大符大回鶻國. Takao Moriyasu, "The Flourishing of Manichaeism under the West Uighur Kingdom. New Edition of the Uighur Charter on the Administration of the Manichaean Monastery in Qočo," in *World History Reconsidered through the Eyes of the Silk Road: Four Lectures at the College de France in May 2003* (Osaka: Osaka University, 2003), 67.
72. L. Ju. Tuguševa, "Ein Fragment eines frühmittelalterlichen uigurischen Textes," in *Turfan, Khotan und Dunhuang: Vorträge der Tagung 'Annemarie v. Gabain und die Turfanforschung,' veranstaltet von der BBAW in Berlin (9.-12.12.1994)*, ed. R. E. Emmerick et al. (Berlin: Akademie Verlag, 1996), 353-359.
73. Boyle, *Genghis Khan*, 59-60.
74. Tieshan Zhang and Peter Zieme, "A Further Fragment of Old Uighur Annals," *Acta Orientalia Academiae Scientiarum Hungaricae* 66, no. 4 (2013): 397-410; Peter Zieme, "Collecting of the Buddhist Scriptures: Notes on Old Uigur 'Annals,'" *Annual Report of the International Research Institute for Advanced Buddhology at Soka University* 27 (2013): 401-422.
75. Herbert Franke, "Tibetans in Yüan China," in *China under Mongol Rule*, ed. John D. Langlois, Jr. (Princeton, NJ: Princeton University Press, 1981), 308. On the Buddhist "two realms" theory of rule, see David S. Ruegg, "The Precept-Donor (*yon mchod*) Relation in Thirteenth Century Tibetan Society and Polity, Its Inner Asian Precursors and Indian Models," in *Tibetan Studies*, ed. H. Krasser et al. (Wien: Österreichische Akademie der Wissenschaft, 1997).
76. H. J. Klimkeit, "The Donor at Turfan," *Silk Road Art and Archaeology: Journal of the Institute of Silk Road Studies, Kamakura* 1 (1990): 179.
77. Peter Zieme, "The West Uigur Kingdom: Views from Inside," *Horizons* 5, no. 1 (2014): 7.
78. Zieme, "The West Uigur Kingdom: Views from Inside," 8.
79. Zieme, "The West Uigur Kingdom: Views from Inside," 8.
80. Clark, *Uygur Manichaean Texts*, 51.
81. Jens Wilkens, *Alttürkische Handschriften Teil 9: Buddhistische Beichttexte* (Stuttgart: Franz Steiner Verlag, 2003), 315.

82. Geng Shimin and H. J. Klimkeit, *Das Zusammentreffen mit Maitreya. Die ersten fünf Kapitel der Hami-Version der Maitrisimit* (Wiesbaden: Otto Harrassowitz, 1988), 10–13.
83. It has, however, been argued that the Uyghur ruler noted in Buddhist stake inscription 3 is actually depicted in a mural at a ruined Buddhist temple in Beshbaliq (Ch. Beiting). Hiroshi Umemura, "A Qočo King Painted in the Buddhist Temple of Beshbaliq," in *Turfan, Khotan und Dunhuang: Vorträge der Tagung 'Annemarie v. Gabain und die Turfanforschung,' veranstaltet von der BBAW in Berlin (9.-12.12.1994)*, ed. R. E. Emmerick et al. (Berlin: Akademie Verlag, 1991), 361-378.
84. Jens Wilkens, "Hatten die alten Uiguren einen buddhistischen Kanon?" in *Kanonisierung und Kanonbildung in der asiatischen Religionsgeschichte*, ed. M. Deeg, O. Freiberger, and C. Kleine (Wien: Verlag der Österreichischen Akademie der Wissenschaft, 2011), 345-378.
85. Takao Moriyasu, "Chronology of West Uighur Buddhism: Re-examination of the Dating of the Wall-paintings in Grünwedel's Cave No. 8 (New: No. 18), Bezeklik," in *Aspects of Research into Central Asian Buddhism: In Memoriam Kōgi Kudara*, ed. Peter Zieme (Turnhout: Brepols 2008), 198.
86. Peter Zieme, "Some Notes on Old Uigur Translations of Buddhist Commentaries," *Annual Report of the International Research Institute for Advanced Buddhology at Soka University* 15 (2012): 147-160.
87. In this regard the Uyghurs were not unique since the tradition of compiling seemingly random texts into new collections is also found in the Dunhuang material and among the Sogdians. Neil Schmid, "Dunhuang and Central Asia (With an Appendix on Dunhuang Manuscript Resources)," in *Esoteric Buddhism and the Tantras in East Asia*, ed. C. D. Orzech et al. (Leiden: Brill, 2011), 365-378; Yutaka Yoshida, "Buddhist Texts Produced by the Sogdians in China," in *Multilingualism and History of Knowledge: Buddhism among the Iranian Peoples of Central Asia*, ed. J. E. Braarvig, M. J. Geller, V. Sadovski, and G. Selz (Wien: Verlag der Österreichischen Akademie der Wissenschaft, 2013), 154-179.
88. Peter Zieme, "Aranemi-Jātaka und ein Sündenbekenntnistext in einer alttürkischen Sammelhandschrift," in *De Dunhuang à Istanbul: Hommage à James Russell Hamilton*, ed. L. Bazin and P. Zieme (Turnhout: Brepols, 2001), 401-421; Kōichi Kitsudō, "Two Chinese Buddhist Texts Written by Uighurs," *Acta Orientalia Academiae Scientiarum Hungaricae* 64, no. 3 (2011): 325-343.
89. Kōichi Kitsudō, "The Lehrtext and *Bodhisattvacaryāmārga* (Pelliot Ouïgour 4521)," in *Beşbalikli Şingko Şali Tutung Anisina Uluslararasi Eski Uygurca Çaliştayi Bildirleri, 4–6 Haziran 2011, Ankara* (Ankara: Türk Dil Kurumu, 2022), 93-105.
90. Geng Shimin, "Study of Two Folios of the Uighur Text 'Abitaki,'" *Acta Orientalia Academiae Scientiarum Hungaricae* 57, no. 1 (2004): 105-113; Geng Shimin, "Study of Another Two Folios of the Uighur Text 'Abitaki,'" *Acta Orientalia Academiae Scientiarum Hungaricae* 59, no. 1 (2006): 47-56; Geng Shimin, "A Study on the Uighur Text Abitaki (4)," *Türkbilig* 14 (2007): 177-183.
91. Peter Zieme, "The Old Uigur Translation of the Siddhaṃ Songs," in *Chán Buddhism in Dūnhuáng and Beyond: A Study of Manuscripts, Texts, and Contexts in Memory of John R. McRae*, ed. C. Anderl and C. Wittern (Leiden: Brill, 2020), 143.

194   2. Buddhist Politics

92. Zieme, "The Old Uigur Translation of the Siddhaṃ Songs," 143. Similarly, the Uyghur translation of the *Guanwuliangshoujing* (T. 365) is a "rather free rendering of the Chinese text by the Uighur translator." Peter Zieme, "The First Leaf of an Old Uyghur *Guanwuliangshoujing* Translation," *Written Monuments of the Orient* 6, no. 1 (2020): 48. On the Uyghur version of the *Guanxin lun* see Abdrishid Yakup, *Prajñāpāramitā Literture in Old Uyghur* (Turnhout: Brepols, 2010), 235-249.

93. W. Radloff, *Suvarṇaprabhāsa (Das Goldglanz Sūtra) aus dem Uigurischen ins Deutsche übersetzt* (Leningrad: Russian Academy of Sciences, 1930), 59; Abdurishid Yakup, "An Old Uyghur Fragment of the Lotus Sutra from the Krotkov Collection in St. Petersburg," *Acta Orientalia Academiae Scientiarum Hungaricae* 64, no. 4 (2011): 411-426.

94. Quoted in Klimkeit, "The Donor at Turfan," 180.

95. Yukiyo Kasai, *Die uigurischen buddhistischen Kolophone* (Turnhout: Brepols, 2008), 145.

96. Kasai, *Der alttürkische Kommentar zum Vimalakīrtinirdeśa-Sūtra*, 2-6.

97. Zieme, "The Old Uigur Translation of the Siddhaṃ Songs," 144. See also Abdurishid Yakup, "On the Quotations from the *Buddhāvataṃsaka-sūtra* and Chan Literature in the Old Uyghur Text KÖNGÜL tözin ukitdaći nom," *Zeitschrift der Deutschen Morgenländischen Gesellschaft* 172, no. 2 (2022): 424-426.

98. Jens Peter Laut and Peter Zieme, "Eine zweisprachiger Lobpreis auf den Bäg von Koćo und seine Gemahlin," in *Buddhistische Erzähllitteratur und Hagiographe in türkischer Überlieferung*, ed. Jens Peter Laut (Wiesbaden: Harrassowitz, 1990), 17-19; Peter Zieme, "An Uighur Instruction Document for Preaching the *Bayangjing* and Other Sutras in Alliterating Verses," in 西域歷史語言研究集刊 (Historical and Philological Studies of China's Western Regions), ed. Shen Weirong (Beijing: Science Press, 2010), 271-282.

99. The importance of the monastic code, the *Vinaya*, in the history and practice of Buddhism cannot be underestimated. Its role among the Uyghurs will be explored in more detail in chapters 3 and 4. Scholars generally recognize the existence of seven different *Vinayas*, representing the different rules—and the underlying theological justifications—of seven different early Buddhist schools: the Theravādins, Mahāsāṃghikas, Mahāsāṃghika-lokottaravādins, Mahīśāsakas, Dharmaguptakas, Sarvāstivādins, and Mūlasarvāstivādins. Nevertheless, "following Louis Renou and Jean Filliozat, leading *vinaya* specialists such as Charles Prebish have categorized the *vinaya* corpus into canonical, paracanonical, and noncanonical literature: (A) canonical literature preserved in the *vinaya-piṭaka* mainly covers three divisions of texts, generally comprising: (1) *sūtravibhaṅga*, or the detailed analyses of offenses and respective punitive measures listed in the *prātimokṣasūtra*, (2) *skandhakas*, or regulations for the organization of the Buddhist community, and (3) appendices, mostly comprising summaries of the monastic rules listed in the two previous sections; (B) paracanonical *vinaya* literature refers to: (1) the set of precepts from the *prātimokṣasūtra* that is recited every fortnight during the so-called *poṣadha* ceremony, and (2) *karmavācanā* texts of correct procedures to settle communal transactions and disputes; and (C) noncanonical *vinaya* literature covering (1) commentaries and (2) miscellaneous texts, which include translations with unclear school affiliation and other *vinaya*-related texts." Klaus Pinte, "Vinaya," *Oxford Bibliographies Online*, www.oxfordbibliographies.com.

100. Jens Peter Laut, "Die Gründung des buddhistischen Nonnenordens in der alttürkischen Überlieferung," in *Türkische Sprachen und Literaturen: Materialien der ersten deutschen*

Turkologen-Konferenz, Bamberg, 3.-6. Juli 1987, ed. Ingeborg Baldauf (Wiesbaden: Harrassowitz, 1991), 257-274.

101. The same phenomenon of using multiple languages and scripts is also evidenced in the Dunhuang documents from the Guiyijun period. Imre Galambos, *Dunhuang Manuscript Culture: End of the First Millennium* (Berlin: DeGruyter, 2020), 139-193.

102. This revival will be explored more in chapter 4. For an introduction to this supposed "renaissance" of learning in the Yuan period see Klaus Röhrborn, "Zum Wanderweg des alttürkischen Lehngutes im Alttürkischen," in *Studien zur Geschichte und Kultur des vorderen Orients: Festschrift für Bertold Spuler zum siebzigsten Geburtstag*, ed. H. R. Roemer and A. Noth (Leiden: Brill, 1984), 340.

103. There is also a Chinese text in Uyghur script in Old Mandarin (which is what they spoke at the time), done by Anzang in the Yuan period; it is the *Tārā-Ekaviṃśatistotra*.

104. On the Uyghur versions of the *Qiānzìwén* see Peter Zieme, "Das *Qiānzìwén* bei den alten Uiguren," in *Writing in the Altaic World*, ed. J. Janhunen and V. Rybatzki (Helsinki: Finnish Oriental Society, 1999), 321-326; M. Shōgaito and A. Yakup, "Four Uyghur Fragments of *Qianziwen* 'Thousand Character Essay,'" *Turkic Languages* 5 (2001): 3-29; M. Shōgaito and A. Yakup, "Four Uyghur Fragments of *Qian-zi-wen* 'Thousand Character Essay,'" *Turkic Languages* 8 (2004): 313-317; Hiroshi Umemura and Peter Zieme, "A Further Fragment of the Old Uighur *Qianziwen*," *Written Monuments of the Orient* 2 (2015): 3-13. On the Uyghur use of the *Qiānzìwén* to catalogue items see Simone-Christiane Raschmann, "Uygur Scribbles On a Wooden Object," in *The Ruins of Kocho: Traces of Wooden Architecture on the Ancient Silk Road*, ed. L. Russell-Smith and I. Konczak-Nagel (Berlin: Museum für Asiatische Kunst, 2016), 43.

105. The following material is drawn from Masahiro Shōgaito, "How Were Chinese Characters Read in Uighur?" in *Turfan Revisited: The First Century of Research into the Arts and Cultures of the Silk Road*, ed. D. Durkin-Meisterernst et al. (Berlin: Dietrich Reimer Verlag, 2004), 321-324; M. Shōgaito, A. Yakup, and S. Fujishiro, *The Berlin Chinese text U 5335 Written in Uighur Script: A Reconstruction of the Inherited Uighur Pronunciation of Chinese* (Turnhout: Brepols, 2015); Masahiro Shōgaito, "Philology and Linguistics: *Ondoku* and *Kundoku* in Old Uighur," trans. Noriko Ohsaki, Mutsumi Sugahara, and Setsu Fujishiro, *Gengo Kenkyu Anthology* 1 (2021): 155-185.

106. Shōgaito et al., *The Berlin Chinese text U 5335*, 158.

107. On Old Uyghur verse see Peter Zieme, *Die Stabreimtexte der Uiguren von Turfan und Dunhuang* (Budapest: Akadémiai Kiadó, 1991).

108. Shōgaito, "How Were Chinese Characters Read in Uighur?," 322.

3. BUDDHIST ECONOMICS

1. F. L. Woodward and E. M. Hare, *The Book of the Gradual Sayings*, 5 vols. (Bristol: Pali Text Society, 1932-1936), vol. 5, 92-94.

2. The main argument of this chapter, and the material in the first section, is drawn from Johan Elverskog, *The Buddha's Footprint: An Environmental History of Asia* (Philadelphia: University of Pennsylvania Press, 2020), 39-49.

3. Max Weber, *The Protestant Ethic and the Spirit of Capitalism*, trans. Talcott Parsons (New York: Routledge, 1994).

4. Max Weber, *Hinduismus und Buddhismus* (Tübingen: Mohr, 1921), 330, 340.

5. David N. Gellner, *The Anthropology of Buddhism and Hinduism: Weberian Themes* (New Delhi: Oxford University Press, 2001), 19–44.
6. For a critical re-evaluation of the Dharma's relation to economics see Richard K. Payne and Fabio Rambelli, "The Economic Study of Buddhism," in *Buddhism under Capitalism*, ed. Richard K. Payne and Fabio Rambelli (London: Bloomsbury Academic, 2022), 1-22.
7. Mark Elvin, *The Retreat of the Elephants: An Environmental History of China* (New Haven, CT: Yale University Press, 2006), 446. Of course, the criticism of Weber was almost immediate, especially regarding the inherent and unique "capitalist" tendencies of Protestantism. Numerous scholars therefore argued that other religions had the same capacities. See, for example, Werner Sombart, *The Jews and Modern Capitalism*, trans. M. Epstein (Kitchener, ON: Batoche Books, 2001); and Peter Gran, *Islamic Roots of Capitalism: Egypt, 1760–1840* (Syracuse, NY: Syracuse University Press, 1979). Similarly, while much has been made of Hinduism's supposedly antimarket tendencies, recent research suggests that early Hindus were also involved with international trade. Richard H. Davies, *Global India Circa 100 CE: South Asia in Early World History* (Ann Arbor: Association for Asian Studies, 2009). Moreover, there is to my knowledge no scholarship looking specifically at the Daoist role in the Chinese market, but it has been argued that the "revival of Daoism during the Sung (with its attendant needs for ritual paraphernalia like ivory, scented wood and mother of pearl) was one reason for the influx of goods [from Southeast Asia]." Eric Tagliacozzo, "Onto the Coasts and into the Forests: Ramifications of the China Trade on the Ecological History of Northwest Borneo, 900-1900 CE," in *Histories of the Borneo Environment*, ed. Reed L. Wadley (Leiden: KITLV, 2005), 28.
8. Jacques Gernet, *Les aspects économiques du bouddhisme dans la société chinoise du Ve au Xe siècle* (Saigon: École française d'Extrême-Orient, 1956), translated into English by Franciscus Verellen, *Buddhism in Chinese Society: An Economic History from the Fifth to the Tenth Centuries* (New York: Columbia University Press, 1995). Other important early works on the link between the Dharma and economics include Lien-sheng Yang, "Buddhist Monasteries and Four Money-Raising Institutions in Chinese History," *Harvard Journal of Asiatic Studies* 13, no. 1-2 (1950): 174-191; D. C. Twitchett, "The Monasteries and China's Economy in Medieval Times," *Bulletin of the School of Oriental and African Studies* 19, no. 3 (1957): 526-549; Robert J. Miller, "Buddhist Monastic Economy: The Jisa Mechanism," *Comparative Studies in Society and History* 3, no. 4 (1961): 427-438; Jean C. Darian, "Social and Economic Factors in the Rise of Buddhism," *Sociological Analysis* 38, no. 3 (1977): 226-238; R. A. H. L. Gunawardana, *Robe and Plough: Monasticism and Economic Interest in Early Medieval Sri Lanka* (Tucson: University of Arizona Press, 1979); and Martin Collcutt, *Five Mountains: The Rinzai Zen Monastic Tradition in Medieval Japan* (Cambridge: Council on East Asian Studies, Harvard University, 1981), 251-253.
9. James Heitzman, "Early Buddhism, Trade, and Empire," in *Studies in the Archaeology and Paleoanthropology of South Asia*, ed. Kenneth A. R. Kennedy and Gregory L. Possehl (New Delhi: Oxford and IBH Publishing/American Institute of Indian Studies, 1984), 121-137; Himanshu P. Ray, *The Winds of Change: Buddhism and the Maritime Links of Early*

       South Asia (Delhi: Oxford University Press, 1994), 121-161; and Jason Neelis, *Early Buddhist Transmission and Trade Networks: Mobility and Exchange within and beyond the Northwestern Borderlands of South Asia* (Leiden: Brill, 2011).

10. Gregory Schopen is the scholar who has done the most to explore the financial realities of early Buddhism. See, for example, his collected works: *Bones, Stones, and Buddhist Monks: Collected Papers on the Archaeology, Epigraphy, and Texts of Monastic Buddhism in India* (Honolulu: University of Hawai'i Press, 1997); *Buddhist Monks and Business Matters: Still More Papers on Monastic Buddhism in India* (Honolulu: University of Hawai'i Press, 2004); *Figments and Fragments of Mahayana Buddhism in India: More Collected Papers* (Honolulu: University of Hawai'i Press, 2005); *Buddhist Nuns, Monks, and Other Worldly Matters: Recent Papers on Monastic Buddhism in India* (Honolulu: University of Hawai'i Press, 2014).

11. For an overview of these developments and a reevaluation of their impact on the development of early Buddhism, see Greg Bailey and Ian Mabbett, *The Sociology of Early Buddhism* (New York: Cambridge University Press, 2003), 13-107. See also Robert N. Bellah, *Religion in Human Evolution: From the Paleolithic to the Axial Age* (Cambridge, MA: Harvard University Press, 2011); and Robert N. Bellah and Hans Joas, eds., *The Axial Age and Its Consequences* (Cambridge, MA: Harvard University Press, 2012).

12. On the so-called sixteen great countries (*soḍaśa mahājanapada*) see Étienne Lamotte, *History of Indian Buddhism: From the Origins to the Śaka Era*, trans. Sara Webb-Boin (Louvain-Paris: Peeters Press, 1988), 7-9. On how these entities were less historical realities than a "technical term" in Buddhist literature, see Richard Gombrich, *Theravada Buddhism: A Social History from Ancient Benares to Modern Colombo* (London: Routledge & Kegan Paul, 1988), 54.

13. For more detailed studies on the shift from these "republics" (*gaṇa-sanghas*) to the more complex political systems of kingdoms and empires, see Romila Thapar, *From Lineage to State: Social Formations in the Mid-first Millennium B.C. in the Ganga Valley* (Bombay: Oxford University Press, 1984); and Uma Chakravarti, *The Social Dimensions of Early Buddhism* (Delhi: Oxford University Press, 1987).

14. Makhan Lal, "Iron Tools, Forest Clearance and Urbanisation in the Gangetic Plains," *Man and Environment* 10 (1986): 83-90.

15. On the relationship among iron, changing methods of warfare, and the rise of centralizing states, see Victor H. Mair, *The Art of War: Sun Zi's Military Methods* (New York: Columbia University Press, 2007), 37-39.

16. William N. Goetzmann, *Money Changes Everything: How Finance Made Civilization Possible* (Princeton, NJ: Princeton University Press, 2017), 1-37.

17. Jonathan P. Berkey, *The Formation of Islam: Religion and Society in the Near East* (New York: Cambridge University Press, 2003), 5.

18. Chakravarti, *Social Dimensions of Early Buddhism*, 19

19. The *Śārdūlakarṇāvadāna*, which was translated into Chinese in 230 CE, notes that the Magadhan *mashaka* is equal to twelve grains of gold; sixteen *mashaka* equal one Chinese *jin*. I thank Brian Baumann for this information.

20. Maurice Walshe, *The Long Discourses of the Buddha: A Translation of the Digha Nikaya* (Boston: Wisdom, 1995), 236.

198   3. Buddhist Economics

21. This passage is from the *Anguttara Nikāya* and is quoted in Chakravarti, *Social Dimensions of Early Buddhism*, 83. For a similar passage see also the *Mahāsīhanāda Sutta* in the *Majjhima Nikāya*, 12.41.
22. Ray, *The Winds of Change*, 132.
23. Jes P. Asmussen, *X^uāstvānīft: Studies in Manichaeism* (Copenhagen: Prostant apud Munksgaard, 1965), 150. See also Ronald M. Davidson, *Indian Esoteric Buddhism: A Social History of the Tantric Movement* (New York: Columbia University Press, 2002), 78.
24. Ray, *The Winds of Change*, 153–154.
25. For studies on how Confucian ideals responded to—or were created in relation to—expanding market economies in the Han and Ming periods, see Tamara T. Chin, *Savage Exchange: Han Imperialism, Literary Style, and the Economic Imagination* (Cambridge, MA: Harvard University Asia Center, 2014); and Timothy Brook, *The Confusions of Pleasure: Commerce and Culture in Ming China* (Berkeley: University of California Press, 1999).
26. Patrick Olivelle, *Dharmasūtras: The Law Codes of Āpastamba, Gautama, Baudhāyana, and Vasiṣṭha* (New York: Oxford University Press, 1999), 105.
27. Gustavo Benavides, "Buddhism, Manichaeism, Markets and Empires," in *Hellenisation, Empire, and Globalisation: Lessons from Antiquity*, ed. Luther H. Martin and Panayotis Pachis (Thessaloniki: Vanias Publications, 2004), 23.
28. For a Uyghur version of the *Catuṣpariṣatsūtra* that includes this story see Abdurishid Yakup, *Dišastvustik: Eine altuigurische Bearbeitung einer Legende aus dem Catuṣpariṣatsūtra* (Wiesbaden: Harrassowitz Verlag, 2006).
29. Michael J. Walshe, "The Economics of Salvation: Toward a Theory of Exchange in Chinese Buddhism," *Journal of the American Academy of Religion* 75, no. 2 (2007): 363.
30. I. B. Horner, *Milinda's Questions*, vol. 1 (London: Luzac and Company, 1963), 171. On the courtesan tradition of treating men of different backgrounds equally, see Ludwick Sternbach, *Gaṇikā-vṛtta-saṃgrahaḥ or Texts on Courtezans in Classical Sanskrit* (Hoshiapur: Vishveshvaranand Institute Publications, 1953), 72–73.
31. Chakravarti, *Social Dimensions of Early Buddhism*, 99.
32. Over time Buddhist texts came to identify more and more jobs; for example, in the *Dīgha Nikāya* there is a standard list of twenty-five occupations (Walshe, *The Long Discourses of the Buddha*, 93), but in the later *Milandapañha* there are seventy-five. Xinru Liu, *Ancient India and Ancient China: Trade and Religious Exchanges, AD 1–600* (Delhi: Oxford University Press, 1988), 37.
33. Gustavo Benavides, "Economy," in *Critical Terms for the Study of Buddhism*, ed. Donald S. Lopez Jr. (Chicago: University of Chicago Press, 2005), 82–83.
34. On the different regulations of the various *prātimokṣa* found in the *Vinaya* see Werner Pachow, *A Comparative Study of the Prātimokṣa on the Basis of Its Chinese, Tibetan, Sanskrit and Pāli Versions* (Delhi: Motilal Banarsidass, 2000).
35. "At the thought: wealth is mine acquired by energetic striving... lawfully gotten, bliss comes to him, satisfaction comes to him. This householder, is called 'bliss of ownership.'... At the thought: By means of wealth acquired... I both enjoy my wealth and do meritorious deeds, bliss comes to him, satisfaction comes to him. This, householder, is called 'bliss of wealth.'... At the thought: I owe no debt, great or small, to

anyone bliss comes to him, satisfaction comes to him. This, householder, is called 'bliss of debtlessness.'" Woodward and Hare, *The Book of the Gradual Sayings*, vol. 2, 77.

36. On some of the ethical issues related to such wealth production see, for example, Frank E. Reynolds, "Ethics and Wealth in Theravāda Buddhism: A Study in Comparative Ethics," in *Ethics, Wealth, and Salvation: A Study in Buddhist Ethics*, ed. R. F. Sizemore and D. K. Swearer (Columbia: University of South Carolina Press, 1990), 59-76; and John S. Strong, "Rich Man, Poor Man, *Bhikku*, King: Aśoka's Great Quinquennial Festival and the Nature of *Dāna*," in *Ethics, Wealth, and Salvation: A Study in Buddhist Ethics*, ed. R. F. Sizemore and D. K. Swearer (Columbia: University of South Carolina Press, 1990), 107-123.

37. Thus, as Michael Walshe has shown in the case of China, it was precisely "those Buddhist monasteries in the Chinese empire that sought to accumulate wealth [that increased] their chances of institutional longevity." *Sacred Economies: Buddhist Monasticism and Territoriality in Medieval China* (New York: Columbia University Press, 2010), 6-8.

38. On monastic involvement in a range of such economic activities, see the collected articles in Gregory Schopen, *Buddhist Monks and Business Matters: Still More Papers on Monastic Buddhism in India* (Honolulu: University of Hawai'i Press, 2004).

39. Walshe, *Sacred Economies*, 6.

40. Yang Hsüan-chih, *A Record of Buddhist Monasteries in Lo-yang*, trans. Yi-t'ung Wang (Princeton, NJ: Princeton University Press, 1984), 5.

41. W. Radloff and Baron A. von Staël-Holstein, *Tišastvustik. Ein in türkischer Sprach bearbeitetes buddhistisches Sūtra*. Bibliotheca Buddhica 12 (St. Petersburg, 1910); Dieter Maue, "Sanskrit-uigurische Fragmente des *Āṭānāṭikasūtra* und des *Āṭānāṭihṛdaya*," *Ural-Altaische Jahrbücher* 5 (1985): 98-122.

42. Oda, *Säkiz Yükmäk Yaruq*, 135-141, 193.

43. Peter Zieme, "The Poor Man in Byzantium: Fragments of an Old Uyghur Tale," *Türkıyät Mecmuasi* 31 (2021): 39-49.

44. Takao Moriyasu and Peter Zieme, "From Chinese to Uighur Documents," *Studies on the Inner Asian Languages* 14 (1999): 73-102; Dai Matsui, "Uigur *käzig* and the Origin of Taxation Systems in the Uigur Kingdom of Qočo," *Türk Dilleri Araştırmaları* 18 (2008): 229-242.

45. On the history of the Uyghur script see György Kara, "Aramaic Scripts for Altaic Languages," in *The World's Writing Systems*, ed. P. T. Daniels and W. Bright (New York: Oxford University Press, 1996), 536-558; Nicholas Sims-Williams, "From Aramaic to Manchu: Prehistory, Life and After-Life of the Sogdian Script," in *Sogdians in China: New Evidence and Archaeological Finds and Unearthed Texts*, ed. Rong Xinjiang and Luo Feng (Beijing: Kexue Chubanshe, 2016), 414-421.

46. On state legibility see James C. Scott, *Seeing Like a State: How Certain Schemes to Improve the Human Condition Have Failed* (New Haven, CT: Yale University Press, 1998).

47. The Uyghur role of linking the Muslim world with China is well captured in the work of Gardīzī: "The Toguz Oguz Xaqan lives in a palace in a palisaded compound or walled town. His floor-coverings are made of felt. But over these are spread carpets made by Muslims and on these latter Chinese brocades... The clothing of their kings

are made of Chinese brocade or silk, that of the common folk silk and cotton. Their garments are quilted, ample sleeved and full skirted. Their king's belt is made up of intertwined strings of pearls and gems, and when a dense crowd of people comes to his audience, a crown is placed on this head." A. P. Martinez, "Gardīzī's Two Chapters on the Turks," *Archivum Eurasiae Medii Aevi* 2 (1982): 135.

48. On the Chanyuan treat see David C. Wright, *From War to Diplomatic Parity in Eleventh-Century China: Sung's Foreign Relations with the Kitan Liao* (Leiden: Brill, 2005).

49. Michal Biran, "Unearthing the Liao Dynasty's Relations with the Muslim World: Migrations, Diplomacy, Commerce, and Mutual Perceptions," *Journal of Song-Yuan Studies* 43 (2013): 234.

50. On the Uyghur role in Qarakhanid trade with the East see Dilnoza Duturaeva, *Qarakhanid Roads to China: The History of Sino-Turkic Relations* (Leiden: Brill, 2022), 41, 48, 55, 107.

51. Gasparini, *Transcending Patterns*, 94. On the importance of *nasīj* in Mongol Eurasia see Thomas T. Allsen, *Commodity and Exchange in the Mongol Empire: A Cultural History of Islamic Textiles* (New York: Cambridge University Press, 1997).

52. On such *ortoq* relationships see Takao Moriyasu, *Corpus of the Old Uighur Letters from the Eastern Silk Road* (Turnhout: Brepols, 2019), no. 58.

53. Takao Moriyasu, "On the Uighur Buddhist Society at Čiqtim in Turfan during the Mongol Period," in *Splitter aus der Gegend von Turfan: Festschrift für Peter Zieme*, ed. Mehmet Ölmez and Simone-Christiane Raschmann (Berlin, Istanbul: 2002), 164.

54. Gerald Clauson, "A Late Uyǧur Family Archive," in *Iran and Islam in Memory of the Late Vladimir Minorsky*, ed. C. E. Bosworth (Edinburgh: Edinburgh University Press, 1971), 196.

55. Thomas T. Allsen, *The Steppe and the Sea: Pearls in the Mongol Empire* (Philadelphia: University of Pennsylvania Press, 2019), 21, 62, 134. See also Eiren Shea, *Mongol Court Dress, Identity Formation, and Global Exchange* (New York: Routledge, 2020).

56. A stater was a Greek coin that over time played a fundamental role in international trade, especially in the Black Sea area. It was adjusted to a standard of 16.05 grams, and this weight subsequently became standard in the trade networks of Inner Asia. A. D. H. Bivar, "Coins," in *The Oxford Encyclopedia of Archaeology in the Near East*, ed. Eric M. Meyers (New York: Oxford University Press, 1997), 41–52.

57. Clauson, "A Late Uyǧur Family Archive," 182–183.

58. Clauson, "A Late Uyǧur Family Archive," 186–187.

59. Nicholas Sims-Williams and James Hamilton, *Turco-Sogdian Documents from 9th-10th Century Dunhuang* (London: Corpus Inscriptionum Iranicum and School of Oriental and African Studies, 2015), 93.

60. Valerie Hansen, *The Silk Road: A New History* (New York: Oxford University Press, 2015). Based on the tenth-century Uyghur letters from Dunhuang, the main products traded were: silk, raw silk, cooked silk, wool or animal hair, cotton, spinning wheels, canvas woven on a straight loom, slaves, musk, dye, sheep, camels pearls, lacquer cups, silver bowls, silver quivers, combs, pans, small steel knives, pickaxes, handkerchiefs, brocade, whey, and dried fruits (James Hamilton, *Manuscrits ouïgours du Ix–X siècle de Touen-Houang*, 2 vols. [Paris: Peeters, 1986], 176–177).

61. Simone-Christiane Raschmann, *Baumwolle im türkischen Zentralasien: Philologische und wirtschaftshistorische Untersuchungen anhand der vorislamischen uigurischen Texte* (Wiesbaden: Harrassowitz Verlag, 1995), 10-11.
62. On the Song horse trade with the Tibetans see Paul J. Smith, *Taxing Heaven's Storehouse: Horses, Bureaucrats, and the Destruction of the Sichuan Tea Industry, 1074–1224* (Cambridge, MA: Harvard Council on East Asian Studies, 1991), 13-48.
63. Smith, *Taxing Heaven's Storehouse*, 257.
64. "When in the ninth century the Uighurs moved into this area they changed the name of the city from Gaochang—47 kilometers south of modern-day Turfan city—to Qocho." Zhang Guangda and Rong Xinjiang, "A Concise History of the Turfan Oasis and Its Exploration," *Asia Major* 11, no. 2 (1998): 21.
65. J. P. Mallory and Victor H. Mair, *The Tarim Mummies: Ancient China and the Mystery of the Earliest Peoples from the West* (New York: Thames & Hudson, 2000), 212. On the history of cotton growing in the Turfan region during the first millennium see Kang Chao, *The Development of Cotton Textile Production in China* (Cambridge, MA: Harvard East Asian Research Center, 1977), 4-7.
66. Michel Cartier, "A propos de l'histoire du coton en Chine. Approche technologique, économique et sociale," *Études chinoises* 13, no. 1-2 (1994): 418-421.
67. On the impact of the medieval warm period on East Asia—the so-called "Song-Yuan Warm Period"—see Philip Jenkins, *Climate, Catastrophe, and Faith: How Changes in Climate Drive Religious Upheaval* (New York: Oxford University Press, 2021), 54-59.
68. Doug Hitch, "The Special Status of Turfan," *Sino-Platonic Papers* 186 (2009): 1-61.
69. Christopher P. Atwood, "Empire of the Mongols: Plantation, Taxation, and Agricultural Innovation in Mongol Yuan China," paper presented at the symposium "Mongol Empire and Its Legacy," University of Washington, February 3, 2017.
70. On the development of East-West trade at this time see Thomas T. Allsen, "Mongolian Princes and Their Merchant Partners 1200-1260," *Asia Major* 3, no. 2 (1989): 86-94.
71. E. I. Kychanov, "The Organization and Control of Embassies in 12th Century Hsi-Hsia—According to the Tangut Law Code," *The Bulletin of Sung-Yuan Studies* 18 (1986): 4-12.
72. Biran, "Unearthing the Liao Dynasty's Relations," 243.
73. Annemarie von Gabain claimed that the Uyghur state benefited from transit tariffs; Peter Zieme has pointed out that we have no evidence to that effect ("Zum Handel im uigurischen Reich von Qočo," *Altorientalische Forschungen* 4 [1976]: 238).
74. Cuilan Liu, "Merit-Making or Financial Fraud? Litigating Buddhist Nuns in Early 10th-Century Dunhuang," *Journal of the International Association of Buddhist Studies* 41 (2018): 186.
75. Yukiyo Kasai, "Zur Verbreitung und Verwendung altuigurischer buddhistischer Texte," in *Eine hundertblättrige Tulpe—Bir sadbarg lāla: Festgabe für Claus Schönig*, ed. I. Hauenschild, M. Kappler, and B. Kellner-Heinkele (Berlin: Klaus Schwarz Verlag, 2016), 225-226; Peter Zieme, "Merit Transfer and Vow According to an Old Uyghur Buddhist Text from Qočo/Gaochang," *Annual Report of the International Research Institute for Advanced Buddhology at Soka University* 24 (2020): 217-230.

76. H. J. Klimkeit, "The Donor at Turfan," *Silk Road Art and Archaeology: Journal of the Institute of Silk Road Studies, Kamakura* 1 (1990): 183.
77. Peter Zieme, "Bägräk Tutung and His Family: Notes on an Old Uygur Colophon," in *Language, Society, and Religion in the World of the Turks: Festschrift for Larry Clark at Seventy-Five*, ed. Zsuzsanna Gulácsi (Turnhout: Brepols, 2018), 166–175.
78. Takao Moriyasu, "Uighur Buddhist Stake Inscriptions from Turfan," n *De Dunhuang à Istanbul: Hommage à James Russell Hamilton*, ed. Louis Bazin and Peter Zieme (Turnhout: Brepols, 2001), 188–190.
79. Takao Moriyasu and Peter Zieme, "Uighur Inscriptions on the Banners from Turfan Housed in the Museum für Indische Kunst, Berlin," in *Central Asian Temple Banners in the Turfan Collection of the Museum für Indische Kunst, Berlin*, ed. Chhaya Bhattacharya-Haesner (Berlin: Dietrich Reimer Verlag, 2003), 463.
80. Dai Matsui, "Mongol Globalism Attested by the Uigur and Mongol Documents from East Turkestan," *Studies in the Humanities (Volume of Cultural Sciences)* 22 (2009): 35; Osman Fikri Sertkaya, "Hukukī Uygur belgelerindeki para birimleri üzerine," in *Eski Türklerde para*, ed. O. F. Sertkaya and R. Alimov (Istanbul: Otuken, 2006), 117–137.
81. Peter Zieme, "An Uigur Monasterial Letter from Toyoq," *Studies on the Inner Asian Languages* 10 (1995): 3.
82. On Buddhists selling land, see, for example, W. Radloff, *Uigurische Sprachdenkmäler: Materialen nach dem Tode des Verfassers mit Ergänzungen von S. Malov herausgegeben* (Leningrad: 1928), 18–20, 44–46; R. R. Arat, "Eski Türk hukuk vesikaları," *Journal de la Société Finno-Ougrienne* 65, no. 1 (1964): 68–69; Nobuo Yamada, *Sammlung uigurischer Kontrakte*, vol. 1, ed. Juten Oda, Peter Zieme, Hiroshi Umemura, and Takao Moriyasu (Osaka: Osaka University Press, 1993), 45.
83. Peter Zieme, "Uigurische Steuerbefreiungsurkunden für buddhistische Klöster," *Altorientalische Forschungen* 7 (1981): 237–263; Dai Matsui, "Taxation Systems as Seen in the Uigur and Mongol Documents from Turfan: An Overview," *Transactions of the International Conference of Eastern Studies* 50 (2005): 67–82.
84. Yi-fu Tuan, *A Historical Geography of China* (New Brunswick: AldineTransaction, 2008), 91.
85. Sem Vermeersch, *The Power of the Buddhas: The Politics of Buddhism During the Koryo Dynasty (918–1392)* (Cambridge, MA: Harvard University Asia Center, 2008), 273.
86. On the question of how much land was granted to the samgha, based on the question of what the measurement "pay" actually meant at that time, see Aye Chan, "The Nature of Land and Labour Endowments to Sasana in Medieval Burmese History: Review of the Theory of 'Merit-path-to-salvation,'" *Southeast Asian Studies* 26, no. 1 (1988): 86–95.
87. Walshe, *Sacred Economies*, 83.
88. Billy K. L. So, *Prosperity, Region, and Institutions in Maritime China: The South Fukien Pattern, 946–1368* (Cambridge, MA: Harvard University Asia Center, 2000), 97; Hugh R. Clark, *Community, Trade, and Networks: Southern Fujian Province from the Third to the Thirteenth Century* (Cambridge: Cambridge University Press, 1991), 142.
89. On the Buddhist monastic production and consumption of alcohol in Dunhuang see Éric Trombert, "Bière et Bouddhisme—La consummation de boissons alcoolisées dans

les monastères de Dunhuang aux VIII-X siècles," *Cahiers d'Extrême-Asie* 11 (1999-2000): 129-181.

90. Harry Falk, "Making Wine in Gandhara under Buddhist Monastic Supervision," *Bulletin of the Asia Institute* 23 (2009): 65-78.

91. Martha L. Carter, "Turfan and the Grape," in *Turfan Revisited: The First Century of Research into the Arts and Cultures of the Silk Road*, ed. D. Durkin-Meisterernst et al. (Berlin: Dietrich Reimer Verlag, 2004), 52. On Manichaeans and wine production see Peter Zieme, "Uigurische Pachtdokumente," *Altorientalische Forschungen* 7 (1980): 199.

92. On the Buddhist monastic involvement with wine production see Simone-Christiane Raschmann, "Der Weingarten des Šabi Tutung," in *Eine hundertblättrige Tulpe–Bir sadbarg lāla: Festgabe für Claus Schonig*, ed. I. Hauenschild et al. (Berlin: Klaus Schwarz Verlag, 2016), 372-388; Simone-Christiane Raschmann, "'In Need For Wine': The Arat Document 112/07," in *Language, Society, and Religion in the World of the Turks: Festschrift for Larry Clark at Seventy-Five*, ed. Zsuzsanna Gulásci (Turnhout: Brepols, 2018): 77-87.

93. Gregory Schopen, "On Monks and Menial Laborers: Some Monastic Accounts of Building Buddhist Monasteries," in *Architetti, Capomastri, Artigiani: L'organizzazione dei cantieri e della produzione artistica nell'Asia ellnistica*, ed. Pierfrancesco Callieri (Roma: Istituto Italiano per l'Africa e l'Oriente, 2006): 225-245.

94. Masao Mori, "A Study on Uyghur Documents of Loans for Consumption," *Memoirs of the Research Department of the Toyo Bunko* 20 (1961): 111-148; Peter Zieme, "Drei neue uigurische Sklavendokumente," *Altorientalische Forschungen* 5 (1978): 145-170; Simone-Christiane Raschmann, "Zur Rolle der Sklaven im uigurischen Königreich von Qočo," *Ausprägung und Entwicklung sozialer Differenzierung in vorkapitalistischen Gessellschaften* (1988): 146-158; Hiroshi Umemura, "The Uyghur Document SI 4b Kr. 71 Concerning the Sale of a Slave and the Loan of Silver," in *Turfan Revisited: The First Century of Research into the Arts and Cultures of the Silk Road*, ed. D. Durkin-Meisterernst et al. (Berlin: Dietrich Reimer Verlag, 2004), 358-360.

95. Craig J. Reynolds, "Monastery Lands and Labour Endowments in Thailand: Some Effects of Social and Economic Change, 1868-1910," *Journal of the Economic and Social History of the Orient* 22, no. 2 (1979): 190-227. On Buddhist justifications for slavery see Gregory Schopen, "Liberation Is Only for Those Already Free: Reflections on Debts to Slavery and Enslavement to Debt in Early Indian Buddhist Monasticism," *Journal of the American Academy of Religion* 82, no. 3 (2014): 606-635; and R. Lingat, *L'esclavage privé dans le vieux droit siamois (avec une traduction des anciennes lois siamoises sur l'esclavage)* (Paris: Les Éditions Domat-Montchrestien, 1931). The most incisive study on the impact of Buddhist slavery is James C. Scott's *The Art of Not Being Governed: An Anarchist History of Upland Southeast Asia* (New Haven, CT: Yale University Press, 2009).

96. Dai Matsui, "Six Uigur Contracts from the West Uigur Period (10th-12th Centuries)," *Jinbun shakai ronsō (Jinbun kagaku hen)* 15 (2006): 37.

97. Buddhist monasteries across Asia have been a major driving force not only in banking but also as facilitators of trade. See, for example, Jason Hawkes, "The Wider Archaeological Contexts of the Buddhist Stūpa Site of Bharhut," in *Buddhist Stupas in South Asia*, ed. Jason Hawkes and Akira Shimada (New Delhi: Oxford University Press, 2009), 170; C. Patterson Giersch, "Across Zomia with Merchants, Monks, and Musk: Process

Geographies, Trade Networks, and the Inner-East-Southeast Asian Borderlands," *Journal of Global History* 5, no. 2 (2010): 215-239; Ethan Isaac Segal, *Coins, Trade, and the State: Economic Growth in Early Medieval Japan* (Cambridge, MA: Harvard University Asia Center, 2011), 93; Gregory Schopen, "On the Legal and Economic Activities of Buddhist Nuns: Two Examples from Early India," in *Buddhism and Law: An Introduction*, ed. Rebecca R. French and Mark A. Nathan (New York: Cambridge University Press, 2014), 91-114.

98. Yamada, *Sammlung uigurischer Kontrakte*, 93.
99. Moriyasu, *Corpus of the Old Uighur Letters*, 69.
100. Yamada, *Sammlung uigurischer Kontrakte*, 125-126.
101. Dai Matsui, "Uigur Peasants and Buddhist Monasteries during the Mongol Period: Reexamination of the Uigur Document U 5330 (Usp 77)," in *"The Way of the Buddha" 2003: The 100th Anniversary of the Otani Mission and the 50th of the Research Society for Central Asian Cultures*, ed. Irisawa Takashi (Osaka: Ryukoku University, 2010), 55-66.
102. Jens Peter Laut, "Uigurische Sünden," in *De Dunhuang à Istanbul: Hommage à James Russell Hamilton*, ed. L. Bazin and P. Zieme (Turnhout: Brepols, 2001), 127-148.
103. "To Burkhan Silavanti, I, Qaytso Tutung, send a letter respectfully. Are you at peace? We treated the new treasury carelessly. Here the seed of ? has run short. If you have any please send it to us. Moreover, if you have plenty of wine in the monastery, can you please send it to us? Moreover, seed to cultivate." Matsui, "Six Uigur Contracts from the West Uigur Period (10th-12th Centuries)," 47.
104. Juten Oda, "A Recent Study on the Uighur Document of Pintung's Petition," *Türk Dilleri Araştımaları* (1992): 35-46.

4. UYGHUR BUDDHISMS

1. Hong Hao, *Songmo jiwen* in *Bishuo xiaoshuo daguan*, vol. 3:3 (Taipei: Xinxin shuju, 1978), 1430-1431. Quoted in Kōichi Kitsudō, "Liao Influence on Uigur Buddhism," in *Studies in Chinese Manuscripts: From the Warring States to the 20th Century*, ed. Imre Galambos (Budapest: Institute of East Asian Studies, Eotvos Lorand University, 2013), 228.
2. The seminal text that ushered in a wave of postcolonial Buddhist studies scholarship was Donald S. Lopez Jr., *Curators of the Buddha: The Study of Buddhism Under Colonialism* (Chicago: University of Chicago Press, 1995). On the development of modern Buddhism see David L. McMahan, *The Making of Buddhist Modernism* (New York: Oxford University Press, 2008); B. Bocking, P. Choompolpaisal, L. Cox, and A. Turner, *A Buddhist Crossroads: Pioneer Western Buddhists and Asian Networks 1860-1960* (New York: Routledge, 2015). For a convenient overview and collection of material on the Western construction of Buddhism, see Donald S. Lopez Jr., ed., *A Modern Buddhist Bible: Essential Readings from East and West* (Boston: Beacon Press, 2002).
3. Peter Zieme, "Ein uigurischer Erntesegen," *Altorientalische Forschungen* 3 (1975): 118.
4. Dai Matsui, "Remarks on Buyan-Qaya, a Uighur Buddhist Pilgrim to Dunhuang," in *Unter dem Bodhi-Baum: Festschrift für Klaus Röhrborn anlässlich des 80. Geburtstags überreicht von Kollegen, Freunden und Schülern*, ed. Z. Özertural and G. Şilfeler (Göttingen: V&R Unipress, 2019), 209-224.

5. Jens Wilkens, "Practice and Rituals in Uyghur Buddhist Texts: A Preliminary Appraisal," in *Buddhism in Central Asia II: Practices and Rituals, Visual and Material Transfer*, ed. Yukiyo Kasai and Henrik H. Sørensen (Leiden: Brill, 2022), 437.
6. Henry Yule, *The Book of Ser Marco Polo the Venetian concerning the Kingdoms and Marvels of the East, Translated and Edited, with Notes, by Colonel Sir Henry Yule, R.E., C.B., K.C.S.I., Corr. Inst. France, Third Edition, Revised Throughout in the Light of Recent Discoveries by Henri Cordier (of Paris)* (New York: Charles Scribner, 1929), 203-204.
7. For convenient overviews of Buddhist thought and its historical development see, for example, Hajime Nakamura, *Indian Buddhism: A Survey with Bibliographical Notes* (Delhi: Motilal Banarsidass, 1987); Peter Harvey, *An Introduction to Buddhism: Teachings, History and Practices* (New York: Cambridge University Press, 1990); Noble Ross Reat, *Buddhism: A History* (Fremont, CA: Jain Publishing, 1994); Donald S. Lopez Jr., *The Story of Buddhism: A Concise Guide to Its History and Teachings* (San Francisco: HarperCollins, 2001).
8. See, for example, the introductory undergraduate textbook by Nicholas S. Brasovan, *Buddhisms in Asia: Traditions, Transmissions, and Transformations* (Albany: State University of New York Press, 2019).
9. Gregory Schopen, "Archaeology and Protestant Presuppositions in the Study of Indian Buddhism," *History of Religions* 31, no. 1 (1991): 1-23.
10. On the importance of the lay donors who paid for the production of these texts see Yukio Kasai, "Ein Kolophon um die Legende von Bokug Kagan," *Studies on the Inner Asian Languages* 19 (2004): 3-5.
11. On the importance of karmic registers in Chinese Buddhism see Cynthia Brokaw, *The Ledgers of Merit and Demerit: Social Change and Moral Order in Late Imperial China* (Princeton, NJ: Princeton University Press, 1991).
12. On the distortions and problems of applying modern categories to Central Asian art and Buddhism see Rob Linrothe, "Periperal Visions: On Recent Finds of Tangut Buddhist Art," *Monumenta Serica* 43 (1995): 235-262.
13. Kate Crosby, *Esoteric Theravada: The Story of the Forgotten Meditation Tradition of Southeast Asia* (Boulder, CO: Shambhala, 2020).
14. In the Berlin collections of Uyghur texts there are about 1,100 fragments of the *Golden Beam Sūtra* that derive from more than 70 different manuscripts and blockprints of the text. Simone-Christiane Raschmann, *Alttürkische Handschriften Teil 7. Berliner Fragmente des Goldglanz-Sutras. Teil 3: Sechstes bis zehntes Buch. Kolophone, Kommentare und Versifizierungen. Gesamtkonkordanz* (Stuttgart: Franz Steiner Verlag, 2005). For a bibliography of about 150 academic works on this text see E. Uçar, "Altun Yaruk Sudur Üzerine Yapılan Çalışmalar Hakkında Açıklamalı Bir Kaynakça Denemesi," *Türük* (2013): 227-251.
15. Yukiyo Kasai, "Ein Kommentar zu einem unbekannten uigurisch-buddhistischen Text, der aus dem Tocharischen übersetzt wurde," *Studies on the Inner Asian Languages* 21 (2006): 21-45. Based on the extant Tokharian *Vinaya* fragments, we also know that they followed both the Sarvāstivādin and Mūlasarvāstivādin monastic codes. Hirotoshi Ogihara, "On the Karmavācanā in Tocharian," in *Buddhism among the Iranian Peoples of Central Asia*, ed. Matteo De Chiara and Jens E. Braarvig (Wien: Verlag der Österreichische Akademie der Wissenschaften, 2013), 324.

16. R. E. Emmerick, *The Sūtra of Golden Light: Being a Translation of the Suvarṇabhāsottama sūtra* (London: Luzac & Company, 1970), 10-11.
17. Peter Zieme, *Buddhistische Stabreimdichtungen der Uiguren* (Berlin: Akademie Verlag, 1985), 87.
18. On these texts see Jens Wilkens, *Alttürkische Handschriften Teil 9: Buddhistische Beichttexte* (Stuttgart: Franz Steiner Verlag, 2003).
19. On the dating of the Uyghur translation to the early eleventh century see Peter Zieme, "Local Literatures: Uighur," in *Brill's Encyclopedia of Buddhism*, ed. Jonathan Silk et al. (Leiden: Brill, 2015), 876.
20. On this work see David W. Chappell, "The Precious Scroll of the Liang Emperor: Buddhist and Daoist Repentance to Save the Dead," in *Going Forth: Visions of Buddhist Vinaya*, ed. Stanley Weinstein and William M. Bodiford (Honolulu: University of Hawai'i Press, 2005), 40-67.
21. Eric M. Greene, *Chan Before Chan: Meditation, Repentance, and Visionary Experience in Chinese Buddhism* (Honolulu: University of Hawai'i Press, 2021), 162.
22. Greene, *Chan Before Chan*, 163-164.
23. Erik Zürcher, "Buddhist Chanhui and Christian Confession in Seventeenth Century China," in *Forgive Us Our Sins*, ed. N. Standaert and A. Dudink (Nettetal: Steyler Verlag, 2006), 103-127.
24. Chappell, "The Precious Scroll of the Liang Emperor," 60.
25. On the continued importance of this worldview and repentance rituals in Chinese Buddhist practice today see Justin R. Ritzinger, "Karma, Charisma, and Community: Karmic Storytelling in a Blue-Collar Taiwanese Buddhist Organization," *Journal of Chinese Buddhist Studies* 33 (2020): 203-232.
26. Jens Wilkens, *Das Buch von der Sündentilgung. Edition des alttürkisch-buddhistischen Kšanti Kılguluk Nom Bitig*, 2 vols. (Turnhout: Brepols, 2007), 9-10. Jens Wilkens, "Hatten die alten Uiguren einen buddhistischen Kanon?" in *Kanonisierung und Kanonbildung in der asiatischen Religionsgeschichte*, ed. M. Deeg, O. Freiberger, and C. Kleine (Wien: Verlag der Österreichischen Akademie der Wissenschaften, 2011), 366. When Uyghurs moved into Yuan China, however, to maintain differences between their subject peoples the Mongols forbade them to practice Han funerary rites such as burning paper money. Haiwei Liu, "Following Their Own Customs: A Reexamination of Khubilai's 1280 Edict on Muslim Practices," *Journal of the American Oriental Society* 142, no. 4 (2022): 941.
27. Kasai, "Ein Kolophon," 106-107.
28. Johan Elverskog, *Uygur Buddhist Literature* (Turnhout: Brepols, 1997), No. 79,135-138.
29. Wilkens, *Das Buch von der Sündentilgung*, 11-12. See also Wilkens, *Buddhistische Beichttexte*, 18-22.
30. Mayfair Yang, *Re-enchanting Modernity: Ritual Economy and Society in Wenzhou, China* (Durham, NC: Duke University Press, 2020), 74.
31. Kirill J. Solonin, "The Glimpses of Tangut Buddhism," *Central Asiatic Journal* 52, no. 1 (2008): 70.
32. Kirill J. Solonin, "Khitan Connection of Tangut Buddhism," in *Heishuicheng ren wen yu huan jing guo ji xue shu* 黑水城人文与环境研究: 黑水城人文与环境国际学术讨论会文集,

ed. Shen Weirong, Masayoshi Nakao, and Shi Jinbo (Beijing: Zhongguo renmin daxue chubanshe, 2007), 392-393.
33. Kirill J. Solonin, "Sinitic Buddhism in the Tangut State," *Central Asiatic Journal* 57 (2014): 170.
34. Kirill J. Solonin, "Buddhist Connections between the Liao and Xixia: Preliminary Considerations," *Journal of Song-Yuan Studies* 43 (2013): 171-219.
35. Abdurishid Yakup, *Buddhāvataṃsaka literature in Old Uyghur* (Turnhout: Brepols, 2021), 240.
36. Kōichi Kitsudō, "The Lehrtext and *Bodhisattvacaryāmārga* (Pelliot Ouïgour 4521)," in *Beşbalıkı Şingko Şeli Tutung anısına uluslararası eski Uygurca çalıştayı bildirleri, 4-6 Haziran 2011, Ankara* (Ankara: Türk Dil Kurumu, 2022), 93-95.
37. Kōichi Kitsudō, "Teachings of the Consciousness Only Inserted in the Chapter 6, Book 4 of the *Altun Yaruk Sudur*," in *Unter dem Bodhi-Baum: Festschrift für Klaus Röhrborn anlässlich des 80. Geburtstags überreicht von Kollegen, Freunden und Schülern*, ed. Z. Özertural and G. Şilfeler (Göttingen: V&R Unipress, 2019), 188.
38. On the Uyghur translation of the *Vimalakīrti Sūtra* itself see Peter Zieme, *Vimalakīrtinirdeśa-sūtra. Edition alttürkischer Übersetzungen nach Handschriftfragmenten von Berlin und Kyoto. Mit einem Appendix von Jorinde Ebert: Ein Vimalakīrti-Bildfragment aus Turfan* (Turnhout: Brepols, 2000).
39. Lambert Schmithausen, *Ālayavijñāna. On the Origin and the Early Development of a Central Concept of Yogācāra Philosophy*, vol. 2 (Tōkyō: The International Institute for Buddhist Studies, 1987).
40. Yukiyo Kasai, "The Outline of the Old Turkish Commentary on the *Vimalakīrtinirdeśa Sūtra*," in *Dunhuang Studies: Prospects and Problems for the Coming Second Century of Research*, ed. Irina Popova and Liu Yi (St. Petersburg: Slavia, 2012), 107-108. For the whole text see Kasai, "The Edition of the Old Turkish Commentary on the *Vimalakīrtinirdeśa-Sūtra*," in *Proceedings of the 1st International Colloquium on Ancient Manuscripts and Literatures of the Minorities of China*, ed. Huang Bianming and Ma Fu (Beijing: Minzu Chubanshe, 2012), and Yukiyo Kasai, "One Further Fragment of the Old Turkish Commentary on the *Vimalakīrtinirdeśa-Sūtra*," *AIBÜ Sosyal Bilimler Enstitüsü Dergesi* 13 (2013): 199-206.
41. "In a Chan Buddhist text T. 2835 *Dacheng kaixin xianxing dunwu zhenzonglun* 大乘開心顯性頓悟真宗論 the same comparison as that of the old Turkish commentary appears. This text was lost a long time ago in central China and was rediscovered among the Dunhuang manuscripts. Yamabe Nobuyoshi points out that in this Chinese Chan-Buddhist text some elements of the Yogacara school are attested, but according to his research the comparison between the four wisdoms and the three bodies of the Buddha in this text does not match any of the theories of the Yogācāra school. Therefore it stems from the author of this Chinese Chan-Buddhist text. The fact that our Old Turkish text uses this special comparison indicates that the Uighur translator knew this Chan text, the teaching that the author based it on, or the ambience in which this text or teaching were studied." Kasai, "The Outline of the Old Turkish Commentary," 109.
42. Kudara Kōgi, "Uiguru-yaku Engakukyō to sono chūshaku (The Uighur Version of the *Yuanjuejing* and the Commentary Belonging to It)," *Ryūkoku Kiyō* 14, no. 1 (1992):

1-23. On Uyghur versions of the *Yuanjuejing* see Peter Zieme, "Ein weiteres alttürkisches Fragment des 'Sūtras von den Vollkommenen Erleuchtung,'" *Acta Orientalia Academiae Scientiarum Hungaricae* 55 (2002): 281-295; Abdurishid Yakup, "On Two St. Petersburg Fragments from the Old Uyghur translation of the Chinese apocryphal text *Yuanjuejing* 圓覺經," *Contributions to the Studies of Eurasian Languages* 20 (2018): 473-483.

43. Abdurishid Yakup, *Prajñāpāramitā Literature in Old Uyghur* (Turnhout: Brepols, 2010), 235-249.
44. Abdurishid Yakup and Li Xiao, "An Old Uyghur Text Written on a Wooden Plate Recently Discovered in the Tuyoq Grottoes," *Acta Orientalia Academiae Scientiarum Hungaricae* 71, no. 3 (2018): 303-317.
45. Peter Zieme, "A Chinese Chan Text from Dunhuang in Uighur Transcription and in Translation from Turfan," in *Dunhuang Studies: Prospects and Problems for the Coming Second Century of Research*, ed. I. F. Popova and Liu Yi (Saint Petersburg: Slavia, 2012), 361-364.
46. Nobuyoshi Yamabe, "Practice of Visualization and the *Visualization Sūtra*: An Examination of Mural Paintings at Toyok, Turfan," *Pacific World: Journal of the Institute of Buddhist Studies* 4 (2002): 123-152.
47. Yakup, *Prajñāpāramitā Literature*, 1-22.
48. Jens-Uwe Hartmann, Klaus Wille, and Peter Zieme, "Aśvaghoṣa's *Buddhacarita* in the Old Uigur Literature," *Annual Report of The International Research Institute of Advanced Buddhology at Soka University* 25 (2022): 173-189.
49. On a slightly shorter version of the Chinese Maudgalyāyana *bianwen* from Dunhuang see Peter Zieme, "Buddhistische Unterweltsberichte-alttürkische Varianten aus der Turfan-Oase," in *Life and Afterlife & Apocalyptic Concepts in the Altaic World*, ed. M. Knüppel and A. van Tongerloo (Wiesbaden: Harrassowitz, 2011), 143-163.
50. Kōichi Kitsudō and Shintarō Arakawa, "New Research on the *Guanxin Shijietu* (*Illustration of the Ten Realms of Mind Contemplation*)—The Case of the Xixia and the Uyghur Kingdoms," *Kokka* 1477 (2018): 5-20.
51. On the "material turn" in Buddhist studies see John Kieschnick, *The Impact of Buddhism on Chinese Material Culture* (Princeton, NJ: Princeton University Press, 2003); Fabio Rambelli, *Buddhist Materiality: A Cultural History of Objects in Japanese Buddhism* (Stanford, CA: Stanford University Press, 2007).
52. In the Chinese case there was a threefold process: 1. a master read or recited from memory the text; 2. this was translated by one or more people and then written down; 3. the translation was re-evaluated and fixed in committee. J. W. de Jong, "Buddha's Word in China," *East Asian History* 11 (1996): 55.
53. Klaus Röhrborn, "Šingko Šäli Tutung und die Organisation der Übersetzungstätigkeit bei den Uiguren," in *Turkologie heute-Tradition und Perspektive*, ed. N. Demir and E. Taube (Wiesbaden: Harrassowitz, 1998), 255-260.
54. The revision of the Uyghur translation of the *Bayangjing*, for example, included the elision of earlier Manichean elements that made the text more Buddhist. See Juten Oda, *A Study of the Buddhist Sutra Säkiz Yükmäk Yaruq or Säkiz Törlügin Yarumïš Yaltrïmïš in Old Turkic* (Turnhout: Brepols, 2015), 5-9.

55. Dieter Maue and Klaus Röhrborn, "Ein Caityastotra aus dem alttürkischen *Goldglanz-Sūtra*," *Zeitschrift der Deutschen Morgenländischen Gesellschaft* 129 (1979): 289. See also Tibor Porció, "On the Technique of Translating Buddhist Texts into Uygur," in *Indien und Zentralasien: Sprach-und Kulturkontakt, Göttingen 7.-10. Mai 2001*, ed. S. Bretfeld and J. Wilkens (Wiesbaden: Harrassowitz, 2003), 85-94.
56. Takao Moriyasu, *Corpus of the Old Uighur Letters from the Eastern Silk Road* (Turnhout: Brepols, 2019), no. 86, 111.
57. On this text—and this particular passage—see Patrick Carré, *Introduction aux pratiques de la non-dualité. Commentaire du Soutra de la Liberté inconcevable* (Paris: Fayard, 2004), 119.
58. Kasai, "The Edition of the Old Turkish Commentary on the *Vimalakīrtinirdeśa-Sūtra*," 403.
59. On the cult of the book see Gregory Schopen, "The Phrase '*sa pṛthivīpradeśaś caityabhūto bhavet*' in the *Vajracchedikā*: Notes on the Cult of the Book in the Mahāyāna," *Indo-Iranian Journal* 17, no. 3-4 (1975): 147-181.
60. Simone-Christiane Raschmann, "What Do We Know About the Use of Manuscripts Among the Old Uighurs in the Turfan Region?" *Eurasian Studies* 12 (2014): 523-540. Yukiyo Kasai, "Central Asian and Iranian Influence in Old Uyghur Buddhist Manuscripts: Book Forms and Donor Colophons," in *The Syntax of Colophons: A Comparative Study Across Pothi Manuscripts*, ed. Nalini Balbir and Giovanni Ciotti (Berlin: Walter de Gruyter, 2022), 375-380. On the use of wood as a writing surface see Abdurishid Yakup, "On the Old Uyghur Wooden Nameplates from the West Zone of the Tuyoq Grottoes in Turfan and the Wooden Objects with Old Uyghur Writing," *Acta Orientalia Academiae Scientiarum Hungaricae* 75, no. 3 (2002): 371-390.
61. On the paleography of the Uyghur script see Takao Moriyasu, "From Silk, Cotton and Copper Coin to Silver: Transition of the Currency Used by the Uighurs during the Period from the 8th to the 14th Centuries," in *Turfan Revisited: The First Century of Research into the Arts and Cultures of the Silk Road*, ed. D. Durkin-Meistererenst et al. (Berlin: Dietrich Reimer, 2004), 228-229.
62. For example, a copy of the *Commentary on the Lotus Sutra* (T 1723) translated by Šingko Šäli Tutung has on the verso "the paper is from Shazhou." T. Thilo, "Fragmente chinesischer Haushaltsregister aus Dunhuang in der Berliner Turfan-Sammlung," *Mitteilungen des Instituts für Orientforschung* XIV (1968): 303-313.
63. Simone-Christiane Raschmann, personal communication, November 18, 2021.
64. Yukiyo Kasai, "Talismans used by the Uyghur Buddhists and Their Relationship with the Chinese Tradition," *Journal of the International Association of Buddhist Studies* 44 (2021): 527-556. For distinctive Uyghur talismans on wood that were presumably worn around the neck see Fu Ma and Xia Lidong, "Philological Study of Several Old Uighur Tantric Manuscripts Recently Unearthed from Tuyuq, Xinjiang," *Acta Orientalia Academiae Scientiarum Hungaricae* 75, no. 1 (2022): 15-31.
65. On the cult of Guanyin see Chün-fang Yü, *Kuan-yin: The Chinese Transformation of Avalokiteśvara* (New York: Columbia University Press, 2000). On the Guanyin cult among the Uyghur see Chen Aifeng 陈爱峰, 高昌回鹘时期吐鲁番观音图研究 (*Study on Turpan Avalokiteśvara Paintings of Qočo Uighur Period*) (Shanghai: Shanghai Guji Chubanshe, 2020); Yukiyo Kasai, "The Avalokiteśvara Cult in Turfan and Dunhuang in the Pre-Mongolian Period," in *Buddhist Rituals in Central Asia II: Practices and Rituals, Visual*

and *Material Transfer*, ed. Yukiyo Kasai and Henrik H. Sørensen (Leiden: Brill, 2022), 246-271.

66. Peter Zieme, "Some Notes on Old Uigur Art and Texts," in *Buddhism and Art in Turfan: From the Perspective of Uyghur Buddhism*, ed. Irisawa Takashi (Kyoto: Research Center for Buddhist Culture in Asia Ryukoku University, 2012), 12.

67. Miki Morita, "Kṣitigarbha Images from the Turfan Region: An Aspect of Uyghur Buddhist Art of the 9th to 14th Centuries" (Ph.D. diss., University of Pennsylvania, 2014).

68. Kōichi Kitsudō and Peter Zieme, "The *Jin'gangjing zuan* in Old Uighur with Parallels in Tangut and Chinese," *Written Monuments of the Orient* 2 (2017): 72.

69. Zhiru, "The Maitreya Connection in the Tang Development of Dizang Worship," *Harvard Journal of Asiatic Studies* 65, no. 1 (2005): 99-132; Zhiru, *The Making of a Savior Bodhisattva: Dizang in Medieval China* (Honolulu: University of Hawai'i Press, 2007).

70. On the Uyghur donors of Chinese style artwork at Dunhuang see Lilla Russell-Smith, *Uygur Patronage in Dunhuang: Regional Art Centres on the Northern Silk Road in the Tenth and Eleventh Centuries* (Leiden: Brill, 2005), 172-189.

71. The Chinese influence can also be seen in the Uyghur representation of Mañjuśrī; see Zheng Huiming, "An Iconographic Study of Pictorial Fragments 'Mañjuśri and His Assistants' from the Bezeklik Caves," in *Sergej Federovič Ol'denburg: učenyj i organizator nauki* (Moscow: NAUKA, 2016), 379-403.

72. Nancy Steinhardt, "The Uighur Ritual Complex in Beiting," *Orientations* 3, no. 1-2 (1999): 35-36.

73. It is unclear what this historical mural represents; however, Nancy Steinhardt has suggested that it is part of a larger death journey narrative. "The location of this man at the entrance, with a monumental Buddha behind him and an image of the death of the Buddha (*parinirvana*), in a niche below him, has led to interpretation of the monument as a Uyghur shrine to Buddhist death, perhaps also the death of a ruler." Nancy Shatzman Steinhardt, *The Borders of Chinese Architecture* (Cambridge, MA: Harvard University Press, 2022), 126.

74. Peter Zieme, "Scenes from the *Lotus Sūtra*: An Old Uygur Temple Banner with Cartouche Inscriptions," *Manuscripta Orientalia* 27, no. 1 (2021): 3-19. See also Chhaya Bhattacharya-Haesner, *Central Asian Temple Banners in the Turfan Collection of the Museum für Indische Kunst, Berlin* (Berlin: Dietrich Reimer Verlag, 2003).

75. For Uyghur texts promoting the practice of visiting holy sites see Maue and Röhrborn, "Ein Caityastotra aus dem alttürkischen *Goldglanz-Sūtra*," 282-320; Peter Zieme, "Caitya Veneration—an Uigur Manuscript with Portraits of Donors," *Journal of Inner Asian Art and Archaeology* 2 (2007): 165-172; Peter Zieme, "The Bodhisattva Sattvauṣadha 'Medicine of all Beings,'" in *"The Way of the Buddha" 2003: The 100th Anniversary of the Otani Missions and the 50th of the Research Society for Central Asian Cultures*, ed. Irisawa Takashi (Kyoto: Ryukoku University, 2010), 35-45.

76. Dai Matsui, "敦煌石窟ウイグル語．モンゴル語題記銘文集成 Tonkō sekkutsu uigurugo mongorugo, daiki meibun shūsei (Uighur and Mongolian Wall Inscriptions of the Dunhuang Grottoes)," in 敦煌石窟多言語資料集成 *Tonkō sekkutsu tagengo shiryō shūsei* (Multilingual Source Materials of the Dunhuang Grottoes), ed. Dai Matsui and

Shintarō Arakawa (Tokyo: Tōkyō gaikokugo daigaku Ajia Afurika gengo bunka kenkyūjo, 2017), 1-161.

77. Dai Matsui, "Uigur Manuscripts Related to the Monks Sivšidu and Yaqšidu at 'Abita-Cave Temple' of Toyoq," in *Essays on the Third International Conference on Turfan Studies: The Origins and Migrations of Eurasian Nomadic Peoples*, ed. Academia Turfanica (Shanghai: Shanghai gu Chubanshe, 2010), 707.

78. Tibor Porció, "Some Peculiarities of the Uygur Buddhist Pilgrim Inscriptions," in *Searching for the Dharma, Finding Salvation—Buddhist Pilgrimage in Time and Space*, ed. Christoph Cueppers and Max Deeg (Lumbini: Lumbini International Research Institute, 2014), 172.

79. Uyghur pilgrim inscriptions are found as far east the White Pagoda in the ancient city of Fengzhou (located 17 km from Hohhot). Simone-Christiane Raschmann, "Pilgrims in Old Uyghur Inscriptions: A Glimpse Behind the Records," in *Buddhism in Central Asia I: Patronage, Legitimation, Sacred Space, and Pilgrimage*, ed. C. Meinert and H. H. Sørensen (Leiden: Brill, 2020), 210.

80. Fu Ma and Xia Lidong, "Comprehensive Study on Old Uighur and Chinese Wall Inscriptions in Room B of Newly Excavated Cave 26 in Tuyuq Grottoes, Turfan," *Acta Orientalia Academiae Scientiarum Hungaricae* 74, no. 2 (2021): 187.

81. Fu and Xia, "Comprehensive Study on Old Uighur and Chinese Wall Inscriptions," 195.

82. Matsui, "Remarks on Buyan Qaya," 210.

83. Fu and Xia, "Comprehensive Study on Old Uighur and Chinese Wall Inscriptions," 184.

84. Maya K. H. Stiller, *Carving Status at Kŭmgangsan: Elite Graffiti in Premodern Korea* (Seattle: University of Washington Press, 2021).

85. Thomas T. Allsen, "Mongolian Princes and their Merchant Partners 1200-1260," *Asia Major* 3, no. 2 (1989): 86-94.

86. Thomas T. Allsen, "The Yüan Dynasty and the Uighurs of the Turfan in the 13th Century," in *China Among Equals*, ed. Morris Rossabi (Berkeley: University of California Press, 1983), 245-246.

87. Michael C. Brose, "Uyghur Technologists of Writing and Literacy in Mongol China," *T'oung Pao* 91, no. 4/5 (2005): 405.

88. I borrow the term "steppe intelligentsia" from Paul D. Buell, "Cinqai (ca. 1169-1252)," in *In the Service of the Khan: Eminent Personalities of the Early Mongol-Yüan Period (1200–1300)*, ed. Igor de Rachewiltz et al. (Wiesbaden: Harrassowitz, 1993), 95. See also Ch'en Yüan, *Western and Central Asians in China under the Mongols: Their Transformation into Chinese*, trans. Ch'ien Hsing-hai and L. Carrington Goodrich (Los Angeles: Monumenta Serica at UCLA, 1966); and Igor de Rachewiltz, "Turks in China under the Mongols: A Preliminary Investigation of Turco-Mongol Relations in the 13th and 14th Centuries," in *China Among Equals: The Middle Kingdom and Its Neighbours, 10th–14th Centuries*, ed. Morris Rossabi (Berkeley: University of California Press, 1983), 281-310; Geng Shimin and Zhang Baoxi, "Yuan huihuwen 'Zhong xiu wen shu si bei,' chu shi," *Kaogu xuebao* 2 (1986): 253-264.

89. This relationship was not unidirectional. Uyghur Buddhism also had a profound effect on the development of Mongolian Buddhism. Masahiro Shōgaito, "Uighur Influence on Indian Words in Mongolian Buddhist Texts," in *Indien und Zentralasien: Sprach und*

Kulturkontakt, ed. Sven Bretfeld and Jens Wilkens (Wiesbaden: Harrassowitz Verlag, 2003), 119-143; Takashi Matsukawa, "Some Uighur Elements Surviving in the Mongolian Buddhist *Sūtra of the Great Bear*," in *Turfan Revisited: The First Century of Research into the Arts and Cultures of the Silk Road*, ed. D. Durkin-Meisterernst et al. (Berlin: Dietrich Reimer Verlag, 2004), 203-207.

90. Peter Zieme, "Notes on Religion in the Mongol Empire," in *Islam and Tibet: Interactions along the Musk Routes*, ed. Anna Akasoy, Charles Burnett and Ronit Yoeli-Tlalim (Farnham: Ashgate, 2011), 177-187.

91. Peter Zieme, *Religion und Gessellschaft im Uigurischen Königreich von Qočo.* (Opladen: Westdeutscher Verlag, 1992), 71-78.

92. Kasai, "Ein Kolophon," 21-22. The Uyghur ruler, the "Idiqut Khan," is also mentioned in three other colophons; see Kasai, "Ein Kolophon," 112-115, and Nrs. 40, 144 and 149.

93. Jan Wilkens, "Buddhism in the West Uygur Kingdom and Beyond," in *Transfer of Buddhism across Central Asian Networks (7th to 13th Centuries)*, ed. Carmen Meinert (Leiden: Brill, 2016), 240.

94. Niu Ruji, "A Fragment of a Buddhist Refuge Formula in Uighur in the Pelliot Collection," in *De Dunhuang à Istanbul: Hommage à James Russell Hamilton*, ed. L. Bazin and P. Zieme (Turnhout: Brepols, 2001), 228.

95. On the building of Buddhist monuments during the reign of Ögedei Khan (1186-1241, r. 1229-1241) see F. W. Cleaves, "The Sino-Mongolian Inscription of 1346," *Harvard Journal of Asiatic Studies* 15 (1952): 1-123; and Christina Franken, *Die "Große Halle" von Karakorum: Zur archäologischen Untersuchung des ersten buddhistischen Tempels der alten mongolischen Hauptstadt* (Wiesbaden: Reichert Verlag. 2015). See also Herbert Franke, *Chinesischer und tibetischer Buddhismus im China der Yüanzeit* (Munich: Kommission für Zentralasiatische Studien/Bayerische Akademie der Wissenschaften, 1996); Leonard van der Kuijp, *The Kālacakra and the Patronage of Buddhism by the Mongol Imperial Family* (Bloomington: Indiana University Department of Central Eurasian Studies, 2004).

96. On early Mongol-Tangut relations see Elliot Sperling, "Lama to the King of Hsia," *The Journal of the Tibet Society* 7 (1987): 31-50; Elliot Sperling, "Notes on References to 'Bri-Gung-pa-Mongol Contact in the Late Sixteenth and Early Seventeenth Centuries," in *Tibetan Studies: Proceedings of the 5th Seminar of the International Association of Tibetan Studies*, ed. Ihara Shoren and Yamaguchi Ziuho (Narita: Naritasan Shinsoji, 1992), 741-750; Ruth W. Dunnell, "The Hsia Origins of the Yüan Institution of Imperial Preceptor," *Asia Major* 5 (1992): 85-111.

97. Karl Debreczeny, "Faith and Empire: An Overview," in *Faith and Empire: The Art of Politics in Tibetan Buddhism*, ed. K. Debreczeny (New York: Rubin Museum of Art, 2019), 31-33.

98. On early Mongol-Tibetan contacts and the conquest of Tibet see Dieter Schuh, *Erlasse und Sendschreiben mongolischer Herrscher für tibetische Geistliche* (St. Augustin: VGH-Wissenschaftsverlag, 1977), 31-41; Christopher P. Atwood, "The First Mongol Contacts with the Tibetans," in *Trails of the Tibetan Tradition: Papers for Elliot Sperling*, ed. Roberto Vitali, 21-46 (Dharamsala: Amnye Machen Institute, 2014).

99. Thomas T. Allsen, *Commodity and Exchange in the Mongol Empire: A Cultural History of Islamic Textiles* (New York: Cambridge University Press, 1997), 50.

100. János Szerb, "Glosses on the Oeuvre of Bla-ma 'Phags-pa: III. The 'Patron-Patronized' Relationship," in *Soundings in Tibetan Civilization*, ed. Barbara Nimri Aziz and Matthew T. Kapstein (New Delhi: Manohar, 1985), 166.
101. On the Pakpa script see Karl-Heinz Everding, *Herrscherurkunden aus der Zeit des mongolischen Großreiches für tibetische Adelshäuser, Geistliche und Klöster. Teil 1: Diplomata Mongolica. Mittelmongolische Urkunden in 'Phags-pa-Schrift. Edition, Übersetzung, Analyse* (Halle: International Institute for Tibetan and Buddhist Studies. 2006); W. South Coblin, *A Handbook of 'Phags-pa Chinese* (Honolulu: University of Hawai'i Press, 2007); and Peter Zieme, "Turkic Fragments in 'Phags-pa Script," *Studies on the Inner Asian Languages* 13 (1998): 63-69.
102. David M. Farquhar, "Emperor as Bodhisattva in the Governance of the Ch'ing Empire," *Harvard Journal of Asiatic Studies* 38, no. 1 (1978): 5-34.
103. Robert M. Gimello, "Wu-t'ai Shan during the Early Chin Dynasty: The Testimony of Chu Pien," *Zhonghua foxue xuebao* 7 (1997): 506-509.
104. Yukiyo Kasai, "The Bodhisattva Mañjuśrī, Mt. Wutai, and Uyghur Pilgrims," *BuddhistRoad Paper* 5, no. 4 (2020): 3-39.
105. This included not only the standard text focusing on Mañjuśrī, the *Mañjuśrīnāmasaṃgīti* (Elverskog, *Uygur Buddhist Literature*, No. 67), but also the *Acintyabuddhaviṣayanirdeśa* (T. 340), which was translated from Chinese into Uyghur by the famous translator Čisön Tutung, as well as the *Mahāyāna Yoga of the Adamantine Ocean, Mañjuśrī with a Thousand Arms and a Thousand Bowls: King of Tantra* (T. 1177), and the *Wutaishanzan* (*Praise of Mount Wutai*), which was not only translated into Uyghur but also prepared in a Chinese transcription. Peter Zieme, "Mount Wutai and Mañjuśrī in Old Uigur Buddhism," in *The Transnational Cult of Mount Wutai: Historical and Comparative Perspectives*, ed. Susan Andrews, Jinhua Chen, and Guang Kuan, 223-237 (Leiden: Brill, 2020); Peter Zieme, "Three Old Turkic *Wutaishanzan* Fragments," *Studies on the Inner Asian Languages* 17 (2002): 223-239.
106. Raschmann, "Pilgrims in Old Uyghur Inscriptions," 207.
107. Henrik H. Sørensen, "Donors and Esoteric Buddhism in Dunhuang during the Reign of the Guiyijun," in *Buddhism in Central Asia I: Patronage, Legitimation, Sacred Space, and Pilgrimage*, ed. Carmen Meinert and Henrik H. Sørensen (Leiden: Brill, 2020), 121.
108. Wilkens, "Practice and Rituals in Uyghur Buddhist Texts," 448-453.
109. György Kara and Peter Zieme, *Die uigurischen Übersetzungen des Guruyogas 'Tiefer Weg' von Sa-skya Paṇḍita und der Mañjuśrīnāmasaṃgīti* (Berlin: Akademie Verlag, 1977).
110. György Kara and Peter Zieme, *Fragmente tantrischer Werke in uigurischer Übersetzung* (Berlin: Akademie Verlag, 1976), 46-62.
111. Peter Zieme and György Kara, *Ein uigurisches Totenbuch: Naropas Lehre in uigurischer Übersetzung* (Budapest: Akadémiai Kiadó, 1979).
112. Peter Zieme, "Zum uigurischen *Tārā-Ekaviṃśatistotra*," *Acta Orientalia Academiae Scientiarum Hungaricae* 36 (1982): 583-597.
113. Kara and Zieme, *Fragmente tantrischer Werke*, 63-69.
114. On the Uyghur intellectuals, scholars, and diplomats working at the Mongol court see Herbert Franke, "A Sino-Uighur Family Portrait: Notes on a Woodcut from Turfan," *The Canada-Mongolia Review* 4, no. 1 (1978): 33-40; Michael C. Brose, *Subjects and Masters:*

Uyghur Elites in Mongol China (Bellingham: Western Washington University Center for East Asian Studies, 2007); Michael C. Brose, "Neo-Confucian Uyghur Semuren in Koryŏ and Chosŏn Korean Society and Politics," in *Eurasian Influences on Yuan China*, ed. Morris Rossabi (Singapore: Institute of Southeast Asian Studies, 2013), 178-199.

115. Herbert Franke, "Chinesische Nachrichten über Karunadaz und seine Familie," in *Turfan, Khotan und Dunhuang*, ed. R. E. Emmerick et al. (Berlin: Akademie Verlag, 1996), 83-93.
116. Yakup, *Buddhāvataṃsaka Literature in Old Uyghur*, 5-6.
117. Herbert Franke, "Chinesische Quellen über den uigurischen Stifter Dhanyasena," in *Memoriae Munusculum: Gedenkband für Annemarie von Gabain*, ed. K. Röhrborn and W. Veenker (Wiesbaden: Harrassowitz, 1994), 55-64.
118. Kōgi Kudara, "Uigur and Tibetan Translations of 'The History of the Buddha Statue of Sandalwood in China," in *Turfan Revisited: The First Century of Research into the Arts and Cultures of the Silk Road*, ed. D. Durkin-Meisterernst et al. (Berlin: Dietrich Reimer Verlag, 2004), 149-154.
119. Abdrishid Yakup, "On an Old Uyghur Fragment of the *Huayan Chanyi* 華嚴懺儀 'Huayan Repentance Ritual' from the Berlin Turfan Collection," *Acta Orientalia Academiae Scientiarum Hungaricae* 74, no. 2 (2021): 171-180.
120. Herbert Franke, "A Note on the Multilinguality in China under the Mongols: The Compilers of the Revised Buddhist Canon, 1285-87," in *Opuscala Altaica: Essays Presented in Honor of Henry Schwarz*, ed. Edward H. Kaplan and Donald W. Whisenhunt (Bellingham: Western Washington University, 1994), 286-298.
121. Peter Zieme, "A Fragment of an Old Uighur Translation of the *Śatapañcāśatka*," *Annual Report of the International Research Institute for Advanced Buddhology at Soka University* XXIII (2019): 333-343.
122. On the use of multiple sources for the translation of Uyghur texts in the Yuan period see Abdurishid Yakup, *Altuigurische Aparimitāyus-Literatur und kleinere tantrische Texte* (Turnhout: Brepols, 2016).
123. Yukiyo Kasai, Simone-Christiane Raschmann, and Peter Zieme, "Introduction," in *The Old Uyghur Āgama fragments preserved in the Sven Hedin collection, Stockholm*, ed. Yukiyo Kasai et al. (Turnhout: Brepols, 2017), 20.
124. Kasai, Raschmann, and Zieme, "Introduction," 20.
125. Johan Elverskog, "Religious Exchange," in *The Cambridge History of the Mongol Empire*, ed. Michal Biran and Hodong Kim (New York: Cambridge University Press, 2023), 525-549.
126. Jens Wilkens, "A Sanskrit Fragment of the *Mañjuśrīnāmasaṃgīti* in Uyghur Script," *International Journal of Old Uygur Studies* 2, no. 1 (2020): 27-35; Ayşe Kılıç Cengiz, "A Fragment of the *Uṣṇīṣavijayā Dhāraṇī* from Turfan Housed in the Museum für Asiatische Kunst in Berlin," *Acta Orientalia Academiae Scientiarum Hungaricae* 74, no. 4 (2021): 651-672; Jens Wilkens, "A Buddhist Spell Transliterated: A Sanskrit Version of the *Uṣṇīṣavijayādhāraṇī* in Uyghur and Brāhmī Scripts," *Annual Report of The International Research Institute for Advanced Buddhology at Soka University* 25 (2022): 191-209.
127. In many cases, however, this seemingly sophisticated philological work was less than stellar, which has led Yukiyo Kasai to surmise that "the use of the Brāhmī script surely

opened the possibility to write Sanskrit words in an accurate way, but it did not seem to be really utilized by most Uyghur Buddhists." Thus in her estimation the Uyghur use of Brāhmī in the Mongol period was more of an affectation than a true scholarly renaissance. Yukiyo Kasai, "Sanskrit Word Forms Written in Brāhmī Script in the Old Uyghur Buddhist Texts," *Journal of the International Association of Buddhist Studies* 38 (2015): 401-422.

128. For a full list of all the *Āgama* fragments see Kasai, Raschmann, and Zieme, "Introduction," 26-31.

129. There are now ten identified Abhidharma texts in Uyghur: 1. *Abhidharmakośa-bhāṣya* (T. 1558); 2. *Abhidharmakośaṭīkātattvārthā* (T. 1561); 3. *Abhidharmakośakārikā* (T. 1560); 4. Commentaries on the gathas in the *Abhidharmakośa-bhāṣya*; 5. *Abhidharmāvatāra* (T. 1554); 6. *Nyāyānusārin/Nyāyānusāra* (T. 1562); 7. An excerpt called "Pratītyasamutpāda of every kind" by Kudara; 8. Commentary on the *Abhidharmakośa-bhāṣya* named *Jinhuachao* ("Golden Flower"); 9. Unknown Abhidharma text; 10. bilingual Sanskrit-Uyghur Abhidharma texts in Brāhmī script. Yukiyo Kasai, "Five Old Uyghur Abhidharma Texts Containing Brāhmī Elements." *BuddhistRoad Paper* 1, no. 1 (2019): 4.

130. Kasai, Raschmann, Zieme, "Introduction," 22.

131. Shōgaito, *The Uighur Abhidharmakośabhāṣya*, 1-5

132. Louis de la Vallée Poussin, *L'Abhidharmakosa de Vasubandhu*, vols. 1-6 (Paris: Paul Geuthner, 1923-1931).

133. Kasai, "Five Old Uyghur Abhidharma Texts," 8.

134. See, for example, the political consequences of the early eighteenth century debate about robes in Burma (Braun, *The Birth of Insight*, 16-17).

135. Peter Zieme, "Das *Pravāraṇā-Sūtra* in alttürkischer Überlieferung," in *Barg-i sabz—A Green Leaf: Papers in Honour of Jes P. Asmussen*, ed. P. O. Skjaervo, et al. (Leiden: Brill, 1988), 445-453; Jens Wilkens, "Buddhist Monastic Life in Central Asia: A Bilingual Text in Sanskrit and Old Uyghur Relating to the *Pravāraṇā* Ceremony," *International Journal of Old Uyghur Studies* 2, no. 2 (2020): 137-152.

136. Peter Zieme, "On some quotations in the Uighur *Insadi-Sutra*," *Bukkyogaku Kenkyu* 60-61 (2006): 1-14.

137. Yang Fuxue, "Three Uighur Inscriptions Quoted from *Altun Yaruq* in Dunhuang Mogao Grottoes 464," in *Beşbalikli Şingko Şali Tutung Anisina Uluslararasi Eski Uygurca Çaliştayi Bildirleri, 4–6 Haziran 2011, Ankara*, ed. (Ankara: Türk Dil Kurumu, 2022), 239-246.

138. Peter Zieme, "Donor and Colophon of an Uigur Blockprint," *Silk Road Art and Archaeology: Journal of the Institute of Silk Road Studies, Kamakura* 4 (1996): 415-416.

139. Timothy H. Barrett, *The Woman Who Discovered Printing* (New Haven, CT: Yale University Press, 2013).

140. Kaiqi Hua, "The White Cloud Movement: Local Activism and Buddhist Printing in China under Mongol Rule (1276-1368 CE)," (Ph.D. diss., University of California Merced, 2016); Hildegaard Diemberger, Franz-Karl Ehrhard, and Peter Kornicki, *Tibetan Printing: Comparisons, Continuities and Change* (Leiden: Brill, 2016); Shi-Shan Susan Huang, "Reassessing Printed Buddhist Frontispieces from Xi Xia," *Zhejiang University Journal of Art and Archaeology* 1 (2014): 129-182.

4. Uyghur Buddhisms

141. There are more than 1,500 fragments of block-printed Uyghur texts, most of which are Buddhist. They comprise about 12 percent of the 8,000 fragments in the Berlin collection, about 1,000; the other 500 are in collections in China, France, Britain, Japan, and Russia. Abdrishid Yakup, "On a Chinese-Old Uyghur bilingual block-printed fragment discovered in the Bezelik caves in Turfan," in *Unter dem Bodhi-Baum: Festschrift für Klaus Röhrborn anlässlich des 80. Geburtstags überreicht von Kollegen, Freunden und Schülern*, ed. Z. Özertural and G. Şilfeler (Göttingen: V&R Unipress, 2019), 411–416.

142. Abdurishid Yakup, *Alttürkische Handschriften Teil 11: Die uigurischen Blockdrucke der Berliner Turfansammlung. Teil 1: Tantrische Texte* (Stuttgart: Franz Steiner Verlag, 2007); Abdrishid Yakup, *Alttürkische Handschriften Teil 12: Die uigurischen Blockdrucke der Berliner Turfansammlung. Teil 2: Apokryphen, Mahāyāna-Sūtren, Erzählungen, Magische Texte, Kommentare und Kolophone* (Stuttgart: Franz Steiner Verlag, 2008); Abdrishid Yakup, *Alttürkische Handschriften Teil 15: Die uigurischen Blockdrucke der Berliner Turfansammlung. Teil 3: Stabreimdichtungen, Kalendarisches, Bilder, unbestimmte Fragmente und Nachträge* (Stuttgart: Franz Steiner Verlag, 2009).

143. Kasai, "Zur Verbreitung und Verwendung altuigurischer buddhistischer Texte," in *Eine hundertblättrige Tulpe—Bir sadbarg lāla: Festgabe für Claus Schönig*, ed. I. Hauenschild, M. Kappler, and B. Kellner-Heinkele (Berlin: Klaus Schwarz Verlag, 2016), 225–226.

5. BECOMING MUSLIM

1. Abdurishid Yakup, "On the Interlinear Uyghur Poetry in the Newly Unearthed Nestorian Text," in *Splitter aus der Gegend von Turfan: Festschrift für Peter Zieme anläßlich seines 60.*, ed. Mehmet Ölmez and Simone-Christiane Raschmann (Istanbul: Türk Dilleri Arastirmalari Dizisi, 2002), 415.

2. On the violent component of Sinhalese Buddhist nationalism see: Stanley J. Tambiah, *Buddhism Betrayed?: Religion, Politics, and Violence in Sri Lanka* (Chicago: University of Chicago Press, 1992); Tessa J. Bartholomeusz and Chandra Richard De Silva, ed., *Fundamentalism and Minority Identities in Sri Lanka* (Albany: State University of New York Press, 1998); Tessa J. Bartholomeusz, *In Defense of Dharma: Just-War Ideology in Buddhist Sri Lanka* (New York: RoutledgeCurzon, 2002); and Ananda Abeyesekara, "The Saffron Army, Violence, Terror(ism): Buddhism, Identity, and Difference in Sri Lanka," *Numen* 48, no. 1 (2001): 1–46. On the Buddhist persecution of Muslims in Myanmar see Melissa Crouch, *Islam and the State in Myanmar: Muslim-Buddhist Relations and the Politics of Belonging* (New York: Oxford University Press, 2016); Francis Wade, *Myanmar's Enemy Within: Buddhist Violence and the Making of a Muslim "Other"* (London: Zed Books, 2017); Michael Walton, *Buddhism, Politics, and Political Thought in Myanmar* (New York: Cambridge University Press, 2018).

3. The Uyghur influence on Mongolian socioeconomic culture is reflected in the fact that many basic terms like "millet," "wheat," "labor service," "loss or damage," "land tax," and others all derive from Uyghur. Dai Matsui, "Uigur-Turkic Influence as Seen in the Qara-Qota Mongolian Documents," in *Actual Problems of Turkic Studies: Dedicated to the 180th Anniversary of the Department of Turkic Philology at the St. Petersburg State University* (St. Petersburg: St. Petersburg State University, 2016), 559–561.

4. Johan Elverskog, "The Uighurs and Shambhala," *The Berlin Journal* 35 (2021): 58–62. Some contemporary scholars have duly noted that the *Kālacakratantra* and related literature does seem to locate Shambhala in relation to the Uyghur kingdom. As John Newman explains: "Although the Buddhist myth of Shambhala derives from the Hindu Kalki myth, this does not mean that the Buddhist Shambhala is a mere fiction. If we assume a Buddhist Shambhala actually existed at the time of the composition of the Sanskrit *Kālacakra* literature, it is not too difficult to determine what historical entity it corresponded to. The primary texts of the *Kālacakra* system came into being around the beginning of the 11th century, so Shambhala must have existed at that time. The *Vimalaprabha* tells us that Shambhala is on a latitude north of Tibet, Khotan and China. Furthermore, the *Vimalaprabha* says again and again that Shambhala is north of the Sita River. The descriptions of the Chinese traveler Xuanzang (7th century), and the Tibetan traveler Man lungs Guru (13th century) both clearly identify the Sita as the Tarim River in Eastern Turkestan. Thus Shambhala must be a special name for the Uighur kingdom centered at Kocho that flourished circa 850–1250." John R. Newman, "A Brief History of the Kalacakra," in *The Wheel of Time: The Kalacakra in Context*, ed. Geshe Lhundub Sopa, Roger Jackson, and John Newman (Ithaca, NY: Snow Lion, 1991), 83–84.
5. Michel Biran, *The Empire of the Qara Khitai in Eurasian History: Between China and the Islamic World* (New York: Cambridge University Press, 2005).
6. The same view of both India and China was also to develop later in Europe. See, for example, David Porter, *Ideographica: The Chinese Cipher in Early Modern Europe* (Stanford, CA: Stanford University Press, 2001).
7. Biran, *The Empire of the Qara Khitai*, 100.
8. A. K. S. Lambton, "Justice in the Medieval Persian Theory of Kingship," *Studia Islamica* 17 (1962): 91–119.
9. Biran, *The Empire of the Qara Khitai*, 171.
10. Thomas T. Allsen, "Mongolian Princes and their Merchant Partners 1200–1260," *Asia Major* 3, no. 2 (1989): 86–94.
11. 'Ala-ad-Din 'Ata-Malik Juvaini, *The History of the World Conqueror*, trans. John A. Boyle (Manchester: Manchester University Press, 1958), 64–65.
12. Devin DeWeese, "'Stuck in the Throat of Chingiz Khan': Envisioning the Mongol Conquests in Some Sufi Accounts from the 14th to 17th Centuries," in *History and Historiography of Post-Mongol Central Asia and the Middle East: Studies in Honor of John E. Woods*, ed. J. Pfeiffer and S. A. Quinn (Wiesbaden: Harrassowitz, 2006), 23–60. Another strategy used to legitimate the Mongols was to parallel them with the great pre-Muslim Iranian kings as found in Firdausi's *Shahnama*. Abolala Soudavar, for example, has argued that the incidents selected for illustration in the Great Mongol *Shahnama* were chosen for their parallels with events in Mongol history ("The Saga of Abu-Sa'id Bahador Khan. The Abu-Sa'idnamé," in *The Court of the Il-khans 1290–1340*, ed. Julian Raby and Teresa Fitzherbert [Oxford: Oxford University Press, 1996], 95–211). On this topic see also the four articles by A. S. Melikian-Chirvani, "Le *Shah-name*, la gnose soufie et le pouvoir mongol," *Journal asiatique* 222 (1984): 249–338; "Le Livre des rois, miroir du destin, I," *Studia Iranica* 17, no. 1 (1988): 7–46; "Le Livre des rois, miroir du destin, II: Takht-e

Soleyman et la symbolique du *Shah-name*," *Studia Iranica* 20, no. 1 (1991): 33-148; "Conscience du passé et résistance culturelle dans l'Iran mongol," in *L'Iran face à la domination mongole*, ed. Denise Aigle (Tehran: Institut Français de Recherche en Iran, 1997), 135-177; as well as Sheila S. Blair, "A Mongol Envoy," in *The Iconography of Islamic Art: Studies in Honour of Robert Hillenbrand*, ed. Bernard O'Kane (Edinburgh: Edinburgh University Press, 2005), 45-46.

13. Biran, *The Empire of the Qara Khitai*, 198.
14. Juvaini, *History of the World Conqueror*, 52.
15. Juvaini, *History of the World Conqueror*, 60, 70-74.
16. Guillaume de Rubrouck, *The Mission of Friar William: His Journey to the court of the Great Khan Möngke 1253-1255*, trans. Peter Jackson (London: The Hakluyt Society, 1990), 151.
17. Biran, *The Empire of the Qara Khitai*, 177 n. 53.
18. Juvaini, *History of the World Conqueror*, 60.
19. Christopher P. Atwood, "A Secular Empire? Estates, *nom*, and religions in the Mongol Empire," *Modern Asian Studies* 56, no. 3 (2022): 796-814.
20. Thomas T. Allsen, "Mahmud Yalavac (?-1254), Mas'ud Beg (?-1289), 'Ali Beg (?-1280); Bujir (fl. 1206-1260)," in *In the Service of the Khan: Eminent Personalities of the Early Mongol-Yüan Period*, ed. Igor de Rachewiltz et al. (Wiesbaden: Harrassowitz Verlag, 1993), 122-135.
21. Tax farming involved tax collectors—usually Muslim merchants—who paid the required amount of tax and then collected it and a surcharge from taxpayers, which often led to discontent among the Chinese populace. Morris Rossabi, "The Muslims in the Early Yüan Dynasty," in *China under Mongol Rule*, ed. John D. Langlois, Jr. (Princeton, NJ: Princeton University Press, 1981), 265.
22. Thomas T. Allsen, *Commodity and Exchange in the Mongol Empire: A Cultural History of Islamic Textiles* (New York: Cambridge University Press, 1997), 50. Although it was Möngke who greatly advanced Mongol power in Islamic lands, Muslim sources surprisingly do not hold him in contempt. The introduction of the *qubchir* tax, however, was roundly despised because it seemed to function very much like the Islamic *jizya* poll tax. Thomas T. Allsen, *Mongol Imperialism: The Policies of the Grand Qan Möngke in China, Russia and the Islamic Lands, 1251-1259* (Berkeley: University of California Press, 1987), 167-168.
23. On the transmission of Muslim science and culture into Yuan China see, for example, Kodo Tasaka, "An Aspect of Islam Culture Introduced into China," *Memoirs of the Research Department of the Toyo Bunko* 16 (1957): 35-74; and Paul D. Buell and Eugene N. Anderson, *A Soup for the "Qan": Chinese Dietary Medicine of the Mongol Era as Seen in Hu Szu-Hui's "Yin-Shan Cheng-Yao"* (London: Kegan Paul International, 2000).
24. For an overview of the role Muslim scholars played in Yuan astronomy see Brian Baumann, *Divine Knowledge: Buddhist Mathematics According to the Anonymous Manual of Mongolian Astrology and Divination* (Leiden: Brill, 2008), 299-307.
25. On Nasir al-Din's career in the Il-khanid court see F. J. Ragep, *Nasr al-Din Tusi's Memoir of Astronomy (al-Tadhkira fi 'ilm al-hay'a)* (New York: Springer-Verlag, 1993), 13-15; George Lane, *Early Mongol Rule in Thirteenth-Century Iran: A Persian Renaissance* (London: Routledge, 2003), chap. 7.

26. Roberto Vitali, *The Kingdoms of Gu.ge Pu.hrang: According to the mkhan.chen Ngag.dbang grags.pa* (Chicago: Serindia, 1997), 418–419.
27. Elliot Sperling, "Hülegü and Tibet," *Acta Orientalia Academicae Scientiarum Hungaricae* 44 (1990): 153.
28. Samuel M. Grupper, "The Buddhist Sanctuary-Vihara of Labnasagut and the Il-Qan Hülegü: An Overview of Il-Qanid Buddhism and Related Matters," *Archivum Eurasiae Medii Aevi* 13 (2004): 5–78.
29. Tegüder converted as a youth to Islam, and when he took the throne he ruled as Sultan Ahmad (r. 1282–1284); however, his reign was a disaster and his conversion had no impact on the Mongol elite, who drove him out of power. See Reuven Amitai, "The Conversion of Tegüder Ilkhan to Islam," *Jerusalem Studies in Arabic and Islam* 25 (2001): 15–43; and Judith Pfeiffer, "Conversion to Islam among the Ilkhans in Muslim Narrative Traditions: The Case of Ahmad Tegüder" (Ph.D. diss., University of Chicago, 2003).
30. Jamal J. Elias, *The Throne Carrier of God: The Life and Thought of 'Ala' ad-dawla as-Simnani* (Albany: State University of New York Press, 1995), 18, 26.
31. Rashiduddin Fazlullah, *Jami'u't-tawarikh: Compendium of Chronicles, A History of the Mongols, Part Three*, trans. W. M. Thackston (Cambridge, MA: Harvard University, Department of Near Eastern Languages and Civilizations, 1999), 664.
32. On the history of Buddhism in Iran during the Ilkhans see Roxann Prazniak, "Ilkhanid Buddhism: Traces of a Passage in Eurasian History," *Comparative Studies in Society and History* 56 (2014): 650–680.
33. Charles Melville, "*Padshah-i Islam*: The Conversion of Sultan Mahmud Ghazan Khan," *Pembroke Papers* 1 (1990): 171–172. On the conversion of the Il-khans and the misguided link often made between Sufism and Mongol shamanism see Reuven Amitai, "Sufis and Shamans: Some Remarks on the Islamization of the Mongols in the Ilkhanate," *Journal of the Economic and Social History of the Orient* 42, no. 1 (1999): 27–46.
34. On the anti-Buddhist and anti-Christian activities of Ghazan's influential advisor Nauraz see Jean Aubin, *Emirs mongols et vizirs persans dans les remous de l'acculturation* (Leuven: Peeters, 1995), 61–68.
35. Devin DeWeese, *Islamization and Native Religion in the Golden Horde: Baba Tükles and Conversion to Islam in Historical and Epic Tradition* (University Park: Pennsylvania State University Press, 1994), 95–100.
36. A. P. Martinez, "The Third Portion of the Story of Gazan Xan in Rasidu'd-Din's *Ta'rix-e Mobarak-e Gazani*," *Archivum Eurasiae Medii Aevi* 6 (1986–1988): 56–72.
37. The classic example of this phenomenon occurred in mid-ninth century Tang dynasty China; see Kenneth Ch'en, "The Economic Background of the Hui-ch'ang Suppression of Buddhism," *Harvard Journal of Asiatic Studies* 19, no. 1/2 (1956): 67–105. See also C. E. Bosworth's comments about the Ghaznavids as not only the "hammers of the pagan Hindus" but also the "bringers into circulation within the eastern Islamic economy of the temple treasures of India" (*The Later Ghaznavids: Splendour and Decay, The Dynasty in Afghanistan and Northern India 1040–1186* [New York: Columbia University Press, 1977], 32).
38. Karl Jahn, *Rashid al-Din's History of India* (The Hague: Mouton, 1965), xxxiii.

39. Prazniak, "Ilkhanid Buddhism," 655. On the role of Uyghur merchants in sustaining these monasteries see Márton Vér, "Uyghur Cultural and Social Influence in Mongol Iran as Mirrored in a Decree of Abaqa Ilkhan," unpublished paper presented at the Ability and Authority Roundtable: Uighur Expertise on the Silk Road, Max Planck Institute, Berlin, November 21, 2021.
40. Thomas Raff, *Remarks on an Anti-Mongol Fatwa by Ibn Taimiya* (Leiden: self-published, 1973), 63.
41. Johan Elverskog, *Buddhism and Islam on the Silk Road* (Philadelphia: University of Pennsylvania Press, 2010).
42. Jonathan Brack, "Chinggisid Pluralism and Religious Competition: Buddhists, Muslims, and the Question of Violence and Sovereignty in Ilkhanid Iran," *Modern Asian Studies* 56, no. 3 (2022): 815–839.
43. Judith Pfeiffer, "Conversion Versions: Sultan Öljeytü's Conversion to Shi'ism (709/1309) in Muslim Narrative Sources," *Mongolian Studies* 22 (1999): 45–46.
44. This story is found in a range of Buddhist literature, including the *Apadāna, Mahāvastu, Divyāvadāna, Ekottarikāgama* (T. 125), *Da Zhidu lun* (T. 1508), *Fenbie gongde lun* (T. 1507), and the *Mahākaruṇapuṇḍarīka* (T. 380). See Jonathan A. Silk, *Riven by Lust: Incest and Schism in Indian Buddhist Legend and Historiography* (Honolulu: University of Hawai'i Press, 2009), 115–122.
45. Jan Nattier, "Namowa buddhay-a: A Note on the Sources of the Mongolian Kanjur," unpublished paper presented at the Annual Meeting of the American Oriental Society, New Haven, CT, 1986.
46. Karl Jahn, "Rashid al-Din and Chinese Culture," *Central Asiatic Journal* 14 (1970): 134–147.
47. Dai Matsui, "Mongol Globalism Attested by the Uigur and Mongol Documents from East Turkestan," *Studies in the Humanities (Volume of Cultural Sciences)* 22 (2009): 39–40.
48. On the Uyghur worship of the Big Dipper as part of the Yuan imperial cult see Johan Elverskog, "The Mongolian *Big Dipper Sutra*," *Journal of the International Association of Buddhist Studies* (2007): 89.
49. In the discussion of Pure Land Buddhism, for example, while it is explained according to a key Chinese Pure Land text, the *Guanwu liang shou jing*, the title in Persian is from the Uyghur: "*Book of Amitayur.*" Jahn, *Rashid al-Din's History of India*, lxxi.
50. One measure of this interaction was that in the thirteenth century the new year in Iran was celebrated not at the vernal equinox according to the Islamic calendar but six weeks before the spring equinox in keeping with the Chinese calendar. See Charles Melville, "The Chinese Uighur Animal Calendar in Persian Historiography of the Mongol Period," *Iran* 32 (1994): 83–98.
51. Michal Biran, "The Mongol Imperial Space: From Universalism to Glocalization," in *The Limits of Universal Rule: Eurasian Empires Compared*, ed. Y. Pines, M. Biran, and J. Rüpke (Cambridge: Cambridge University Press, 2021), 220–256.
52. Thomas T. Allsen, "Sharing out the Empire: Apportioned Lands under the Mongols," in *Nomads in the Sedentary World*, ed. Anatoly M. Khazanov and André Wink (Richmond: Curzon Press, 2001), 172–190.

53. Jean Richard, "La conversion de Berke et les debuts de l'islamisation de la horde d'or," *Revue des Études Islamiques* 35 (1967): 173-184; István Vásáry, "'History and Legend' in Berke Khan's Conversion to Islam," in *Aspects of Altaic Civilization III*, ed. Denis Sinor (Bloomington: Indiana University, Research Institute for Inner Asian Studies, 1990), 230-252; Devin DeWeese, "Problems of Islamization in the Volga-Ural Region: Traditions about Berke Khan," in *Proceedings of the International Symposium on Islamic Civilisation in the Volga-Ural Region, Kazan, 8–11 June 2001*, ed. Ali Çaksu and Radik Mukhammetshin (Istanbul: Research Centre for Islamic History, Art and Culture, 2004), 3-13.
54. Charles J. Halperin, "The Kipchak Connection: The Ilkhans, the Mamluks and Ayn Jalut," *Bulletin of the School of Oriental and African Studies* 63, no. 2 (2000): 229-245.
55. On the conflict between these two see Reuven Amitai Preiss, *Mongols and Mamluks: The Mamluk-Ilkhanid War, 1260–1281* (Cambridge: Cambridge University Press, 1995).
56. Michal Biran, *Qaidu and the Rise of the Independent Mongol State in Central Asia* (Richmond: Curzon, 1997).
57. On Möngke Khan's historiographical projects see Christopher P. Atwood, "The Date of the *Secret History of the Mongols* Reconsidered," *Journal of Song-Yuan Studies* 37 (2007): 1-48.
58. Christopher P. Atwood, "The Uyghur Stone: Archaeological Revelations in the Mongol Empire," in *The Steppe Lands and the World Beyond Them: Studies in honor of Victor Spinei on his 70th Birthday*, ed. F. Curta and B. P. Maleon (Iasi: Editura Universitatii, 2013), 331.
59. Martón Vér, *Old Uyghur Documents Concerning the Postal System of the Mongol Empire* (Turnhout: Brepols, 2019), 103-106.
60. The following history is drawn largely from Thomas T. Allsen, "The Yüan Dynasty and the Uighurs of Turfan in the 13th Century," in *China Among Equals: The Middle Kingdom and Its Neighbours, 10th-14th Centuries*, ed. Morris Rossabi (Berkeley: University of California Press, 1983), 243-280; Biran, *Qaidu*; and Michal Biran, "The Mongols in Central Asia from Chinggis Khan's Invasion to the Rise of Temür: The Ögedeid and Chaghadaid Realms," in *The Cambridge History of Inner Asia: The Chinggisid Age*, ed. N. Di Cosmo et al. (New York: Cambridge University Press, 2009), 46-66.
61. On the Mongols' changing tax exemption policies see Wonhee Cho, "Negotiated Privilege: Strategic Tax Exemptions Policies for Religious Groups and the Mongol-Yuan Dynasty in 13th-Century China," *Journal of the Economic and Social History of the Orient* 63 (2020): 1-37. On Mongol tax policies among the Uyghurs see Dai Matsui, "Bezeklik Uigur Administrative Orders Revisited," in *Tujue yuwenxue yanjiu. Geng Shimin jiaoshu 80 huadan jinian wenji* (Studies in Turkic Philology. Festschrift in Honour of the 80th Birthday of Geng Shimin), ed. Zhang D. and A. Yakup (Beijing: Minzu Daxue Chubanshe, 2009), 339-350; Martón Vér, "Religious Communities and the Postal System of the Mongol Empire," in *Role of Religions in the Turkic Culture*, ed. Mária Ivanics and Zsuzsanna Olach (Budapest: Péter Pázmány Catholic University, 2017), 291-306.
62. Biran, *Qaidu*, 42.
63. Allsen, "The Yüan Dynasty and the Uighurs," 256
64. Fu Ma and Xia Lidong, "Comprehensive Study on Old Uighur and Chinese Wall Inscriptions in Room B of Newly Excavated Cave 26 in Tuyuq Grottoes, Turfan," *Acta Orientalia Academiae Scientiarum Hungaricae* 74, no. 2 (2021): 197.

65. Allsen, "The Yüan Dynasty and the Uighurs," 255.
66. Dai Matsui, "An Uigur Decree of Tax Exemption in the Name of Duwa-Khan," *Shinjlex Uxaani Akademiin Medee* 4 (2007): 60-68.
67. Biran, *Qaidu*, 73.
68. Biran, *Qaidu*, 62.
69. Quote from the *Yuan Shi* cited in Allsen, "The Yüan Dynasty and the Uighurs."
70. Jens Wilkens, "Buddhism in the West Uyghur Kingdom and Beyond," in *Transfer of Buddhism across Central Asian Networks (7th to 13th Centuries)*, ed. Carmen Meinert (Leiden: Brill, 2016), 242.
71. As Peter Jackson has noted, on account of the importance of pluralism in the Yasa of Chinggis Khan, Mongol converts who went too fast, like Tarmashirin, were rejected, and only those who went slowly, paying heed to pluralism, enabled Islamization to proceed apace. "Reflections on the Islamization of Mongol Khans in Comparative Perspective," *Journal of the Economic and Social History of the Orient* 62 (2019): 367-379.
72. Michal Biran, "The Chaghataids and Islam: The Conversion of Tarmashirin Khan," *Journal of the American Oriental Society* 122, no. 4 (2002): 750.
73. György Kara, "Mediaeval Mongol Documents from Khara Khoto and East Turkestan in the St. Petersburg Branch of the Institute of Oriental Studies," *Manuscripta Orientalia* 9, no. 2 (2003): 28.
74. Dai Matsui, "A Mongolian Decree from the Chaghataid Khanate Discovered at Dunhuang," in *Aspects of Research into Central Asian Buddhism: In Memoriam Kōgi Kudara*, ed. Peter Zieme (Turnout: Brepols, 2008), 170.
75. On the possible role of Chagataid policies exacerbated by drought on generating this plague outbreak see Philip Slavin, "Death by the Lake: Mortality Crisis in Early Fourteenth-Century Central Asia," *Journal of Interdisciplinary History* 1 (2019): 59-90.
76. On the rise of Timur see Beatrice F. Manz, *The Rise and Rule of Tamerlane* (New York: Cambridge University Press, 1989), 41-89.
77. The term "Moghul" reflects the Persian and Arabic adaptation of the Turkic rendering of "Mongol," and is used to identify the dynastic lineage of Chagatai that ruled Central Asia from the fourteenth to seventeenth centuries. Unfortunately, it is also the term commonly used to refer to the descendants of Babur who ruled in India, though it is often misspelled as "Mughal," apparently an English adaptation of Indian pronunciation. Regardless, it is a misnomer because the descendants of Babur never used this term. They saw themselves as Timurids (see Lisa Balabanlilar, "The Lords of the Auspicious Conjunction: Turco-Mongol Imperial Identity on the Subcontinent," *The Journal of World History* 18, no. 1 [2007]: 1-39). To make matters even more complicated, as the descendants of Chagatai came to be known as the Moghuls, the term "Chagatai" came to be applied to the Timurids.
78. Kim Hodong, "The Early History of the Moghul Nomads: The Legacy of the Chagatai Khanate," in *The Mongol Empire and Its Legacy*, ed. Reuven Amitai-Preiss and David O. Morgan (Leiden: Brill, 1999), 290-318.
79. Nimrod Hurwitz, Christian C. Sahner, Uriel Simonsohn, and Luke Yarbrough, *Conversion to Islam in the Premodern Age: A Sourcebook* (Berkeley: University of California Press, 2020), 16.

80. *Catalogue of the Old Uyghur Manuscripts and Blockprints in the Serindia Collection of the Institute of Oriental Manuscripts, RAS*, vol. 1, ed. IOM, RAS, and the Toyo Bunko (Tokyo: The Toyo Bunko, 2021), 68-69. See also Yukiyo Kasai, "Ein Kolophon um die Legende von Bokug Kagan," *Studies on the Inner Asian Languages* 19 (2004): 1-25.
81. Semih Tezcan and Peter Zieme, "Antiislamische Polemik in einem alttürkischen buddhistischen Gedicht aus Turfan," *Altorientalische Forschungen* 17, no. 1 (1990): 146-151.
82. Peter Zieme, "Some Notes on Old Uigur Art and Texts," in *Buddhism and Art in Turfan: From the Perspective of Uyghur Buddhism*, ed. Irisawa Takashi (Kyoto: Research Center for Buddhist Culture in Asia Ryukoku University, 2012), 6.
83. Semih Tezcan, *Das uigurische Insadi-Sūtra* (Berlin: Akademie Verlag, 1974).
84. The *Kālacakratantra* was compiled between 1025 and 1040. John R. Newman, "The Epoch of the *Kālacakra Tantra*," *Indo-Iranian Journal* 41 (1998): 319-349.
85. John R. Newman, "Islam in the Kālacakra Tantra," *Journal of the International Association of Buddhist Studies* 21, no. 2 (1998): 334.
86. J. de Somogyi, "A *Qasida* on the Destruction of Baghdad by the Mongols," *Bulletin of the School of Oriental and African Studies* 7 (1933-5): 41-48; J. A. Boyle, "The Death of the Last 'Abbasid Caliph of Baghdad: A Contemporary Muslim Account," *Journal of Semitic Studies* 6 (1961): 145-161; and G. M. Wickens, "Nasir ad-Din Tusi on the Fall of Baghdad: A Further Study," *Journal of Semitic Studies* 7 (1962): 23-35.
87. H. G. Raverty, *Tabakat-i-Nasiri: A General History of the Muhammadan Dynasties of Asia, including Hindustan, from A.H. 194 [810 A.D.] to A.H. 658 [1260 A.D.], and the Irruption of the Infidel Mughals into Islam* (London: Gilbert & Rivington, 1881), 1157-1159.
88. Igor de Rachewiltz, "Turks in China under the Mongols: A Preliminary Investigation of Turco-Mongol Relations in the 13th and 14th Centuries." In *China Among Equals: The Middle Kingdom and Its Neighbours, 10th-14th Centuries*, ed. Morris Rossabi (Berkeley: University of California Press, 1983), 287. On the historiography of Güyüg see Kim Hodong, "A Reappraisal of Güyüg Khan," in *Mongols, Turks and Others: Eurasian Nomads and the Sedentary World*, ed. Reuven Amitai and Michal Biran (Leiden: Brill, 2005), 309-338.
89. Zhang Tieshan and Peter Zieme, "A Memorandum about the King of the 'On Uygur' and His Realm," *Acta Orientalia Academiae Scientiarum Hungaricae* 64, no. 2 (2011): 129-159.
90. Biran, *Qaidu*, 64.
91. K. M. Maitra, *A Persian Embassy to China: Being an Extract from Zubdatu't Tawarikh of Hafiz Abru* (New York: Paragon Book Reprint Corp., 1970), 12-13.
92. Maitra, *A Persian Embassy*, 14-15.
93. Luo Yuejiong, *Xian bin lü* (Beijing: Zhonghua shuju, 1983). I thank Abdurishid Yakup for this reference.
94. David Brophy, *Uyghur Nation: Reform and Revolution on the Russia-China Frontier* (Cambridge, MA: Harvard University Press, 2016), 24-25.
95. Matsui, "A Mongolian Decree from the Chaghataid Khanate Discovered at Dunhuang," 160.
96. Juten Oda, "Indian Buddhist Missions to Uighuristan, based on Chinese Sources," in *Indien und Zentralasien: Sprach-und Kulturkontakt: Vorträge des Göttinger Symposions vom*

7. bis 10. Mai 2001, ed. Sven Bretfeld and Jens Wilkens (Wiesbaden: Harrassowitz, 2003), 30.
97. Oda, "Indian Buddhist Missions to Uighuristan," 31.
98. Abdurishid Yakup, "Two Alliterative Uighur Poems from Dunhuang," *Linguistic Research* 17-18 (1999): 11-12.
99. Yakup, "On the Interlinear Uyghur Poetry in the Newly Unearthed Nestorian Text," 415.
100. Peter Zieme and György Kara, *Ein uigurisches Totenbuch: Naropas Lehre in uigurischer Übersetzung* (Budapest: Akadémiai Kiadó, 1979), 27-29, 161-162.
101. Herbert Franke, "Mittelmongolische Glossen in einer arabischen astronomischen Handschrift von 1366," *Oriens* 31 (1988): 95-118. On the scientific contents of al-Sanjufini's *zij* see E. S. Kennedy and Jan Hogendijk, "Two Tables from an Arabic Astronomical Handbook for the Mongol Viceroy of Tibet," in *A Scientific Humanist: Studies in Memory of Abraham Sachs*, ed. Erie Leichty et al. (Philadelphia: The University Museum, 1988), 233-242; E. S. Kennedy, "Eclipse Predictions in Arabic Astronomical Tables Prepared for the Mongol Viceroy of Tibet," *Zeitschrift für Geschichte der Arabisch-Islamischen Wissenschaften* 4 (1990): 60-80.
102. Kara, "Mediaeval Mongol Documents from Khara Khoto and East Turkestan," 30-34.
103. On the conversion of Tughlugh Temür see Kim, "The Early History of the Moghul Nomads," 301-307.
104. Devin DeWeese suggests that Tughluq Temür's conversion may have "played a role in shoring up political alignments." "Islamization in the Mongol Empire," in *The Cambridge History of Inner Asia: The Chinggisid Age*, ed. Nicola Di Cosmo, Allen J. Frank, and Peter B. Golden (New York: Cambridge University Press, 2014), 132.
105. On the history of the Kataki and the connection between Sufism and urban renewal see Kim Hodong, "Muslim Saints in the 14th to the 16th Centuries of Eastern Turkestan," *International Journal of Central Asian Studies* 1 (1996): 287-296, 314-319.
106. Devin DeWeese, "The *Mashā'ikh-i Turk* and the *Khojagān*: Rethinking the Links Between the Yasavī and Naqshbandī Sufi Traditions," *Journal of Islamic Studies* 7, no. 2 (1996): 206-27.
107. Beatrice F. Manz, "Timur and the Symbolism of Sovereignty," *Iranian Studies* 21, no. 1-2 (1988): 105-122.
108. David Roxburgh, *Turks: A Journey of a Thousand Years, 600–1600* (London: Royal Academy of Arts, 2005), 196-197.
109. On the spiritual and historical struggles between the Yasaviyya and Naqshbandiyya see Devin DeWeese, "The *Masha'-ikh-i* Turk and the *Khojagan*: Rethinking the Links between the Yasavi and Naqshbandi Sufi Traditions," *Journal of Islamic Studies* 7, no. 2 (1996): 180-207.
110. This particular phrase (*sharr-i rusūm-i bīgānegān*) is found in several Naqshbandiyya letters. Jo-Ann Gross and Asom Urunbaev, *The Letters of Khwāja 'Ubayd Allāh Aḥrār and his Associates* (Leiden: Brill, 2002), 114, 128, 166.
111. On the Mongol response to this predicament, in particular, their attempt at reclaiming this new territory by means of the cult of Chinggis Khan, see Johan Elverskog, "The Legend of Muna Mountain," *Inner Asia* 8, no. 1 (2006): 99-122.

112. For the court debates and different Ming views on the Mongols see David M. Robinson, *In the Shadow of the Mongol Empire: Ming China and Eurasia* (New York: Cambridge University Press, 2020).
113. The Ming hatred of the Mongols would reach its most pathological extreme during the later reign of the Jiajing emperor (r. 1522-1566), who mandated that the Chinese characters for "barbarians" (i.e., Mongols) should be written as small as possible in all official records. James Geiss, "The Chia-ching reign, 1522-1566," in *The Cambridge History of China, Vol. 8: 1*, ed. F. W. Mote and D. Twitchett (Cambridge: Cambridge University Press, 1988), 441.
114. Hidehiro Okada, "Origins of the Dörben Oyirad," *Ural-Altaische Jahrbücher* 7 (1987): 181-211; Junko Miyawaki, "The Birth of Oyirad Khanship," *Central Asiatic Journal* 41 (1997): 39-41.
115. On the Ming-Mongol horse trade see Henry Serruys, *Sino-Mongol Relations during the Ming, III: Trade Relations: The Horse Fairs* (Brussels: Institut Belge des Hautes Études Chinoises, 1975).
116. Elliot Sperling, "The Szechwan-Tibet Frontier in the Fifteenth Century," *Ming Studies* 26 (1988): 37-55.
117. Johan Elverskog, *The Jewel Translucent Sutra: Altan Khan and the Mongols in the Sixteenth Century* (Leiden: Brill, 2003), 148-149 n. 257.
118. Morris Rossabi, "Ming Foreign Policy: The Case of Hami," in *China and Her Neighbours: Borders, Visions of the Other, Foreign Policy 10th to 19th Century*, ed. Sabine Dabringhaus and Roderich Ptak (Wiesbaden: Harrassowitz, 1997), 79-97.
119. In fact, this westward orientation extended all the way to Egypt, where Oirad men served in the army and Oirad women were joyfully accepted as wives by the Mamluk elite; see Linda S. Northrup, *From Slave to Sultan: The Career of Al-Mansur Qalawun and the Consolidation of Mamluk Rule in Egypt and Syria (678–689 A.H./1279–1290 A.D.)* (Stuttgart: Franz Steiner Verlag, 1998), 117-118, 191.
120. Anthony Reid, "Islamization and Christianization in Southeast Asia: The Critical Phase, 1550-1650," in *Southeast Asia in the Early Modern Era: Trade, Power, Belief*, ed. Anthony Reid (Ithaca, NY: Cornell University Press, 1993), 151-179.
121. André Wink, *Al-Hind: The Making of the Indo-Islamic World, Vol. 1, Early Medieval India and the Expansion of Islam 7th-11th Centuries* (Leiden: E. J. Brill, 1990), 331.
122. Mirza Haydar Dughlat, *Tarikh-i-Rashidi: A History of the Khans of Moghulistan*, trans. W. M. Thackston (Cambridge, MA: Harvard University, Department of Near Eastern Studies, 1996), 35-36, 48.
123. Joseph F. Fletcher, "China and Central Asia, 1368-1884," in *The Chinese World Order*, ed. John K. Fairbank (Cambridge, MA: Harvard University Press, 1968), 216-218. On the continued trade through the fifteenth century see Hiroshi Watanabe, "An Index of Embassies and Tribute Missions from Islamic Countries to Ming China (1368-1644) as recorded in the *Ming Shih-lu* Classified According to Geographic Area," *Memoirs of the Research Department of the Toyo Bunko* 33 (1975): 285-348; and F. W. Cleaves, "The Sino-Mongolian Edict of 1453 in The Topkapı Sarayı Müsezi," *Harvard Journal of Asiatic Studies* 13, no. 3-4 (1950): 431-446.
124. Juten Oda, "Uighuristan," *Acta Asiatica* 34 (1978): 43.

125. Chu Hung-lam, "Intellectual Trends in the Fifteenth Century," *Ming Studies* 27 (1989): 9.
126. Timothy Brook, "Commerce: The Ming in the World," in *Ming: 50 Years that Changed China*, ed. Craig Clunas and Jessica Harrison-Hall (Seattle: University of Washington Press, 2014), 274.
127. On the history and meaning of the Great Wall see Nicola Di Cosmo, *Ancient China and Its Enemies: The Rise of Nomadic Power in East Asian History* (Cambridge: Cambridge University Press, 2002); and Arthur Waldron, *The Great Wall of China: From Myth to History* (Cambridge: Cambridge University Press, 1990). On the move to the sea trade, see Morris Rossabi, "The Decline of the Central Asian Caravan Trade," in *The Rise of Merchant Empires: Long Distance Trade in the Early Modern World, 1350–1750*, ed. James D. Tracy (New York: Cambridge University Press, 1990), 351–370.
128. On the reorientation of Eurasian trade in the early modern period, especially toward traders in Central Asia, see Scott C. Levi, *The Bukharan Crisis: A Connected History of 18th Century Central Asia* (Pittsburgh: University of Pittsburgh Press, 2020).
129. Kim Hodong, "The Rise and Fall of the Hami Kingdom (ca. 1389-1513)," in *Land Routes of the Silk Roads and the Cultural Exchanges between the East and West before the 10th Century* (Beijing: New World Press, 1996).
130. Morris Rossabi, "A Translation of Ch'en Ch'eng's *Hsi-Yu Fan-kuo Chih*," *Ming Studies* 17 (1983): 49-59.
131. Derryl N. MacLean, *Religion and Society in Arab Sind* (Leiden: E. J. Brill, 1989), 75.
132. Himanshu P. Ray, *The Winds of Change: Buddhism and the Maritime Links of Early South Asia* (Delhi: Oxford University Press, 1994), 122.
133. "Spiritual capital" is a term used to describe "the power, influence, knowledge, and dispositions created by participation in a particular religious tradition." Peter L. Berger and Gordon Redding, *The Hidden Form of Capital: Spiritual Influences in Societal Progress* (New York: Anthem Press, 2010).
134. Brophy, *Uyghur Nation*, 25.
135. On the importance of healing in Inner Asian Islamic conversion narratives see DeWeese, *Islamization and Native Religion in the Golden Horde*; and on medical knowledge and the spread of Buddhism see C. Pierce Salguero, *A Global History of Buddhism and Medicine* (New York: Columbia University Press, 2022).
136. In thinking about these issues it is also interesting that in an Indian law compilation, the *Devalasmṛti* (ca. 800–1000 CE), "converting to Islam is only a minor contamination and might be made null and void by a minor ritual." Andreas Kaplony, "The Conversion of the Turks of Central Asia to Islam as Seen by Arabic and Persian Geography," in *Islamisation de l'Asie centrale: Processus locaux d'acculturation du VIIe au XIe siècle*, ed. Etienne de la Vaissière (Paris: Association pour l'avancement des etudes iraniennes, 2008), 328.
137. Peter Brown, *Authority and the Sacred: Aspects of Christianization of the Roman World* (New York: Cambridge University Press, 1995), 6.

CONCLUSION

1. Jeff Eden, *Warriors Saints of the Silk Road: Legends of the Qarakhanids* (Leiden: Brill, 2019), 31.

2. Ron Sela, "Central Asian Muslims on Tibetan Buddhism, 16th-18th Centuries," in *Trails of the Tibetan Tradition: Papers for Elliot Sperling*, ed. Roberto Vitali (Dharamshala: Amnye Machen Institute, 2014), 345-358; Muhammad Sadiq Kashghari, *In Remembrance of the Saints: The Rise and Fall of an Inner Asian Sufi Dynasty*, trans. David Brophy (New York: Columbia University Press, 2021).
3. Rian Thum, *The Sacred Routes of Uyghur History* (Cambridge, MA: Harvard University Press, 2014); Jeff Eden, *The Life of Muhammad Sharīf: A Central Asian Sufi Hagiography in Chagatay* (Vienna: Verlag der Österreichischen Akademie der Wissenschaften, 2015).
4. At Toyuq the Uyghur Buddhist cave temples became the seat of Sufi dervishes "who considered the caves to be the abode of the 'Seven Sleepers' of Islamic hagiography." David A. Scott, "Buddhism and Islam: Past to Present Encounters and Interfaith Lessons," *Numen* 42, no. 2 (1995): 146. See also Rian Thum, "'Sunni' Veneration of the Twelve Imams in Khotan," *Journal of the American Oriental Society* 142, no. 3 (2022): 636-637.
5. On the Uyghur ethnic revival, especially its relation to Soviet nationality policies in Central Asia, see David Brophy, *Uyghur Nation: Reform and Revolution on the Russia-China Frontier* (Cambridge, MA: Harvard University Press, 2016), 173-203. See also Ondřej Klimeš, *Struggle by the Pen: The Uyghur Discourse of Nation and National Interest, c. 1900–1949* (Leiden: Brill, 2015), 86-97.
6. Edmund Waite, "From Holy Man to National Villain: Popular Historical Narratives About Apaq Khoja amongst Uyghurs in Contemporary Xinjiang," *Inner Asia* 8, no. 1 (2006): 13-15. On forging a unified identity of the heterogenous inhabitants of Xinjiang as part of the Uyghur national project see James A. Millward, *Eurasian Crossroads: A History of Xinjiang* (New York: Columbia University Press, 2007), 40-76; Gardner Bovingdon, *The Uyghurs: Strangers in Their Own Land* (New York: Columbia University Press, 2010), 23-39.

Bibliography

Abeyesekara, Ananda. "The Saffron Army, Violence, Terror(ism): Buddhism, Identity, and Difference in Sri Lanka." *Numen* 48, no. 1 (2001): 1-46.
Adolphson, Mikael S. *The Gates of Power: Monks, Courtiers, and Warriors in Premodern Japan.* Honolulu: University of Hawai'i Press, 2000.
Allsen, Thomas T. "The Yüan Dynasty and the Uighurs of the Turfan in the 13th Century." In *China Among Equals: The Middle Kingdom and Its Neighbours, 10th–14th Centuries*, ed. Morris Rossabi, 243-280. Berkeley: University of California Press, 1983.
———. *Mongol Imperialism: The Policies of the Grand Qan Möngke in China, Russia and the Islamic Lands, 1251–1259.* Berkeley: University of California Press, 1987.
———. "Mongolian Princes and Their Merchant Partners 1200-1260." *Asia Major* 3, no. 2 (1989): 86-94.
———. "Mahmud Yalavac (?-1254), Mas'ud Beg (?-1289), 'Ali Beg (?-1280), Bujir (fl. 1206-1260)." In *In the Service of the Khan: Eminent Personalities of the Early Mongol-Yüan Period*, ed. Igor de Rachewiltz et al., 122-135. Wiesbaden: Harrassowitz Verlag, 1993.
———. "Spiritual Geography and Political Legitimacy in the Eastern Steppe." In *Ideology and the Formation of Early States*, ed. H. J. M. Claessen and J. G. Oosten, 116-135. Leiden: Brill, 1996.
———. *Commodity and Exchange in the Mongol Empire: A Cultural History of Islamic Textiles.* New York: Cambridge University Press, 1997.
———. "Sharing out the Empire: Apportioned Lands under the Mongols." In *Nomads in the Sedentary World*, ed. Anatoly M. Khazanov and André Wink, 172-190. Richmond: Curzon Press, 2001.
———. *The Steppe and the Sea: Pearls in the Mongol Empire.* Philadelphia: University of Pennsylvania Press, 2019.
Amitai, Reuven. "Sufis and Shamans: Some Remarks on the Islamization of the Mongols in the Ilkhanate." *Journal of the Economic and Social History of the Orient* 42, no. 1 (1999): 27-46.
———. "The Conversion of Tegüder Ilkhan to Islam." *Jerusalem Studies in Arabic and Islam* 25 (2001): 15-43.
Amitai Preiss, Reuven. *Mongols and Mamluks: The Mamluk-Ilkhanid War, 1260–1281.* Cambridge: Cambridge University Press, 1995.
———. *The Masters Revived: The Occult Lives of Nikolai and Elena Roerich.* Leiden: Brill, 2014.

Apple, James B. "Eschatology and World Order in Buddhist Formations." *Religious Studies and Theology* 29, no. 1 (2010): 109-122.
Arat, R. R. "Eski Türk hukuk vesikaları." *Journal de la Société Finno-Ougrienne* 65, no. 1 (1964): 11-77.
Asmussen, Jes P. *X^uāstvānīft: Studies in Manichaeism*. Copenhagen: Prostant apud Munksgaard, 1965.
Atwood, Christopher P. "The Date of the *Secret History of the Mongols* Reconsidered." *Journal of Song-Yuan Studies* 37 (2007): 1-48.
———. "The Notion of Tribe in Medieval China: Ouyang Xiu and the Shatou Dynastic Myth." In *Miscellanea Asiatica: Festschrift in Honour of Françoise Aubin*, ed. Denise Aigle et al., 593-621. Sankt Augustin: Steyler Verlag, 2010.
———. "The Uyghur Stone: Archaeological Revelations in the Mongol Empire." In *The Steppe Lands and the World Beyond Them: Studies in honor of Victor Spinei on his 70th Birthday*, ed. F. Curta and B. P. Maleon, 315-344. Iasi: Editura Universitatii, 2013.
———. "The First Mongol Contacts with the Tibetans." In *Trails of the Tibetan Tradition: Papers for Elliot Sperling*, ed. Roberto Vitali, 21-46. Dharamsala: Amnye Machen Institute, 2014.
———. "Empire of the Mongols: Plantation, Taxation, and Agricultural Innovation in Mongol Yuan China." Unpublished paper presented at the symposium "Mongol Empire and Its Legacy," University of Washington, February 3, 2017.
———. "A Secular Empire? Estates, Nom, and Religions in the Mongol Empire." *Modern Asian Studies* 56, no. 3 (2022): 796-814.
Aubin, Jean. *Emirs mongols et vizirs persans dans les remous de l'acculturation*. Leuven: Peeters, 1995.
Bailey, Greg and Ian Mabbett. *The Sociology of Early Buddhism*. New York: Cambridge University Press, 2003.
Bailey, H. W. "A Turkish-Khotanese Vocabulary." *Bulletin of the School of Oriental and African Studies* 11 (1944): 290-296.
Balabanlilar, Lisa. "The Lords of the Auspicious Conjunction: Turco-Mongol Imperial Identity on the Subcontinent." *The Journal of World History* 18, no. 1 (2007): 1-39.
Balkwill, Stephanie and James A. Benn. *Buddhism and Statecraft in East Asia*. Leiden: Brill, 2022.
Bang, Willi and Annemarie von Gabain. "Türkische Turfan-Texte I: Bruchstücke eines Wahrsagebuches." *Sitzungsberichte der Preußischen Akademie der Wissenschaften* (1929): 241-268.
Barrett, Timothy H. *The Woman Who Discovered Printing*. New Haven, CT: Yale University Press, 2013.
Bartholomeusz, Tessa J. *In Defense of Dharma: Just-War Ideology in Buddhist Sri Lanka*. New York: Routledge Curzon, 2002.
Bartholomeusz, Tessa J. and Chandra Richard De Silva. *Fundamentalism and Minority Identities in Sri Lanka*. Albany: State University of New York Press, 1998.
Baumann, Brian. *Divine Knowledge: Buddhist Mathematics According to the Anonymous Manual of Mongolian Astrology and Divination*. Leiden: Brill, 2008.
Bechert, Heinz. *Buddhismus, Staat und Gesellschaft in den Ländern des Theravāda-Buddhismus*. Frankfurt: A. Metzner (vol. 1, 1966); Wiesbaden: Otto Harrassowitz (vol. 2, 1967; vol. 3, 1973).
Becker, Jasper. *City of Heavenly Tranquility: Beijing in the History of China*. New York: Oxford University Press, 2008.

Beckwith, Christopher I. "The Impact of the Horse and Silk Trade on the Economies of Tang China and the Uighur Empire: On the Importance of International Commerce in the Early Middle Ages." *Journal of the Economic and Social History of the Orient* 34 (1991): 183-198.

BeDuhn, Jason. *The Manichaean Body: In Discipline and Ritual.* Baltimore, MD: Johns Hopkins University Press, 2000.

———. "The Metabolism of Salvation: Manichaean Concepts of Human Physiology." In *The Light and the Darkness: Studies in Manichaeism and Its World*, ed. P. Mirecki and J. BeDuhn, 5-37. Leiden: Brill, 2001.

Belka, Lubos. "The Myth of Shambhala: Visions, Visualizations, and the Myth's Resurrection in the Twentieth Century in Buryatia." *Archiv Orientální* 71, no. 3 (2003): 247-262.

Bellah, Robert N. *Religion in Human Evolution: From the Paleolithic to the Axial Age.* Cambridge, MA: Harvard University Press, 2011.

Bellah, Robert N. and Hans Joas. *The Axial Age and Its Consequences.* Cambridge, MA: Harvard University Press, 2012.

Benavides, Gustavo. "Buddhism, Manichaeism, Markets and Empires." In *Hellenisation, Empire, and Globalisation: Lessons from Antiquity*, ed. Luther H. Martin and Panayotis Pachis, 21-44. Thessaloniki: Vanias Publications, 2004.

———. "Economy." In *Critical Terms for the Study of Buddhism*, ed. Donald S. Lopez Jr., 77-104. Chicago: University of Chicago Press, 2005.

Berger, Peter L. and Gordon Redding, *The Hidden Form of Capital: Spiritual Influences in Societal Progress.* New York: Anthem Press, 2010.

Berkey, Jonathan P. *The Formation of Islam: Religion and Society in the Near East.* New York: Cambridge University Press, 2003.

Bernbaum, Edwin. *The Way to Shambhala: A Search for the Mythical Kingdom Beyond the Himalayas.* Los Angeles: Jeremy P. Tarcher, 1980.

Bhattacharya-Haesner, Chhaya. *Central Asian Temple Banners in the Turfan Collection of the Museum für Indische Kunst, Berlin.* Berlin: Dietrich Reimer Verlag, 2003.

Biran, Michal. *Qaidu and the Rise of the Independent Mongol State in Central Asia.* Richmond: Curzon, 1997.

———. "The Chaghataids and Islam: The Conversion of Tarmashirin Khan." *Journal of the American Oriental Society* 122, no. 4 (2002): 742-752.

———. *The Empire of the Qara Khitai in Eurasian History: Between China and the Islamic World.* New York: Cambridge University Press, 2005.

———. "True to Their Ways: Why the Qara Khitai Did Not Convert to Islam." In *Mongols, Turks and Others: Eurasian Nomads and the Sedentary World*, ed. Reuven Amitai and Michal Biran, 175-200. Leiden: Brill, 2005.

———. "The Mongols in Central Asia from Chinggis Khan's Invasion to the Rise of Temür: The Ögedeid and Chaghadaid Realms." In *The Cambridge History of Inner Asia: The Chinggisid Age*, ed. N. Di Cosmo et al., 46-66. New York: Cambridge University Press, 2009.

———. "Unearthing the Liao Dynasty's Relations with the Muslim World: Migrations, Diplomacy, Commerce, and Mutual Perceptions." *Journal of Song-Yuan Studies* 43 (2013): 221-251.

———. "The Mongol Imperial Space: From Universalism to Glocalization." In *The Limits of Universal Rule: Eurasian Empires Compared*, ed. Y. Pines, M. Biran, and J. Rüpke, 220-256. Cambridge: Cambridge University Press, 2021.

Bivar, A. D. H. "Coins." In *The Oxford Encyclopedia of Archaeology in the Near East*, ed. Eric M. Meyers, 41-52. New York: Oxford University Press, 1997.

Blackburn, Anne M. "Buddhist Technologies of Statecraft and Millennial Moments." *History and Theory* 56, no. 1 (2017): 71-79.

Blair, Sheila S. "A Mongol Envoy." In *The Iconography of Islamic Art: Studies in Honour of Robert Hillenbrand*, ed. Bernard O'Kane, 45-60. Edinburgh: Edinburgh University Press, 2005.

Bocking, B., P. Choompolpaisal, L. Cox, and A. Turner. *A Buddhist Crossroads: Pioneer Western Buddhists and Asian Networks 1860–1960*. New York: Routledge, 2015.

Bosworth, C. E. *The Ghaznavids: Their Empire in Afghanistan and Eastern Iran 994–1040*. Edinburgh: Edinburgh University Press, 1963.

——. *The Later Ghaznavids: Splendour and Decay, The Dynasty in Afghanistan and Northern India 1040–1186*. New York: Columbia University Press, 1977.

Bovingdon, Gardner. *The Uyghurs: Strangers in Their Own Land*. New York: Columbia University Press, 2010.

Boyle, John A. "The Death of the Last 'Abbasid Caliph of Baghdad: A Contemporary Muslim Account." *Journal of Semitic Studies* 6 (1961): 145-161.

——. *Genghis Khan: The History of the World Conqueror by Ata-Malik Juvaini*. Seattle: University of Washington Press, 1997.

Brack, Jonathan. "Chinggisid Pluralism and Religious Competition: Buddhists, Muslims, and the Question of Violence and Sovereignty in Ilkhanid Iran." *Modern Asian Studies* 56, no. 3 (2022): 815-839.

Brasovan, Nicholas S. *Buddhisms in Asia: Traditions, Transmissions, and Transformations*. Albany: State University of New York Press, 2019.

Braun, Erik. *The Birth of Insight: Meditation, Modern Buddhism, and the Burmese Monk Ledi Sayadaw*. Chicago: University of Chicago Press, 2013.

Brokaw, Cynthia. *The Ledgers of Merit and Demerit: Social Change and Moral Order in Late Imperial China*. Princeton, NJ: Princeton University Press, 1991.

Brook, Timothy. *The Confusions of Pleasure: Commerce and Culture in Ming China*. Berkeley: University of California Press, 1999.

——. "Commerce: The Ming in the World." In *Ming: 50 Years that Changed China*, ed. Craig Clunas and Jessica Harrison-Hall, 254-295. Seattle: University of Washington Press, 2014.

Brophy, David. *Uyghur Nation: Reform and Revolution on the Russia-China Frontier*. Cambridge, MA: Harvard University Press, 2016.

Brose, Michael C. "Uyghur Technologists of Writing and Literacy in Mongol China." *T'oung Pao* 91, nos. 4/5 (2005): 396-435.

——. *Subjects and Masters: Uyghur Elites in Mongol China*. Bellingham: Western Washington University Center for East Asian Studies, 2007.

——. "Neo-Confucian Uyghur Semuren in Koryŏ ansd Chosŏn Korean Society and Politics." In *Eurasian Influences on Yuan China*, ed. Morris Rossabi, 178-199. Singapore: Institute of Southeast Asian Studies, 2013.

Brown, Peter. *Authority and the Sacred: Aspects of Christianization of the Roman World*. New York: Cambridge University Press, 1995.

Bryson, Megan. "The Great Kingdom of Eternal Peace: Buddhist Kingship in Tenth-Century Dali." *Asia Major* 32, no. 1 (2019): 87-111.

Buell, Paul D. "Cinqai (ca. 1169-1252)." In *In the Service of the Khan: Eminent Personalities of the Early Mongol-Yüan Period (1200–1300)*, ed. Igor de Rachewiltz et al., 95-111. Wiesbaden: Harrassowitz, 1993.

Buell, Paul D. and Eugene N. Anderson. *A Soup for the "Qan": Chinese Dietary Medicine of the Mongol Era as Seen in Hu Szu-Hui's "Yin-Shan Cheng-Yao."* London: Kegan Paul International, 2000.

Carré, Patrick. *Introduction aux pratiques de la non-dualité. Commentaire du Soutra de la Liberté inconcevable.* Paris: Fayard, 2004.

Cartier, Michel. "A propos de l'histoire du coton en Chine. Approche technologique, économique et sociale." *Études chinoises* 13, nos. 1-2 (1994): 417-435.

Calobrisi. Thomas. "Review of Williams, Duncan Ryuken, *American Sutra: A Story of Faith and Freedom in the Second World War.*" H-Buddhism, H-Net Reviews. March 2021. https://www.h-net.org/reviews/showrev.php?id+55929.

Carter, Martha L. "Turfan and the Grape." In *Turfan Revisited: The First Century of Research into the Arts and Cultures of the Silk Road*, ed. D. Durkin-Meisterernst et al., 49-53. Berlin: Dietrich Reimer Verlag, 2004.

Chakravarti, Uma. *The Social Dimensions of Early Buddhism.* Delhi: Oxford University Press, 1987.

Chan, Aye. "The Nature of Land and Labour Endowments to Sasana in Medieval Burmese History: Review of the Theory of 'Merit-path-to-salvation.'" *Southeast Asian Studies* 26, no. 1 (1988): 86-95.

Chang, Maria Hsia. *Falun Gong: The End of Days.* New Haven, CT: Yale University Press, 2004.

Chao, Kang. *The Development of Cotton Textile Production in China.* Cambridge, MA: Harvard East Asian Research Center, 1977.

Chappell, David W. "The Precious Scroll of the Liang Emperor: Buddhist and Daoist Repentance to Save the Dead." In *Going Forth: Visions of Buddhist Vinaya*, ed. Stanley Weinstein and William M. Bodiford, 40-67. Honolulu: University of Hawai'i Press, 2005.

Chavannes, Edouard. *Documents sur les Tou-kiue (Turcs) occidentaux.* Saint Petersburg: Académie Imperiale des Sciences, 1903.

Chen Aifeng 陈爱峰, 高昌回鹘时期吐鲁番观音图研究 [Study on Turpan Avalokiteśvara paintings of the Qočo Uighur period]. Shanghai: Shanghai Guji Chubanshe, 2020.

Chen, Hao. *A History of the Second Türk Empire (ca. 682–745 A.D.).* Leiden: Brill, 2021.

Ch'en, Kenneth. "The Economic Background of the Hui-ch'ang Suppression of Buddhism." *Harvard Journal of Asiatic Studies* 19, nos. 1/2 (1956): 67-105.

Chin, Tamara T. "The Invention of the Silk Road, 1877." *Critical Inquiry* 40, no. 1 (2013): 194-219.

——. *Savage Exchange: Han Imperialism, Literary Style, and the Economic Imagination.* Cambridge, MA: Harvard University Asia Center, 2014.

Cho, Wonhee. "Negotiated Privilege: Strategic Tax Exemptions Policies for Religious Groups and the Mongol-Yuan Dynasty in 13th-Century China." *Journal of the Economic and Social History of the Orient* 63 (2020): 1–37.

Chu, Hung-lam. "Intellectual Trends in the Fifteenth Century." *Ming Studies* 27 (1989): 1-33.

Clark, Hugh R. *Community, Trade, and Networks: Southern Fujian Province from the Third to the Thirteenth Century.* Cambridge: Cambridge University Press, 1991.

Clark, Larry V. "The Manichean Turkic Pothi-Book." *Altorientalische Forschungen* 9 (1982): 145-218.
———. "The Early Turkic and Sarig Yugur Counting Systems." In *Turfan, Khotan und Dunhuang*, ed. R. E. Emmerick et al., 18-49. Berlin: BBAW Akademie Verlag, 1996.
———. "The Conversion of Bügü Khan to Manichaism." In *Studia Manichaica. IV*, ed. R. E. Emmerick, W. Sunderman, P. Zieme, 82-123. Berlin: Berlin-Brandenburgische Akademie der Wissenschaften, 2000.
———. "Manichaeism among the Uygurs: The Uygur Khan of the Bokug Clan." In *New Light on Manichaeism: Papers from the Sixth International Congress on Manichaeism*, ed. Jason D. BeDuhn, 61-71. Leiden: Brill, 2009.
———. "The Turkic Script and the *Kutadgu Bilig*." In *Turkologie in Mainz*, ed. H Boeschoten and J. Rentzsch, 89-106. Wiesbaden: Harrassowitz, 2010.
———. *Uygur Manichaean Texts: Texts, Translations, Commentary* vol. III. Turnhout: Brepols, 2017.
Clauson, Gerald. "A Late Uyğur Family Archive." In *Iran and Islam in Memory of the Late Vladimir Minorsky*, ed. C. E. Bosworth, 167-196. Edinburgh: Edinburgh University Press, 1971.
Cleaves, F. W. "The Sino-Mongolian Edict of 1453 in The Topkapı Sarayı Müsezi." *Harvard Journal of Asiatic Studies* 13, nos. 3-4 (1950): 431-446.
———. "The Sino-Mongolian Inscription of 1346." *Harvard Journal of Asiatic Studies* 15 (1952): 1-123.
Coblin, W. South. *A Handbook of 'Phags-pa Chinese*. Honolulu: University of Hawai'i Press, 2007.
Colditz, Iris. "Manichaean Time-Management: Laymen between Religious and Secular Duties." In *New Light on Manichaeism: Papers from the Sixth International Congress on Manichaeism*, ed. Jason D. BeDuhn, 73-99. Leiden: Brill, 2009.
Collcutt, Martin. *Five Mountains: The Rinzai Zen Monastic Tradition in Medieval Japan*. Cambridge, MA: Council on East Asian Studies, Harvard University, 1981.
Čolmon. *Mongγol tamaγ-a sayilumal*. Kökeqota: Öbör mongγol-un surγan kümüjil-ün keblel-ün qoriy-a, 1996.
Cook, David. *Studies in Muslim Apocalyptic*. Princeton, NJ: The Darwin Press, 2002.
Cook, Joanna. *Meditation in Modern Buddhism: Renunciation and Change in Thai Monastic Life*. New York: Cambridge University Press, 2010.
Coq, Albert von Le. *Chotscho: Facsimile-Wiedergaben der wichtigeren Funde der ersten Königlich Preussischen Expedition nach Turfan in Ost-Turkistan*. Berlin: Dietrich Reimer, 1913.
Crosby, Kate. *Esoteric Theravada: The Story of the Forgotten Meditation Tradition of Southeast Asia*. Boulder, CO: Shambhala, 2020.
Crouch, Melissa. *Islam and the State in Myanmar: Muslim-Buddhist Relations and the Politics of Belonging*. New York: Oxford University Press, 2016.
Dankoff, Robert. "Three Turkic Verse Cycles Relating to Inner Asian Warfare." *Harvard Ukrainian Studies* 3-4, no. 1 (1979-80): 151-165.
Darian, Jean C. "Social and Economic Factors in the Rise of Buddhism." *Sociological Analysis* 38, no. 3 (1977): 226-238.
Davidovich, E. O. "The Karakhanids." In *History of Civilizations of Central Asia, vol. IV: The Age of Achievement: AD 750 to the end of the fifteenth century*, ed. M. S. Asimov and C. E. Bosworth, 119-144. Paris: UNESCO, 1998.
Davidson, Ronald M. *Indian Esoteric Buddhism: A Social History of the Tantric Movement*. New York: Columbia University Press, 2002.

———. *Tibetan Renaissance: Tantric Buddhism in the Rebirth of Tibetan Culture*. New York: Columbia University Press, 2005.

Davies, Richard H. *Global India Circa 100 CE: South Asia in Early World History*. Ann Arbor: Association for Asian Studies, 2009.

Debreczeny, Karl. "Faith and Empire: An Overview." In *Faith and Empire: The Art of Politics in Tibetan Buddhism*, ed. K. Debreczeny, 19-51. New York: Rubin Museum of Art, 2019.

de Jong, J. W. "Buddha's Word in China." *East Asian History* 11 (1996): 45-58.

de Somogyi, J. "A *Qasida* on the Destruction of Baghdad by the Mongols." *Bulletin of the School of Oriental and African Studies* 7 (1933-5): 41-48.

DeWeese, Devin. *Islamization and Native Religion in the Golden Horde: Baba Tükles and Conversion to Islam in Historical and Epic Tradition*. University Park: Pennsylvania State University Press, 1994.

———. "The *Masha'-ikh-i Turk* and the *Khojagan*: Rethinking the Links between the Yasavi and Naqshbandi Sufi Traditions." *Journal of Islamic Studies* 7, no. 2 (1996): 180-207.

———. "Sacred Places and 'Public' Narratives: The Shrine of Ahmad Yasavi in Hagiographical Traditions of the Yasavi Sufi Order, 16th-17th Centuries." *Muslim World* 90 (2000): 353-376.

———. "Problems of Islamization in the Volga-Ural Region: Traditions about Berke Khan." In *Proceedings of the International Symposium on Islamic Civilisation in the Volga-Ural Region, Kazan, 8–11 June 2001*, ed. Ali Çaksu and Radik Mukhammetshin, 3-13. Istanbul: Research Centre for Islamic History, Art and Culture, 2004.

———. "'Stuck in the Throat of Chingiz Khan': Envisioning the Mongol Conquests in Some Sufi Accounts from the 14th to 17th Centuries." In *History and Historiography of Post-Mongol Central Asia and the Middle East: Studies in Honor of John E. Woods*, ed. J. Pfeiffer and S. A. Quinn, 23-60. Wiesbaden: Harrassowitz, 2006.

———. "Islamization in the Mongol Empire." In *The Cambridge History of Inner Asia: The Chinggisid Age*, ed. Nicola Di Cosmo, Allen J. Frank, Peter B. Golden, 120-134. New York: Cambridge University Press, 2014.

Di Cosmo, Nicola. *Ancient China and Its Enemies: The Rise of Nomadic Power in East Asian History*. Cambridge: Cambridge University Press, 2002.

———. "Maligned Exchanges: The Uyghur-Tang Trade in the Light of Climate Data." In *Texts and Transformations: Essays in Honor of the 75th Birthday of Victor H. Mair*, ed. Haun Saussy, 117-136. Amherst, MA: Cambria Press, 2018.

Diemberger, Hildegaard, Franz-Karl Ehrhard, and Peter Kornicki. *Tibetan Printing: Comparisons, Continuities and Change*. Leiden: Brill, 2016.

Drompp, Michael R. "The Uighur-Chinese Conflict of 840-848." In *Warfare in Inner Asian History (500–1800)*, ed. Nicola Di Cosmo, 73-104. Leiden: Brill, 2002.

———. *Tang China and the Collapse of the Uighur Empire: A Documentary History*. Leiden: Brill, 2005.

Dunhuang Wenwu Yanjiusuo 敦煌文物研究所. *Zhongguo shiku.5. Dunhuang Mogaoku* 中國石窟. 敦煌莫高窟 5. Beijing: Wenwu Chubanshe, 1987.

Dunnell, Ruth W. "The Hsia Origins of the Yüan Institution of Imperial Preceptor." *Asia Major* 5 (1992): 85-111.

———. "Esoteric Buddhism Under the Xixia (1038-1227)." In *Esoteric Buddhism and the Tantras in East Asia*, ed. C. D. Orzech et al., 465-477. Leiden: Brill, 2011.

Duturaeva, Dilnoza. *Qarakhanid Roads to China: The History of Sino-Turkic Relations*. Leiden: Brill, 2022.

Ecsedy, Hilda. "Trade-and-War Relations between the Turks and China in the Second Half of the 6th Century." *Acta Orientalia Academiae Scientiarum Hungaricae* 21 (1968): 131-180.

Eden, Jeff. *The Life of Muhammad Sharīf: A Central Asian Sufi Hagiography in Chagatay*. Vienna: Verlag der Österreichischen Akademie der Wissenschaften, 2015.

———. *Warrior Saints of the Silk Road: Legends of the Qarakhanids*. Leiden: Brill, 2019.

El-Hibri, Tayeb. *Reinterpreting Islamic Historiography: Harun al-Rashid and the Narrative of the 'Abbasid Caliphate*. New York: Cambridge University Press, 1999.

Elias, Jamal J. *The Throne Carrier of God: The Life and Thought of 'Ala' ad-dawla as-Simnani*. Albany: State University of New York Press, 1995.

Elverskog, Johan. *Uygur Buddhist Literature*. Turnhout: Brepols, 1997.

———. *The Jewel Translucent Sutra: Altan Khan and the Mongols in the Sixteenth Century*. Leiden: Brill, 2003.

———. "The Legend of Muna Mountain." *Inner Asia* 8, no. 1 (2006): 99-122.

———. "The Mongolian *Big Dipper Sutra*." *Journal of the International Association of Buddhist Studies* (2007): 87-124.

———. *Buddhism and Islam on the Silk Road*. Philadelphia: University of Pennsylvania Press, 2010.

———. *The Buddha's Footprint: An Environmental History of Asia*. Philadelphia: University of Pennsylvania Press, 2020.

———. "The Uighurs and Shambhala." *The Berlin Journal* 35 (2021): 58-62.

———. "Religious Exchange." In *The Cambridge History of the Mongol Empire*, ed. Michal Biran and Kim Hodong, 525-549. New York: Cambridge University Press, 2023.

Elvin, Mark. *The Retreat of the Elephants: An Environmental History of China*. New Haven, CT: Yale University Press, 2006.

Emmerick, R. E. *The Sūtra of Golden Light: Being a Translation of the Suvarṇabhāsottama Sūtra*. London: Luzac, 1970.

Erdosy, George. "City States of North India and Pakistan at the Time of the Buddha." In *The Archaeology of Early Historic South Asia: The Emergence of Cities and States*, ed. F. R. Allchin, 99-122. New York: Cambridge University Press, 1995.

Ess, Hans van. "Der Name der Uiguren." In *Über den Alltag hinaus: Festschrift für Thomas O. Höllmann zum 65. Geburtstag*, ed. Shing Müller and Armin Selbitschka, 253-266. Wiesbaden: Harrassowitz, 2017.

Everding, Karl-Heinz. *Herrscherurkunden aus der Zeit des mongolischen Großreiches für tibetische Adelshäuser, Geistliche und Klöster. Teil 1: Diplomata Mongolica. Mittelmongolische Urkunden in 'Phags-pa-Schrift. Edition, Übersetzung, Analyse*. Halle: International Institute for Tibetan and Buddhist Studies, 2006.

Falk, Harry. "Making Wine in Gandhara under Buddhist Monastic Supervision." *Bulletin of the Asia Institute* 23 (2009): 65-78.

Farquhar, David M. "Emperor as Bodhisattva in the Governance of the Ch'ing Empire." *Harvard Journal of Asiatic Studies* 38, no. 1 (1978): 5-34.

Fedakar, Durdu. "Das Alttürkische in sogdischer Schrift: Textmaterial und Orthographie (Teil I)." *Ural-Altaische Jahrbücher* NF 10 (1991): 85-98.

———. "Das Alttürkische in sogdischer Schrift: Textmaterial und Orthographie (Teil II)." *Ural-Altaische Jahrbücher* NF 13 (1991): 133-157.

Fletcher, Joseph F. "China and Central Asia, 1368-1884." In *The Chinese World Order*, ed. John K. Fairbank, 205-219. Cambridge, MA: Harvard University Press, 1968.

——. "Turco-Mongolian Monarchic Tradition in the Ottoman Empire." In *Eucharisterion: Essays Presented to Omeljan Pritsak*, ed. I. Sevcenko and F. E. Sysyn, 237-242. Cambridge, MA: Ukranian Research Institute, 1979-1980.

Forte, Antonino. *Mingtang and Buddhist Utopias in the History of the Astronomical Clock: The Tower, Statue and Armillary Sphere Constructed by Empress Wu*. Rome: École Française d'Extreme-Orient, 1988.

Frasch, Tilman. "The Theravāda Buddhist Ecumene in the Fifteenth Century: Intellectual Foundations and Material Representations." In *Buddhism across Asia: Networks of Material, Intellectual, and Cultural Exchange*, vol. 1, ed. Tansen Sen, 347-368. Singapore: Institute for Southeast Asian Studies, 2014.

Franke, Herbert. "A Sino-Uighur Family Portrait: Notes on a Woodcut from Turfan." *The Canada-Mongolia Review* 4, no. 1 (1978): 33-40.

——. "Tibetans in Yüan China." In *China under Mongol Rule*, ed. John D. Langlois, Jr., 296-328. Princeton, NJ: Princeton University Press, 1981.

——. "Mittelmongolische Glossen in einer arabischen Astronomischen Handschrift von 1366." *Oriens* 31 (1988): 95-118.

——. "A Note on the Multilinguality in China under the Mongols: The Compilers of the Revised Buddhist Canon, 1285-87." In *Opuscala Altaica: Essays Presented in Honor of Henry Schwarz*, ed. Edward H. Kaplan and Donald W. Whisenhunt, 286-298. Bellingham: Western Washington University Center for East Asian Studies, 1994.

——. "Chinesische Quellen über den uigurischen Stifter Dhanyasena." In *Memoriae Munusculum: Gedenkband für Annemarie von Gabain*, ed. K. Röhrborn and W. Veenker, 55-64. Wiesbaden: Harrassowitz, 1994.

——. "Chinesische Nachrichten über Karundaz und seine Familie." In *Turfan, Khotan und Dunhuang: Vorträge der Tagung 'Annemarie v. Gabain und die Turfanforschung,' veranstaltet von der BBAW in Berlin (9.-12.12.1994)*, ed. R. E. Emmerick et al., 83-93. Berlin: Akademie Verlag, 1996.

——. *Chinesischer und tibetischer Buddhismus im China der Yüanzeit*. Munich: Kommission für Zentralasiatische Studien/Bayerische Akademie der Wissenschaften, 1996.

Franken, Christina. *Die "Große Halle" von Karakorum: Zur archäologischen Untersuchung des ersten buddhistischen Tempels der alten mongolischen Hauptstadt*. Wiesbaden: Reichert Verlag, 2015.

Fu Ma 付马. *Sichouzhilu shang xizhou huihu wangchao: 9–13 shiji zhongya dongbu lishi yanjiu* 絲綢之路上的西州回鶻王朝：9-13世紀中亞東部歷史研究 (The West Uygur Kingdom on the Silk Road: Study on the History of Eastern Central Asia during the 9th-13th centuries). Beijing: Social Science Academic Press, 2019.

Fu Ma and Xia Lidong. "Comprehensive Study on Old Uighur and Chinese Wall Inscriptions in Room B of Newly Excavated Cave 26 in Tuyuq Grottoes, Turfan." *Acta Orientalia Academiae Scientiarum Hungaricae* 74, no. 2 (2021): 181-206.

Fu Ma and Xia Lidong, "Philological Study of Several Old Uighur Tantric Manuscripts Recently Unearthed from Tuyuq, Xinjiang." *Acta Orientalia Academiae Scientiarum Hungaricae* 75, no. 1 (2022): 27-30.

Fuchs, Walther. "Huei-ch'ao's Pilgerreise durch Nordwest-Indien und Zentralasien um 726." *Sitzungsberichte der Preußischen Akademie der Wissenschaften* 30 (1938): 1-46.

Fujieda, Akira. "Sha-shū Kigi-gun setsudoshi shimatsu." *Tōhō Gakuhō* 13 (1942): 48-51.
Fussman, Gérard. "Upāya-kauśalya: l'implantation du bouddhisme au Gandhāra." In *Bouddhisme et cultures local. Quelques cas de reciproques adaptations*, ed. Fukui Fumimasa and Gérard Fussman, 17-51. Paris: École Française d'Extrême-Orient, 1994.
——. "Kushan Power and the Expansion of Buddhism Beyond the Soleiman Mountains." In *Kushan Histories: Literary Sources and Selected Papers from a Symposium at Berlin, December 5 to 7, 2013*, ed. Harry Falk, 153-202. Bremen: Hempen Verlag, 2015.
Gabain, Annemarie von. "Buddhistische Türkenmission." In *Asiatica: Festschrift Friedrich Weller zum 65. Geburtstag*, ed. J. Schubert and U. Schneider, 161-173. Leipzig: O. Harrassowitz, 1954.
——. *Das Leben im uigurischen Königreich von Qočo: (850–1250)*. Wiesbaden: Harrassowitz, 1973.
Galambos, Imre. "Non-Chinese Influence in Medieval Chinese Manuscript Culture." In *Frontiers and Boundaries: Encounters on China's Margins*, ed. Zsombor Rajkai and Ildikó Bellér-Hann, 72-86. Wiesbaden: Harrassowitz Verlag, 2012.
——. *Dunhuang Manuscript Culture: End of the First Millennium*. Berlin: DeGruyter, 2020.
Gasparini, Mariachiara. *Transcending Patterns: Silk Road Cultural and Artistic Interactions through Central Asian Textile Images*. Honolulu: University of Hawai'i Press, 2020.
Geiss, James. "The Chia-ching reign, 1522-1566." In *The Cambridge History of China, Vol. 8: 1*, ed. F. W. Mote and D. Twitchett, 440-510. Cambridge: Cambridge University Press, 1988.
Gellner, David N. *The Anthropology of Buddhism and Hinduism: Weberian Themes*. New Delhi: Oxford University Press, 2001.
Geng, Shimin. "Study of Two Folios of the Uighur Text 'Abitaki.'" *Acta Orientalia Academiae Scientiarum Hungaricae* 57, no. 1 (2004): 105-113.
——."Study of Another Two Folios of the Uighur Text 'Abitaki.'" *Acta Orientalia Academiae Scientiarum Hungaricae* 59, no. 1 (2006): 47-56.
——. "A Study on the Uighur Text Abitaki (4)." *Türkbilig* 14 (2007): 177-183.
Geng, Shimin and H. J. Klimkeit. *Das Zusammentreffen mit Maitreya. Die ersten fünf Kapitel der Hami-Version der Maitrisimit*. Wiesbaden: Otto Harrassowitz, 1988.
Geng, Shimin and Zhang Baoxi. "Yuan huihuwen 'Zhong xiu wen shu si bei,' chu shi." *Kaogu xuebao* 2 (1986): 253-264.
Gernet, Jacques. *Les aspects économiques du bouddhisme dans la société chinoise du Ve au Xe siècle*. Saigon: École française d'Extrême-Orient, 1956.
——. *Buddhism in Chinese Society: An Economic History from the Fifth to the Tenth Centuries*. Trans. Franciscus Verellen. New York: Columbia University Press, 1995.
Giersch, C. Patterson. "Across Zomia with Merchants, Monks, and Musk: Process Geographies, Trade Networks, and the Inner-East-Southeast Asian Borderlands." *Journal of Global History* 5, no. 2 (2010): 215-239.
Gimello, Robert M. "Wu-t'ai Shan during the Early Chin Dynasty: The Testimony of Chu Pien." *Zhonghua foxue xuebao* 7 (1997): 501-612.
Glahn, Richard von. *The Sinister Way: The Divine and the Demonic in Chinese Religious Culture*. Berkeley: University of California Press, 2004.
Goetzmann, William N. *Money Changes Everything: How Finance Made Civilization Possible*. Princeton, NJ: Princeton University Press, 2017.
Golden, Peter B. "The Migrations of the *Oguz*." *Archivum Ottomanicum* 4 (1972): 45-84.

———. "Imperial Ideology and the Sources of Political Unity amongst the pre-Chinggisid Nomads of Western Eurasia." *Archivum Eurasiae Medii Aevi* 2 (1982): 37-77.

———. "The Karakhanids and Early Islam." In *The Cambridge History of Early Inner Asia*, ed. Denis Sinor, 343-370. New York: Cambridge University Press, 1990.

———. "The Türk Imperial Tradition in the Pre-Chinggisid Era." In *Imperial Statecraft: Political Forms and Techniques of Governance in Inner Asia, 6th–20th Centuries*, ed. D. Sneath, 23-59. Bellingham: Western Washington University Center for East Asian Studies, 2006.

Gombrich, Richard. *Theravada Buddhism: A Social History from Ancient Benares to Modern Colombo*. London: Routledge & Kegan Paul, 1988.

Gran, Peter. *Islamic Roots of Capitalism: Egypt, 1760–1840*. Syracuse, NY: Syracuse University Press, 1979.

Greene, Eric M. *Chan Before Chan: Meditation, Repentance, and Visionary Experience in Chinese Buddhism*. Honolulu: University of Hawai'i Press, 2021.

Gross, Jo-Ann and Asom Urunbaev. *The Letters of Khwāja 'Ubayd Allāh Aḥrār and his Associates*. Leiden: Brill, 2002.

Grupper, Samuel M. "The Buddhist Sanctuary-Vihara of Labnasagut and the Il-Qan Hülegü: An Overview of Il-Qanid Buddhism and Related Matters." *Archivum Eurasiae Medii Aevi* 13 (2004): 5-78.

Gulácsi, Zsuzsanna. *Mani's Pictures: The Didactic Images of the Manichaeans from Sasanian Mesopotamia to Uygur Central Asia and Tang-Ming China*. Leiden: Brill, 2015.

———. "The Manichaean Roots of a Pure Land Banner from Kocho (III 4524) in the Asian Art Museum, Berlin." In *Language, Society, and Religion in the World of the Turks: Festschrift for Larry Clark at Seventy-Five*, ed. Zsuzsanna Gulácsi, 187-204. Turnhout: Brepols, 2018.

Gunawardana, R. A. H. L. *Robe and Plough: Monasticism and Economic Interest in Early Medieval Sri Lanka*. Tucson: University of Arizona Press, 1979.

Halperin, Charles J. "The Kipchak Connection: The Ilkhans, the Mamluks and Ayn Jalut." *Bulletin of the School of Oriental and African Studies* 63, no. 2 (2000): 229-245.

Hamilton, James "Toquz-Oguz et On-Uygur." *Journal asiatique* 250 (1962): 23-64.

———. *Manuscrits ouïgours du Ix–X siècle de Touen-Houang*. 2 vols. Paris: Peeters, 1986.

Hansen, Valerie. "The Tribute Trade with Khotan in Light of Materials Found at the Dunhuang Library Cave." *Bulletin of the Asia Institute* 19 (2005): 37-46.

———. *The Silk Road: A New History*. New York: Oxford University Press, 2015.

Hansen, Valerie, François Louis, and Daniel Kane. "Perspectives on the Liao." Special issue, *Journal of Song-Yuan Studies* 43 (2013): 1-412.

Harris, Ian. "'A vast unsupervised recycling plant': Animals and the Buddhist Cosmos." In *A Communion of Subjects: Animals in Religion, Science, and Ethics*, ed. Paul Waldau and Kimberley Patton, 207-217. New York: Columbia University Press, 2006.

Hartmann, Jens-Uwe, Klaus Wille, and Peter Zieme. "Indrasenas Beichte: Ein Sanskrit-Text in uigurischer Schrift aus Turfan." *Berliner Indologische Studien* 9/10 (1996): 203-216.

———. "Aśvaghoṣa's Buddhacarita in the Old Uigur Literature." *Annual Report of The International Research Institute of Advanced Buddhology at Soka University* 25 (2022): 173-189.

Harvey, Peter. *An Introduction to Buddhism: Teachings, History and Practices*. New York: Cambridge University Press, 1990.

Hawkes, Jason. "The Wider Archaeological Contexts of the Buddhist Stūpa Site of Bharhut." In *Buddhist Stupas in South Asia*, ed. Jason Hawkes and Akira Shimada, 146-175. New Delhi: Oxford University Press, 2009.
Haydar Dughlat, Mirza. *Tarikh-i-Rashidi: A History of the Khans of Moghulistan*. Trans. W. M. Thackston. Cambridge, MA: Harvard University, Department of Near Eastern Studies, 1996.
Hedin, Sven. *Southern Tibet: Discoveries in Former Times Compared with My Own Researches in 1906-1908*. Vol. 8. Stockholm: Lithographic Institute of the General Staff of the Swedish Army, 1922.
Heitzman, James. "Early Buddhism, Trade, and Empire." In *Studies in the Archaeology and Paleoanthropology of South Asia*, ed. Kenneth A. R. Kennedy and Gregory L. Possehl, 121-137. New Delhi: Oxford and IBH Publishing/American Institute of Indian Studies, 1984.
Hitch, Doug. "The Special Status of Turfan." *Sino-Platonic Papers* 186 (2009): 1-61.
Horlemann, Bianca. *Aufstieg und Niedergang der Tsong Kha-Stammeskonföderation im 11./12. Jahrhundert an der Schnittstelle von Tibet, China und Zentralasien*. Frankfurt: Peter Lang, 2004.
———. "The Relations of the Eleventh-Century Tsong Kha Tribal Confederation to Its Neighbour States on the Silk Road." In *Contributions to the Early History of Tibet*, ed. M. T. Kapstein and B. Dotson, 83-106. Leiden: Brill, 2007.
Horner, I. B. *Milinda's Questions*, vol. 1. London: Luzac, 1963.
Hua, Kaiqi. "The White Cloud Movement: Local Activism and Buddhist Printing in China under Mongol Rule (1276-1368 CE)." Ph.D. diss., University of California Merced, 2016.
Huang, Chi-Chiang. "Imperial Rulership and Buddhism in the Early Northern Song." In *Imperial Rulership and Cultural Change in Traditional China*, ed. F. P. Brandauer and Chun-Chieh Huang, 144-187. Seattle: University of Washington Press, 1994.
Huang, Shi-Shan Susan. "Reassessing Printed Buddhist Frontispieces from Xi Xia." *Zhejiang University Journal of Art and Archaeology* 1 (2014): 129-182.
Huber, Toni. *The Holy Land Reborn: Pilgrimage and the Tibetan Reinvention of Buddhist India*. Chicago: University of Chicago Press, 2008.
Hughes, April D. *Worldly Saviors and Imperial Authority in Medieval Chinese Buddhism*. Honolulu: University of Hawai'i Press, 2021.
Hurwitz, Nimrod, Christian C. Sahner, Uriel Simonsohn, and Luke Yarbrough. *Conversion to Islam in the Premodern Age: A Sourcebook*. Berkeley: University of California Press, 2020.
Institute of Oriental Manuscripts, Russian Academy of Sciences, and the Toyo Bunko, eds. *Catalogue of the Old Uyghur Manuscripts and Blockprints in the Serindia Collection of the Institute of Oriental Manuscripts, RAS*. Vol. 1. Tokyo: The Toyo Bunko, 2021.
Iwasaki, Tsutomu. "The Tibetan Tribes of Ho-hsi and Buddhism during the Northern Sung Period." *Acta Asiatica* 64 (1993): 17-37.
Jackson, Peter. "Reflections on the Islamization of Mongol Khans in Comparative Perspective." *Journal of the Economic and Social History of the Orient* 62 (2019): 356-387.
Jahn, Karl. *Rashid al-Din's History of India*. The Hague: Mouton, 1965.
———. "Rashid al-Din and Chinese Culture." *Central Asiatic Journal* 14 (1970): 134-147.
Jan, Yün-hua. "Buddhist Relations between India and Sung China." *History of Religions* 6, no. 1 (1966): 24-42.

———. "Buddhist Relations between India and Sung China." *History of Religions* 6, no. 2 (1966): 135-168.

Jenkins, Philip. *Climate, Catastrophe, and Faith: How Changes in Climate Drive Religious Upheaval.* New York: Oxford University Press, 2021.

———. "Climate Shocks and the Fate of Empires (and of World Religions)." https://patheos.com/blogs/anxiousbench/2022/-2/climate-shocks-and-the-fate-of-empires-and-of-world-religions/.

Jones, J. J. *The Mahāvastu.* Vol. 3. London: Luzac, 1956.

Jülch, Thomas. *The Middle Kingdom and the Dharma Wheel: Aspects of the Relationship Between the Buddhist Samgha and the State in Chinese History.* Leiden: Brill, 2016.

Julien, Stanislas. "Concordance sinico-sanskrite d'un nombre considérable de titres d'ouvrages bouddhiques recueillé dans un catalogue chinois de l'an 1306." *Journal asiatique* 14 (1849): 353-446.

Juvaini, 'Ala-ad-Din 'Ata-Malik. *The History of the World Conqueror.* Trans. John A. Boyle. Manchester: Manchester University Press, 1958.

Kaplony, Andreas. "The Conversion of the Turks of Central Asia to Islam as Seen by Arabic and Persian Geography." In *Islamisation de l'Asie centrale: Processus locaux d'acculturation du VIIe au XIe siècle*, ed. Etienne de la Vaissière, 319-338. Paris: Association pour l'avancement des études iraniennes, 2008.

Kara, György. "Aramaic Scripts for Altaic Languages." In *The World's Writing Systems*, ed. P. T. Daniels and W. Bright, 536-558. New York: Oxford University Press, 1996.

———."Mediaeval Mongol Documents from Khara Khoto and East Turkestan in the St. Petersburg Branch of the Institute of Oriental Studies." *Manuscripta Orientalia* 9, no. 2 (2003): 3-40.

Kara, György and Peter Zieme. *Die uigurischen Übersetzungen des Guruyogas 'Tiefer Weg' von Saskya Pandita und der Mañjuśrīnāmasamgīti.* Berlin: Akademie Verlag, 1977.

———. *Fragmente tantrischer Werke in uigurischer Übersetzung.* Berlin: Akademie Verlag, 1976.

Kasai, Yukiyo. "Ein Kolophon um die Legende von Bokug Kagan." *Studies on the Inner Asian Languages* 19 (2004): 1-25.

———. "Ein Kommentar zu einem unbekannten uigurisch-buddhistischen Text, der aus dem Tocharischen übersetzt wurde." *Studies on the Inner Asian Languages* 21 (2006): 21-47.

———. *Die uigurischen buddhistischen Kolophone.* Turnhout: Brepols, 2008.

———. *Der alttürkische Kommentar zum Vimalakīrtinirdeśa-Sūtra.* Turnhout: Brepols, 2011.

———. "The Outline of the Old Turkish Commentary on the *Vimalakīrtinirdeśa Sūtra*." In *Dunhuang Studies: Prospects and Problems for the Coming Second Century of Research*, ed. Irina Popova and Liu Yi, 106-111. St. Petersburg: Slavia, 2012.

———. "The Edition of the Old Turkish Commentary on the *Vimalakīrtinirdeśa-Sūtra*." In *Proceedings of the 1st International Colloquium on Ancient Manuscripts and Literatures of the Minorities of China*, ed. Huang Bianming and Ma Fu, 401-409. Beijing: Minzu Chubanshe, 2012.

———. "One Further Fragment of the Old Turkish Commentary on the *Vimalakīrtinirdeśa-Sūtra*." *AIBÜ Sosyal Bilimler Enstitüsü Dergesi* 13 (2013): 199-206.

———. "Der Ursprung des alttürkischen Maitreya-Kults." In *Die Erforschung des Tocharischen und die alttürkische Maitrisimit*, ed. Y. Kasai, A. Yakup, and D. Durkin-Meistererenst, 67-104. Turnhout: Brepols, 2013.

——. "Sanskrit Word Forms Written in Brāhmī Script in the Old Uyghur Buddhist Texts." *Journal of the International Association of Buddhist Studies* 38 (2015): 401-422.

——."Zur Verbreitung und Verwendung altuigurischer buddhistischer Texte." In *Eine hundertblättrige Tulpe—Bir sadbarg lāla: Festgabe für Claus Schönig*, ed. I. Hauenschild, M. Kappler, B. Kellner-Heinkele, 224-231. Berlin: Klaus Schwarz Verlag, 2016.

——. "Five Old Uyghur Abhidharma Texts Containing Brāhmī Elements." *BuddhistRoad Papers* 1, no. 1 (2019): 1-24.

——. "The Bodhisattva Mañjuśrī, Mt. Wutai, and Uyghur Pilgrims." *BuddhistRoad Papers* 5, no. 4 (2020): 3-39.

——. "Uyghur Legitimation and the Role of Buddhism." In *Buddhism in Central Asia I: Patronage, Legitimation, Sacred Space, and Pilgrimage*, ed. C. Meinert and H. H. Sørensen, 61-90. Leiden: Brill, 2020.

——. "Talismans Used by the Uyghur Buddhists and Their Relationship with the Chinese Tradition." *Journal of the International Association of Buddhist Studies* 44 (2021): 527-556.

——. "The Avalokiteśvara Cult in Turfan and Dunhuang in the Pre-Mongolian Period." In *Buddhist Rituals in Central Asia II: Practices and Rituals, Visual and Material Transfer*, ed. Yukiyo Kasai and Henrik H. Sørensen, 246-271. Leiden: Brill, 2022.

——. "Central Asian and Iranian Influence in Old Uyghur Buddhist Manuscripts: Book Forms and Donor Colophons." In *The Syntax of Colophons: A Comparative Study Across Pothi Manuscripts*, ed. Nalini Balbir and Giovanni Ciotti, 373-398. Berlin: Walter de Gruyter, 2022.

Kasai, Yukiyo, Simone-Christiane Raschmann, and Peter Zieme. "Introduction." In *The Old Uyghur Āgama fragments preserved in the Sven Hedin collection, Stockholm*, ed. Yukiyo Kasai et al., 17-36. Turnhout: Brepols, 2017.

al-Kāšγarī, Maḥmūd. *Compendium of the Turkic Languages (Diwan Lugat at-Turk) Volume 1*. Trans. Robert Dankoff and James Kelly. Cambridge, MA: Harvard University Press, 1982.

Kashghari, Muhammad Sadiq. *In Remembrance of the Saints: The Rise and Fall of an Inner Asian Sufi Dynasty*. Trans. David Brophy. New York: Columbia University Press, 2021.

Kennedy, E. S. "Eclipse Predictions in Arabic Astronomical Tables Prepared for the Mongol Viceroy of Tibet." *Zeitschrift für Geschichte der Arabisch-Islamischen Wissenschaften* 4 (1990): 60-80.

Kennedy, E. S. and Jan Hogendijk. "Two Tables from an Arabic Astronomical Handbook for the Mongol Viceroy of Tibet." In *A Scientific Humanist: Studies in Memory of Abraham Sachs*, ed. Erie Leichty et al., 233-242. Philadelphia: The University Museum, 1988.

Kieschnick, John. *The Impact of Buddhism on Chinese Material Culture*. Princeton, NJ: Princeton University Press, 2003.

Kılıç Cengiz, Ayşe. "A Fragment of the *Uṣṇīṣavijayā Dhāraṇī* from Turfan Housed in the Museum für Asiatische Kunst in Berlin." *Acta Orientalia Academiae Scientiarum Hungaricae* 74, no. 4 (2021): 651-672.

Kim, Hodong, "The Cult of Saints in Eastern Turkestan: The Case of Alp Ata in Turfan." In *Proceedings of the 35th Permanent International Altaistic Conference*, ed. Chieh-hsien Ch'en, 199-226. Taipei: National Taiwan University, 1993.

——. "The Rise and Fall of the Hami Kingdom (ca. 1389-1513)." In *Land Routes of the Silk Roads and the cultural exchanges between the East and West before the 10th century*. Beijing: New World Press, 1996.

———. "Muslim Saints in the 14th to the 16th Centuries of Eastern Turkestan." *International Journal of Central Asian Studies* 1 (1996): 285-322.
———. "The Early History of the Moghul Nomads: The Legacy of the Chagatai Khanate." In *The Mongol Empire and Its Legacy*, ed. Reuven Amitai-Preiss and David O. Morgan, 290-318. Leiden: Brill, 1999.
———. "A Reappraisal of Güyüg Khan." In *Mongols, Turks and Others: Eurasian Nomads and the Sedentary World*, ed. Reuven Amitai and Michal Biran, 309-338. Leiden: Brill, 2005.
Kitsudō, Kōichi. "Supplements to *Uigurische Āgama-Fragmente*." In *Aspects of Research into Central Asian Buddhism*, ed. Peter Zieme, 95-113. Turnhout: Brepols, 2008.
———. "Two Chinese Buddhist Texts Written by Uighurs." *Acta Orientalia Academiae Scientiarum Hungaricae* 64, no. 3 (2011): 325-343.
———. "Historical Significance of Bezeklik Cave 20 in the Uygur Buddhism." In *Buddhism and Art in Turfan: From the Perspective of Uyghur Buddhism*, ed. Irisawa Takashi, 141-152. Kyoto: Research Center for Buddhist Culture in Asia Ryukoku University, 2012.
———. "Liao Influence on Uigur Buddhism." In *Studies in Chinese Manuscripts: From the Warring States to the 20th Century*, ed. Imre Galambos, 225-248. Budapest: Institute of East Asian Studies, Eotvos Lorand University, 2013.
———. "Teachings of the Consciousness Only Inserted in the Chapter 6, Book 4 of the *Altun Yaruk Sudur*." In *Unter dem Bodhi-Baum: Festschrift für Klaus Röhrborn anlässlich des 80. Geburtstags überreicht von Kollegen, Freunden und Schülern*, ed. Z. Özertural and G. Şilfeler, 187-196. Göttingen: V&R Unipress, 2019.
———. "The Lehrtext and *Bodhisattvacaryāmārga* (Pelliot Ouïgour 4521)." In *Beşbalıkı Şingko Şeli Tutung anısına uluslararası eski Uygurca çalıştayı bildirleri, 4-6 Haziran 2011, Ankara*, 93-105, ed. Mustafa S. Kaçalin. Ankara: Türk Dil Kurumu, 2022.
Kitsudō, Kōichi and Shintarō Arakawa. "New Research on the *Guanxin Shijietu* (*Illustration of the Ten Realms of Mind Contemplation*)—The Case of the Xixia and the Uyghur Kingdoms." *Kokka* 1477 (2018): 5-20.
Kitsudō, Kōichi and Peter Zieme. "The *Jin'gangjing zuan* in Old Uighur with Parallels in Tangut and Chinese." *Written Monuments of the Orient* 2 (2017): 43-87.
Klimeš, Ondřej. *Struggle by the Pen: The Uyghur Discourse of Nation and National Interest, c. 1900-1949*. Leiden: Brill, 2015.
Klimkeit, H. J. "The Donor at Turfan." *Silk Road Art and Archaeology: Journal of the Institute of Silk Road Studies, Kamakura* 1 (1990): 179-201.
Konczak, Ines. "Origin, Development and Meaning of the *Praṇidhi* Paintings on the Northern Silk Road." In *Buddhism and Art in Turfan: From the Perspective of Uyghur Buddhism*, ed. Irisawa Takashi, 43-55. Kyoto: Research Center for Buddhist Culture in Asia Ryukoku University, 2012.
Konczak-Nagel, Ines. "Praṇidhi-Darstellungen an der Nördlichen Seidenstraße: Das Bildmotiv der Prophezeiung der Buddhaschaft Śākyamunis in den Malereien Xinjiang." Ph.D. diss., Ludwig-Maximilians-Universität, 2014.
Kudara, Kōgi. "'Pelliot ouïgour 218': Its Significance." In *Documents et archives provenant de l'Asie Centrale: actes du colloque franco-japonais*, ed. Akira Haneda, 167-174. Kyoto: Association Franco-Japonais des Études Orientales, 1990.
———. "Uiguru-yaku Engakukyō to sono chūshaku [The Uighur version of the *Yuanjuejing* and the commentary belonging to it]." *Ryūkoku Kiyō* 14, no. 1 (1992): 1-23.

———. "Uigur and Tibetan Translations of 'The History of the Buddha Statue of Sandalwood in China.'" In *Turfan Revisited: The First Century of Research into the Arts and Cultures of the Silk Road*, ed. D. Durkin-Meisterernst et al., 149-154. Berlin: Dietrich Reimer Verlag, 2004.

Kuijp, Leonard W. J.van der. *The Kālacakra and the Patronage of Buddhism by the Mongol Imperial Family*. Bloomington: Indiana University Department of Central Eurasian Studies, 2004.

Kychanov, E. I. "The Organization and Control of Embassies in 12th Century Hsi-Hsia— According to the Tangut Law Code." *The Bulletin of Sung-Yuan Studies* 18 (1986): 4-12.

Lahiri, Nayanjot. *Ashoka in Ancient India*. Cambridge, MA: Harvard University Press, 2015.

Lal, Makhan. "Iron Tools, Forest Clearance and Urbanisation in the Gangetic Plains." *Man and Environment* 10 (1986): 83-90.

Lambton, A. K. S. "Justice in the Medieval Persian Theory of Kingship." *Studia Islamica* 17 (1962): 91-119.

Lamotte, Étienne. *History of Indian Buddhism: From the Origins to the Śaka Era*. Trans. Sara Webb-Boin. Louvain-Paris: Peeters Press, 1988.

Lane, George. *Early Mongol Rule in Thirteenth-Century Iran: A Persian Renaissance*. London: Routledge, 2003.

Laut, Jens Peter. "Die Gründung des buddhistischen Nonnenordens in der alttürkischen Überlieferung." In *Türkische Sprachen und Literaturen: Materialien der ersten deutschen Turkologen-Konferenz, Bamberg, 3.-6. Juli 1987*, ed. Ingeborg Baldauf, 257-274. Wiesbaden: Harrassowitz, 1991.

———. "Uigurische Sünden." In *De Dunhuang à Istanbul: Hommage à James Russell Hamilton*, ed. L. Bazin and P. Zieme, 127-148. Turnhout: Brepols, 2001.

———. "Gedanken zum alttürkischen Stabreim." In *Splitter aus der Gegend von Turfan: Festschrift für Peter Zieme anläßlich seines 60. Geburtstags*, ed. Mehmet Ölmez and Simone-Christiane Raschmann, 134-135. Istanbul: Türk Dilleri Araştırmaları Dizisi, 2002.

———. "Göttingen Üniversitesindeki Maitrisimit Projesi Üzerine." In *Beşbalıkı Şingko Şeli Tutung anısına uluslararası eski Uygurca çalıştayı bildirleri, 4-6 Haziran 2011*, ed. Mustafa S. Kaçalin, 9-18. Ankara: Türk Dil Kurumu, 2022.

Laut, Jens Peter and Jens Wilkens. *Alttürkische Handschriften Teil 3: Die Handschriftenfragmente der Maitrisimit aus Sängrim und Murtuk in der Berliner Turfansammlung*. Stuttgart: Franz Steiner Verlag, 2015.

Laut, Jens Peter and Peter Zieme. "Eine zweisprachiger Lobpreis auf den Bäg von Koĉo und seine Gemahlin." In *Buddhistische Erzählliteratur und Hagiographe in türkischer Überlieferung*, ed. Jens Peter Laut, 15-36. Wiesbaden: Harrassowitz, 1990.

Lee, Sonya S. "Repository of Ingenuity: Cave 61 and Artistic Appropriation in Tenth-Century Dunhuang." *Art Bulletin* 94, no. 2 (2012): 199-200.

Leidy, Denise P. "Bezeklik Temple 20 and Early Esoteric Buddhism." *Silk Road Art and Archaeology* 7 (2001): 201-222.

Levi, Scott C. *The Bukharan Crisis: A Connected History of 18th-Century Central Asia*. Pittsburgh: University of Pittsburgh Press, 2020.

Li, Yiwen. "Chinese Objects Recovered from Sutra Mounds in Japan, 1000-1300." In *Visual and Material Cultures in Middle Period China*, ed. P. B. Buckley and S. S. S. Huang, 284-317. Leiden: Brill, 2017.

Lieu, Samuel N.C. *Manichaeism in the Later Roman Empire and Medieval China.* Tübingen: J. C. B. Mohr, 1992.

Ligeti, Louis. "Un vocabulaire Sino-ouigour des Ming: Le *Kao-tch'ang-kou an yi-chou* du Bureau des Traducteurs," *Acta Orientalia Academiai Scientiarum Hungaricae* 19, no. 3 (1966): 290.

Lingat, R. *L'esclavage privé dans le vieux droit siamois (avec une traduction des anciennes lois siamoises sur l'esclavage.* Paris: Les Éditions Domat-Montchrestien, 1931.

Linrothe, Rob. "Peripheral Visions: On Recent Finds of Tangut Buddhist Art." *Monumenta Serica* 43 (1995): 235-262.

———. "Xia Renzong and the Patronage of Tangut Buddhist Art: The Stupa and Ushnīshavijayā Cult." *Journal of Song-Yuan Studies* 28 (1998): 91-121.

Liu, Cuilan. "Merit-Making or Financial Fraud? Litigating Buddhist Nuns in Early 10th-Century Dunhaung." *Journal of the International Association of Buddhist Studies* 41 (2018): 169-208.

Liu, Haiwei. "Following Their Own Customs: A Reexamination of Khubilai's 1280 Edict on Muslim Practices." *Journal of the American Oriental Society* 142, no. 4 (2022): 935-953.

Liu, Mau-Tsai. *Die chinesischen Nachrichten zur Geschichte der Ost-Türken (T'u-Küe).* 2 vols. Wiesbaden: Harrassowitz, 1958.

Liu, Xinru. *Ancient India and Ancient China: Trade and Religious Exchanges, AD 1–600.* Delhi: Oxford University Press, 1988.

Lopez Jr., Donald S. *Curators of the Buddha: The Study of Buddhism Under Colonialism.* Chicago: University of Chicago Press, 1995.

———. *The Story of Buddhism: A Concise Guide to Its History and Teachings.* San Francisco: HarperCollins, 2001.

———. *A Modern Buddhist Bible: Essential Readings from East and West.* Boston: Beacon Press, 2002.

Luo, Yuejiong. *Xian bin lü.* Beijing: Zhonghua shuju, 1983.

Mackerras, Colin. *The Uighur Empire according to the T'ang Dynastic Histories: A Study in Sino-Uighur Relations 744–840.* Columbia: University of South Carolina Press, 1972.

MacLean, Derryl N. *Religion and Society in Arab Sind.* Leiden: E. J. Brill, 1989.

Mair, Victor H. *The Art of War: Sun Zi's Military Methods.* New York: Columbia University Press, 2007.

Maitra, K. M. *A Persian Embassy to China: Being an Extract from Zubdatu't Tawarikh of Hafiz Abru.* New York: Paragon Book Reprint Corp., 1970.

Mallory, J. P. and Victor H. Mair. *The Tarim Mummies: Ancient China and the Mystery of the Earliest Peoples from the West.* New York: Thames & Hudson, 2000.

Manz, Beatrice F. "Tamerlane and the Symbolism of Sovereignty." *Iranian Studies* 21 (1988): 105-122.

———. *The Rise and Rule of Tamerlane.* New York: Cambridge University Press, 1989.

Martinez, A. P. "Gardīzī's Two Chapters on the Turks." *Archivum Eurasiae Medii Aevi* 2 (1982): 109-217.

———. "The Third Portion of the Story of Gazan Xan in Rasidu'd-Din's *Ta'rix-e Mobarak-e Gazani.*" *Archivum Eurasiae Medii Aevi* 6 (1986-1988): 56-72.

Matsui, Dai. "Taxation Systems as Seen in the Uigur and Mongol Documents from Turfan: An Overview." *Transactions of the International Conference of Eastern Studies* 50 (2005): 67-82.

———. "Six Uigur Contracts from the West Uigur Period (10th-12th Centuries)." *Jinbun shakai ronsō (Jinbun kagaku hen)* 15 (2006): 37-62.

———. "An Uigur Decree of Tax Exemption in the Name of Duwa-Khan." *Shinjlex Uxaani Akademiin Medee* 4 (2007): 60-68.

———. "A Mongolian Decree from the Chaghataid Khanate Discovered at Dunhuang." In *Aspects of Research into Central Asian Buddhism: In Memoriam Kōgi Kudara*, ed. Peter Zieme, 159-177. Turnout: Brepols, 2008.

———. "Uigur *käzig* and the Origin of Taxation Systems in the Uigur Kingdom of Qočo." *Türk Dilleri Araştırmaları* 18 (2008): 229-242.

———. "Bezeklik Uigur Administrative Orders Revisited." In *Studies in Turkic Philology. Festschrift in Honour of the 80th Birthday of Geng Shimin*, ed. Zhang D. and A. Yakup, 339-350. Beijing: Minzu Daxue Chubanshe, 2009.

———. "Mongol Globalism Attested by the Uigur and Mongol Documents from East Turkestan." *Studies in the Humanities (Volume of Cultural Sciences)* 22 (2009): 33-42.

———. "Uigur Peasants and Buddhist Monasteries during the Mongol Period: Re-examination of the Uigur Document U 5330 (Usp 77)." In *"The Way of the Buddha" 2003: The 100th Anniversary of the Otani Mission and the 50th of the Research Society for Central Asian Cultures*, ed. Irisawa Takashi, 55-66. Osaka: Ryukoku University, 2010.

———. "Uigur Manuscripts Related to the Monks Sivšidu and Yaqšidu at 'Abita-Cave Temple' of Toyoq." In *Essays on the Third International Conference on Turfan Studies: The Origins and Migrations of Eurasian Nomadic Peoples*, ed. Academia Turfanica, 697-714. Shanghai: Shanghai gu Chubanshe, 2010.

———. "Uighur Almanac Divination Fragments from Dunhuang." In *Dunhuang Studies: Prospects and Problems for the Coming Second Century of Research*, ed. I. Popova and Liu Yi, 154-166. St. Petersburg: Slavia, 2012.

———. "Uighur Scribble Attached to a Tangut Buddhist Fragment from Dunhuang." In *Tanguty v Czentral'noj Azii: Sbornik statej v chest' 80-letija professor E.I. Kychanova*, ed. Rossiskaja Akademija Nauk Institut Vostochnykh Rukopisej, 238-243. Moscow: Rossiskaja Akademija Nauk Institut, 2012.

———. "Uigur-Turkic Influence as Seen in the Qara-Qota Mongolian Documents." In *Actual Problems of Turkic Studies: Dedicated to the 180th Anniversary of the Department of Turkic Philology at the St. Petersburg State University*, 559-565. St. Petersburg: St. Petersburg State University, 2016.

———. "敦煌石窟ウイグル語．モンゴル語題記銘文集成 *Tonkō sekkutsu uigurugo mongorugo, daiki meibun shūsei* (Uighur and Mongolian Wall Inscriptions of the Dunhuang Grottoes)." In 敦煌石窟多言語資料集成 *Tonkō sekkutsu tagengo shiryō shūsei* [Multilingual source materials of the Dunhuang grottoes], ed. Dai Matsui and Shintaro Arakawa, 1-161. Tokyo: Tōkyō gaikokugo daigaku Ajia Afurika gengo bunka kenkyūjo, 2017.

———. "An Old Uigur Account Book for Manichaean and Buddhist Monasteries from Temple α in Qočo." In *Zur lichten Heimat: Studien zu Manichäismus, Iranistik und Zentralasienkunde im Gedenken an Werner Sundermann*, ed. Team Turfanforschung, 409-419. Wiesbaden: Harrassowitz, 2017.

———. "Remarks on Buyan-Qaya, a Uighur Buddhist Pilgrim to Dunhuang." In *Unter dem Bodhi-Baum: Festschrift für Klaud Röhrborn anlässlich des 80. Geburtstags überreicht von Kollegen, Freunden und Schülern*, ed. Z. Özertural and G. Şilfeler, 209-224. Göttingen: V&R Unipress, 2019.

Matsukawa, Takashi. "Some Uighur Elements Surviving in the Mongolian Buddhist Sūtra of the Great Bear." In *Turfan Revisited: The First Century of Research into the Arts and Cultures of the Silk Road*, ed. D. Durkin-Meisterernst et al., 203-207. Berlin: Dietrich Reimer Verlag, 2004.

Maue, Dieter. "Sanskrit-uigurische Fragmente des *Āṭānāṭikasūtra* und des *Āṭānāṭihṛdaya*." *Ural-Altaische Jahrbücher* 5 (1985): 98-122.

———. *Alttürkische Handschriften Teil 1: Dokumente in Brāhmī und tibetischer Schrift*. Stuttgart: Franz Steiner Verlag, 1996.

———. "The Equanimity of the Tathāgata." In *Aspects of Research into Central Asian Buddhism: In Memoriam Kōgi Kudara*, ed. Peter Zieme, 179-190. Turnout: Brepols, 2008.

———. "Three Languages on One Leaf: On IOL Toch 81 with Special Regard to the Turkic Part." *Bulletin of the School of Oriental and African Studies* 71, no. 1 (2008): 59-73.

———. "An Uighur Version of Vāgbhaṭa's *Aṣṭāngahṛdayasaṃhitā*." *Asian Medicine* 4 (2008): 113-173.

———. "Uigurisches in Brāhmī in nicht-uigurischen Brāhmī-Handschriften." *Acta Orientalia Academiae Scientiarum Hungaricae* 62, no. 1 (2009): 1-36.

———. "Uigurisches in Brāhmī in nicht-uigurischen Brāhmī-Handschriften Teil II." *Acta Orientalia Academiae Scientiarum Hungaricae* 63, no. 3 (2011): 319-361.

Maue, Dieter and Niu Ruji. "80 TBI 774 b: A Sanskrit-Uigur Bilingual Text from Bezeklik." *Studies on the Inner Asian Languages* 27 (2012): 43-92.

Maue, Dieter and Klaus Röhrborn. "Ein Caityastotra aus dem alttürkischen *Goldglanz-Sūtra*." *Zeitschrift der Deutschen Morgenländischen Gessellschaft* 129 (1979): 282-320.

———. "Ein buddhistischer Katechismus in alttürkischer Sprache und tibetischer Schrift (Teil I)." *Zeitschrift der Deutschen Morgenländischen Gessellschaft* 134 (1984): 286-313.

———. "Ein buddhistischer Katechismus in alttürkischer Sprache und tibetischer Schrift (Teil II)." *Zeitschrift der Deutschen Morgenländischen Gessellschaft* 135 (1985): 68-91.

McMahan, David L. *The Making of Buddhist Modernism*. New York: Oxford University Press, 2008.

Melikian-Chirvani, A. S. "Le *Shah-name*, la gnose soufie et le pouvoir mongol." *Journal asiatique* 222 (1984): 249-338.

———. "Le Livre des rois, miroir du destin, I." *Studia Iranica* 17, no. 1 (1988): 7-46.

———. "Le Livre des rois, miroir du destin, II: Takht-e Soleyman et la symbolique du *Shah-mame*." *Studia Iranica* 20, no. 1 (1991): 33-148.

———. "Conscience du passé et résistance culturelle dans l'Iran mongol." In *L'Iran face à la domination mongole*, ed. Denise Aigle, 135-177. Tehran: Institut Français de Recherche en Iran, 1997.

Melville, Charles. "*Padshah-i Islam*: The Conversion of Sultan Mahmud Ghazan Khan." *Pembroke Papers* 1 (1990): 159-177.

———. "The Chinese Uighur Animal Calendar in Persian Historiography of the Mongol Period." *Iran* 32 (1994): 83-98.

Miller, Robert J. "Buddhist Monastic Economy: The Jisa Mechanism." *Comparative Studies in Society and History* 3, no. 4 (1961): 427-438.

Millward, James A. *Eurasian Crossroads: A History of Xinjiang*. New York: Columbia University Press, 2007.

Minorsky, Vladimir. *Sharaf al-Zaman Tahir Marvazi on China, the Turks and India*. London: The Royal Asiatic Society, 1942.

Miyawaki, Junko. "The Birth of Oyirad Khanship." *Central Asiatic Journal* 41 (1997): 39-41.

Moerman, D. Max. "The Archaeology of Anxiety: An Underground History of Heian Religion." In *Heian Japan, Centers and Peripheries*, ed. M. Adolphson, E. Kamens, and S. Matsumoto, 245-271. Honolulu: University of Hawai'i Press, 2007.

Molé, M. "Les Kubrawiya entre le Sunnisme et Shiisme aux Huitième et Neuvième Siécles de l'Hégire." *Revue des Études Islamiques* 29 (1961): 76-90.

Mori, Masao. "A Study on Uygur Documents of Loans for Consumption." *Memoirs of the Research Department of the Toyo Bunko* 20 (1961): 111-148.

Morita, Miki. "Ksitigarbha Images from the Turfan Region: An Aspect of Uygur Buddhist Art of the 9th to 14th Centuries." Ph.D. diss., University of Pennsylvania, 2014.

Morrison, Kathleen D. "Trade, Urbanism, and Agricultural Expansion: Buddhist Monastic Institutions and the State in Early Historic Western Deccan." *World Archaeology* 27, no. 2 (1995): 203-221.

Moriyasu, Takao. "Qui des Ouigours ou des Tibétaines ont gagné en 789-792 à Beš-balïq?" *Journal asiatique* 269, nos. 1-2 (1981): 193-205.

———. "Étude sur un catéchisme boudhique ouigour en écriture tibétaine (P.t. 1292)." *Memoirs of the Faculty of Letters, Osaka University* 25 (1985): 1-85.

———. "L'origine du bouddhisme chez les Turcs et l'apparition des textes bouddhiques en turc ancient." In *Documents et archives provenant de l'Asie Centrale. Actes du Colloque Franco-Japonais*, ed. Akira Haneda, 147-165. Kyoto: Dohosha, 1990.

———. "The West Uighur Kingdom and Tun-huang around the 10th-11th Centuries." *Berichte und Abhandlungen: Berlin-Brandenburgische Akademie der Wissenschaften* 8 (2000): 337-368.

———. "The Sha-chou Uighurs and the West Uighur Kingdom." *Acta Asiatica* 78 (2000): 28-48.

———. "Uighur Buddhist Stake Inscriptions from Turfan." In *De Dunhuang à Istanbul: Hommage à James Russell Hamilton*, ed. Louis Bazin and Peter Zieme, 149-223. Turnhout: Brepols, 2001.

———. "On the Uighur Buddhist Society at Čiqtim in Turfan during the Mongol Period." In *Splitter aus der Gegend von Turfan: Festschrift für Peter Zieme anläßlich seines 60. Geburtstags*, ed. Mehmet Ölmez and Simone-Christiane Raschmann, 153-177. Istanbul: Türk Dilleri Araştırma Dizis, 2002.

———. "Introduction à l'histoire de Ouïghours et de leurs relations avec le Manichéisme et le Bouddhisme." In *Shiruku Rōdo to sekaische* [World history reconsidered through the Silk Road], 24-38. Osaka: Osaka University, 2003.

———. "The Flourishing of Manichaeism under the West Uighur Kingdom. New Edition of the Uighur Charter on the Administration of the Manichaean Monastery in Qočo." In *World History Reconsidered through the Eyes of the Silk Road. Four Lectures at the College de France in May 2003*, 63-83. Osaka: Osaka University, 2003.

———. "From Silk, Cotton and Copper Coin to Silver: Transition of the Currency Used by the Uighurs during the Period from the 8th to the 14th Centuries." In *Turfan Revisited: The First Century of Research into the Arts and Cultures of the Silk Road*, ed. D. Durkin-Meisterernst et al., 228-239. Berlin: Dietrich Reimer, 2004.

———. *Die Geschichte des uigurischen Manichäismus an der Seidenstraße: Forschungen zu manichäischen Quellen und ihrem geschichtlichen Hintergrund.* Trans. Christian Steineck. Wiesbaden: Harrassowitz Verlag, 2004.

———. "Chronology of West Uighur Buddhism: Re-examination of the Dating of the Wallpaintings in Grünwedel's Cave No. 8 (New: No. 18), Bezeklik." In *Aspects of Research into Central Asian Buddhism: In Memoriam Kōgi Kudara*, ed. Peter Zieme, 191-227. Turnhout: Brepols 2008.

———. *Corpus of the Old Uighur Letters from the Eastern Silk Road*. Turnhout: Brepols, 2019.

Moriyasu, Takao and Peter Zieme. "From Chinese to Uighur Documents." *Studies on the Inner Asian Languages* 14 (1999): 73-102.

———. "Uighur Inscriptions on the Banners from Turfan Housed in the Museum für Indische Kunst, Berlin." In *Central Asian Temple Banners in the Turfan Collection of the Museum für Indische Kunst, Berlin*, ed. Chhaya Bhattacharya-Haesner, 461-474. Berlin: Dietrich Reimer Verlag, 2003.

Nakamura, Hajime. *Indian Buddhism: A Survey with Bibliographical Notes*. Delhi: Motilal Banarsidass, 1987.

Nattier, Jan. "Namowa buddhay-a: A Note on the Sources of the Mongolian Kanjur." Unpublished paper presented at the Annual Meeting of the American Oriental Society, New Haven, CT, 1986.

———. "The Meanings of the Maitreya Myth: A Typological Analysis." In *Maitreya: The Future Buddha*, ed. A. Sponberg and H. Hardacre, 23-47. New York: Cambridge University Press, 1988.

———. *Once Upon a Future Time: Studies in a Buddhist Prophecy of Decline*. Berkeley, CA: Asian Humanities Press, 1991.

Neelis, Jason. *Early Buddhist Transmission and Trade Networks: Mobility and Exchange within and beyond the Northwestern Borderlands of South Asia*. Leiden: Brill, 2011.

Newman, John R. "A Brief History of the Kalacakra." In *The Wheel of Time: The Kalacakra in Context*, ed. Geshe Lhundub Sopa, Roger Jackson, and John Newman, 51-90. Ithaca, NY: Snow Lion, 1991.

———. "Islam in the Kālacakra Tantra." *Journal of the International Association of Buddhist Studies* 21, no. 2 (1998): 311-371.

———. "The Epoch of the *Kālacakra Tantra*." *Indo-Iranian Journal* 41 (1998): 319-349.

Niu, Ruji. "A Fragment of a Buddhist Refuge Formula in Uighur in the Pelliot Collection." In *De Dunhuang à Istanbul: Hommage à James Russell Hamilton*, ed. L. Bazin and P. Zieme, 225-231. Turnhout: Brepols, 2001.

Niu, Ruji and Peter Zieme. "The Buddhist Refuge Formula: An Uigur Manuscript from Dunhuang." *Türk Dilleri Araştırmaları* 6 (1996) 41-56.

Northrup, Linda S. *From Slave to Sultan: The Career of Al-Mansur Qalawun and the Consolidation of Mamluk Rule in Egypt and Syria (678–689 A.H./1279–1290 A.D.)*. Stuttgart: Franz Steiner Verlag, 1998.

Oda, Juten. "Uighuristan." *Acta Asiatica* 34 (1978): 22-45.

———. "On Manichaean Expressions in the *Säkiz yükmäk yaruq*." In *Splitter aus der Gegend Turfan: Festschrift für Peter Zieme anläßlich seines 60. Geburtstags*, ed. Mehmet Ölmez and Simone-Christiane Raschmann, 179-198. Istanbul: Türk Dilleri Araştırmaları Dizisi, 2002.

———. "Indian Buddhist Missions to Uighuristan, based on Chinese Sources." In *Indien und Zentralasien: Sprach-und Kulturkontakt: Vorträge des Göttinger Symposions vom 7. bis 10. Mai 2001*, ed. Sven Bretfeld and Jens Wilkens, 25-43. Wiesbaden: Harrassowitz, 2003.

———. *A Study of the Buddhist Sutra Säkiz Yükmäk Yaruq or Säkiz Törlügin Yarumïš Yaltrïmïš in Old Turkic*. Turnhout: Brepols, 2015.

Ogihara, Hirotoshi. "On the *Karmavācanā* in Tocharian." In *Buddhism among the Iranian Peoples of Central Asia*, ed. Matteo De Chiara and Jens E. Braarvig, 311–331. Wien: Verlag der Österreichische Akademie der Wissenschaften, 2013.

Okada, Hidehiro. "Origins of the Dörben Oyirad." *Ural-Altaische Jahrbücher* 7 (1987): 181–211.

Okada, Y. and S. Sakamoto. "Virtual Reconstruction of the Bezeklik Wall Paintings." In *Rongshe yu chuangxin: Guoji Dunhuang xiangmu di liu cihui yilun wenji = Tradition and Innovation: Proceedings of the 6th IDP Conservation Conference*, ed. Shitian Lin and A. Morrison, 259–263. Beijing: Beijing tushuguan chubanshe, 2007.

Olivelle, Patrick. *Dharmasūtras: The Law Codes of Āpastamba, Gautama, Baudhāyana, and Vasiṣṭha*. New York: Oxford University Press, 1999.

———. "Aśoka's Inscriptions as Text and Ideology." In *Reimagining Aśoka: Memory and History*, ed. P. Olivelle, J. Leoshko, and H. P. Ray, 157–183. Delhi: Oxford University Press, 2012.

Orzech, Charles D. *Politics and Transcendent Wisdom: The Scripture of the Humane King in the Creation of Chinese Buddhism*. University Park: Pennsylvania State University Press, 1998.

Özertural, Zekine and Michael Knüppel. "Die uigurischen Texte in sogdischer Schrift und die Vermittlung der sogdischen Schreibkultur an die Uiguren." *Ural-Altaische Jahrbücher* NF 18 (2003/4): 148–160.

Pachow, Werner. *A Comparative Study of the Prātimokṣa on the Basis of Its Chinese, Tibetan, Sanskrit and Pāli Versions*. Delhi: Motilal Banarsidass, 2000.

Payne, Richard K. "Introduction: Just How Much Is Enough?" In *How Much is Enough: Buddhism, Consumerism, and the Human Environment*, ed. Richard K. Payne, 1–16. Somerville, MA: Wisdom, 2010.

Payne, Richard K. and Fabio Rambelli. "The Economic Study of Buddhism." In *Buddhism under Capitalism*, ed. Richard K. Payne and Fabio Rambelli, 1–22. London: Bloomsbury Academic, 2022.

Peyrot, Michaël, Georges-Jean Pinault, and Jens Wilkens. "Vernaculars of the Silk Road–A Tocharian B–Old Uyghur Bilingual." *Journal Asiatique* 301, no. 1 (2019): 65–90.

Pfeiffer, Judith. "Conversion to Islam among the Ilkhans in Muslim Narrative Traditions: The Case of Ahmad Tegüder." Ph.D. diss., University of Chicago, 2003.

———. "Conversion Versions: Sultan Öljeytü's Conversion to Shi'ism (709/1309) in Muslim Narrative Sources." *Mongolian Studies* 22 (1999): 35–67.

Piggott, Joan. *Emergence of Japanese Kingship*. Stanford, CA: Stanford University Press, 1997.

Pinault, Georges-Jean. "Le tokharien pratiqué par les Ouïgours. À propos d'un fragment en tokharien A du Musée Guimet." In *Études de Dunhuang et Turfan*, ed. Jean-Pierre Drège and Olivier Venture, 327–366. Genève: Droz, 2007.

Pinks, Elisabeth. *Die Uiguren von Kan-chou in der frühen Sung-Zeit (960–1028)*. Wiesbaden: Otto Harrassowitz, 1968.

Pinte, Klaus. "Vinaya." *Oxford Bibliographies Online*. www.oxfordbibliographies.com.

Pollock, Sheldon. "Axialism and Empire." In *Axial Civilizations and World History*, ed. Johann P. Arnason, S. N. Eisenstadt, and Björn Wittrock, 397–450. Leiden: Brill, 2005.

Popova, I. F. *Russian Expeditions to Central Asia at the Turn of the 20th Century*. St. Petersburg: Slavia Publishers, 2008.

Porció, Tibor. "On the Technique of Translating Buddhist Texts into Uygur." In *Indien und Zentralasien: Sprach-und Kulturkontakt, Göttingen 7.-10. Mai 2001*, ed. S. Bretfeld and J. Wilkens, 85-94. Wiesbaden: Harrassowitz, 2003.

———. "Some Peculiarities of the Uygur Buddhist Pilgrim Inscriptions." In *Searching for the Dharma, Finding Salvation—Buddhist Pilgrimage in Time and Space*, ed. Christoph Cueppers and Max Deeg, 157-178. Lumbini: Lumbini International Research Institute, 2014.

Porter, David. *Ideographica: The Chinese Cipher in Early Modern Europe*. Stanford, CA: Stanford University Press, 2001.

Prazniak, Roxann. "Ilkhanid Buddhism: Traces of a Passage in Eurasian History." *Comparative Studies in Society and History* 56 (2014): 650-680.

Rachewiltz, Igor de. "Turks in China under the Mongols: A Preliminary Investigation of Turco-Mongol Relations in the 13th and 14th Centuries." In *China Among Equals: The Middle Kingdom and Its Neighbours, 10th–14th Centuries*, ed. Morris Rossabi, 281-310. Berkeley: University of California Press, 1983.

Radloff, W. *Uigurische Sprachdenkmäler: Materialen nach dem Tode des Verfassers mit Ergänzungen von S. Malov herausgegeben*. Leningrad: Verlag der Akademie der Wissenschaften der USSR, 1928.

———. *Suvarṇaprabhāsa (Das Goldglanz Sūtra) aus dem Uigurischen ins Deutsche übersetzt*. Leningrad: Russian Academy of Sciences, 1930.

Radloff, W. and Baron A. von Staël-Holstein. *Tišastvustik. Ein in türkischer Sprach bearbeitetes buddhistisches Sūtra*. St. Petersburg: Bibliotheca Buddhica, 1910.

Raff, Thomas. *Remarks on an Anti-Mongol Fatwa by Ibn Taimiya*. Leiden: Self-published, 1973.

Ragep, F. J. *Nasr al-Din Tusi's Memoir of Astronomy (al-Tadhkira fi 'ilm al-hay'a)*. New York: Springer-Verlag, 1993.

Rambelli, Fabio. *Buddhist Materiality: A Cultural History of Objects in Japanese Buddhism*. Stanford, CA: Stanford University Press, 2007.

Raschmann, Simone-Christiane. "Zur Rolle der Sklaven im uigurischen Königreich von Qočo." *Ausprägung und Entwicklung sozialer Differenzierung in vorkapitalistischen Gessellschaften* (1988): 146-158.

———. *Baumwolle im türkischen Zentralasien: Philologische und wirtschaftshistorische Untersuchungen anhand der vorislamischen uigurischen Texte*. Wiesbaden: Harrassowitz Verlag, 1995.

———. *Alttürkische Handschriften Teil 7. Berliner Fragmente des Goldglanz-Sutras. Teil 3: Sechstes bis zehntes Buch. Kolophone, Kommentare und Versifizierungen. Gesamtkonkordanz*. Stuttgart: Franz Steiner Verlag, 2005.

———. "The Old Turkish Fragments of the Scripture on the Ten Kings (*Shiwangjing*) in the Collection of the Institute of Oriental Manuscripts, RAS." In *Dunhuang Studies: Prospects for the Coming Second Century of Research*, ed. I. F. Popova and Liu Yi, 209-216. St Petersburg: Slavia, 2012.

———. "What Do We Know About the Use of Manuscripts Among the Old Uighurs in the Turfan Region?" *Eurasian Studies* 12 (2014): 523-540.

———. "Uygur Scribbles On a Wooden Object." In *The Ruins of Kocho: Traces of Wooden Architecture on the Ancient Silk Road*, ed. L. Russell-Smith and I. Konczak-Nagel, 42-48. Berlin: Museum für Asiatische Kunst, 2016.

———. "S. F. Oldenburg's Cooperation with German Scholars and Explorers of Central Asia at the Beginning of the 20th C. and the Significance of His Finds for the Uighur Studies." In *Sergei Fedorovic Oldenburg*, ed. I. F. Popova, 285-305. Moscow: Nauka, 2016.

———. "Der Weingarten des Šabi Tutung." In *Eine hundertblättrige Tulpe–Bir sadbarg lāla: Festgabe für Claus Schönig*, ed. I. Hauenschild et al., 372-388. Berlin: Klaus Schwarz Verlag, 2016.

———. "'In Need For Wine': The Arat Document 112/07." In *Language, Society, and Religion in the World of the Turks: Festschrift for Larry Clark at Seventy-Five*, ed. Zsuzsanna Gulácsi, 77-87. Turnhout: Brepols, 2018.

———. "Pilgrims in Old Uyghur Inscriptions: A Glimpse Behind the Records." In *Buddhism in Central Asia I: Patronage, Legitimation, Sacred Space, and Pilgrimage*, ed. C. Meinert and H. H. Sørensen, 204-229. Leiden: Brill, 2020.

Rashiduddin Fazlullah. *Jami'u't-tawarikh: Compendium of Chronicles, A History of the Mongols, Part Three*. Trans. W. M. Thackston. Cambridge, MA: Harvard University, Department of Near Eastern Languages and Civilizations, 1999.

Raverty, H. G. *Tabakat-i-Nasiri: A General History of the Muhammadan Dynasties of Asia, including Hindustan, from A.H. 194 [810 A.D.] to A.H. 658 [1260 A.D.], and the Irruption of the Infidel Mughals into Islam*. London: Gilbert & Rivington, 1881.

Ray, Himanshu P. *The Winds of Change: Buddhism and the Maritime Links of Early South Asia*. Delhi: Oxford University Press, 1994.

Reat, Noble Ross. *Buddhism: A History*. Fremont, CA: Jain Publishing, 1994.

Reid, Anthony. "Islamization and Christianization in Southeast Asia: The Critical Phase, 1550-1650." In *Southeast Asia in the Early Modern Era: Trade, Power, Belief*, ed. Anthony Reid, 151-179. Ithaca, NY: Cornell University Press, 1993.

Reynolds, Craig J. "Monastery Lands and Labour Endowments in Thailand: Some Effects of Social and Economic Change, 1868-1910." *Journal of the Economic and Social History of the Orient* 22, no. 2 (1979): 190-227.

———. "Power." In *Critical Terms for the Study of Buddhism*, ed. Donald S. Lopez Jr., 211-228. Chicago: University of Chicago Press, 2005.

Reynolds, Frank E. "Ethics and Wealth in Theravāda Buddhism: A Study in Comparative Ethics." In *Ethics, Wealth, and Salvation: A Study in Buddhist Ethics*, ed. R. F. Sizemore and D. K. Swearer, 59-76. Columbia: University of South Carolina Press, 1990.

Richard, Jean. "La conversion de Berke et les debuts de l'islamisation de la horde d'or." *Revue des Études Islamiques* 35 (1967): 173-184.

Ritzinger, Justin R. "Karma, Charisma, and Community: Karmic Storytelling in a Blue-Collar Taiwanese Buddhist Organization." *Journal of Chinese Buddhist Studies* 33 (2020): 203-232.

Robinson, David M. *In the Shadow of the Mongol Empire: Ming China and Eurasia*. New York: Cambridge University Press, 2020.

Röhrborn, Klaus. "Zum Wanderweg des alttürkischen Lehngutes im Alttürkischen." In *Studien zur Geschichte und Kultur des vorderen Orients: Festschrift für Bertold Spuler zum siebzigsten Geburtstag*, ed. H. R. Roemer and A. Noth, 337-343. Leiden: Brill, 1984.

———. "Šingko Šäli Tutung und die Organisation der Übersetzungstätigkeit bei den Uiguren." In *Turkologie heute-Tradition und Perspektive*, ed. N. Demir and E. Taube, 255-260. Wiesbaden: Harrassowitz, 1998.

Rong, Xinjiang. "The Relationship of Dunhuang with the Uighur Kingdom in the Tenth Century." In *De Dunhuang à Istanbul: Hommage à James Russell Hamilton*, ed. L. Bazin and P. Zieme, 275-298. Turnhout: Brepols, 2001.

——. "Cultural Contacts between China and India from the Late Tang to the Early Song in Light of the Dunhuang Manuscripts." In *The Silk Road and Cultural Exchanges between East and West*, ed. Sally K. Church, 152-186. Leiden: Brill, 2022.
Rossabi, Morris. "The Muslims in the Early Yüan Dynasty." In *China under Mongol Rule*, ed. John D. Langlois, Jr., 257-295. Princeton, NJ: Princeton University Press, 1981.
——. "A Translation of Ch'en Ch'eng's *Hsi-Yu Fan-kuo Chih*." *Ming Studies* 17 (1983): 49-59.
——. "The Decline of the Central Asian Caravan Trade." In *The Rise of Merchant Empires: Long Distance Trade in the Early Modern World, 1350–1750*, ed. James D. Tracy, 351-370. New York: Cambridge University Press, 1990.
——. "The Silk Trade in China and Central Asia." In *When Silk was Gold: Central Asian and Chinese Textiles*, ed. James C.Y. Watt and Anne E. Wardwell, 7-19. New York: The Metropolitan Museum of Art, 1997.
——. "Ming Foreign Policy: The Case of Hami." In *China and Her Neighbours: Borders, Visions of the Other, Foreign Policy 10th to 19th Century*, ed. Sabine Dabringhaus and Roderich Ptak, 79-97. Wiesbaden: Harrassowitz, 1997.
Rowe, Mark. *Bonds of the Dead: Temples, Burials, and the Transformation of Contemporary Japanese Buddhism*. Chicago: University of Chicago Press, 2011.
Roxburgh, David. *Turks: A Journey of a Thousand Years, 600–1600*. London: Royal Academy of Arts, 2005.
Rubrouck, Guillaume de. *The Mission of Friar William: His Journey to the court of the Great Khan Möngke 1253–1255*. Trans. Peter Jackson. London: The Hakluyt Society, 1990.
Ruegg, David S. "The Precept-Donor (*yon mchod*) Relation in Thirteenth Century Tibetan Society and Polity, Its Inner Asian Precursors and Indian Models." In *Tibetan Studies*, ed. H. Krasser et al., 857-872. Wien: Österreichische Akademie der Wissenschaft, 1997.
Russell-Smith, Lilla. *Uygur Patronage in Dunhuang: Regional Art Centres on the Northern Silk Road in the Tenth and Eleventh Centuries*. Leiden: Brill, 2005.
——. "Stars and Planets in Chinese and Central Asian Buddhist Art in the Ninth to Fifteenth Centuries." *Culture and Cosmos* 10, 1 & 2 (2006): 99-124.
——. "The Formation of Uygur Buddhist Art: Some Remarks on Work in Progress." In *Buddhism and Art in Turfan: From the Perspective of Uyghur Buddhism*, ed. Irisawa Takashi, 141-152. Kyoto: Research Center for Buddhist Culture in Asia Ryukoku University, 2012.
Salguero, C. Pierce. *A Global History of Buddhism and Medicine*. New York: Columbia University Press, 2022.
Schaik, Sam van. "Tibetan Buddhism in Central Asia: Geopolitics and Group Dynamics." In *Transfer of Buddhism Across Central Asian Networks (7th to 13th Centuries)*, ed. Carmen Meinert, 55-81. Leiden: Brill, 2016.
——. "Fakes, Delusions, or the Real Thing? Albert Grünwedel's Maps of Shambhala." *Journal of the American Oriental Society* 140, no. 2 (2020): 273-286.
Schluessel, Eric. *Land of Strangers: The Civilizing Project in Qing Central Asia*. New York: Columbia University Press, 2020.
Schmid, Neil. "Dunhuang and Central Asia (With an Appendix on Dunhuang Manuscript Resources)." In *Esoteric Buddhism and the Tantras in East Asia*, ed. C. D. Orzech et al., 365-378. Leiden: Brill, 2011.
Schmithausen, Lambert. *Ālayavijñāna. On the Origin and the Early Development of a Central Concept of Yogācāra Philosophy*, vol. 2. Tōkyō: The International Institute for Buddhist Studies, 1987.

———. *Buddhism and Nature: The Lecture Delivered on the Occasion of the EXPO 1990, an Enlarged Version with Notes.* Tokyo: International Institute for Buddhist Studies, 2003.

Schopen, Gregory. "The Phrase 'sa pṛthivīpradeśaś caityabhūto bhavet' in the *Vajracchedikā*: Notes on the Cult of the Book in the Mahāyāna." *Indo-Iranian Journal* 17, no. 3-4 (1975): 147-181.

———. "Archaeology and Protestant Presuppositions in the Study of Indian Buddhism." *History of Religions* 31, no. 1 (1991): 1-23.

———. *Bones, Stones, and Buddhist Monks: Collected Papers on the Archaeology, Epigraphy, and Texts of Monastic Buddhism in India.* Honolulu: University of Hawai'i Press, 1997.

———. *Buddhist Monks and Business Matters: Still More Papers on Monastic Buddhism in India.* Honolulu: University of Hawai'i Press, 2004.

———. *Figments and Fragments of Mahāyāna Buddhism in India: More Collected Papers.* Honolulu: University of Hawai'i Press, 2005.

———. "On Monks and Menial Laborers: Some Monastic Accounts of Building Buddhist Monasteries." In *Architetti, Capomastri, Artigiani: L'organizzazione dei cantieri e della produzione artistica nell'Asia ellnistica*, ed. Pierfrancesco Callieri, 225-245. Roma: Istituto Italiano per l'Africa e l'Oriente, 2006.

———. *Buddhist Nuns, Monks, and Other Worldly Matters: Recent Papers on Monastic Buddhism in India.* Honolulu: University of Hawai'i Press, 2014.

———. "Liberation Is Only for Those Already Free: Reflections on Debts to Slavery and Enslavement to Debt in Early Indian Buddhist Monasticism." *Journal of the American Academy of Religion* 82, no. 3 (2014): 606-635.

———. "On the Legal and Economic Activities of Buddhist Nuns: Two Examples from Early India." In *Buddhism and Law: An Introduction*, ed. Rebecca R. French and Mark A. Nathan, 91-114. New York: Cambridge University Press, 2014.

Schuh, Dieter. *Erlasse und Sendschreiben mongolischer Herrscher für tibetische Geistliche.* St. Augustin: VGH-Wissenschaftsverlag, 1977.

Scott, David A. "Buddhism and Islam: Past to Present Encounters and Interfaith Lessons." *Numen* 42, no. 2 (1995): 141-155.

Scott, James C. *Seeing Like a State: How Certain Schemes to Improve the Human Condition Have Failed.* New Haven, CT: Yale University Press, 1998.

———. *The Art of Not Being Governed: An Anarchist History of Upland Southeast Asia.* New Haven, CT: Yale University Press, 2009.

Segal, Ethan Isaac. *Coins, Trade, and the State: Economic Growth in Early Medieval Japan.* Cambridge, MA: Harvard University Asia Center, 2011.

Sela, Ron. "Central Asian Muslims on Tibetan Buddhism, 16th-18th Centuries." In *Trails of the Tibetan Tradition: Papers for Elliot Sperling*, ed. Roberto Vitali, 345-358. Dharamshala: Amnye Machen Institute, 2014.

Serruys, Henry. *Sino-Mongol Relations during the Ming, III: Trade Relations: The Horse Fairs.* Brussels: Institut Belge des Hautes Études Chinoises, 1975.

Sertkaya, Osman Fikri. "Hukukī Uygur belgelerindeki para birimleri üzerine." In *Eski Türklerde para*, ed. O. F. Sertkaya and R. Alimov, 117-137. Istanbul: 2006.

Sharf, Robert. "Buddhist Modernism and the Rhetoric of Meditative Experience." *Numen* 32, no. 3 (1995): 228-283.

Shea, Eiren. *Mongol Court Dress, Identity Formation, and Global Exchange.* New York: Routledge, 2020.

Shōgaito, Masahiro. "Uighur Influence on Indian Words in Mongolian Buddhist Texts." In *Indien und Zentralasien: Sprach und Kulturkontakt*, ed. Sven Bretfeld and Jens Wilkens, 119-143. Wiesbaden: Harrassowitz Verlag, 2003.

———. "How Were Chinese Characters Read in Uighur?" In *Turfan Revisited: The First Century of Research into the Arts and Cultures of the Silk Road*, ed. D. Durkin-Meisterernst et al., 321-324. Berlin: Dietrich Reimer Verlag, 2004.

———. *The Uighur Abhidharmakośabhāsya preserved at the Museum of Ethnography in Stockholm.* Wiesbaden: Harrassowitz Verlag, 2014.

———. "Philology and Linguistics: *Ondoku* and *Kundoku* in Old Uighur." Trans. Noriko Ohsaki, Mutsumi Sugahara and Setsu Fujishiro. *Gengo Kenkyu Anthology* 1 (2021): 155-18.

Shōgaito, M. and A. Yakup. "Four Uyghur Fragments of *Qianziwen* 'Thousand Character Essay.'" *Turkic Languages* 5 (2001): 3-29.

———. "Four Uyghur Fragments of *Qian-zi-wen* 'Thousand Character Essay.'" *Turkic Languages* 8 (2004): 313-317.

Shōgaito, M., A. Yakup, and S. Fujishiro. *The Berlin Chinese Text U 5335 Written in Uighur Script: A Reconstruction of the Inherited Uighur Pronunciation of Chinese.* Turnhout: Brepols, 2015.

Silk, Jonathan A. *Riven by Lust: Incest and Schism in Indian Buddhist Legend and Historiography.* Honolulu: University of Hawai'i Press, 2009.

Sims-Williams, Nicholas. "The Manichaean Commandments: A Survey of the Sources." In *Papers in Honour of Professor Mary Boyce (Acta Iranica 25)*, 573-582. Leiden: E. J. Brill, 1985.

———. "From Aramaic to Manchu: Prehistory, Life and After-Life of the Sogdian Script." In *Sogdians in China: New Evidence and Archaeological Finds and Unearthed Texts*, ed. Rong Xinjiang and Luo Feng, 414-421. Beijing: Kexue Chubanshe, 2016.

Sims-Williams, Nicholas and James Hamilton. *Turco-Sogdian Documents from 9th–10th century Dunhuang.* London: Corpus Inscriptionum Iranicum and School of Oriental and African Studies, 2015.

Sinor, D., Geng Shimin, and Y. I. Kychanov. "The Uighurs, the Kyrgyz and the Tangut (Eighth to the Thirteenth Century)." In *History of Civilizations of Central Asia*, volume 4, ed. I. Iskender-Mochiri, 191-214. Paris: UNESCO, 1998.

Slavin, Philip. "Death by the Lake: Mortality Crisis in Early Fourteenth-Century Central Asia." *Journal of Interdisciplinary History* 1 (2019): 59-90.

Smith, Paul J. *Taxing Heaven's Storehouse: Horses, Bureaucrats, and the Destruction of the Sichuan Tea Industry, 1074–1224.* Cambridge, MA: Harvard Council on East Asian Studies, 1991.

So, Billy K. L. *Prosperity, Region, and Institutions in Maritime China: The South Fukien Pattern, 946–1368.* Cambridge, MA: Harvard University Asia Center, 2000.

Sombart, Werner. *The Jews and Modern Capitalism.* Trans. M. Epstein. Kitchener, ON: Batoche Books, 2001.

Solonin, Kirill J. "Khitan Connection of Tangut Buddhism." In *Heishuicheng ren wen yu huan jing guo ji xue shu* 黑水城人文与环境研究: 黑水城人文与环境国际学术讨论会文集, ed. Shen Weirong, Masayoshi Nakao, and Shi Jinbo, 371-395. Beijing: Zhongguo renmin daxue chubanshe, 2007.

———. "The Glimpses of Tangut Buddhism." *Central Asiatic Journal* 52, no. 1 (2008): 64-127.

———. "Buddhist Connections between the Liao and Xixia: Preliminary Considerations." *Journal of Song-Yuan Studies* 43 (2013): 171-219.
———. "Sinitic Buddhism in the Tangut State." *Central Asiatic Journal* 57 (2014): 157-183.
———. "The Formation of Tangut Ideology: Buddhism and Confucianism." In *Buddhism in Central Asia I: Patronage, Legitimation, Sacred Space, and Pilgrimage*, ed. Carmen Meinert and Henrik H. Sørensen, 123-147. Leiden: Brill, 2020.
Sørensen, Henrik H. "Astrology and the Worship of the Planets in Esoteric Buddhism of the Tang." In *Esoteric Buddhism and the Tantras in East Asia*, ed. C. D. Orzech et al., 230-244. Leiden: Brill, 2011.
———. "Esoteric Buddhism Under the Liao." In *Esoteric Buddhism and the Tantras in East Asia*, ed. C. D. Orzech et al., 456-464. Leiden: Brill, 2011.
———. "Donors and Esoteric Buddhism in Dunhuang during the Reign of the Guiyijun." In *Buddhism in Central Asia I: Patronage, Legitimation, Sacred Space, and Pilgrimage*, ed. Carmen Meinert and Henrik H. Sørensen, 91-122. Leiden: Brill, 2020.
———. "The Life and Times of Daozhen—A Samgha Leader and Monk Official in Dunhuang During the 10th Century." *BuddhistRoad Papers* 5, no. 3 (2020): 3-32.
Soudavar, Abolala. "The Saga of Abu-Sa'id Bahador Khan. The Abu-Sa'idnamé." In *The Court of the Il-khans 1290–1340*, ed. Julian Raby and Teresa Fitzherbert, 95-211. Oxford: Oxford University Press, 1996.
Sperling, Elliot. "Lama to the King of Hsia." *The Journal of the Tibet Society* 7 (1987): 31-50.
———. "The Szechwan-Tibet Frontier in the Fifteenth Century." *Ming Studies* 26 (1988): 37-55.
———. "Hülegü and Tibet." *Acta Orientalia Academicae Scientiarum Hungaricae* 44 (1990): 145-157.
———. "Notes on References to 'Bri-Gung-pa-Mongol Contact in the Late Sixteenth and Early Seventeenth Centuries." In *Tibetan Studies: Proceedings of the 5th Seminar of the International Association of Tibetan Studies*, ed. Ihara Shoren and Yamaguchi Ziuho, 741-750. Narita: Naritasan Shinsoji, 1992.
Sponberg, Alan and Helen Hardacre. *Maitreya: The Future Buddha*. New York: Cambridge University Press, 1988.
Steinhardt, Nancy S. *Liao Architecture*. Honolulu: University of Hawai'i Press, 1997.
———. "The Uighur Ritual Complex in Beiting." *Orientations* 3, no. 1-2 (1999): 28-37.
———. *The Borders of Chinese Architecture*. Cambridge, MA: Harvard University Press, 2022.
Sternbach, Ludwick. *Gaṇikā-vṛtta-saṃgrahaḥ or Texts on Courtesans in Classical Sanskrit*. Hoshiapur: Vishveshvaranand Institute Publications, 1953.
Stiller, Maya K. H. *Carving Status at Kŭmgangsan: Elite Graffiti in Premodern Korea*. Seattle: University of Washington Press, 2021.
Strong, John S. "Rich Man, Poor Man, *Bhikku*, King: Aśoka's Great Quinquennial Festival and the Nature of *Dāna*." In *Ethics, Wealth, and Salvation: A Study in Buddhist Ethics*, ed. R. F. Sizemore and D. K. Swearer, 107-123. Columbia: University of South Carolina Press, 1990.
———. *Relics of the Buddha*. Princeton, NJ: Princeton University Press, 2004.
Sundermann, Werner. "Completion and Correction of Archaeological Work by Philological Means: The Case of the Turfan Texts." In *Histoire et cultes de l'Asie centrale préislamique*, ed. Paul Bernard and Frantz Grenet, 283-289. Paris: Editions du Centre National de la Recherche Scientifique, 1991.

———. "Manichaeism Meets Buddhism: The Problem of Buddhist Influence on Manichaeism." In *Bauddhavidyāsudhākaraḥ: Studies in Honour of H. Bechert on the Occasion of his 65th Birthday*, ed. P. Kieffer-Pülz and J.-U. Hartmann, 647-656. Swisttal-Odendorf: Indica et Tibetica Verlag, 1997.

———. "A Manichaean Liturgical Instruction on the Act of Almsgiving." In *The Light and the Darkness: Studies in Manichaeism and its World*, ed. P. Mirecki and J. BeDuhn, 200-208. Leiden: Brill, 2001.

Szerb, János. "A Note on the Tibetan-Uigur Treaty of 822/23 A.D." In *Contributions on Tibetan Language, History and Culture*, ed. E. Steinkellner, 375-386. Wien: Wien Arbeitskreis für Tibet. u. Buddhist. Studien, 1983.

———. "Glosses on the Oeuvre of Bla-ma 'Phags-pa: III. The 'Patron-Patronized' Relationship." In *Soundings in Tibetan Civilization*, ed. Barbara Nimri Aziz and Matthew Kapstein, 165-173. New Delhi: Manohar, 1985.

Tagliacozzo, Eric. "Onto the Coasts and into the Forests: Ramifications of the China Trade on the Ecological History of Northwest Borneo, 900-1900 CE." In *Histories of the Borneo Environment*, ed. Reed L. Wadley, 25-60. Leiden: KITLV, 2005.

Takeuchi, Tsuguhito. "Sociolinguistic Implications of the Use of Tibetan in East Turkestan from the End of Tibetan Domination through the Tangut Period (9th-12th c.)." In *Turfan Revisited: The First Century of Research into the Arts and Cultures of the Silk Road*, ed. D. Durkin-Meisterernst et al., 341-348. Berlin: Dietrich Reimer Verlag, 2004.

Tambiah, Stanley J. *World Conqueror and World Renouncer: A Study of Buddhism and Polity in Thailand*. New York: Cambridge University Press, 1976.

———. *Buddhism Betrayed? Religion, Politics, and Violence in Sri Lanka*. Chicago: University of Chicago Press, 1992.

Tan, Shutong and An Chunyang. *Shinkyō no hekiga—Kijirusenbutsudō (Murals of Xinjiang: The Thousand Buddha Caves at Kizil)*. 2 vols. Beijing: Zhongguo waiwen chubanshe, 1981.

Tezcan, Semih. *Das uigurische Insadi-Sūtra*. Berlin: Akademie Verlag, 1974.

Tezcan, Semih and Peter Zieme. "Antiislamische Polemik in einem alttürkischen buddhistischen Gedicht aus Turfan." *Altorientalische Forschungen* 17, no. 1 (1990): 146-151.

Thapar, Romila. *From Lineage to State: Social Formations in the Mid-first Millennium B.C. in the Ganga Valley*. Bombay: Oxford University Press, 1984.

Tasaka, Kodo. "An Aspect of Islam Culture Introduced into China." *Memoirs of the Research Department of the Toyo Bunko* 16 (1957): 35-74.

Thiel, Joseph. "Der Streit der Buddhisten und Taoisten zur Mongolenzeit." *Monumenta Serica* (1961): 1-81.

Thilo, T. "Fragmente chinesischer Haushaltsregister aus Dunhuang in der Berliner Turfan-Sammlung." *Mitteilungen des Instituts für Orientsforschung* 14 (1968): 303-313.

Thomas, F. W. and G. L. M. Clauson. "A Second Chinese Buddhist Text in Tibetan Characters." *Journal of the Royal Asiatic Society* 2 (1927): 281-306.

Thum, Rian. *The Sacred Routes of Uyghur History*. Cambridge, MA: Harvard University Press, 2014.

———. "'Sunni' Veneration of the Twelve Imams in Khotan." *Journal of the American Oriental Society* 142, no. 3 (2022): 621-642.

Tongerloo, Aloïs van. "The Buddha's First Encounter in a Manichaean Old Turkic Text." In *Il Manicheismo Nuove Prospettive Della Rechercha: Dipartimento Di Studi Asiatica Università Degli*

Studi Di Napoli "L'Orientale." Napoli, 2–8 Settembre 2001, ed. Aloïs van Tongerloo and Luigi Cirillo, 385-396. Turnhout: Brepols, 2005.

Torma, Franziska. *Turkestan-Expeditionen. Zur Kulturgeschichte deutscher Forschungsreisen nach Mittelasien (1890–1930)*. Bielefeld: Transcript, 2011.

Tōru, Saguchi. "Historical Development of the Sarïgh Uyghurs." *Memoirs of the Research Department of the Toyo Bunko* 44 (1986): 1-21.

Tremblay, Xavier. *Pour une histoire de la Sérinde. Le manichéisme parmi les peuples et religions d'Asie Centrale d'après les sources primaires*. Wien: Verlag der Österreichischen Akademie der Wissenschaften, 2001.

———. "The Spread of Buddhism in Serindia—Buddhism among Iranians, Tocharians and Turks before the 13th Century." In *The Spread of Buddhism*, ed. Ann Heirman and Stephan Peter Bumbacher, 75-130. Leiden: Brill, 2007.

Trombert, Éric. "La fête du 8ème jour du 2ème mois à Dunhuang a'après les comptes de monastères." In *De Dunhuang au Japon: Etudes chinoises et bouddhiques offertes à M. Soymié*, ed. J.-P. Drège, 25-72. Genève: Droz, 2000.

———. "Bière et Bouddhisme—La consommation de boissons alcoolisées dans les monastères de Dunhuang aux VIII-X siècles." *Cahiers d'Extreme-Asie* 11 (1999-2000): 129-181.

Trümpler, Ch. *Das große Spiel. Archäologie und Politik zur Zeit des Kolonialismus (1860–1940)*. Essen/Köln: Dumont, 2008.

Tuan, Yi-fu. *A Historical Geography of China*. New Brunswick: AldineTransaction, 2008.

Tugusheva, L. Ju. "Three Letters of Uighur Princes from the MS Collection of the Leningrad Section of the Institute of Oriental Studies." *Acta Orientalia Academiae Scientiarum Hungaricae* 24, no. 2 (1971): 173-187.

———. "Ein fragment eines frühmittelalterlichen uigurischen Textes." In *Turfan, Khotan und Dunhuang: Vorträge der Tagung 'Annemarie v. Gabain und die Turfanforschung,' veranstaltet von der BBAW in Berlin (9.-12.12.1994)*, ed. R. E. Emmerick et al., 353-359. Berlin: Akademie Verlag, 1996.

Twitchett, D. C. "The Monasteries and China's Economy in Medieval Times." *Bulletin of the School of Oriental and African Studies* 19, no. 3 (1957): 526-549.

Uçar, E. "*Altun Yaruk Sudur* Üzerine Yapılan Çalışmalar Hakkında Açıklamalı Bir Kaynakça Denemesi." *Türük* (2013): 227-251.

Umemura, Hiroshi. "A Qočo King Painted in the Buddhist Temple of Beshbaliq." In *Turfan, Khotan und Dunhuang: Vorträge der Tagung 'Annemarie v. Gabain und die Turfanforschung,' veranstaltet von der BBAW in Berlin (9.-12.12.1994)*, ed. R. E. Emmerick et al., 361-378. Berlin: Akademie Verlag, 1991.

———. "The Uyghur Document SI 4b Kr. 71 Concerning the Sale of a Slave and the Loan of Silver." In *Turfan Revisited: The First Century of Research into the Arts and Cultures of the Silk Road*, ed. D. Durkin-Meistererernst et al., 358-360. Berlin: Dietrich Reimer Verlag, 2004.

Umemura, Hiroshi and Peter Zieme. "A Further Fragment of the Old Uighur *Qianziwen*." *Written Monuments of the Orient* 2 (2015): 3-13.

Uray, Géza. "L'emploi du tibétain dans les chancelleries des états du Kan-sou et de Khotan postérieurs à la domination tibétaine." *Journal asiatique* 269 (1981): 81-90.

Vaissière, Étienne de la. *Sogdian Traders: A History*. Trans. James Ward. Leiden: Brill, 2005.

Vallée Poussin, Louis de la. *L'Abhidharmakośa de Vasubandhu*, vols. 1–6. Paris: Paul Geuthner, 1923-1931.

Vásáry, István. "'History and Legend' in Berke Khan's Conversion to Islam." In *Aspects of Altaic Civilization III*, ed. Denis Sinor, 230-252. Bloomington: Indiana University, Research Institute for Inner Asian Studies, 1990.

Vér, Márton. "Religious Communities and the Postal System of the Mongol Empire." In *Role of Religions in the Turkic Culture*, ed. Mária Ivanics and Zsuzsanna Olach, 291-306. Budapest: Péter Pázmány Catholic University, 2017.

———. *Old Uyghur Documents Concerning the Postal System of the Mongol Empire*. Turnhout: Brepols, 2019.

———. "Uyghur Cultural and Social Influence in Mongol Iran as Mirrored in a Decree of Abaqa Ilkhan." Unpublished paper presented at "Ability and Authority Roundtable: Uighur Expertise on the Silk Road," Max Planck Institute, Berlin, November 21, 2021.Vermeersch, Sem. "Buddhism and State-Building in Song China and Goryeo Korea." *Asia Pacific Perspectives* 1, no. 1 (2004): 4-11.

———. *The Power of the Buddhas: The Politics of Buddhism During the Koryo Dynasty (918–1392)*. Cambridge, MA: Harvard University Asia Center, 2008.

———. "Who in Legitimating Whom? On Justifying Buddhism's Place in the Body Politic." In *Buddhism in Central Asia I: Patronage, Legitimation, Sacred Space, and Pilgrimage*, ed. C. Meinert and H. H. Sørensen, 15-39. Leiden: Brill, 2020.

Vitali, Roberto. *The Kingdoms of Gu.ge Pu.hrang: According to the mkhan.chen Ngag.dbang grags.pa*. Chicago: Serindia, 1997.

Vryonis, Jr., S. *The Decline of Medieval Hellenism in Asia Minor and the Process of Islamization from the Eleventh through the Fifteenth Century*. Berkeley: University of California Press, 1971.

Wade, Francis. *Myanmar's Enemy Within: Buddhist Violence and the Making of a Muslim "Other."* London: Zed Books, 2017.

Waite, Edmund. "From Holy Man to National Villain: Popular Historical Narratives About Apaq Khoja amongst Uyghurs in Contemporary Xinjiang." *Inner Asia* 8, no. 1 (2006): 5-28.

Waldron, Arthur. *The Great Wall of China: From Myth to History*. Cambridge: Cambridge University Press, 1990.

Waley, Arthur. *A Catalogue of Paintings Recovered from Tun-huang by Sir Aurel Stein, K.C.I.E. Preserved in the Sub-Department of Oriental Prints and Drawings in the British Museum, and in the Museum of Central Asian Antiquities, Delhi*. London: Trustees of the British Museum, 1931.

Wallis, Glenn. *Mediating the Power of Buddhas: Ritual in the Mañjuśrīmūlakalpa*. Albany: State University of New York Press, 2002.

Walshe, Maurice. *The Long Discourses of the Buddha: A Translation of the Dīgha Nikāya*. Boston: Wisdom, 1995.

Walshe, Michael J. "The Economics of Salvation: Toward a Theory of Exchange in Chinese Buddhism." *Journal of the American Academy of Religion* 75, no. 2 (2007): 353-382.

———. *Sacred Economies: Buddhist Monasticism and Territoriality in Medieval China*. New York: Columbia University Press, 2010.

Walter, Michael L. *Buddhism and Empire: The Political and Religious Culture of Early Tibet*. Leiden: Brill, 2009.

Walton, Michael. *Buddhism, Politics, and Political Thought in Myanmar*. New York: Cambridge University Press, 2018.

Wang, Ding. "Ch 3586–ein khitanisches Fragment mit uigurischen Glossen in der Berlin Turfansammlung." In *Turfan Revisited: The First Century of Research into the Arts and Cultures of the Silk Road*, ed. D. Durkin-Meisterernst et al., 371-379. Berlin: Dietrich Reimer Verlag, 2004.

Wang-Toutain, F. "Le sacre du printemps: les cérémonies bouddhiques de 8ᵉ du 2ᵉ mois." In *De Dunhuang au Japon: Etudes chinoises et bouddhiques offertes à M. Soymié*, ed. J.-P. Drège, 25-72. Genève: Droz, 2000.

Watanabe, Hiroshi. "An Index of Embassies and Tribute Missions from Islamic Countries to Ming China (1368-1644) as recorded in the *Ming Shih-lu* Classified According to Geographic Area." *Memoirs of the Research Department of the Toyo Bunko* 33 (1975): 285-348.

Waugh, Daniel. "Richthofen's 'Silk Roads': Toward the Archaeology of a Concept." *The Silk Road* 5, no. 1 (2007): 1-10.

Weber, Claudia. *Buddhistische Beichten in Indien und bei den Uiguren*. Wiesbaden: Harassowitz Verlag, 1999.

Weber, Max. *Hinduismus und Buddhismus*. Tübingen: Mohr, 1921.

———. *The Religion of India*. New York: The Free Press, 1967.

———. *The Protestant Ethic and the Spirit of Capitalism*. Trans. Talcott Parsons. New York: Routledge, 1994.

Whitfield, Susan. "A Place of Safekeeping? The Vicissitudes of the Bezeklik Murals." In *Conservation of the Ancient Sites on the Silk Road*, ed. Neville Agnew, 95-106. Los Angeles: Getty Conservation Institute, 2010.

Wickens, G. M. "Nasir ad-Din Tusi on the Fall of Baghdad: A Further Study." *Journal of Semitic Studies* 7 (1962): 23-35.

Wilkens, Jens. *Alttürkische Handschriften Teil 9: Buddhistische Beichttexte*. Stuttgart: Franz Steiner Verlag, 2003.

———. *Das Buch von der Sündentilgung. Edition des alttürkisch-buddhistischen Kšanti Kılguluk Nom Bitig*, 2 vols. Turnhout: Brepols, 2007.

———. "Ein Bildnis der Göttin Ötükän." In *Studies in Turkic Philology: Festschrift in Honour of the 80th Birthday of Professor Geng Shimin*, ed. Zhang Dingjing and Abdurishid Yakup, 449-461. Beijing: China Minzu University Press, 2009.

———. "Hatten die alten Uiguren einen buddhistischen Kanon?" In *Kanonisierung und Kanonbildung in der asiatischen Religionsgeschichte*, ed. M. Deeg, O. Freiberger, C. Kleine, 345-378. Wien: Verlag der Österreichischen Akademie der Wissenschaft, 2011.

———. "Buddhismus bei den türkischen Völkern in Zentralasien." In *Der Buddhismus II: Theravāda-Buddhismus und Tibetischer Buddhismus*, ed. Manfred Hutter, 469-490. Stuttgart: Kohlhammer, 2016.

———. "Buddhism in the West Uyghur Kingdom and Beyond." In *Transfer of Buddhism across Central Asian Networks (7th to 13th Centuries)*, ed. Carmen Meinert, 189-249. Leiden: Brill, 2016.

———. "A Sanskrit Fragment of the *Mañjuśrīnāmasaṃgīti* in Uyghur Script." *International Journal of Old Uygur Studies* 2, no. 1 (2020): 27-35.

———. "Buddhist Monastic Life in Central Asia: A Bilingual Text in Sanskrit and Old Uyghur Relating to the *Pravāraṇā* Ceremony." *International Journal of Old Uygur Studies* 2, no. 2 (2020): 137-152.

———. "Sacred Space in Uyghur Buddhism." In *Buddhism in Central Asia: Patronage, Legitimation, Sacred Space and Pilgrimage*, ed. C. Meinert and H. H. Sørensen, 189-203. Leiden: Brill, 2020.
———. *Handwörterbuch des Altuigurischen: Altuigurisch-Deutsch-Türkisch*. Göttingen: Universitätverlag, 2021.
———. "A Buddhist Spell Transliterated: A Sanskrit Version of the *Uṣṇīṣavijayādhāraṇī* in Uyghur and Brāhmī Scripts." *Annual Report of The International Research Institute for Advanced Buddhology at Soka University* 25 (2022): 191-209.
———. "Practice and Rituals in Uyghur Buddhist Texts: A Preliminary Appraisal." In *Buddhism in Central Asia II: Practices and Rituals, Visual and Material Transfer*, ed. Yukiyo Kasai and Henrik H. Sørensen, 430-464. Leiden: Brill, 2022.
Wink, André. *Al-Hind: The Making of the Indo-Islamic World, Vol. 1, Early Medieval India and the Expansion of Islam 7th–11th Centuries*. Leiden: E. J. Brill, 1990.
Wong, Dorothy C. "A Reassessment of the Representation of Mt. Wutai from Dunhuang Cave 61." *Archives of Asian Art* 46 (1993): 27-28.
Woodward, F. L. and E. M. Hare. *The Book of the Gradual Sayings*. 5 vols. Bristol: Pali Text Society, 1932-1936.
Wright, David C. *From War to Diplomatic Parity in Eleventh-Century China: Sung's Foreign Relations with the Kitan Liao*. Leiden: Brill, 2005.
Wu, Jiang, Lucille Chia, and Chen Zhichao. "The Birth of the First Printed Canon: The Kaibao Edition and Its Impact." In *Spreading Buddha's Word in East Asia: The Formation and Transformation of the Chinese Buddhist Canon*, ed. Jiang Wu and Lucille Chia, 145-180. New York: Columbia University Press, 2016.
Yakup, Abdurishid. "Two Alliterative Uighur Poems from Dunhuang." *Linguistic Research* 17-18 (1999): 1-25.
———. "On the Old Uyghur Wooden Nameplates from the West Zone of the Tuyoq Grottoes in Turfan and the Wooden Objects with Old Uyghur Writing." *Acta Orientalia Academiae Scientiarum Hungaricae* 75, no. 3 (2002): 371-390.
———. "On the Interlinear Uyghur Poetry in the Newly Unearthed Nestorian Text." In *Splitter aus der Gegend von Turfan: Festschrift für Peter Zieme anläßlich seines 60. Geburtstags*, ed. Mehmet Ölmez and Simone-Christiane Raschmann, 409-417. Istanbul: Türk Dilleri Araştırmaları Dizisi, 2002.
———. *Diśastvustik: Eine altuigurische Bearbeitung einer Legende aus dem Catuṣpariṣatsūtra*. Wiesbaden: Harrassowitz Verlag, 2006.
———. *Alttürkische Handschriften Teil 11: Die uigurischen Blockdrucke der Berliner Turfansammlung. Teil 1: Tantrische Texte*. Stuttgart: Franz Steiner Verlag, 2007.
———. *Alttürkische Handschriften Teil 12: Die uigurischen Blockdrucke der Berliner Turfansammlung. Teil 2: Apokryphen, Mahāyāna-Sutren, Erzählungen, Magische Texte, Kommentare und Kolophone*. Stuttgart: Franz Steiner Verlag, 2008.
———. *Alttürkische Handschriften Teil 15: Die uigurischen Blockdrucke der Berliner Turfansammlung. Teil 3: Stabreimdichtungen, Kalendarisches, Bilder, unbestimmte Fragmente und Nachträge*. Stuttgart: Franz Steiner Verlag, 2009.
———. *Prajñāpāramitā Literature in Old Uyghur*. Turnhout: Brepols, 2010.
———. "An Old Uyghur Fragment of the Lotus Sutra from the Krotkov Collection in St. Petersburg." *Acta Orientalia Academiae Scientiarum Hungaricae* 64, no. 4 (2011): 411-426.

—. *Altuigurische Aparimitāyus-Literatur und kleinere tantrische Texte*. Turnhout: Brepols, 2016.

—. "An Old Uyghur Fragment of an Astrological Treatise Kept in the Beijing National Library." In *Zur Lichten Heimat: Studien zu Manichäismus, Iranistik und Zentralasienkunde im Gedenken an Werner Sundermann*, ed. Team Turfanforschung, 711-718. Wiesbaden: Harrassowitz Verlag, 2017.

—. "On Two St. Petersburg Fragments from the Old Uyghur Translation of the Chinese Apocryphal Text *Yuanjuejing* 圓覺經." *Contributions to the Studies of Eurasian Languages* 20 (2018): 473-483.

—. "On a Chinese-Old Uyghur bilingual block-printed fragment discovered in the Bezelik caves in Turfan." In *Unter dem Bodhi-Baum: Festschrift für Klaus Röhrborn anlässlich des 80. Geburtstags überreicht von Kollegen, Freunden und Schülern*, ed. Z. Özertural and G. Şilfeler, 411-416. Göttingen: V&R Unipress, 2019.

—. "An Old Uyghur Appeal to T(ä)ngrikän Tegin T(ä)ngrim to Renounce Secular Life." *Turkic Languages* 23 (2019): 6-30.

—. "On an Old Uyghur Fragment of the Huayan Chanyi 華嚴懺儀 'Huayan Repentance Ritual' from the Berlin Turfan Collection." *Acta Orientalia Academiae Scientiarum Hungaricae* 74, no. 2 (2021): 171-180.

—. *Buddhāvataṃsaka Literature in Old Uyghur*. Turnhout: Brepols, 2021.

—. "On the Quotations from the *Buddhāvataṃsaka-sūtra* and Chan Literature in the Old Uyghur Text *KÖNGÜL tözin ukitdačï nom*." *Zeitschrift der Deutschen Morgenländischen Gesellschaft* 172, no. 2 (2022): 415-428.

Yakup, Abdurishid and Li Xiao. "An Old Uyghur Text Written on a Wooden Plate Recently Discovered in the Tuyoq Grottoes." *Acta Orientalia Academiae Scientiarum Hungaricae* 71, no. 3 (2018): 303-317.

Yamabe, Nobuyoshi. "Practice of Visualization and the *Visualization Sūtra*: An Examination of Mural Paintings at Toyok, Turfan." *Pacific World: Journal of the Institute of Buddhist Studies* 4 (2002): 123-152.

Yamada, Nobuo. *Sammlung uigurischer Kontrakte*. Vol. 1. Ed. Juten Oda, Peter Zieme, Hiroshi Umemura, and Takao Moriyasu. Osaka: Osaka University Press, 1993.

Yang Fuxue 楊福學. *Huihu wenxian yu huihu wenhua* 回鶻文獻與回鶻文化 [Uyghur literature and Uygur culture]. Beijing: Minzu chubanshe, 2003.

Yang, Fuxue. "Three Uighur Inscriptions Quoted from Altun Yaruq in Dunhuang Mogao Grottoes 464." In *Beşbalıkı Şingko Şeli Tutung anısına uluslararası eski Uygurca çalıştayı bildirleri, 4-6 Haziran 2011, Ankara*, ed. Mustafa S. Kaçalin, 239-246. Ankara: Türk Dil Kurumu, 2022.

Yang, Hsüan-chih. *A Record of Buddhist Monasteries in Lo-yang*. Trans. Yi-t'ung Wang. Princeton, NJ: Princeton University Press, 1984.

Yang, Lien-sheng. "Buddhist Monasteries and Four Money-Raising Institutions in Chinese History." *Harvard Journal of Asiatic Studies* 13, no. 1-2 (1950): 174-191.

Yang, Mayfair. *Re-enchanting Modernity: Ritual Economy and Society in Wenzhou, China*. Durham, NC: Duke University Press, 2020.

Yiengpruksawan, Mimi Hall. *Hiraizumi: Buddhist Art and Regional Politics in Twelfth-Century Japan*. Cambridge, MA: Harvard University Asia Center, 1998.

—. "A Pavilion for Amitabha: Yorimichi's Phoenix Hall in Transcultural Perspective." In *Buddhist Transformations and Interactions: Essays in Honor of Antonino Forte*, ed. Victor H. Mair, 401-516. Amherst, MA: Cambria Press, 2017.

———. "Countdown to 1051: Some Preliminary Thoughts on the Periodization of the Buddhist Eschaton in Heian and Liao." In *Texts and Transformations: Essays in Honor of the 75th Birthday of Victor H. Mair*, ed. Haun Saussy, 369-434. Amherst, MA: Cambria Press, 2018.

Yoshida, Yutaka. "Die buddhistischen sogdischen Texte in der Berliner Turfansammlung und die Herkunft des buddhistischen sogdischen Wortes für Bodhisattva." *Acta Orientalia Academiae Scientiarum Hungaricae* 61, no. 3 (2008): 325-358.

———. "Turco-Sogdian Features." *Iranica* 17 (2009): 571-586.

———. "Buddhist Texts Produced by the Sogdians in China." In *Multilingualism and History of Knowledge: Buddhism among the Iranian Peoples of Central Asia*, ed. J. E. Braarvig, M. J. Geller, V. Sadovski, and G. Selz, 154-179. Wien: Verlag der Österreichischen Akademie der Wissenschaft, 2013.

Yü, Chün-fang. *Kuan-yin: The Chinese Transformation of Avalokiteśvara*. New York: Columbia University Press, 2000.

Yüan, Ch'en. *Western and Central Asians in China under the Mongols: Their Transformation into Chinese*. Trans. Ch'ien Hsing-hai and L. Carrington Goodrich. Los Angeles: Monumenta Serica at UCLA, 1966.

Yule, Henry. *The Book of Ser Marco Polo the Venetian concerning the Kingdoms and Marvels of the East, Translated and Edited, with Notes, by Colonel Sir Henry Yule, R.E., C.B., K.C.S.I., Corr. Inst. France, Third Edition, Revised Throughout in the Light of Recent Discoveries by Henri Cordier (of Paris)*. New York: Charles Scribner, 1929.

Zhang Guangda and Rong Xinjiang. "A Concise History of the Turfan Oasis and Its Exploration." *Asia Major* 11, no. 2 (1998): 13-36.

Zhang, Tieshan and Peter Zieme. "A Memorandum about the King of the 'On Uygur' and His Realm." *Acta Orientalia Academiae Scientiarum Hungaricae* 64, no. 2 (2011): 129-159.

Zhang, Tieshan and Peter Zieme. "A Further Fragment of Old Uighur Annals." *Acta Orientalia Academiae Scientiarum Hungaricae* 66, no. 4 (2013): 397-410.

Zheng, Huiming. "An Iconographic Study of Pictorial Fragments 'Mañjuśri and His Assistants' from the Bezeklik Caves." In *Sergej Federovič Ol'denburg: učenyj i organizator nauki*, 379-403. Moscow: NAUKA, 2016.

Zhiru. "The Maitreya Connection in the Tang Development of Dizang Worship." *Harvard Journal of Asiatic Studies* 65, no. 1 (2005): 99-132.

Zhiru. *The Making of a Savior Bodhisattva: Dizang in Medieval China*. Honolulu: University of Hawai'i Press, 2007.

Zhongguo Shehui Kexueyuan Yanjiusiu. *Beiting Gaochang Huihu Fosi Yizhi (Remains of a Uygur Monastery Gaochang-Beiting)*. Shenyang: Liaoning meishu chubanshe, 1991.

Zieme, Peter. "Ein uigurischer Erntesegen." *Altorientalische Forschungen* 3 (1975): 109-143.

———. "Zum Handel im uigurischen Reich von Qočo." *Altorientalische Forschungen* 4 (1976): 235-249.

———. "Drei neue uigurische Sklavendokumente." *Altorientalische Forschungen* 5 (1978): 145-170.

———. "Uigurische Pachtdokumente." *Altorientalische Forschungen* 7 (1980): 197-245.

———. "Uigurische Steuerbefreiungsurkunden für buddhistische Klöster." *Altorientalische Forschungen* 7 (1981): 237-263.

———. "Zum uigurischen *Tārā-Ekaviṃśatistotra*." *Acta Orientalia Academiae Scientiarum Hungaricae* 36 (1982): 583-597.

———. *Buddhistische Stabreimdichtungen der Uiguren*. Berlin: Akademie Verlag, 1985.
———. "Das *Pravāraṇā-Sūtra* in alttürkischer Überlieferung." In *Barg-i sabz—A Green Leaf: Papers in Honour of Jes P. Asmussen*, ed. P. O. Skjaervo, et al., 445-453. Leiden: Brill, 1988.
———. *Die Stabreimtexte der Uiguren von Turfan und Dunhuang*. Budapest: Akadémiai Kiadó, 1991.
———. *Religion und Gesellschaft im Uigurischen Königreich von Qočo*. Opladen: Westdeutscher Verlag, 1992.
———. "Zum Maitreya-Kult in uigurischen Kolophonen." *Rocznik Orientalistyczny* 49 (1994): 536-549.
———. "An Uigur Monasterial Letter from Toyoq." *Studies on the Inner Asian Languages* 10 (1995): 1-8.
———. "Donor and Colophon of an Uigur Blockprint." *Silk Road Art and Archaeology: Journal of the Institute of Silk Road Studies, Kamakura* 4 (1996): 409-424.
———. "Old Turkish Versions of the 'Scripture on the Ten Kings.'" In *Proceedings of the 38th PIAC, Kawasaki, Japan: August 7–12, 1995*, ed. Giovanni Stary, 401-425. Wiesbaden: Harrassowitz, 1996.
———. "Turkic Fragments in 'Phags-pa Script." *Studies on the Inner Asian Languages* 13 (1998): 63-69.
———. "Das *Qiānzìwén* bei den alten Uiguren." In *Writing in the Altaic World*, ed. J. Janhunen and V. Rybatzki, 321-326. Helsinki: Finnish Oriental Society, 1999.
———. "An Old Uigur Idiyut Text." In *The History behind the Languages: Essays of Turfan Forum on Old Languages of the Silk Road*, ed. Academia Turfanica, 1-12. Shanghai: Shanghai Guji Chubanshe, 2000.
———. *Vimalakīrtinirdeśasūtra. Edition alttürkischer Übersetzungen nach Handschriftfragmenten von Berlin und Kyoto. Mit einem Appendix von Jorinde Ebert: Ein Vimalakīrti-Bildfragment aus Turfan*. Turnhout: Brepols, 2000.
———. "*Araṇemi-Jātaka* und ein Sündenbekenntnistext in einer alttürkischen Sammelhandschrift." In *De Dunhuang à Istanbul: Hommage à James Russell Hamilton*, ed. L. Bazin and P. Zieme, 401-421. Turnhout: Brepols, 2001.
———. "Ein weiteres alttürkisches Fragment des 'Sūtras von der Vollkommenen Erleuchtung.'" *Acta Orientalia Academiae Scientiarum Hungaricae* 55 (2002): 281-295.
———. "Three Old Turkic *Wutaishanzan* Fragments." *Studies on the Inner Asian Languages* 17 (2002): 223-239.
———. *Magische Texte des uigurischen Buddhismus*. Turnhout: Brepols, 2005.
———. "On Some Quotations in the Uighur *Insadi-Sutra*." *Bukkyogaku Kenkyu* 60-61 (2006): 1-14.
———. "Notes on Uighur Medicine, Especially on the Uighur Siddhasāra Tradition." *Asian Medicine* 3 (2007): 308-322.
———. "Caitya Veneration—an Uigur Manuscript with Portraits of Donors." *Journal of Inner Asian Art and Archaeology* 2 (2007): 165-172.
———. "The Bodhisattva Sattvauṣadha 'Medicine of All Beings.'" In *"The Way of the Buddha" 2003: The 100th Anniversary of the Otani Missions and the 50th of the Research Society for Central Asian Cultures*, ed. Irisawa Takashi, 35-45. Kyoto: Ryukoku University, 2010.
———. "Chinese Classical Works in Uighur Tradition." In *Tulufan xue yanjiu: di san jie Tulufan xueji Ou-Ya youmu minzu de qiyuan yu qianxi guoji xueshu yantao huilun wenji*, 459-471. Shanghai: Shanghai Guji Chubanshe, 2010.
———. "An Uighur Instruction Document for Preaching the *Bayangjing* and Other Sutras in Alliterating Verses." In 西域歷史語言研究集刊 [Historical and philological studies of China's western regions], ed. Shen Weirong, 271-282. Beijing: Science Press, 2010.
———. "Buddhistische Unterweltsberichte-alttürkische Varianten aus der Turfan-Oase." In *Life and Afterlife & Apocalyptic Concepts in the Altaic World*, ed. M. Knüppel and A. van Tongerloo, 143-163. Wiesbaden: Harrassowitz, 2011.

———. "Notes on Religion in the Mongol Empire." In *Islam and Tibet: Interactions along the Musk Routes*, ed. Anna Akasoy, Charles Burnett, and Ronit Yoeli-Tlalim, 177-187. Farnham: Ashgate, 2011.

———. "Some Notes on Old Uigur Art and Texts." In *Buddhism and Art in Turfan: From the Perspective of Uyghur Buddhism*, ed. Irisawa Takashi, 5-18. Kyoto: Research Center for Buddhist Culture in Asia Ryukoku University, 2012.

———. "Some Notes on Old Uigur Translations of Buddhist Commentaries." *Annual Report of the International Research Institute for Advanced Buddhology at Soka University* 15 (2012): 147-160.

———. "A Chinese Chan Text from Dunhuang in Uighur Transcription and in Translation from Turfan." In *Dunhuang Studies: Prospects and Problems for the Coming Second Century of Research*, ed. I. F. Popova and Liu Yi, 361-364. Saint Petersburg: Slavia, 2012.

———. "Collecting of the Buddhist Scriptures: Notes on Old Uigur 'Annals.'" *Annual Report of the International Research Institute for Advanced Buddhology at Soka University* 23 (2013): 401-422.

———. "The West Uigur Kingdom: Views from Inside." *Horizons* 5, no. 1 (2014): 1-29.

———. "Local Literatures: Uighur." In *Brill's Encyclopedia of Buddhism*, ed. Jonathan Silk et al., 871-882. Leiden: Brill, 2015.

———. "Bägräk Tutung and His Family: Notes on an Old Uygur Colophon." In *Language, Society, and Religion in the World of the Turks: Festschrift for Larry Clark at Seventy-Five*, ed. Zsuzsanna Gulásci, 166-175. Turnhout: Brepols, 2018.

———. "A Fragment of an Old Uighur Translation of the *Śatapañcāśatka*." *Annual Report of the International Research Institute for Advanced Buddhology at Soka University* 27 (2019): 333-343.

———. "Mount Wutai and Mañjuśrī in Old Uigur Buddhism." In *The Transnational Cult of Mount Wutai: Historical and Comparative Perspectives*, ed. Susan Andrews, Jinhua Chen, and Guang Kuan, 223-237. Leiden: Brill, 2020.

———. "Die Lehre des Buddha und das Königshaus des Westuigurischen Reichs: Die vier Begegnungen." *Journal of Old Turkic Studies* 4, no. 2 (2020): 546-731.

———. "The Old Uigur Translation of the Siddhaṃ Songs." In *Chán Buddhism in Dūnhuáng and Beyond: A Study of Manuscripts, Texts, and Contexts in Memory of John R. McRae*, ed. C. Anderl and C. Wittern, 143-193. Leiden: Brill, 2020.

———. "The First Leaf of an Old Uyghur *Guanwuliangshoujing* Translation." *Written Monuments of the Orient* 6, no. 1 (2020): 47-55.

———. "Merit Transfer and Vow According to an Old Uyghur Buddhist Text from Qočo/Gaochang." *Annual Report of the International Research Institute for Advanced Buddhology at Soka University* 24 (2020): 217-230.

———. "The Poor Man in Byzantium: Fragments of an Old Uyghur Tale." *Türkiyat Mecmuasi* 31 (2021): 39-49.

———. "Scenes from the *Lotus Sūtra*: An Old Uygur Temple Banner with Cartouche Inscriptions." *Manuscripta Orientalia* 27, no. 1 (2021): 3-19.

Zieme, Peter and György Kara. *Ein uigurisches Totenbuch: Naropas Lehre in uigurischer Übersetzung*. Budapest: Akadémiai Kiadó, 1979.

Zieme, Peter, György Kara, and Liliya Tugusheva. *Avalokiteśvara-Sūtras: Edition altuigurischer Übersetzungen nach Fragmenten aus Turfan und Dunhuang*. Turnhout: Brepols, 2022.

Zürcher, Erik. "Buddhist Chanhui and Christian Confession in Seventeenth Century China." In *Forgive Us Our Sins*, ed. N. Standaert and A. Dudink, 103-127. Nettetal: Steyler Verlag, 2006.

Index

Abaqa Khan, 139
Abbasid caliphate, 7, 20, 21, 156
Abhidharmakośa-bhāṣya, 130, 215n129
abhidharma literature, 129, 130, 131, 215n129
Abitaki Sūtra, 61
Acintyabuddhaviṣayanirdeśa, 213n105
Ädiz clan, 9, 10, 15, 35, 58
Afghanistan, 17, 21, 117, 170
āgama literature, 127, 129, 130
Āgama Sūtra (Ahan jing), 62
'Ala' ad-Dawla as-Simnani, 139, 141
Alan Qoa (legendary figure), 163
ālaya-vijñāna (eighth consciousness), 102
alcohol consumption, 89, 92, 93
Alexander Romance, 137
Algu, 147, 150, 153
Ali Sultan, 154
Alp Qutluq Bilgä Khan, 9
Altisharis, 2
Amir Fakhru'd-Din, 160
Amitābha Buddha, 102, 143
Amitābha Cave Temple, 117
Amitābha Sūtra (Amituo jing), 101
Ananda, 95
Aṅguttara Nikāya, 66, 70–71, 198n21
animal sacrifice, 89, 93
An Lushan rebellion, 7–8
Anzang, 125
Arabic script, 143, 184n80
Arakawa Shintaro, 103
Aranemi Jātaka, 61, 102

Arghun Khan, 139
Ariq Böke, 123, 125, 146, 147
Arslan Bilgä Tängri Ellig the Fourth, 20
Ārya Śūra, 102
Aśoka, 5, 40, 55, 72
Aṣṭāṅgahṛdayasaṃhitā (Vagbhaṭa), 188n15
astronomical events, 51
Astūd Frazend, 20
Asuday, Prince, 162
Āṭānāṭikasūtra, 59
Atwood, Christopher, 146
Augustine of Hippo, 26
avadāna literature, 95
Avalokiteśvara (bodhisattva), 45, 46, 125, 191n63
Avalokiteśvara Sūtra, 123
Avataṃsaka Repentance Ritual, 127
Avataṃsaka Sūtra (Huayan jing), 101, 125, 127
axial age, 24, 67, 71, 186n1

Babur, 222n77
Baghdad, 23, 156
Bagučak, 158
banks, monasteries as, 89–90
Barchug Art Tegin, 120, 121, 146
Basa Togril, 76–77
Basmil tribe, 7
Batu Khan, 144
Bema festival, 15, 16
Benavides, Gustavo, 71

Berkey, Jonathan, 70
Beshbaliq (Beiting), 11, 14, 113, 138, 193n83; Bezeklik cave murals compared with, 116–17; donor portraits in, 118; horse market and, 81; map, 3; Mongol garrison in, 146; Yuan postal relay system and, 147–48
Besma (Chagatid prince), 147
Bezeklik caves, artwork from, 35, 113, 180n38; Cave Temples Restoration Project (Ryukoku Museum, Japan), 36; ḍākinī, 126; distinctive Uyghur style in, 117; donor portraits, 56, 57, 86, 87; murals in Museum für Völkerkunde (Berlin), 34, 36; outside views of cave temple complex, 116; praṇidhi scenes, 32–33, 35, 54–55; Tejaprabha's Paradise, 47; Vaiśravaṇa (guardian deity), 44, 45
Bhallika, 71–72
Bhrum Bhrum Vajrapāṇi, 87
Big Dipper Sūtra, 134, 143
"big script," Khitan, 31, 31
Bilgä Bukha, 120
Biography of Xuanzang, 61, 106
Biran, Michal, 76, 136, 149
block printing, 103, 104, 132, 133, 134, 216n141
bodhisattvas, 97, 123
Book for the Redemptions of Sins (*Cibei daochang chanfa*), 62, 98, 99
Book of Changes (Ch. *Yijing*), 43
Book of the Dead (Naropa), 125, 162
Boz Bay Tiräk, 54
Brahmajāla Sūtra (*Fangwang jing*), 62
Brahmans, 71, 72, 84
Brāhmī script, 17, 18, 128, 128, 129
Brown, Peter, 3, 169
Buddha, the, 35, 58; animals sacrificed to, 93; on creation of nun order, 61; first lay disciples of, 71–72; imagined as political "radical," 70; politics of axial age India and, 67, 186n1; relics of, 41, 179n36; stories about previous lives of, 95, 141; wealth production and, 71, 73, 74–75, 198–99n35

Buddhacarita, 103
Buddhism: golden age of, 1, 156; Khitan canon, 31, 31; meaning of, 3–4; meeting with Islam, 3, 22; monks traveling between India and China, 29; mutual influence with Manichaeanism, 27; as pan-Asian faith, 4, 27–39, 28; political power and, 40; transcendence of material world, 24. *See also specific schools and traditions*
Buddhism, Chinese, 2, 95, 98, 110; Chinese (Kaibao) canon, 28–29, 30, 51; monks depicted in Bezeklik, 36, 38; "north Chinese Buddhist complex," 31, 100, 101; *Vinaya* (monastic code) of, 132; Yogācāra school, 55
Buddhism, economics and: Eurasian trade, 75–83; "field of merit," 73; monastic economy, 83–91; wealth accumulation and Buddhism, 66–75
Buddhism, Mongolian, 122, 211n89
Buddhism, Tibetan, 94, 95, 134; Mongol connection to, 123–25; *Vinaya* (monastic code) of, 132
Buddhism, Uyghur, 65, 92–93, 143; absence of canon, 60; adoption of Maitreya cult, 190n51; Buddhism beyond the state, 40–50; Buddhist history erased by Islamic conversion, 1–2, 173; consolidation of Buddhist kingdom, 6–17; conversion as defense against Qarakhanids, 20–24; conversion as drawn-out process, 39; disengagement with politics as distinctive Buddhist realm, 59–65; distinctive and pluralistic nature of, 92–106; elite adoption of Buddhism, 5–6, 15, 18; end of, 170; golden age of, 119–34, 135; gradual embrace of Buddhism, 17–20; history in stages, 95–96; Khitan Liao and, 34, 35; materiality of manuscripts, 106–19, 108–16
Buddhism in Chinese Society (Gernet, 1956), 67
"Buddhist Catechism," 17, 19
Bukhara, 20, 21

Bulmiš, 153
Buyids, 21
Büyük Tarih-i Umumi (Refik, 1912), 1
Byzantine Empire, 23

cakravartin (wheel-turning king), 141, 191n63
Cao family, 12, 14, 41
Cao Yijin, 12; Ganzhou Uyghur wife of, 13, *13*
Carter, Martha, 89
Cave 17 (Dunhuang), 56
Cave 20 (Bezeklik), 35, 36, *37–38*
Cave 38 (Bezeklik), 180n38
Cave 39 (Yulinku), 45
Cave 98 (Dunhuang), 12, *13*
Cave 130 (Dunhuang), 53
Central Asia, 7, 9, 10, 23, 89; geopolitical shifts in, 136; Mongol civil wars in, 146, 147, 149; Muslim subjects of Qara Khitai in, 137; post-Abbasid, 20–21, *21*; Qarakhanid conquests in, 23; Yuan dynasty map of, 150, *151–52*
Chagatai (son of Chinggis Khan), 144, 145, 146, 222n77
Chagataids, 144, 147, 148, 150, 153–54, 163
Chagatai Khanate, 147, 148, 154
Chan Buddhism, 31, 61, 94, 100, 102. *See also* Zen Buddhism
Chang'an (Xi'an), 6, 62
chanhui (remorseful apology), 98–99
Chanyuan Treaty (1005), 29, 76
Chaoyang, northern pagoda at, 52
Chapar, 150
Chappell, David, 99
Chen Cheng, 160
China, 4, 117; fears about "end of the Dharma," 50; market for horses in, 79–80; Muslim knowledge of, 136; People's Republic of China, 14, 164; Songmo region, 92; Uyghur pilgrim inscriptions in, 117, 211n79; Uyghurs' role in economy, 9–10. *See also specific dynasties*

Chinese characters, 17, 130; in Khitan canon, 31, *31*; Uyghur texts with, 63, *63*, 64–65
Chinese language, Uyghur transcriptions of, 62, *63*
Chinggis Khan, 120–21, 137–38, 143–44, 145, 146; Buddhist and Muslim advisers of, 138; rulers as direct descendants of, 162–63, 164, 166
Christianity, 2, 4, 56, 59, 94, 154, 158; Christianization of Roman Empire, 3; Christian subjects of West Uyghur Kingdom, 17; confession of sins in, 99; hard doctrinal boundaries within, 96; Nestorian, 89; Protestant theology and capitalism, 66–67, 196n7
Čisön Tutung, 213n105
Ciyun Zunshi, 103
climate change, 3, 27, 82
codex format, 108, *110*
Collected Commentaries on the Vimalakīrti Sūtra from "Inside the Passes" (Ch. *Jingmingjing jijie guanzhongshu*), 101–2
Commentary on the Lotus Sūtra, 209n62
Commentary on the Vimalakīrti Sūtra (Kumārajīva), 107
Compendium of Chronicles [Jami' al-tawarikh] (Rashid al-Din), 139, 141
concertina format, 108, *109*
confessional texts, 97–100
Confucianism, 71
cotton cultivation, 81–82

Daizong (Tang emperor), 9
Dalai Lama, 141
Dali kingdom, 24, 27, 28, 41
Daocheng, 51
Daoism, 196n7
Daoye, 101
Daśakarmapathāvadānamāla, 39
Dehli Sultanate, *145*, 153
Delbeg, 165
Devalasmṛti, 226n136
Devaśāntika (Ch. Tianxizai), 51
DeWeese, Devin, 224n104
Dhanyasena, 127

Dharma, 1, 4, 29, 91, 102, 128; abandoned for Islam, 135, 168, 169; Asia-wide turn to, 27; comprehensibility of, 107; economics and, 67, 71, 72; end of, 50, 51, 113; golden age of, 51; Il-khanid rulers and, 139, 140; laissez faire approach to, 60; Maitreya Buddha and, 50; political power/legitimacy and, 40, 45, 191n63; preservation of, 60; prosperity theology of, 72, 74; as protective shield, 43; Turks and, 7; universalist dispensation of, 58; urban trade and, 70. *See also* Buddhism
Dharmaguptaka Vinaya, 132
Diamond Sūtra, 101
Dīgha Nikāya, 198n32
Dīpaṃkara, 55
disease outbreaks, 51
Divan Lugat al-Turk (1070s), 22
donors: generation of merit and, 83–86; portraits of, 48, 49, 56, 57, 86, 117, *118*
Döre Temür, 150
Dorjé Tashi Pelzangpo, 160
Drigungpa order, 124, 139, 148
Dum (Ch. Longjia "dragon families"), 11–12
Dunhuang, city of, 14, 30, 34, 53, 93, 95, 162; Avalokiteśvara depiction, 45, 46; Cave of a Thousand Buddhas pavilion, 12; Guanyin painting, 113, *115*; map, *3*; Middle Chinese spoken in Song period, 62; multiple languages and scripts used in Guiyijun documents, 195n101; Silk Road and, 11; sixteen great temples of, 13; as source of paper, 108; Tanguts' recapture of, 17; tenth-century artistic efflorescence, 189n32; "transformation texts" (*bianwen*), 103; Uyghur elites and, 62; West Uyghur Kingdom control of, 15, 180n43; Yogācāra Faxiang school in, 55
dutong (leader of Chinese Buddhist community), 60
Duwa (Chagatid prince), 147, 148, 149–50, 153

Eight Yang Sūtra (*Bayang jing*), 39, 96
Ekottarāgama (*Zengyi Ahan jing*), 62
El-Altun, 146
Eljigdai, 153
Emperor White Robe, 12
Engke Temür, 165
Esen Buqa, 150, 167
Essential Readings for Buddhists [Ch. *Shishi yaolan*] (Daocheng), 51
Eurasia, 1, 4, 174; Buddhism and trade throughout, 75–83; Buddhists and Muslims in, 136–43; in fifteenth century, 166; reordering of political alignments in, 7

Fabao, 12
Fayuan, 41
Fazang, 100
"field of merit," 73, 83, 89, 95
Filliozat, Jean, 194n99
Firdausi, 217n12
Five Dynasties period (China), 12, 29, 100
Five Peak Mountain [Wutai Shan] (China), 125, 127

Gaikhatu (Rinchen Dorjé), 139
Gandhara, 89, 93
Gansu corridor, 8, 12, 147
Ganzhou Uyghur Kingdom, 10, 11, 12; map, *10*; Tangut attack on, 14, 42
Garlands of Legends Pertaining to the Ten Courses of Action (*Daśakarmapathāvadānamālā*), 95, 96
geopolitics, 3, 136
Gernet, Jacques, 67
Ghazan, 139–40
Ghaznavids, 21, *21*, 23, 219n37
Ghost Festival, 99
"giving" (*dāna*), 73, 83
Glahn, Richard von, 100
Golden Horde, 144, *145*, 154
Golden Light Sūtra, 43, 45, 61, 101, 155, 205n14; "The Dream of the Golden Drum of Penitence," 47–48; mixing of traditions and, 97–98
Grahamātṛkādhāraṇī, 129
Great Game, in nineteenth century, 2
Greek philosophy, 70

Greene, Eric M., 98
Guanyin (Bodhisattva of Compassion), 110, *111*, *112*, 113, *115*, 143
Güchlüg Khan, 137, 138
Guifeng Zongmi, 100
Guiyijun ("Return to Righteousness Army"), 11, 12, 13, 14, 83, 195n101
Gülichi, 165
Guruyoga of Sakya Pandita, 125
Güyük Khan, 123, 157-58

al-Hamadani, Abu Yusuf, 163
Hami, city-state of, *3*, 165, 167
Hand Mirror of the Dragon Niche (*Longkan shoujian*), 42
Han dynasty (China), 82
Hanlin Academy, 127
Haribhaṭṭa, 102
Heian state (Japan), 27, 28, 41
Hinayāna [Small Vehicle] (Nikāya), 94
Hinduism, 24, 67, 71, 196n7
History of the Sandalwood Buddha Statue in China, The, 127
History of the Yuan Dynasty, 120
Hongfasi monastery, 132
Hong Hao, 92, 93
horses, trade in, 9, 79-81, *81*, 164-65
Huayan Buddhism, 31, 94, 100, 101, 106
Hui Chao, 7
Huilin, 7
Hülegü, 139, 156

"Idiyut Text," 185n103
Idukkur Khan, 122
Il-khanid realm, 139-40, 141, 144, 155, 170; Four Ulus of Mongol empire and, *145*; map, *140*
Illustration of the Ten Realms of Mind Contemplation in the Perfect and Immediate Teaching [*Yuandun Guanxin Shifaijietu*] (Ciyun Zunshi), 103
India, 5, 29, 50-51, 58; in axial age, 67; Buddhist wine production in Gandhara, 89, 93; Mauryan Empire, 69, *69*, 71; Mughal rulers of, 222n77; republics in early India, 67, *68*; urbanization and iron technology in, 67-68, 70
individualism, 60, 62, 70, 100
Inquiry into Divine Thinking (*Siyi fantian suowen jing*), 102
Insadi Sūtra, 156
intermediaries, Uyghurs' role as, 76, 80, 82, 199-200n47
Iran, 89, 139
Islam, 3, 4, 22; advance into Buddhist India, 50; Buddhists and Muslims in Mongol Eurasia, 136-43; prosperity theology of, 168; stereotypes about, 154; Uyghurs' slow conversion to, 1, 2, 3, 135-36, 154-69, 170

Jackson, Peter, 222n71
Jainism, 24, 67
Jankeshi, 153
Japan, 43, 48, 149; apocalyptic visions in, 51; "Kan-on" system, 62
jātaka literature, 95, 134
Jātakamālā (*Haribhaṭṭa*), 102
Jesus, 70
Jinagupta, 7
Jin dynasty. *See* Jurchen Jin dynasty
Jinggim, 124
Jingzong (Tangut emperor), 42
Jochi Khan, 143-44, 145
Julien, Stanislas, 2
Jumada II, 160
Jurchen Jin dynasty, 62, 83, 92, 120
Juvaini, 138
Juzjani, 156-58, 159

Käd Ogul Xoštir, 18
Kagyü (Tibetan lineage), 123, 139
Kālacakra literature, 217n4
Kālacakratantra, 51, 156, 217n4
Kanakamuni (historical buddha), 50
Karluk tribe, 7
karma, 72, 73, 84, 91, 94, 107; *chanhui* (remorseful apology) and, 98; Maitreya and karmic registers, 95; Muslims and, 162; printing of texts and, 134

Karma Pakshi, 123, 138
Kasai, Yukiyo, 214-15n127
Kashgar, 2, 22
kāši ačari (leader of Tokharian monks), 60
Kaśyapa (historical buddha), 50, 55
Kebek Khan, 150, 153
Kesmes, 146
Kharakhoja, 45
Khitan Liao dynasty, 13, 14, 15, 28; alliance with West Uyghur Kingdom, 119-20; Buddhism of, 100, 101; fall of, 82; influence on Japanese Buddhist architecture, 30, 30; Maitreya worship in, 51; as part of Buddhist Asia, 27, 28, 29, 34, 41; Song dynasty conflict with, 76, 80; Uyghur ties to, 22, 29, 42, 62, 76; wars of, 57; Yogācāra Faxiang school and, 55. *See also* Qara Khitai (Western Liao)
Khoja Abdusattar, 168
Khoran, 50-51
Khotan, city-state of, 22, 41, 76, 138, 173
Khubilai Khan, 2, 29, 123, 124, 127, 138, 146; death of, 149; failure of Central Asia strategy, 148; rebellions against, 149; Uyghurs allied with, 147. *See also* Yuan dynasty
Kim, Youn-mi, 52-53
Kingdom of the Golden Mountain of the Western Han, 12
Kirghiz, 10
Kitsudō Kōichi, 103
Kizil Cave, 53
Klaproth, Julius, 2
Köl Bilgä Khan (Ch. Huairen), 7
Könchek, 150
Korea, 62; Koryo kingdom, 27, 28, 41; monastic landownership in, 88
Krakucchanda (historical buddha), 50
Kṣitigarbha (Ch. Dizang), Bodhisattva, 112-13, *114*
Kucha, 3
Kulika Rudracakrin, 51
Külüg Bilgä Khan, 8, 9
Kumārajīva, 107
Kutlug Bars, 60

Langdarma, 11
Legends of the Bughra Khans, 170
Leidy, Denise, 45
Li, Lady, 12
Liang dynasty, 98
Literary Sinitic, 107
Li Ziye, 141
Lopez, Donald, 4
"Lord of Auspicious Conjunction" (*ṣāḥibqirān*), 141
Lotus Sūtra, 39, 43, 45, 48, 117; apocalyptic rituals and, 51; *Avalokiteśvara Sūtra*, 101; texts paired with, 61; Uyghur translation/ transcription of, 61, 62
Luoyang, monasteries around, 88
Luo Yuejiong, 160
Lu Tao, 29

Madhyamāgama (*Zhong ahanjing*), 129, 130
Mahākāla (deity), 123
Mahāparinirvāṇa Sūtra, 7
Mahāvatsu, 55
Mahāyāna (Great Vehicle), 94, 95, 134
Mahmud (Oirad ruler), 165
Mahmud of Ghazna, 17, 23
Maitreya (Buddha of the future), 39, 50-59, 61, 64, 143, 190n51, 191n63; confessional texts and, 100; in Japan, 52; karmic register and, 95; meritorious deeds and, 84, 85; return of, 112; Tuṣita heaven as abode of, 50, 54, 55, 153
Maitrisimit, 39, 53-54, 60, 95, 188n21
Malikshah, Sultan, 23
Malov, S. E., 2
Mamluks, 145, 153, 225n119
Manchuria, 76, 148, 149
Manchus, 1, 2, 155
Mäng Tekin, 10
Mani, 24-25, 26
Manichaeism, 2, 6, 35, 179n35, 183n74, 191n64; abandoned for Buddhism, 20; commercial ties of, 8; confessional texts, 100; envoys to courts of China, 15, 179n35; loss of royal support, 15, 180n39; Maitreya worship in, 190n51; new year

bendiction, 49–50; reasons for Uyghurs' rejection of, 24–27; of Sogdians, 9, 14; "Table of God" ritual, 25–26; "two orders" (*iki törlüg*), 58–59; West Uyghur Kingdom and, 56; as "world religion," 26
Manistan, 20
Mañjuśrī (bodhisattva of wisdom), 125, 127, 153, 191n63, 210n71, 213n105
Mañjuśrīnāmasaṃgīti, 62, 125, 213n105
Man lungs Guru, 217n4
Mārīcī, 87
Marzavi, Sharaf al-Zaman Tahir, 23–24
Matsui, Dai, 141, 180n39
Maudgalyāyana *bianwen*, 103
Maue, Dieter, 188n15
Mauryan Empire, 69, 69, 71
Menander, 72
merchants, 29, 82–83, 88, 92; the Buddha and, 71; Eurasian trade and, 75, 135; as middlemen, 80; ritual protection of, 74; tax farming and, 218n21; wealth and conspicuous consumption of, 78–79
Merkits, 121
Merv, 23
Milindapañhā, 72, 198n32
Ming dynasty (China), 160–61, 164, 170, 225n113; Great Wall and, 167; horse market and, 164–65, 167
Minlaq, 22
Mirāj Name, 170, 172
Moerman, D. Max, 51–52
Mofa (Latter Dharma), 52, 53
Mogao caves (Dunhuang), 12
Moghulistan, 154
Moghuls, 136, 154, 155, 159, 222n77; Mongol legacy and, 164; "nomadic Islam" of, 162; Oirads and, 166–67
monasteries, 7, 17; coexistence with mosques, 160; land owned by, 88–89, 202n86; monastic economy, 83–91; Shizong emperor's closing of, 27–28; stripped of assets by Tang emperor, 8; violence against, 91; wealth production and, 73, 74, 199n37
moneylending, 9, 83

Möngke Khan, 123, 125, 138, 144, 146, 147, 218n22
Mongol empire, 58, 82, 95, 136; Buddhists and Muslims in, 137–43; Chinggis Khan's conquests, *144*; civil wars and decline of, 82, 91, 143–54; collapse of, 121; Four Ulus, 143–44, *145*; *pax mongolica*, 132, 134; tax farming in, 138, 218n21; Uyghurs as "steppe intelligentsia" of, 2, 121, 135
Mongolia, 76
Mongolian language, written in Uyghur script, 120, *121*
monks, 7, 60, 73, 88, 90, 154; Bezeklik cave depictions of, 36, *37–38*; economic trade and, 71; forced to become soldiers, 8; at Ming court, 161; slave trade and, 89; at Song court, 41–42; Uyghur monks in Tokharian-style robes, 131, *131*. *See also* monasteries
Mughals (rulers of India), 141
Muhammad, Prophet, 137, 163
Muhan Khan, 7
Mūlasarvāstivādin Vinaya, 132, 205n15
Müller, F. W. K., 2
Museum für Völkerkunde (Berlin), *34, 36*
Muslims, Uyghurs as, 1
Myanmar, 135

Nāgasena, 72
Naimans, 120
Names of the Buddha Sūtra, The (*Foming Jing*), 13
Namo buddhayah prayer, 141
Nanda Kingdom, 69
Nandaśri, 161
Nanzhao Kingdom, 7
Naqshband, Baha ad-Din, 163
Naqshbandiyya (Sufi order), 163, 166, 168
Naropa, 125, 162
Nayan, 149
Ne'üril Tegin, 148, 150
Newman, John, 217n4
Nikāya schools, 55, 94, 95
"Nine Tribes" (Toquz Oguz), 7, 20, 58, 191n64
nirvana (Ch. *niepan*), 31, 72
Northern Qi dynasty, 7, 8

Northern Zhou dynasty, 6
nuns, 73, 83, 89

Ögedeids, 150, 154
Ögedei Khan, 138, 144–46
Ögrünch, 146
Oirad (Western Mongols), 164, 165–67, 225n119
Old Uyghur Annals, 50
Öljeitü Khan, 140, 141
One Thousand Character Classic (Ch. *Qianziwen*), 62
On Uygur (ten clans), 9
orientalism, European, 2, 174
Orkhon Valley, 7
ortoq (financial institution), 76, 79
Ottoman Turks, 23
Özbek Khan, 150, 154

Pakistan, 51, 156
Pakmo Drukpa, 139
Pakpa Lama, 123–24, 125, 127
Pakpa script, 124, *124*, 170
paper money, 147, 161
Paramartaśri, 161
pastoralism, nomadic, 68, 70
Perfect Enlightenment Sūtra (*Yuanjue jing*), 101, 102
"Perfect Teaching" (*yuanjiao*), 100, 101, 102
Performing Confession Scripture, The, 100
Persian language, 139, 141, 143
Phoenix Temple (Kyoto, Japan), 30, *30*
pilgrims/pilgrimage, 4, 94, 117, 173–74, *173*; inscriptions by, 93, 117, 211n79; intelligence agents in guise of, 29; Maitreya and, 55
Piratyaśri, 161, 167
poetry, Uyghur, 64, 102, 135, 155–56, 161–62, 182n57
Polo, Marco, 93
poṣadha ceremony, 73
Prabhakhamitra, 7
praṇidhi scenes, *32–33*, *35*, *53*; king presenting umbrella to the Buddha, *53*, *54*; *Mahavatsu* and, 54–55

pravaraṇā ceremony, 132
Prebish, Charles, 194n99
Primary Ritual Ordinance of Mañjuśri, The (Skt. *Mañjuśrimulakalpa*; Ch. *Wenshushili genben yigui jing*), 51, 190n43
prosperity theology, 72, 74, 75, 168
prostitution, 79, 80
"Protestant presupposition" problem, 94, 96, 102
Punyashri, 165
Pure Land Buddhism, 50, 61, 94
pustaka format, 107, *108*

Qaidu, 146, 147, 149, 150
Qarakhanids, 6, 51, 173; conversion to Islam, 21; expansion into Tarim Basin, 21–22; Manichaeans and, 27, 184n80; maps, *3, 21*; Nine Tribes and, 20; as trading partners of Khitan Liao, 76
Qara Khitai (Western Liao), 23, 24, 120, 136; Chinggis Khan's conquest of, 138; East-West trade and, 82; Muslim subjects of, 137. *See also* Khitan Liao dynasty
Qatwan, Battle of (1141), 23
Qian-zi-wen, 143
Qing dynasty (China), 2, 155
Qingliang Chengguan, 100
Qocho (Xizhou/Gaochang), city of, 35, 55, 81, 116, 150; besieged during Mongol civil wars, 147; Buddhist monasteries in, 17; Manichaean temple in, 26; map, *3*
Qočqar, 147, 148
Quanming, 101

Radloff, Wilhelm, 2
Radna, Prince, 162
Rashid al-Din, 120, 139, 141
Ray, Himanshu, 168
Record of Tribute Guests [*Xian bin lü*] (Luo Yuejiong), 160
Records of an Embassy to Qocho (Wang Yande, ca. 982 CE), 5
Records of the History of the Liao Dynasty (*Liao shi jishi benmo*), 42
Records of the Jade Casket (Ch. *Yuxiaji*), 43

Refik, Ahmet, 1
relics, 15, 179n36
Religion of India, The (Weber), 40
Renou, Louis, 194n99
Report on Songmo (Hong Hao, ca. 1150), 92

sādhāna texts, 125
Saffarids, 21
Säkiz Yükmäk Yaruk Sūtra, 108
Śākyamuni (buddha of contemporary era), 50, 55, 94, 112, 160
Sakya order, 123, 124, 149
Sakya Pandita Kungga Gyeltsen, 123
Sälindi, 146, 147
samādhi, 107
Samanids, 20, 21, *21*, 23
Samantabhadra, 100
Samarkand, *21*
Saṃyukta-Āgama, 61
Samyuktāgama, 130
Sanjar, Sultan, 23
Sanjie monastery (Dunhuang), 12
al-Sanjufini, Khwaja Ghazi, 162
Sanskrit language, 41, 59, 106, 127; in Brahmi script, 17, *18*; in Uyghur script, 128
Śaraki, 123
Śārdūlakarṇāvadāna, 102, 197n19
Śariputra, 95
Sarvāstivādin monastic code, 130, 205n15
Śatapañcāśatka, 127
Satuq Bughra Khan, Sultan, 170, 173
Sautrāntika school, 130
šazin ayguči (leader of Uyghur monks), 60
Schopen, Gregory, 197n10
Scripture on the Ten Kings, 39, 110, *113*
scroll format, 108, *109*
Seljuk Turks, 23
Shahnama (Firdausi), 217n12
Shahrukh Khan, 159, 163
shamans/shamanism, 58
Shambhala, myth of, 1, 51, 136, 156, 217n4
shari'a (Islamic law), 163
Shenxiu, 61
Shingon Buddhism, 94
Shizong emperor, 27, 28

Shōgaito, Masahiro, 65, 143
Shushi Huiyao (Tao Zongyi), 170, *171*
Siddhasāra, 187n15
Śikhin (historical buddha), 50
Silk Road, 1, 8, 9, 11, 167; lost civilizations of, 2; products traded through, 79, 200n60; Uyghurs' role as middlemen and, 76
Šingko Šäli Tutung, 101, 106, 209n62
Sino-Uyghur dictionaries, 170, *171*
slavery, 66, 74, 79; military, 21; monastic economy and, 83, 89, 91
Sogdian language, 15, 177n5
Sogdians, 8–9, 14–15, 193n87; Buddhists, 17; influence on early Uyghur Buddhism, 180n45
Song dynasty (China), 13, 14, 34, 100, 125; Buddhist redemption rituals in, 48; Chinese (Kaibao) canon and, 51; commercialized economy of, 100; cotton market and, 81–82; Khitan victory over, 76; Khubilai Khan's campaign against, 147; market for horses and, 79–80; Mongol conquest of, 29; as part of Buddhist Asia, 27, 41; Tiantai Buddhism and, 103, 104; Uyghur elites and, 62; wars of, 57
Songsten Gampo, 5
Soudavar, Abolala, 217n12
Śrīcakraśamvara, 125
Sri Lanka, 135
stake inscriptions, 15, *16*, 20, 54, 59, 193n83
Steinhardt, Nancy, 210n73
Stiller, Maya, 119
Sufism, 141, 162, 163–64, 173, 227n4
Sukhāvatīvyūha Sūtra, 39
Sulayman, prince of Xining, 161, 162
Sūtra of the Divine Talismans of the Seven Thousand Buddhas to Increase the Account, 110
Sūtra on Maitreya's Ascent to Tuṣita (*Guan Mile shangsheng Doushuai tian jing*), 101
Sūtra That Teaches the Mind Essence, The, 61

Taibudu Tölemiš, 153
Taizong (Tang emperor), 29
Taizu (Song emperor), 27, 28

Takao Moriyasu, 190n51
Talas, Battle of (751), 7
Tang dynasty (China), 5, 10, 12, 29, 100, 136; cotton excluded by, 82; influence on West Uyghur Kingdom, 75; Uyghur military assistance to, 7–8
Tang emperors: Daizong, 9; Taizong, 29; Xuanzong, 8
Tängri Bögü El Bilgä Arslan, 60
Tängridä Ülüg Bolmïš Alp Qutlug Ulug Bilgä Khan (Ch. Huaixin), 9, 58
Tangut language, 42, 127
Tanguts, 14, 17, 27; blockprints of, 103, *104*; East-West trade and, 82–83; expansionism of, 24, 41; Mongol campaigns against, 121, 123; Song dynasty conflict with, 80. *See also* Xixia dynasty
Tansuq Name (Rashid al-Din, 1313), 141, *142*, 143
tantric Buddhism, 31
Tao Zongyi, 170
Tārā-Ekavimśatistotra (*Praise of the Twenty-One Taras*), 125
Tarim Basin, 2, 82
Tarmashirin, 153, 222n71
Taš Yegän Totok, 54
Tatar Tongga, 120
Tatpar Khan, 7
Tejaprabha ["Lord of Constellations"] (esoteric Buddhist deity), 45, 47
Temple α (Turfan), 45
Temür (Yuan emperor), 149
Ten Uyghur, 58, 59, 159
Theravāda Buddhism, 94, 96
Thousand Buddhas motif, 117
Tianshan Mountains, 10, 14, 27
Tiantai Buddhism, 94, 100, 101-2, 103, 106
Tibet, 4, 5, 41, 76; Amdo Tibetans, 80; Hexi Tibetans, 14, 27; Il-khanid relations with, 141; Mongol policy toward, 123–24; rebellion against Yuan dynasty, 148; tea-horse trade and, 165
Tibetan empire, 7, 8, 11
Tibetan language, 17, *19*, 127

Tibetan Renaissance, 27
Timur, 154, 162–63
Timurids, 141, 162, 163–64, 165
Toghan (Oirad ruler), 167
Toghan Temür, 164
Tokharian language, 17, *18*, 39, 95, 131
Tokharians, 34, 35, 53; Buddhists, 17; monks, 36, 37, 60; Nikaya schools and, 55
Toluids, 146
Tolui Khan, 144
Tözün, 54
"transformation texts" (*bianwen*), 103
Trapusa, 71-72
Treatise on Contemplating the Mind [*Guanxin lun*] (Shenxiu), 61, 102
tribute system, 42
Tripiṭaka, 132
Tsongkha kingdom (Tibet), 14; market for horses and, 80, *81*; as part of Buddhist Asia, 27, 41
Tughluq Temür, 154, 159, 162, 164, 224n104
Tugh Temür, 123
Turfan Basin, 2, 27, 81, 89, 174
Turk Empire: First, 6, *6*; Second, 7
Turkestan, Eastern, 143, 157, 160, 174
Turkic languages, 64, 184n80
Turkmenistan, 23
Turks, 6, 21, 23
Tusi, Nasir al-Din, 139
Tuṣita heaven, 50, 54, 55, 58, 117, 153
"two realms" model, 58–59, 124-25

Umayyads, 7
urbanization, 68–69, 70
Uṣṇīṣavijayā dhāraṇī (Superlative Spell of the Buddha's Crown), 52–53
Uways Khan, 163, 166-67
Uyghur empire, 7, 8, 9, *10*
Uyghur language, 2, 17, 30, 127; influence on Mongolian socioeconomic culture, 216n3; Manichaean texts in, 15; in Pakpa script, 124; in Tibetan script, 17, *19*
Uyghur language, translations into, 71, 95; Chinese texts, 39, 61, 96–97, *129*, 130;

Indian medical treatises, 43, 187-88n15; Sanskrit texts, 127; Tangut texts, 43, 127; Tokharian texts, 95, 97
Uyghur script, 17, 170, 195n103; Aramaic derivation of, 128; Chinese texts in, 62; instituted as standard in West Uyghur Kingdom, 75

Vagbhaṭa, 188n15
Vairocana Buddha, 100, *133*
Vaiśravaṇa (guardian deity), 43
Vajrapāṇi (bodhisattva), 125
Vajravidaraṇa, 87
Vajrayāna [Diamond Vehicle] (Tantric Buddhism), 94, 123, 162
Vali, Ishaq, 168
Vasubandhu, 130
Veritable Records of the Ming Dynasty [*Ming shi lü*] (1408), 160-61
Vimalakīrti Sūtra, 61, 101
Vimalaprabhā, 217n4
Vinaya (monastic code), 61, 73, 94, 131-32, 194n99, 205n15
Vipaśyin (historical buddha), 50
virtue (Skt. *guṇa*), 48
Visualization Maṇḍala of the Heart and Ten Worlds of Kumano (*Kumano Kanjin Jikkai Mandara*), 103
Viśvabhu (historical buddha), 50
Viśvantara Jātaka, 102, *103*
Vow of Samantabhadra (*Puxian xingyuan*), 101

wall paintings, Uyghur, 103-4, *105*
Walshe, Michael, 199n37
Wang Yangde, 4
warfare, persistence and threat of, 48-49
Weber, Max, 40, 66-67, 196n7
Wei dynasty, 88
West Uyghur Kingdom, 10, 12, 29, 39, 57, 82, 158; alliance with Khitan Liao dynasty, 119-20; Buddhism adopted by elites of, 41; Buddhist monasteries in, 94-95; Chinese laws and, 148; Chinggis Khan and, 121; confessional literature and, 98;

envoys from Dunhuang to, 13; ethnic and cultural diversity of, 56; Manichaeanism of nobility, 14, 15; map, *3*, *10*; monastic economy in, 83, 89, 91; paper supply for manuscripts, 108; regulatory system of, 75; as Shambhala, 136, 217n4; *Vinaya* (monastic code) and, 130
What Is to Be Known [*Shes bya rab gsal*] (Pakpa), 124
Wilkens, Jens, 100
William of Rubruck, 138
women donors of Buddhist community, 57, 61-62, 87
Wu, Emperor (Liang dynasty), 98
Wu, Empress (Tang dynasty), 125

Xiangfa (Semblance Dharma), 52, 53
Xiao Ming Di, 6
Xifanzi maijue jijue (Li Ziye), 141, 143
Xiliangfu (Liangzhou), 14
Xilin, 101
Xinjiang ("New Frontier"), 2, 6, 23, 174
Xixia dynasty, 14, 28-29, 62; Buddhist scriptures translated into Tangut, 42-43; as part of Buddhist Asia, 27, 28, 41; wars of, 57. *See also* Tanguts
Xuanzang, 55, 217n4
Xuanzong (Tang emperor), 8

Yaglakar clan, 9, 10, 15
Yamabe Nobuyoshi, 207n41
yānas ["vehicles"] (Buddhist traditions), 94
Yasavi, Ahmad, 163
Yasaviyya (Sufi order), 162, 163
Yellow Uyghurs, 14
Yidläk, 54
Yiengpruksawan, Mimi, 48, 52
Yisün Temür, 153, 154
Yixiu, 41
Yogācāra school, 55, 61, 207n41; *ālaya-vijñāna* (eighth consciousness), 102; Faxiang school, 55, 101; six forms of consciousness, 106
Yogaśataka, 187n15

Yuan dynasty, 58, 62, 82, 122, 129, 206n26; Buddhist culture promoted by Mongol court, 128, 134; cult of Mañjuśrī and, 125; fall of, 164; Four Ulus of Mongol empire and, *145*; Islamic intellectual elites and, 139; map of Central Asia (1331), 150, *151–52*; Mongol civil wars and, 146; Uyghur alliance with, 147–48
Yulin caves, 117, 189n32
Yunhua Zhiyan, 100
Yunus, 167
Yu Yiqiejing yinyi, 101

Zen Buddhism, 50, 94. *See also* Chan Buddhism
Zhang Chengfeng, 12
Zhang Huaishen, 12
Zhang Yichao, victory over Tibetans, 11, *11*
Zhentong emperor, capture of, 167
Zhiyuan fabao kantong zonglu, 127
Zhou dynasty (China), 179n35
Zhu Yuanzhang, 164
Zieme, Peter, 61, 191n66, 201n73
Zoroastrians, 191n64

GPSR Authorized Representative: Easy Access System Europe, Mustamäe tee 50, 10621 Tallinn, Estonia, gpsr.requests@easproject.com